The Economics of Health and Medical Care

Fourth Edition

Philip Jacobs, PhD
University of Alberta
Edmonton, Alberta, Canada

AN ASPEN PUBLICATION®
Aspen Publishers, Inc.
Gaithersburg, Maryland
1997

Library of Congress Cataloging-in-Publication Data

Jacobs, Philip, 1943–
The economics of health and medical care / Philip Jacobs. — 4th
ed.
p. cm.
Includes bibliographical references and index.
ISBN 0-8342-0803-2
1. Medical economics. 2. Medical economics—United States.
I. Title.
RA410.J32   1996
338.4′73621—dc20
96-9475
CIP

Orders: (800) 638-8437
Customer Service: (800) 234-1660

About Aspen Publishers • For more than 35 years, Aspen has been a leading professional
publisher in a variety of disciplines. Aspen's vast information resources are available in both
print and electronic formats. We are committed to providing the highest quality information
available in the most appropriate format for our customers. Visit Aspen's Internet site for more
information resources, directories, articles, and a searchable version of Aspen's full catalog,
including the most recent publications: http://www.aspenpub.com
Aspen Publishers, Inc. • The hallmark of quality in publishing
Member of the worldwide Wolters Kluwer group

Editorial Resources: Sandra L. Lunsford
Library of Congress Catalog Card Number: 96-9475
ISBN: 0-8342-0803-2

Printed in the United States of America

1   2   3   4   5

Table of Contents

Preface

The primary purpose of this book is to provide the reader with the elements necessary to understand and apply basic economic principles to the health care field. It is assumed that the reader has no prior background in economics, and a minimum of mathematics is needed to follow the discussion of topics. The concepts presented are explained at a level of exposition characteristic of introductory economics texts. Emphasis is placed on those tools that are of particular relevance to health care. The reader will find that, even at this introductory level, economic analysis can provide pertinent and systematic insights into the workings of the health care system and the advantages and disadvantages of health care policies. The book is designed for use in undergraduate or graduate health care economics courses in public health, health care administration, and other health-related disciplines.

One goal of this book is to present usable economic concepts. Another is to give the reader a "task" focus to make him or her aware of the questions being answered by the analysis. The subject matter is divided into three parts. The tasks that correspond to these parts are description, explanation (or prediction), and evaluation (or prescription). The book is organized in a progressive manner, the concepts developed in Part III (Prediction) build on those of Parts II (Explanation) and Part I (Description).

In response to the very rapid changes in health care in the United States, the contents of the new edition have been broadened. The overall didactic organization remains the same. The basic structure of economic science forms the foundation for the book. Specific applications are presented in their appropriate analytical places. The previous editions focused on medical care markets. This edition includes more complete treatments of health insurance and prepaid care markets and labor markets. This permitted the inclusion of several additional topics related to "health care reform," notably health care finance and health insurance market reform. In addition, a section on antitrust policy in health care has been prepared by Ronald Wilder of the University of South Carolina, and additional material has been added on extra-welfarist principles, managed care, and cost-effectiveness analysis.

Because of the expansion of the contents, instructors using the book may want to be selective in choosing topics for a one-semester course. Selection suggestions based on my and others' experiences are included.

The field of health care is changing very rapidly, and the economics of health care has been changing as well. The interested reader who wants to keep up with these changes should consult current periodicals, policy-oriented books, and documents from various bodies, such as the Health Care Financing Administration, Congressional Budget Office, General Accounting Office, Prospective Payment Assessment Commission, and Health Insurance Association, to name a few.

Acknowledgments

A number of people provided me with comments and material, and I would like to acknowledge their help. They include Sy Banner, Tony Culyer, George Gisin, David Hemenway, Lanis Hicks, Judith Lave, Scott Optenberg, and Ronald Wilder. Thomas Noseworthy, chair of the Department of Public Health Sciences, University of Alberta, was very understanding in allowing me to have time to work on this manuscript. I very much appreciate the support of Thomas Palakkamanil and the students from several introductory health economics courses at Athabasca University/Yellowhead Tribal Council where new materials were tried out. Konrad Fassbender provided a great deal of help in preparing materials and conducting literature searches. My family has been very patient with me while I was preparing the revisions for this manuscript. Thanks to them, I was able to complete the necessary work, and so I dedicate this book to Frosso, Louis, Alex, and Jo.

Introduction

This book is an introduction to the economic approach to understanding health care problems. Our approach is based on the identification of scarcity as a major cause of many of today's health care problems. Scarcity can be defined as a deficiency in the quantity or quality of available goods and services as compared with the amounts that people desire. Perhaps the most glaring deficiency in the United States today is the lack of health insurance coverage on the part of roughly 40 million people, many of whom consequently have difficulty obtaining adequate care, especially primary care. Although there are others as well who have inadequate access to care, the size of the uninsured population has become a bellwether of the access problems in the U.S. health care system.

Yet the fundamental difficulty is not merely that there is "not enough" to go around. Side by side with problems of scarcity are problems of "too much." In 1995 total expenditures on health care in the United States reached just over $1 trillion, over 14 percent of the gross national product (GNP), the dollar sum of all final goods and services produced. In 1965, health care expenditures were only 5.6 percent of the GNP. Included in these expenditures are high-cost services whose impact on health has been questioned, including large-volume "little ticket" items, such as radiographs and lab tests, which make up about a quarter of all hospital costs (Angell 1985); high-cost procedures, such as coronary artery bypass grafting and transplants, and costly intensive care services, whose effectiveness is often still undocumented; and some hospital services for the terminally ill, which consume a disproportionate share of the health care dollar (Zook and Moore 1980; Long et al. 1984). A number of commentators have asserted that a considerable amount of ineffective or "flat of the curve" medicine is being practiced (Enthoven 1980). Accusations of "too much," when uttered side by side with cries of "not enough," point to the importance of studying the entire resource allocation process in health care.

Economics is the science that deals with the consequences of resource scarcity, and health economics deals with the consequences of resource scarcity in the health care industry. Because of its very broad scope, economics does not provide a body of rigid doctrines about scarce resources. Rather, economics offers an over-all viewpoint intended to help in understanding the many problems related to vari-ous types of scarcity.

This book focuses on how to *do* economics; that is, how to think about eco-nomic problems in a systematic way. It divides the discipline into three separate areas, which can be regarded as the three main tasks of economics: description, explanation, and evaluation. The exposition of these tasks in a health context is the object of the book; the performance of these tasks should be regarded as the object of the reader.

Accomplishing the tasks involves asking specific questions and searching for answers to them. It should be stressed that searching for relevant questions is as critical a part of the process of analyzing economic problems as searching for answers. By formulating a problem in the context of scarcity, a deeper understand-ing of it can be obtained, and discovery of a solution or a means of accommodation might be the end result.

THREE MAJOR TASKS OF ECONOMICS

The three major tasks of economics covered in this book—description, explana-tion, and evaluation—will usually not be performed in isolation from one another. Rather, descriptive economics will be used to complement explanations and evaluations of events. But even though these tasks may be intermingled in eco-nomic analysis, the specific task being performed should be kept clearly in mind.

Descriptive Economics

Description involves the identification, definition, and measurement of phe-nomena. By performing this task, we obtain some notion of the existing facts. It should be pointed out that this task basically amounts to fact-finding. There is, at this stage, no explanation of why the facts are what they are and no evaluative pronouncement or judgment.

The statement that, for example, in 1992 Americans 65 years and older visited physicians' offices on the average of 5.5 times per year while those in the 15- to 44-year-old age group paid 2.5 visits per year (U.S. Department of Health and Human Services, 1995, 173) falls with the realm of description.

Explanatory Economics

The second task of economics is explaining and predicting certain phenomena. This task involves conducting a cause-and-effect analysis. In undertaking such a task we are moving one step beyond description; we are now identifying the causes of certain events that have occurred. This task is performed with the aid of models that classify various causal factors (assuming there is more than one) in a systematic framework. Based on this framework, hypotheses are developed about the net effect of each causal factor on the phenomena we want to explain. We do not do any further analysis at this stage. That is, we do not pass judgment on whether the phenomena we have observed are present in the desired amounts.

As an example of an explanation, suppose we want to determine why those in the 65-year-old and above age group utilized more medical care than those in the 15- to 44-year-old age group. First, we would develop a framework that incorporates the major causal factors relevant to this phenomenon. Let us say that our framework contains two essential causal factors: (1) the health status of each group and (2) the price paid by the members of each group for their medical care. Using these causal factors, we might then hypothesize that quantity of medical care demanded will increase when health status is lowered and when consumers pay less for their medical care. These causal factors relate to our example because (1) the health status of the older group is lower and (2) government-sponsored health insurance for the elderly reduces the amount the older group pay for medical care. Assuming these facts to be true, our hypothesis would predict that the older group will demand medical care in greater quantities. Should these increased quantities also be available, then the older group will utilize more.

Evaluative Economics

The third task of economics is evaluation. This task involves judging or ranking alternative phenomena according to some standard. An acceptable standard is first chosen, then used to rank alternative ways of distributing scarce resources. In choosing the standard, one major criterion is acceptability. Standards are easy to come by; however, many are controversial, and the standard chosen should have some degree of acceptability.

Using the standard, alternative quantities of economic variables—that is, alternative uses of scarce resources—can be evaluated. For example, if we choose a standard that says that the more medical care one has the better off one is, then, according to this standard, the older group in our example is better off than the younger group. Furthermore, any measure that raises the utilization of the younger group (by lowering the price paid by this group and by increasing the resources available for use by this group) would, according to our standard, lead to a better allocation of resources (Hemenway 1982).

TOOLS USED IN ECONOMIC ANALYSIS

Several tools are used in economic analysis. One general tool is graphic analysis. The purpose of graphic analysis is to illustrate relations between economic variables. Also helpful are models that allow us to draw inferences about the relations we might expect to occur when specific underlying conditions are present. Such tools help us to be explicit about the underlying factors that are present in the workings of the resource-allocation process.

Economic Variables

An economic variable is an economically relevant phenomenon whose value or magnitude may vary. Examples of economic variables include prices, costs, incomes, and quantities of commodities. An economic variable can be measured along a scale once appropriate units of measurement have been chosen. For example, price can be measured in cents or dollars per unit, and quantities can be expressed in terms of number of visits, number of hospital days, number of hospital beds, and so on. Two examples of units of measurement are shown in Figure I–1. Along the vertical axis, values of the price of medical care are shown. The price per visit to a physician, which is the economic variable being examined, is expressed in terms of cents. Along this axis, the price can be 0, 100, 200, 300, and so on. Along the horizontal axis are alternative values of the quantity of visits to a physician's office. These are measured in terms of number of visits.

Relations between Economic Variables

The next step after the identification and measurement of economic variables is to determine the relations between these variables. The relations show how one variable changes with respect to another variable.

These relations can be causal or noncausal. For example, we can state that one variable (total health care costs) has increased while another variable (time) has also increased. This is an example of a noncausal relation, because it is not time itself that has caused the costs to increase. As time has passed, other influencing variables have changed, and these have caused the health care costs to increase.

In a causal relation, when the value of one economic variable changes, the value of a second economic variable also changes as a result. For example, if the price falls for a visit to the doctor, the lower price causes more visits to be demanded.

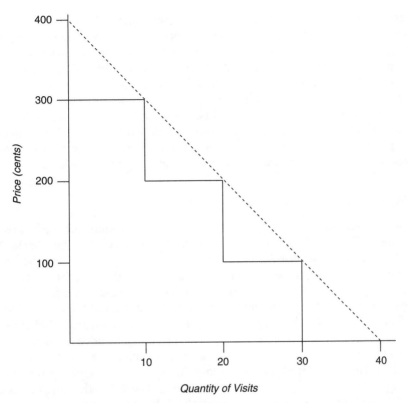

Figure I–1 Relation between price and quantity of visits. The dashed line shows continuous values, and the solid line shows discrete values.

Causal relations are usually expressed in the form of hypothetical statements (e.g., "If price falls, then the quantity demanded will increase").

Graphic Representation of Relations

Let us start with a simple relation between price and quantity of visits: When the price is 400 cents, the quantity of visits is 0; when the price is 300, the quantity of visits is 10; when the price is 200, the quantity of visits is 20; and when the price is 100, the quantity of visits is 30. Associated with each price is a specific quantity: 0 visits with 400 cents, 10 visits with 300 cents, and so on. Each of the associations can be represented by a point, as shown in Figure I–1. All these points together form the relation. If we knew only these values, we could draw this relation diagrammatically as the solid line in Figure I–1. This solid line is known as a step function and relates only to the values specified. However, we could go further and generalize about the nature of our function by saying that the values between 0 and 100 cents (or 100 and 200 cents) and between 0 and 10 visits (or 10 and 20 visits) could also be specified as part of the relation. We could draw a continuous curve joining all the points specified in the relation in order to represent the values not explicitly expressed, such as 155 cents, 5 visits, and so on (consider the dashed line in Figure I–1). Once we have drawn a continuous curve, we have a more complete specification of the relation between price and quantity. Any value of price, within our specified ranges, has an associated quantity of visits.

The Direction of Relations

We can now be more specific about the nature of the relation between the two variables. The first characteristic to be examined is the direction of the relation. A relation can have four possible directions, as shown in Figure I–2. First, the relation may be positive, as shown by curve B. Here higher values of price are associated with higher values of quantity of visits. If there was a causal relation between them, and if the direction of causation ran from price to quantity, we would hypothesize that, as price increases, so does quantity. The opposite type of relation is shown by curve D. The relation is a negative: the greater the price, the smaller the quantity. Thus higher values of price are associated with lower values of quantity of visits. The third type of relation is shown by curve C. In this relation (or, to be more precise, nonrelation), whatever the quantity of visits, the price stays the same (i.e., 200 cents). The final type of relation, shown by curve A, could also be interpreted as a nonrelation. Curve A shows that, whatever the price may be, the quantity of visits will remain the same (i.e., 30 visits).

The Slope of Relations

The slope of a geometric relation shows how much of a change in one variable is associated with a given change in a related variable. In causal terms, slope can be expressed as the magnitude of response. Several examples are shown in Figure I–3.

Let us first look at the slope of relation, or curve, F. Relation F touches the price axis where the price equals 200 cents. This price is associated with a quantity of visits of 0. If we raise the price by 50 cents to a level of 250 cents, the associated new quantity of visits, as shown by F, is 10. A 50-cent increase in the price is associated with a 10-visit increase in quantity. The slope of F is thus 50/10 with regard to the quantity axis (or 10/50 with regard to the price axis). Because F is a straight line, the slope remains constant at every point on the line. (Some nonlinear relations are presented later.)

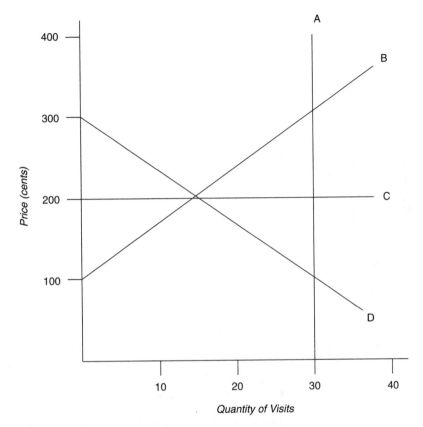

Figure I–2 Direction of relations: curve *A*, constant quantity of visits for all prices; curve *B*, price and quantity positively related; curve *C*, constant price; and curve *D*, price and quantity negatively related.

Relation *E* also has a positive slope. As can be seen in Figure I–3, *E* shows a greater change in price associated with a given change in quantity than does *F*. From the initial price of 200 cents and 0 visits, a quantity change of 10 visits is associated with a price change from 200 to 300 cents. The slope is thus 100/10 with regard to the quantity axis (or 10/100 with regard to the price axis). Comparing *E* and *F*, we can say that for the same quantity change, the price change in *E* must be double that in *F*.

Relations *G* and *H* can be regarded in a similar manner, but now the direction of these relations is such that a higher price is associated with a lower quantity. In relation *G*, a fall in price of 50 cents is associated with an increase in quantity of 10 visits. The slope is thus the same as the slope of *F* but in the opposite direction.

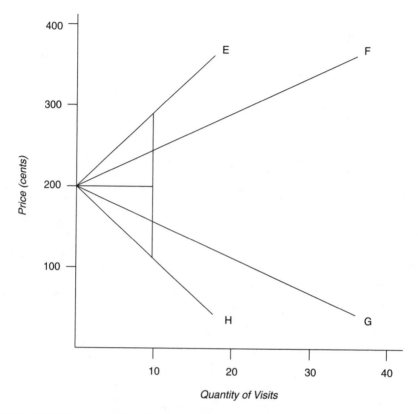

Figure I–3 Slope of relations. In relation E, the price increases more than in relation F for a given increase in quantity. In relation H, the price decreases more than in relation G for a given increase in quantity.

Relation H shows a change in price of 100 associated with a quantity change of 10—the same as relation E, except the slope is in the opposite direction.

The Position of Relations

The next characteristic of a relation is its position. In Figure I–4, two relations, J and K, are shown with similar slopes but different positions. Each relation exhibits a 100-cent change in price associated with a change of 10 visits. Relation J shows no visits at a price of 300 cents, 10 visits at a price of 200, and so on. By comparison, K shows 10 visits at a price of 300 cents, 20 visits at a price of 200, and so on. The essential point of this figure is to show how the two relations are

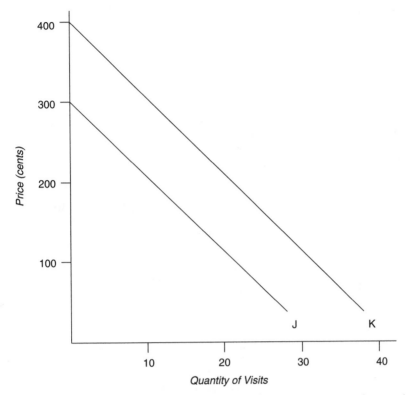

Figure I–4 Position of relations. *K* shows a greater quantity of visits than *J* for any given price.

positioned with respect to each other. Relation *K* is greater than *J* in the same sense that, at any specific price, the related quantity of visits for *K* is greater than the related quantity for *J*.

The Shape of Relations

The examples so far have involved only linear relations, in which the change in one variable with regard to a given change in another variable is fixed. This is not the only type of relation, however. Sometimes we also encounter nonlinear relations. For this type of relation, the magnitude of the response will vary along the curve. Relations *L* and *M* in Figure I–5 are both nonlinear relations.

M indicates the correspondence between the total cost of production of lab tests and the number of tests produced. At a quantity of 0, the total cost is $10; at a

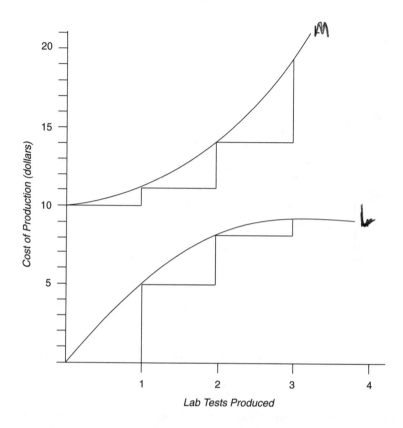

Figure I–5 Shape of relations. *M* shows additional higher costs at successively higher levels of lab tests produced. *L* shows lower additional costs at successively higher levels of tests.

quantity of 1, it is $11; at a quantity of 2, it is $14; and at a quantity of 3, it is $19. The slope of the relation changes as more lab tests are produced. For the first test, the slope is such that a $1 change in cost is associated with a change of one lab test. The next change of one lab test is associated with a $3 change in cost, and the next with a $5 change in cost. The slope with reference to the lab test axis increases as the number of lab tests increases. *M* is a smoothed-out version of this relation.

Relation *L* shows declining slopes with increasing production. A total cost of 0 is associated with a 0 level of output. An output level of 1 is associated with a cost of $5, an output level of 2 is associated with a cost of $8, and an output level of 3 is associated with a cost of $9. The slope of the relation between 0 and 1 units of production, with regard to the production axis, is 5/1; for the next unit of production, it is 3/1; and for the next it is 1/1.

The Nature of Economic Propositions

Many statements in this book regarding the resource allocation process in the health care field are basically attempts to spell out the consequences of certain conditions. The propositions are hypothetical statements of the form "if ... then ... " For example, we might claim that if certain conditions x, y, and z hold, then, as a consequence, phenomenon q will occur. In making this statement, we essentially make a prediction of what will cause the phenomenon we want to explain. The "if" portions of these statements are called *conditions* or *assumptions;* the "then" portions are *conclusions*, *implications*, or *predictions*.

As an example, let us form a model to explain how much medical care an individual will demand. Our model contains initial assumptions. The first, A1, is that the price of medical care charged to an individual is $5 per visit; this $5 includes all services provided by the doctor, including transfusions, intravenous feedings (should they be needed), and so on. The second assumption, A2, states that the individual has a weekly income of $100 that can be spent on any of a number of commodities. This assumption brings the example within the realm of economics, since scarcity is now introduced. The third assumption, A3, is about the behavior of the individual; the individual has as an objective the consumption of medical care only; he does not want to consume any other commodity. We also assume that this is entirely feasible. If the individual does not consume food, for example, he would begin to starve and have to visit a physician, where, for a fee of $5, he could receive nutrition intravenously.

What are the implications of these assumptions? The main implication is that the individual will consume 20 physician's office visits. Given his economic situation, this is all he can afford to consume, and given that he wants only medical care and can survive by consuming this commodity, then he will not consume less than 20 visits. This implication is a prediction of our model; the prediction is based on the initial conditions or assumptions of the model. Predictions are derivatives of the assumptions and can be regarded as the consequences that would result if the assumptions were to hold.

Let us now replace one of our initial assumptions, A1, with the assumption that the price of medical care is $1 per visit. Now our model implies that the quantity of visits will be 100. With a fall in price, the quantity demanded will increase. This is a prediction of our model when we consider all the assumptions and do a comparative analysis.

We can also predict the consequences that would result if the individual's income increases. Suppose we replace assumption A2 with the assumption that the individual's weekly income is $110. This new assumption, coupled with the original assumptions A1 and A3, yields the conclusion that the quantity of visits demanded will increase. By performing a comparative analysis of the original conditions and the new conditions, we can conclude that an increase in income will lead to an increase in the quantity of medical care demanded.

The mere predicting or deriving conclusions about the resource allocation process is not the end of our task, however. Our conclusions are hypotheses. They are suggestions about how the world might behave if the assumptions we have posited in the model are adequate approximations of the conditions that exist in reality. In explanatory economics, implications are tested against actual data to see if what we predicted actually does occur. The true test of an explanatory model is how well it explains or predicts actual phenomena. In evaluative economics, our task is somewhat different: we compare actual against ideal sets of events. Nevertheless, whether we are deriving explanatory or evaluative principles, we put our propositions into a logical form that allows us to incorporate a number of variables into our analysis simultaneously.

OUTLINE OF CONTENTS

This book introduces the analysis of health care economics in the context of the three tasks mentioned above: description, explanation, and evaluation. Part I, which consists of Chapters 1 and 2, describes the economic dimensions of the health care field. Part II, consisting of Chapters 3–9, presents explanatory analyses of a number of health-related issues. Part III, which consists of Chapters 10–15, develops evaluative analyses of several important aspects of health care resource use. The analyses in the book focus on three distinct markets: the medical care market, the health insurance market, and the labor market. Throughout the book, tools are developed to analyze the economic behavior of all three markets.

Chapter 1 contains a discussion of the output of the health care sector. Three types of output are identified: (1) health care, which consists of activities designed to improve health; (2) health itself; and (3) health insurance coverage. (Types of input, such as the hiring of health care personnel, are also discussed.) Measurements of each type of output are presented. In Chapter 2, economic dimensions of the health care sector are identified and some measures of these dimensions are presented. In particular, economic flows of the various components of the health care system are described, and the concept of cost is analyzed.

Chapter 3, the first explanatory chapter, develops a model to explain the demand for medical care by consumers. A number of separate factors are identified as influences on the demand for medical care. These are incorporated into a single model that allows us to predict the effects of each factor when all other relevant factors are held constant. In this chapter, the demand for medical care is presented as if medical care were an ordinary commodity in the consumer's budget. However, medical care has characteristics that combine to warrant special treatment. These include the importance of medical care in influencing health status, uncertainty when illness occurs, people's concern about others' health status and health care consumption, and the asymmetry in the medical knowledge possessed by providers and consumers.

In Chapter 4 a number of these characteristics are introduced and analyzed in light of the standard model developed in Chapter 3. In addition to discussing the way that medical care's unique characteristics influence the demand for care, Chapter 4 provides an introductory account of the demand for health insurance and the supply of labor. The demand for medical care and the demand for health insurance figure importantly in an analysis of the demand for "managed care," which combines these two elements.

Chapters 5 and 6 focus the behavior of health care suppliers, such as doctors, hospitals, and laboratories. Chapter 5 discusses the relationships between resource use and output, quality of care and output, and cost of care and output. All these relationships are examined with regard to each individual supplying organization. Also examined is the supply of health maintenance organizations (HMOs), which are insurer-providers.

Chapter 6 presents an analysis of the supply behavior of individual providers and of groups of providers (i.e., market supply). The behavior of for-profit providers and the behavior of nonprofit providers are treated separately, since nonprofit and government providers play such an important role in the health care field. The chapter also considers a model of the supply behavior of health care providers and health insurers as well as a model of the demand for labor (which is based on the supply model).

Chapter 7 examines a standard textbook explanation of how the market resource allocation process works. This is the competitive market model, which has drawn a good deal of attention recently. Variants of the model are developed for the medical care, health insurance, and labor markets.

However, not all market behavior is competitive. Chapter 8 looks at the concept of market power: how it is acquired by suppliers and demanders and, when they acquire it, how its acquisition affects market phenomena (i.e., prices and quantity and quality of output).

Some economists have stated that, because of unique characteristics of medical care, medical care markets are special, and so in order to address these unique features they have developed models tailored to these markets. Chapter 9 examines several such models, including those where supplier-induced demand predominates and where consumers can selectively choose health insurance and managed care providers. Analyses of the health insurance and medical care markets focus on the phenomenon of "information asymmetry" (the possession of better data or more knowledge by some players in a given market).

Chapter 10 introduces the topic of evaluation by identifying several alternative standards that have been used in evaluating resource use in the health care field. These standards include efficiency and equity. Two frameworks used to evaluate efficiency are presented: the narrower efficiency framework and the broader "extra-welfarist" framework. A set of specific goals for the health care system are derived from these welfare analyses.

Chapter 11 discusses alternative types of health care finance: out-of-pocket reimbursement, health insurance, and taxation. It uses economic models to identify the burden of each type.

Chapter 12 presents a description of two major public insurance programs, Medicare and Medicaid. Specific policy problems are presented and, using the explanatory economic models developed in Chapters 3–9, the effects of specific policy measures are evaluated in light of specific policy goals.

Chapter 13 focuses on methods to reform health insurance and health care markets. It discusses various proposals for restructuring the health insurance market so that the preferred risk selection of the health insurers might discriminate less against high-risk individuals, thereby increasing the equity of these markets. It also explains how antitrust policies might make health care markets more competitive and possibly more efficient.

The role of government policy in influencing the performance of the health care market is the topic of Chapter 14. Two views of regulation are presented there. According to the first, the public-interest approach, the government establishes regulations to ensure that providers act in the public interest. Evidence of the effectiveness of this approach has not been very convincing. The second view of regulation is based on a wider picture of the market. According to this view, the government is a participant in a marketplace that encompasses both the suppliers and demanders of the traded product as well as politicians and regulators. In this marketplace, various regulations and laws that have an impact on the supply-demand situation are "traded." The market outcome is thus influenced by regulation. Faced with discontent over the results of traditional market regulation, some observers have proposed that the medical market should be reshaped in the competitive mold.

There is a great deal of controversy over whether health care markets can ensure that health care is delivered efficiently to consumers. One way to study this is to gauge whether specific interventions improve health status in an efficient way. Cost-benefit and cost-effectiveness analyses are two techniques by which we can judge the economic impact of various interventions and policies on health status. Chapter 15 offers an introduction to these tools.

Table I–1 Alternative Orientations for Health Economics Courses and Recommended Contents

Orientation of Course	Suggested Materials To Be Covered
Basic health economics course	Chapters 1, 2, 3, 4.1, 4.2, 5, 6.1–6.3, 6.7.1–6.7.8, 7.1–7.4, 8.1–8.3, 9, 10, 12, 13
Emphasis on population health and evaluation	1, 2, 3, 4.1–4.2, 5, 6.1–6.7, 7.1–7.5, 8.1, 8.2, 9.2, 10 (except 10.4), 15
Health policy orientation with an institutional focus (a little more advanced)	1, 2, 3, 4.1–4.2, 5, 6.1–6.7, 7.1–7.6, 8, 9.1, 10, 11, 12, 13, 14
Health finance emphasis (more advanced still)	1.5, 2, 3, 4.3, 4.4, 5, 6 (Sections 1, 2, 3, 4, 5, 7, 9), 7, 8.1, 8.2, 9.3, 10, 11, 12, 13

HOW TO USE THIS BOOK

There is a considerable amount of material in this book, much more than would be included in a typical introductory course in health care economics. Instructors will probably want to be selective in covering the subjects. The book could be used as the main text for a basic health care economics course, a course with an emphasis on population health, and courses incorporating more advanced materials on health care policy and institutions and on health care finance. Table I–1 lists recommended reading materials for the four types of courses. The materials cited are just suggestions, of course, and instructors will want to design their own outlines based on their own interests and the needs of their students.

BIBLIOGRAPHY

Aaron, H.J., and Schwartz, W.B. 1984. *The painful prescription.* Washington, D.C.: Brookings Institution.

____. 1990. Rationing health care. *Science* 247:418–422.

Angell, M. 1985. Cost containment and the physician. *JAMA* 253:1203–1207.

Arrow, K.H. 1972. Problems of resource allocation in United States medical care. In *The challenge of life*, ed. R.M. Kunz, H. Fehr. Basel: Birkhauser-Verlag.

Enthoven, A.C. 1980. *Health plan.* Reading, Mass.: Addison-Wesley.

Fuchs, V. 1974. *Who shall live?* New York: Basic Books.

Hemenway, D. 1982. The optimal location of doctors. *New England Journal of Medicine* 306:397–401.

Littenberg, B., and Newhauser, D. 1981. To hell with economics? *American Journal of Public Health* 71:363–365.

Long, S.H., et al. 1984. Medical expenditures of terminal cancer patients during the last year of life. *Inquiry* 21:315–327.

Reinhardt, U. 1985. Future trends in the economics of medical practice and care. *American Journal of Cardiology* 56:50C–58C.

___. 1987. Resource allocation in health care. *Milbank Quarterly* 65:153–176.

U.S. Department of Health and Human Services. 1995. *Health United States, 1994.* Hyattsville, Md.: U.S. Department of Health and Human Services, Public Health Service.

Weisbrod, B. 1975. Research in health economics: a survey. *International Journal of Health Services* 5:643–661.

___. 1991. The health care quadrilemma: An essay on technological change, insurance, quality of care, and cost containment. *Journal of Economic Literature* 29:523–552.

Zook, C., and Moore, F.D. 1980. High cost users of medical care. *New England Journal of Medicine* 302:996–1002.

Part I

Descriptive Economics

Chapter 1

Output of the Health Care Sector

1.1 INTRODUCTION

In this chapter we introduce the first task of our study of the health care system, the task of description. This involves identifying the phenomena with which we are concerned, defining them so we can know their nature precisely, and measuring them so we can obtain an understanding of their magnitude. At this stage, we only wish to discover what phenomena exist, not what causes them (the task of explanation) or in what quantities they should exist (the task of evaluation).

The processes generated within the health care system can be looked at in two ways. The first approach is to directly examine the components of health care that are part of the process of influencing health. These health-influencing factors can be classified as lifestyle factors, such as diet, sleep, and other individual behaviors; environmental factors, such as air and water purification; genetic factors; and medical care, such as examinations and treatments. Section 1.2 focuses on the definition and measurement of medical care. It identifies and defines the phenomena associated with medical care and discusses measures that indicate how much medical care is provided.

The second approach stems from the assertion that the true end of the health care sector is not the care itself but rather the health that results from this care. When measuring the output of health care, according to this approach, we should be measuring how much health is being produced. In some cases we may be satisfied with knowing how much *medical care* is being utilized. If, however, we feel that changes in the quantity of medical care may not necessarily be beneficial, a more logical approach would be to measure what medical care is ideally supposed to produce, that is, health. Section 1.3 examines issues of definition and measurement associated with health, and in Section 1.4 actual measurements are discussed.

3

In Section 1.5 another output of the health care system is described: risk shifting. Because most medical expenditures do not occur with certainty, individuals will place a value on buying insurance to cover merely possible losses. Risk shifting provides benefits to consumers and is an important output of the health care sector. Section 1.6 focuses on the output of the health care system derived from the education of health care personnel. The health care system includes the training of the professionals who work within the system, and these individuals will produce output (health care) during their training and after it is completed.

1.2   MEDICAL CARE

Medical care is a process in which certain inputs or factors of production (e.g., physician services, medical instrument and equipment services, and pharmaceuticals) are combined in varying quantities, usually under a doctor's supervision, to yield an output. An individual visiting a doctor's office receives an examination involving the services of the doctor, a nurse, or a paramedic and the use of some equipment. The inputs vary from one visit to another. One patient may receive more friendly treatment than another, and physicians vary in their thoroughness, knowledge, and technique. Thus the quality of one visit may differ considerably from the quality of another.

Much of the difficulty in measuring the medical care process stems from the issue of quality. If we measure doctor care by the number of patient visits to a doctor's office, two cursory examinations count as two visits. But one cursory examination followed by a thorough examination involving a battery of tests also counts as two visits, even though more medical care was provided.

It should be stressed that *quality* is a very broad term and its meaning is elusive (Donabedian 1988). For example, medical care units can have substantially different characteristics. They differ, among other ways, in the amount of personal attention they devote to consumers in the process of providing medical care. Examples of quality-of-care measures that reflect the degree of personal attention given to consumers include the volume of services performed per individual and patient evaluations of physician performance.

Another set of characteristics is associated with the accuracy of diagnoses and the effectiveness of treatments in producing health. Examples of measures reflecting this set of characteristics include hospital mortality rates adjusted for patient condition and other adverse events in hospitals such as postsurgical infections. A third set of characteristics relates to the amount and type of training of the care providers and the type of medical equipment used. Associated with this set are different techniques used in the provision of care. For example, a CAT scan machine that takes cross-sectional x-ray pictures is generally considered to provide a higher-quality product than a standard x-ray machine (Sisk et al. 1990).

All the above characteristics, as well as others, have been identified as aspects of quality. The challenge of measuring quality, then, derives from the fact that there are many ways of viewing quality—many different ideas as to what constitutes it. For this reason, the raw measure "visits" should be only guardedly used as a measure of physician care.

Hospital care requires the same caution. Hospital output has frequently been measured by bed days or by the number of cases admitted to the hospital. Over time, however, the average admitted patient receives a greater intensity of services as a result of advances in technology. To count an admission in 1965 as having the same output as an admission in 1996 (given the type of case) would be to neglect the greater intensity of services likely to be provided at the later date.

Despite these objections, (1) physician visits to measure the output of medical care and (2) hospital admission or bed days have frequently been used to measure the output of hospital care because of their immediate availability. Recently, efforts have been made to develop additional measures that incorporate the changing quality of inputs per admission or per bed day. These measures are discussed in Section 1.4.2.

Using changes or differences in the number of physician visits or the number of days of in-hospital treatment as measures of movements or differences in the output of the medical care industry gives rise to another issue: What is the actual nature of the industry's output? People seek medical care not in and of itself but to maintain and improve their health. Thus the output of the medical care sector should perhaps be regarded as the health produced by medical care rather than the medical care itself. If this is the case, we should try to identify and measure health and use the changed health status caused by the medical care as a measure of the industry's output. The next section discusses this topic.

1.3   HEALTH STATUS

The concept of health seems so familiar to us that we can almost reach out and touch it. It seems easy to distinguish the 97-pound weakling from the bodybuilder who kicks sand in his face at the beach or to recognize a radiant complexion when we see one in a facial soap commercial on television. More precise measures, however, are harder to obtain. The two categories of "healthy" and "unhealthy" are not exact. The main reason for this is that we have not defined health precisely. Lacking such a definition, two observers can have different opinions as to whether one person is healthier than another. An essential task of the scientific method is to obtain widespread agreement about the nature of a phenomenon. If we lack an implementable definition, we can hardly expect two independent observers to reach agreement about the status of the phenomenon. A definition is useful if it helps pinpoint the characteristics of the phenomenon we are trying to describe and eventually measure.

Health is not an easy concept to define with any degree of precision. As the English epidemiologist Sir Richard Doll remarked concerning the concept of health, "Positive health seems to be as elusive to measure as love, beauty, and happiness" (Doll 1974). Yet in an effort to give some hold on the concept, the World Health Organization has defined health as "a complete state of physical, mental and social well-being, and not merely the absence of illness or disease." This is a very broad definition, and the characteristics of health suggested by it are not easy to pinpoint and measure. Yet one thing that is obvious is that health is viewed a positive good, not something merely neutral. Thus, one individual with a well-functioning body can be healthier (closer to a state of health) than another individual with a well-functioning body.

For many years health was measured by illness (morbidity) or death (mortality) rates in the community; the lower the death rate (adjusting for differences in age levels, sex ratios, or racial makeup), the healthier the community. More recently researchers have been looking for other measures of health. As the death rate has fallen, it has become increasingly recognized that a community with a low death rate is not necessarily a healthy community. To arrive at what is a healthy community, the concept of positive health has become the point of focus.

Attempts at identifying and measuring health have focused on certain characteristics we would expect in a healthy person. These characteristics include the physical functioning of the individual's body in relation to some norm, the physical capability of the individual to perform certain acts (e.g., getting up or dressing), the social capabilities of the individual (i.e., how well he or she interacts with others), and how the individual feels. These characteristics are by no means distinct from one another, a fact that has led to much disagreement among researchers who have tried to invent a unique measurement of health status. Different research efforts have focused on clinical characteristics, on individual capabilities (Boyle and Torrance 1984; Culyer 1976), on the physical functioning of people's bodies in relation to some norm (Kass 1975; Williamson 1971), and on a mixture of physical, mental, and social characteristics (Breslow 1972).

Despite the considerable difficulties in arriving at widely acceptable indexes of health status, the importance of the topic ensures that researchers will keep trying. To appreciate some of the difficulties, let us construct a simple health status indicator with two dimensions or attributes: physical mobility (M) and pain (P). First, we need an index scaling each dimension. Our mobility index might be as follows: 5 = "able to leap tall buildings in a single bound"; 4 = normal mobility; 3 = mildly incapacitated; 2 = severely incapacitated; 1 = fully incapacitated but alive; and 0 = dead. Our pain index might be 5 = no pain; 4 = slight pain; 3 = moderate pain; 2 = severe pain; 1 = excruciating pain; and 0 = dead.

For these scales to be operable, we must have specific information as to the correspondence of each number on the scale to readily identifiable patient conditions. Assuming that we have this and that there is a good degree of correspondence among ratings across raters, we must then develop a formula to combine M and P to obtain our overall health status index (HS). A number of mathematical formulas are usable; two of the more popular are $HS = M + P$ and $HS = M \times P$ (Boyle and Torrance 1984). Using the multiplicative formula, the healthiest individual would have an index value of 36, whereas a dead individual would have a value of 0. Most individuals would fall somewhere between these extremes. Therefore, the use of such an index, when aggregated, would allow a more refined estimate of group health status.

At a more specific level, a single-dimension index for specific diseases has been developed (Gonnella et al. 1984). This index classifies cases of a disease according to stages, which range from extremely mild to fatal, and it permits the development of a case to be tracked through various stages. Its use in the measurement of output is discussed in more detail later.

Health status indexes have been developed for most disease groups and for the overall health of individuals. Their construction has been characterized by a considerable degree of subjectivity, and they offer an enormous variety of descriptive elements to choose from. The increase in health index construction is a result of the growing skepticism about the effectiveness of health care practices.

1.4 MEASURING OUTPUT

Output measurements are usually conducted to make comparisons, either against other output measures or against some standard. There are two types of output comparisons: time series and cross-sectional. A time series comparison measures the output of the same commodity at different times. A cross-sectional comparison measures the output of the commodity among different groups at the same time. For example, the medical care provided to consumers in different age groups, ethnic groups, or geographic areas or with different diagnoses can be compared.

1.4.1 Medical Care Output

Medical care output can be measured at three sources:

1. The providers can be surveyed to determine how much medical care they have produced.
2. The payers for medical care can be surveyed to determine how much medical care they have paid for.
3. The consumers can be surveyed to determine the quantity of consumption.

With perfect measurement, all three sources will yield the same results; however, because of measurement difficulties, considerable differences will arise. A continuing source of data on medical care received by consumers is the National Health Survey, an annual nationwide sample survey of households on health-related matters compiled for the U.S. Public Health Service. Much of the information from this survey is summarized in the Public Health Service's annual compendium of health-related data, *Health United States*.

The National Health Survey is also the major source of data on medical care administered by physicians outside the hospital; this care is measured by the number of visits to physicians (the numbers of visits are often adjusted for the size of the relevant populations to yield utilization rates). As an illustration of the use of time series data, comparisons were made of physician's office visits per year for individuals in the 45–64 and 65 and over age groups. For the 45–64 age group, visits per person were 3.4 in 1975, 3.1 in 1985, and 3.2 in 1992; the numbers of visits for the 65 and over group were 4.5, 4.5, and 4.9, respectively. These data do not indicate that there was increase in the output of ambulatory care for these groups (see U.S. Department of Health and Human Services, *Health United States* 1994). Also, one visit in 1975 was counted as the equivalent of one visit in 1992 even though quality-difference adjustments were not made. It is very likely that quality did increase in this period because of new technology, better equipment, and better training. Unfortunately, this aspect of output is usually neglected in data collection efforts (Freiman 1985).

An alternative way of measuring physician output is to focus on procedures. Procedures (e.g., an appendectomy) can be measured in a number of dimensions (e.g., average time of performance, complexity, overhead expenses), and based on these comparable weights can be developed for each procedure (Hsiao and Stason 1979; Hsiao et al. 1992). This approach better captures the differences between various physician tasks.

The data for hospitals also show decreasing use for the under 65 age groups and increasing use for the over 65 age group. The numbers of discharges from short-stay hospitals per 1,000 population in the 45–64 age group were 146.2 in 1964, 135.7 in 1990, and 121.5 in 1993. Comparable data for the 65 and over group were 190.0, 248.8, and 265.9 (U.S. Department of Health and Human Services, *Health United States* 1994). These statistics can be translated into total output by multiplying them by the number of individuals in the relevant populations. When this is done, the 45–64 group exhibits a decline, whereas the 65 and over age group exhibits an increase.

To gather a picture of hospital product quality, we must look at data collected from hospitals. Hospital output data are available from the *Vital and Health Statistics* (Series 13), published by the Public Health Service, the American Hospital Association's (AHA) annual compendium of hospital data (*Hospital Statistics*), and various issues of *Hospitals: Journal of the American Hospital Association*.

The AHA formerly published a series of indexes that extensively covered the concept of measuring quality changes in hospital care over time (Phillip 1977). This index attempted to measure the quality change of a day of care by changes in service intensity, which was defined as the quantity of real services that go into one typical day of hospitalization. The AHA's Hospital Intensity Index (HII) incorporated 46 services, including the number of dialysis treatments, obstetric unit worker hours, and pharmacy worker hours. A weighted average of these 46 services was calculated annually for data from a sample of hospitals to derive an average number of services per patient day offered during the year. Compared with 1969 (whose value equaled 100), these annual averages formed an index that measured changes in the service intensity component of output over time. Although these data are no longer published, they provide an excellent illustration of how important service intensity is as a component of medical care output.

In Table 1–1, national data are shown for three components of hospital care: services per day, average length of hospital stay, and number of admissions. Services per day are presented in the form of an index (the HII, with 1969 = 100). Average length of stay is presented in average days per stay and as an index (1969 = 100) in parentheses beside the average-length figure. Admissions are shown in millions and also as an index (1969 = 100). As can be seen from the three indexes, service intensity was by far the largest growth component of hospital output, increasing by 68 percent in seven years. Admissions rose by 18 percent, while the length of stay fell slightly. This indicates the importance of intensity of output in medical care. However, although we often equate intensity with quality, this presupposition has been questioned because additional intensity of services may not always result in additional health.

1.4.2 Measuring Changes in Health Status: Outcome

The final output of the health care sector is health. If there is a close relationship between health and medical care, then indicators of medical care output can be

---

Table 1–1 Components of Output in Short-Term Hospital Care in the United States

Year	Index of Services per Day (1969 = 100)[a]	Average Length of Stay in Days and as Index (1969 = 100)[b]	Total Admissions in Millions and as Index (1969 = 100)
1969	100.0	8.2 (100)	20.3 (100)
1970	108.7	8.2 (100)	20.9 (102)
1971	115.5	8.1 (98)	21.5 (106)
1972	119.5	8.0 (97)	21.8 (107)
1973	125.4	7.9 (96)	22.4 (110)
1974	136.9	7.9 (96)	23.3 (114)
1975	153.5	7.8 (95)	23.7 (116)
1976	168.6	7.9 (96)	24.1 (118)

[a]Data compiled from the Hospital Intensity Index, American Hospital Association.
[b]Data compiled from *Hospital Statistics: 1978 Edition*, American Hospital Association.

used as indicators of the true output of the medical care sector. It has been contended that there is not necessarily such a correspondence, and so medical care should not be used as a positive indicator of the medical care sector.

The true output of the health care sector is measured by the net change in health that was produced by the medical care provided. That is, output is measured, not by the level of the health index (e.g., by the infant mortality rate), but rather by the *change* in the index that was due to the medical care—in other words, the outcome of the care. For example, if the infant mortality rate fell from 12 to 10 deaths per 1,000 births subsequent to the introduction of an intensive maternity program, the output of the program would be that proportion of the reduction in infant mortality that was due to the program. It may be that other factors, such as the mothers' diets, also contributed to the change in infant mortality. The presence of such confounding factors creates difficulties in finding an accurate measure of output; medical care is seldom the only factor contributing to changes in health status. Other factors may be difficult to identify (e.g., changes in personal behaviors) and equally difficult to measure.

In addition to the identification of confounding factors, there is the problem of measuring changes in health status. We have seen how many difficulties are posed in trying to measure levels of health status. The measurement of changes in health status merely adds to these problems. For example, consider the categories of disease severity ranked (but not indexed) on the vertical axis in Figure 1–1 (for an index, see Williams 1974). Stages of disease range from no disease present to death (although it may well be that some states of health are even worse than death) (Hornbrook 1983). The horizontal axis represents the duration of the illness (see Williams 1974). On the graph we plot two courses of a given disease: the course with treatment and the course with no treatment. The output of medical care is the difference in disease states with and without the medical care. This is shown as the striped area between the curves. In this version, output is depicted as differences in severity of illness.

It has been contended that, in general, there is a limit to how much good medical care can do; as more medical care is provided (to the same cases), the additional output becomes less. This is illustrated in Figure 1–2, where health is shown on the vertical axis and the quantity of medical care on the horizontal axis. The medical care "outcome" curve showing the relation between health and medical care is drawn so as to indicate that there would be some level of health without any medical care (H_o) and that additional levels of medical care make some contribution to health. However, the additional contribution declines as the output of medical care increases. Such an output curve assumes all other factors (environmental, genetic, personal) are held constant and only medical care varies. The additional output is expressed as $\Delta H/\Delta M$, where ΔM is the additional medical care and ΔH is the additional health. Note that, because of the way the curve is drawn, $\Delta H/\Delta M$ declines in value as more medical care (M) is provided. This eventual flattening of the output

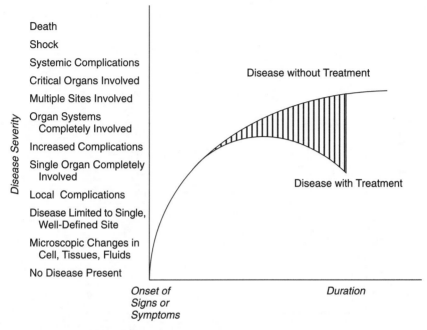

Figure 1–1 Representation of alternative courses of disease in terms of stages of disease severity. In this example, treatment is associated with reduced severity. The difference between the "with treatment" and the "without treatment" curves represents the impact of medical care.

curve has given rise to the expression "flat of the curve medicine" (Enthoven 1980). Drawing the curve in this way illustrates geometrically that, as medical care provision is increased, the additional effectiveness of medical care declines.

Researchers have attempted to establish the relation between medical care and health in different ways. Several early studies attempted to identify statistically a relation between mortality rates and various measures of medical input per capita using state data (Auster et al. 1969) and national data (Stewart 1971). Both studies found a small relationship or none at all. One explanation given was that we may have reached the leveling-out point on the curve. Furthermore, it was estimated that the self-care components of health care (e.g., quitting smoking, eating right, getting exercise) may indeed be more important than the medical care components (Newhouse and Freidlander 1979). However, subsequent statistical research that examined specific groups such as infants did find significant evidence of the impact of medical care (Hadley 1982).

Because such studies are so broadly focused, their results are often difficult to interpret, and it may be that health output is more reasonably measured only by

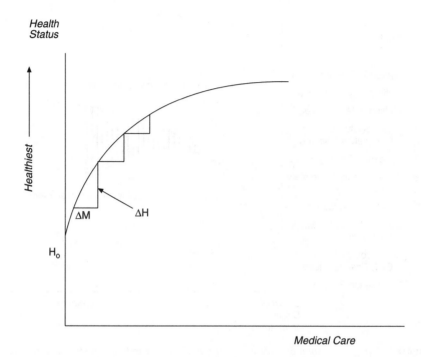

Figure 1–2 Hypothesized relationship between health and medical care. In this representation, additional doses of medical care have a diminishing impact on health; eventually, a situation of low medical productivity, termed "flat of the curve medicine," is reached.

experimental means. Setting up clinical trials in which one group receives a certain treatment and another group with similar characteristics (a control group) does not is an experimental method of establishing output. The difference in cure rates, if any, between the two groups could be taken as a measure of the output produced by the resources (Cochrane 1972). In a number of instances less aggregated studies have sometimes failed to turn up evidence that certain medical practices impact health (e.g., no relationship was found between appendicitis death rates and appendectomies performed) (see Enthoven 1980, chap. 2). However, such findings should not automatically be generalized (Angell 1985). Although it may have some analytic appeal, a broad-brush approach may pass over many situations where we are not on the "flat of the curve."

1.5   RISK SHIFTING AND HEALTH INSURANCE

Another type of output of the health care sector is of health insurance. Illnesses are usually unexpected and are often accompanied by monetary losses. These losses can be in the form of medical expenses, lost earnings from work, and other expenses. Because these losses are uncertain, individuals can be said to face a *risk* of losing some of their wealth. This risk creates concern on the part of the consumers, and they are usually willing to pay something to avoid the risk.

One way of dealing with the risk is to shift it to someone else. Insurers are organizations that specialize in accepting risk. When an insurer accepts a large amount of risk, the average loss to the insurer becomes predictable. Of course, there are costs of operating such a risk-sharing organization. These include the administrative expenses associated with determining probabilities, setting prices, selling policies, and adjudicating claims. The owners also expect a return on their investment (profits). These expenses and profits are included in the fee (called a *premium*) that each individual must pay to obtain insurance. The essential point here is that, in its own right, risk shifting is an additional output that is distinct from the output called *medical care*. Someone can obtain medical care without the risk shifting (by paying for it when the product is received). The individual is still faced with the risk of incurring losses, should they occur. It is the *additional* activity of shifting the risk—the reduction of the loss should illness occur—that is the output.

There are a variety of ways in which a risk can be shifted. It can be done privately, by the purchase of insurance. Insurance organizations such as Blue Cross, Blue Shield, Prudential, and Aetna sell health insurance policies either directly to individuals (individual policies) or through groups such as employers and professional associations (group policies). In addition, health maintenance organizations (HMOs) act as both insurers and providers of care. The government also acts as a payer of health care bills for large numbers of individuals, although strictly speaking it is not an insurer: Most of its revenues are in the form of taxes, not premiums, and often the covered individuals are not the ones who pay these taxes. Thus the government does not manage its health care–related expenditures on an insurance (risk assessment) basis. Government-style risk sharing is referred to as *risk pooling*.

The product, health insurance, can cover all an individual's expenses. Full insurance has become quite costly, and so insurers have come to resort to "cost-sharing" provisions according to which insureds pay a portion of their health care bills and the insurer covers the rest. These provisions allow the insurers to limit expected payouts and charge the insureds lower premium rates. In cost-sharing arrangements, the risk shifting is not complete.

Cost sharing can be done in several ways. The insurance policy can require the individual to cover the first dollars of expenses, and the insurer then pays all, or a portion, of the rest. For example, the individual might be required to pay a deductible of $100 before the insurer begins to kick-in. The insurer can also specify a limit above which payments will cease. For example, it might cover expenses up to a lifetime limit of $100,000. Beyond that, the individual would again bear the risk. So-called catastrophic insurance can be obtained to cover very large losses.

The amount and type of insurance coverage is inextricably tied to the workings of the medical care market. Thus, although insurance and medical care should be thought of as separate products, they do affect one another. In the case of insurance coverage, distribution issues have arisen as a cause for concern. In the United States in 1993, roughly 39 million people under age 65, 17.3 percent of the under 65 population, were uninsured (Short et al. 1988; U.S. Department of Health and Human Services, *Health United States* 1994). Among those lacking insurance were a large number of children (14.8 percent of those under 15), a fact that has generated an extra amount of concern. Additionally, many employed individuals have no insurance. Since employment is the traditional source of health insurance in the United States, the lack of insurance among workers is viewed as a worrisome development (Monheit and Short 1989).

The mere possession of some sort of coverage does not guarantee adequate risk protection. Medicare is a government plan that covers hospital expenses and (optionally) medical expenses for individuals over 65. Because of the cost-sharing arrangements incorporated into the program, many of those who are covered under Medicare still face a substantial financial risk should they become ill. Indeed, 75 percent of those who are over 65 now purchase private "Medigap" coverage to cover the risk resulting from the cost-sharing elements (Cafferata 1984;U.S. Department of Health and Human Services, *Health United States* 1994).

At the same time, it also should be pointed out that a complete absence of risk on the part of insureds (the shifting of the entire risk onto insurers) has its problems as well. A totally riskless policy may be very expensive, since individuals are more prone to demand care when it has a zero price (as under full insurance coverage). The costs of such care must still be covered by the insurer, and so premiums must increase to cover these costs.

1.6   CONSUMPTION AND INVESTMENT OUTPUT

The production of any output requires the use of inputs, including services and supplies. These inputs themselves have to be produced. Many of them are capital inputs, which means that they are durable and last for fairly long periods of time. The totality of resources at any point in time is called a *stock*. In contrast, the amount of activity that occurs during a given time period is called a *flow*.

An output is measured over a given period of time, such as a year. Outputs fall into two classes: those that serve current wants, such as the treatment of patients, and those that serve future wants, such as the production of capital inputs. The production of output for current wants is called *consumption* activity. In health care, much of the output is used up as soon as it is produced. Treating a sore throat by performing a tonsillectomy is a consumption activity; although the outcome lasts for a long period of time, the treatment itself is brief. The production of capital resources is called *investment* activity; the resources themselves are designed to last for several years or more.

Capital inputs can be of the physical variety (radiological equipment) or the human variety (trained radiologists and radiology technicians). Physical capital is the stock of physical means of production. Examples include equipment and buildings. Human capital is the stock of talents, skills, and knowledge embodied in individuals. An example of investment in physical capital is the production of x-ray machines. Undergraduate and postgraduate medical education is an example of investment in human capital.

One feature of the health care sector is that much of the human capital investment activity is a byproduct of medical care consumption activity. Much undergraduate medical education and most postgraduate medical education occurs in hospitals and clinics. In many cases, education and patient care activities are inseparable, physically and financially. For many years teaching hospitals have relied on labor from medical interns and residents for patient care. Because the supply of doctors, including the ratio of specialists to primary care physicians, has become such an important issue in the United States, much attention is being paid to the process by which doctors and specialists are produced.

There is a distinct relationship between capital and production activities. Imagine a given stock of capital at the beginning of 1995 (e.g., magnetic resonance imaging [MRI] machines). Net new investment is the additional stock added during the year (new machines produced minus any machines retired). The stock at the beginning of 1996 is the original capital stock plus the net new investment in MRIs. Important related concepts include the capacity of the capital equipment, actual production, and the percent utilization (or occupancy) rate. If there are 1,000 MRIs in existence, and it takes one hour to produce one image, then the daily capacity is 24,000 images and the yearly capacity is 8.76 million images. If, in any year, 2 million images were produced, the utilization rate would be 23 percent.

Measures of capacity have a particular importance in the health care field. Some analysts believe that the supply of resources directly influences the demand. Commonly used terms and sayings such as "supplier-induced demand" and "an available bed is a filled bed" draw attention to this view. One of its implications is that, in order to control consumption activity, the investment of capital inputs must be controlled.

BIBLIOGRAPHY

Measurement of Medical Care

Bailey, R. 1970. Philosophy, faith, fact and fiction in the production of medical services. *Inquiry* 7:37–53.

Berry, R.E. 1973. On grouping hospitals for economic analysis. *Inquiry.* 10:5–12.

Freiman, M.P. 1985. The rate of adoption of new procedures among physicians. *Medical Care* 23:939–945.

Hornbrook, M. 1982. Hospital case mix: its definition, measurement, and use. Parts 1, 2. *Medical Care Review* 39:1–43, 73–123.

Hsiao, W.C., and Stason, W.B. 1979. Toward developing a relative value scale for medical and surgical services. *Health Care Financing Review* 1:23–39.

Hsiao, W.C., et al. 1992. An overview of the development and refinement of the resource-based relative value scale. *Medical Care* 30 (suppl.): NS1.

Lave, J.R., and Lave, L.B. 1971. The extent of role differentiation among hospitals. *Health Services Research* 5:15–38.

Phillip, P.J. 1977. HCI/HII: Two new AHA indexes measure cost, intensity. *Hospital Financial Management*, April, 20–26.

Reder, M.W. 1967. Some problems in the measurement of productivity in the medical care industry. In *Production and productivity in the service industries*, ed. V.R. Fuchs. New York: Columbia University Press.

Russell, L.B. 1976. The diffusion of new hospital technologies in the United States. *International Journal of Health Services* 6:557–580.

Sisk, J.E., et al. Assessing information for consumers on the quality of medical care. *Inquiry* 27:263–272.

Measurement of Health

Boyle, M.H., and Torrance, G.W. 1984. Developing multiattribute health indexes. *Medical Care* 22:1045–1057.

Breslow, L. 1972. A quantitative approach to the World Health Organization definition of health: Physical, mental, and social well being. *International Journal of Epidemiology* 1:347–355.

Culyer, A.J. 1972. Appraising government expenditure on health services: The problems of "need" and "output." *Public Finance* 27:205–211.

____. 1976. *Need and the national health service.* London: Martin Robertson Co.

Donaldson, C., et al. 1988. Should QALYs be programme-specific? *Journal of Health Economics* 7:239–257.

Goldsmith, S.B. 1973. A re-evaluation of health status indicators. *Health Services Reports* 88:937–941.

Gonnella, J.S., et al. 1984. Staging of disease. *JAMA* 251:637–644.

Hellinger, F.J. 1989. Expected utility theory and risky choices with health outcomes. *Medical Care* 27:273–279.

Hornbrook, M.C. 1983. Allocative medicine. *Annals: American Association of Political and Social Science.* 468:12–29.

Israel, S., and Teeling-Smith, G. 1967. The submerged iceberg of sickness in society. *Social Policy and Administration* 1:43–57.

Kass, L.R. 1975. The pursuit of health. *Public Interest* 40:11–42.

Smith, G.T. 1988. *Measuring health: A practical approach.* Chichester, England: Wiley.

Sullivan, D.F. 1966. *Conceptual problems in developing an index of health.* Vital and Health Statistics, series 2, no. 17, pub. no. (HRA) 74-1017. Washington, D.C.: U.S. Department of Health, Education and Welfare.

U.S. Congress, Office of Technology Assessment. *The quality of medical care.* Washington, D.C.: US Government Printing Office. Publication OTA-H-386 (1988).

Williams, A. 1985. The nature, meaning, and measurement of health and illness. *Social Science and Medicine* 20:1023–1027.

___. 1988. The importance of quality of life in policy decisions. In *Quality of life: assessment and application*, ed. S.R. Walker and R.M. Rossier. Lancaster, England: MTP Press Limited.

Williamson, J.W. Evaluating quality of patient care. *JAMA* 218:564–569.

The Health–Medical Care Relationship

Angell, M. 1985. Cost containment and the physician. *JAMA* 254:1203–1207.

Auster, R., et al. 1969. The production of health. *Journal of Human Resources* 4:412–436.

Cochrane, A. 1972. *Effectiveness and efficiency.* New York: Oxford University Press.

Doessel, D.P., and Marshall, J.V. 1985. A rehabilitation of health outcome in quality assessment. *Social Science and Medicine* 21:1319–1328.

Doll, R. 1974. Surveillance and monitoring. *International Journal of Epidemiology* 3:305–314.

Donabedian, A. 1988. The quality of care. *JAMA* 260:1743–1748.

Enthoven, A.C. 1980. *Health plan.* Reading, Mass.: Addison-Wesley.

Erickson, P., et al. 1989. Using composite health status measures to assess the nation's health. *Medical Care* 27:S66–S76.

Hadley, J. 1982. *More medical care, better health?* Washington, D.C.: Urban Institute.

Newhouse, J.P., and Friedlander, L.J. 1979. The relationship between medical resources and measures of health. *Journal of Human Resources* 15:200–218.

Russell, L.B. 1986. *Is prevention better than cure?* Washington, D.C.: The Brookings Institution.

Scheffler, R.M., et al. 1982. Severity of illness and the relationship between intensive care and survival. *American Journal of Public Health* 72:449–454.

Stewart, C.T. 1971. Allocation of resources to health. *Journal of Human Resources* 6:103–122.

Williams, A. 1974. Measuring the effectiveness of the health care system. *British Journal of the Preventive Medicine Society* 28:196–202.

Health Insurance

Cafferata, G.C. 1984. *Private health insurance coverage of the Medicare population.* National Health Care Expenditures Study, data preview, 18 September 1984. Rockville, Md.: National Center for Health Services Research.

Monheit, A.C., and Short, P.F. 1989. Mandating health coverage for working Americans. *Health Affairs* 8 (winter):22–38.

Short, P.F., et al. 1988. *Uninsured Americans: A 1987 profile.* Rockville, Md.: National Center for Health Services Research.

Data Sources

American Hospital Association. *Hospital statistics.* Chicago: American Hospital Association. Various years.

U.S. Department of Health and Human Services. *Health United States.* Rockville, Md.: National Center for Health Statistics. Annual publication; includes health and medical care trends.

U.S. Department of Health and Human Services. *Morbidity and Mortality Weekly Report.* Atlanta, Ga.: Centers for Disease Control. Weekly epidemiologic report.

U.S. Department of Health and Human Services. *NCHS Monthly Vital Statistics Report.* Monthly data on births and deaths.

U.S. Department of Health and Human Services. *Vital and Health Statistics.* Rockville, Md.: National Center for Health Statistics. Periodical and occasional reports on a wide variety of topics, including population-based utilization data, mortality data, worker hours, and special studies. Known as the Rainbow Series. Early releases of data can be obtained in the "Advancedata" series.

CHAPTER 2

Economic Dimensions of the Health Care System

2.1 INTRODUCTION

The purpose of this chapter is twofold: to introduce readers to some basic concepts used in describing health care activity and to provide a basic description of some of the key elements of health care in the United States. To do this, it focuses on three aspects of economic activity. First, it will examine the basic economic units that participate in the health care economy. Second, it explains how simple flow analysis can be used to describe the economic relationships between the various units. Finally, it presents a concept that is used in measuring the amount of economic activity performed to produce economic output. This concept is called *cost*, and the common measuring rod is money.

It should be pointed out that this chapter is again simply describing what is going on. It identifies the economic units and their characteristics and describes the flows of money and services that occur. (Parts II and III are where the causes and evaluation of output and cost are discussed.)

Section 2.2 identifies the main "actors" in our analysis—the economic units of the health care sector—and describes some of their central characteristics. It also identifies the concepts economists use to study how these units are organized. Finally, using flow diagrams, it shows how transactions between the various economic units can be understood.

Of considerable importance is the measurement of the magnitude of economic activity. Section 2.3 elucidates the concept of "economic cost," which is a measure of economic activity in terms of money. This concept is used to measure various aspects of health care activity, including the total expenditures on health care services, the total economic costs of illness, and the burden of economic costs on various groups. Section 2.3 also discusses the growth of costs over time and how this growth can be divided into components. Section 2.4 introduces a formula for measuring the contribution of each of several components of growth to total growth in expenditures.

2.2   ECONOMIC UNITS AND ECONOMIC FLOWS

2.2.1 Economic Units

Economic units are the basic unit of observation in economic analysis. In examining the activity of consuming health care, one can take the economic unit to be an individual or a household. Both alternatives are commonly employed by economists in describing and explaining economic activity. One reason the household is so frequently used is that more consistent data can be collected at this level. For example, if one examined housewives' consumption of health care in relation to their *personal* incomes, a biased picture of the relationship might emerge, because their consumption of health care is more closely related to the income of their households. (One can, of course, combine the concepts [if data are available] so that housewives' consumption can be related to family income.) The basic roles of consumers include the roles of demanders of health care and health insurance, employees, and taxpayers. Employers are also economic units in the health care system, primarily in their role as demanders of health care insurance for their employees.

Insurers are units that have the function of taking on the health care expenditures risk of their customers. They collect premiums from their customers and reimburse the providers for the care they provide for their customers. Providers of health care can include physicians, hospitals, nursing homes, and providers of various forms of ambulatory care.

There are several economic characteristics of economic units that are believed to affect their behavior and the terms on which they transact business with other economic units. The first of these characteristics is *size*. Economic units can vary considerably in size, and the size of a unit is believed to affect the unit's efficiency and at times its ability to obtain a better price for its product.

Physicians can practice as individuals or in multiphysician units called groups. In 1986, about 30 percent of physicians practiced in groups. There is a trend toward group practice, especially single-specialty group practice and practices connected with HMOs.

A recent phenomenon in the health care field has been the growth of hospital and nursing home chains. Many providers are now members of multiunit systems. The concept of a multiunit system is vague, and the terms of association between the individual provider and the chain vary considerably. In 1987, 40 percent of all hospitals were members of one of 278 multihospital systems. Forty-one percent of nursing homes were chain members, 52 percent were independent, and 5 percent were government owned. There is considerable economic significance attached to chain membership. The ability of a chain to standardize functions (accounts receivable, admissions, etc.) might result in economies of scale. Further, a large chain might be able to exert economic influence over its suppliers (by purchasing in larger quantities) and its customers (by obtaining larger volume contracts).

Providers can also vary by ownership status. A provider can be a *for-profit* unit, meaning its assets are owned privately by shareholders who can sell their share in the organization and have a claim to any profits (revenues over expenses) that the organization might make. A *nonprofit* organization is incorporated for the purposes of providing a service. It is, in a sense, community owned, and no individual is considered an owner. Any profits that the organization earns are returned to the organization. Nonprofit organizations gain certain benefits. For example, a nonprofit organization that is accepted as such under Section 501(c) of the Internal Revenue Code is exempt from paying any taxes on its profits. Although such an organization thus benefits from tax exemption, it is expected to behave in a community-oriented fashion. A good deal of controversy has existed over whether nonprofits do, in fact, behave in such a manner. Much economic literature has been devoted to issues such as whether the operating efficiency of nonprofits differs from that of for-profits. A third type of provider is a *government-owned* unit.

The hospital sector of the health care economy has been predominantly nonprofit, but in recent years for-profits, especially chain members, have grown in importance. Between 1976 and 1992, for-profits have increased from 12.7 to 13.5 percent of all nongovernment short-term hospitals. Government-owned units have been declining, with state and local units falling from 30 percent to 26.6 percent of all nonfederal, short-term hospitals. Nursing homes are mainly for-profit with that form of ownership accounting for about 75 percent of all nursing homes.

The health insurance sector is a mixture of for-profit and nonprofit organizations. Blue Cross and Blue Shield, which insure hospital and physician care, respectively, are nonprofit organizations, though some tax advantages they once possessed have been rescinded. The other major group of traditional insurers consists of the "commercials," which include for-profit and nonprofit ownership types. Classified in this group are the large insurance companies such as Aetna, Sun Life, and Prudential. A growing number of employers are beginning to self-insure (i.e., operate their own insurance funds), and HMOs are now a major force in the health insurance market.

2.2.2 Market Structure

Economic units are organized into "markets" whose size can be measured by the volume of business transacted between buyers and sellers. The market shares of the various individual units volume determine the degree to which the markets are concentrated. Concentration is believed to influence the terms of the transactions. For example, in a market with only a few sellers, buyers tend to pay a higher price for services. When considering flows, and transactions, one must keep in mind that the economic units may be organized in different ways, resulting in differing degrees of concentration.

2.2.3 Flows between Units

Economic flows can be flows of money or services. Generally, a flow will summarize a transaction in which a service or commodity is exchanged for money. Such transactions occur in simple markets, with the degree of concentration influencing the terms of the exchange. The market for lettuce is a simple market in which vendors provide lettuce to consumers in exchange for money. Behind the exchange is a price, which is determined, in part, by how concentrated the vendor market is. In this section, we are concerned merely with describing which flows take place, not with the terms of the transactions. Further, as we shall see presently, the flows in typical health care markets are much more complex than those in markets for lettuce, since they often contain two sets of flows—one for insurance and one for health care services.

2.2.3.1 Flows in a "Generic" Health Care Market

The flows in a simple, or "generic," health care market are shown in Figure 2–1. In this market, consumers purchase health insurance from insurers. The cash payments by the consumers are called *premiums*. When a consumer uses services that are covered by the insurer, the insurer *reimburses* the provider for the services.

The contract between the insurer and the consumer can have another very important dimension. The consumer can purchase varying degrees of insurance coverage. If the consumer is partially covered, the insurer reimburses the provider for only a portion of the bill; the consumer must pay the remainder. The consumer's portion is called a copayment (or an *out-of-pocket payment*). If the consumer is fully insured, there is no out-of-pocket payment. The reimbursement paid by the insurer is payment in full for the services.

The economic importance of out-of-pocket payments is that each one is a cost the consumer is responsible for as a result of his/her consumption. It is this cost that governs the consumer's decision as to how much of the service he or she demands. Among the types of direct consumer payments are deductibles, which are fixed upfront payments, and copayments, which are payments related to quantity used. For example, an insurance policy might have a deductible of $200 and a copayment of 10 percent. This means that the consumer pays the first $200 for services rendered before insurance coverage begins. After the deductible is used

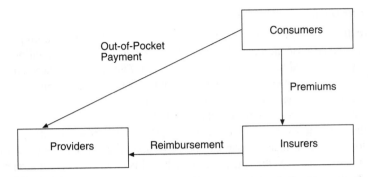

Figure 2–1 Diagrammatic representation of the flow of funds in a typical health care market. Consumers purchase insurance from third-party insurers, who reimburse providers for services. Providers include physicians, hospitals, nursing homes, and other health care organizations.

up, the consumer pays 10 percent of the bill and the insurer reimburses the other 90 percent. Typically, hospital care has the highest coverage, with 90 percent of expenses being covered; physician care has a lower degree of coverage (75 percent on average), and nursing home care has less still (50 percent).

With regard to insurer reimbursement, there are numerous bases on which providers can be reimbursed. Hospitals can be reimbursed on the basis of a given budget or on a unit basis—per patient day, per case, or per service. In the past decade there has been a movement on the part of some insurers toward reimbursing hospitals on a per case basis, recognizing differences in resource use among different case types. In this instance, hospital cases are categorized into *diagnosis-related groups* (DRGs), and a separate reimbursement rate is set for each DRG. Each time a patient is admitted to the hospital, the hospital is paid a rate corresponding to the patient's particular DRG. Physicians are largely reimbursed on a fee-for-service basis and nursing homes on a per diem basis.

The insurer retains the difference between the reimbursement and the premium, which is called the *loading charge*. This charge covers the insurer's administrative costs and profits. It is related to the retention ratio. The retention ratio can be expressed as the ratio of reimbursement or benefits (payout) to premiums. This ratio will vary by type of policy. A group policy, in which the individual is covered as a member of a group, will typically have a 75-percent retention ratio. An individual policy, in which the individual purchases insurance directly from the insurer and not as a member of a group, will have roughly a 60-percent ratio. Much of the difference is accounted for by higher costs of administering individual policies.

2.2.3.2 Introducing the Employer

Almost three-quarters of all health insurance is provided through employers (Health Insurance Association of America 1989). A basic set of flow relationships for employer-provided health insurance is shown in Figure 2–2. In these circumstances both the employer and the employee pay a share of the premiums. Typically, the employer pays about two-thirds of the premium, though the percentage will vary depending on the plan (Levit et al. 1989).

Note that the employer's share of the premiums is not a "free" benefit given to the employee. It is, rather, a form of compensation received by the employee. Total compensation takes the form of money benefits (wages), and nonmonetary benefits, such as health insurance coverage. The employer is probably indifferent regarding the form of compensation: a dollar in wages costs the same to the employer as a dollar in noncash benefits. But the employee will have a preference because of income tax regulations.

Unlike wages, many noncash benefits are not subject to income tax. Thus noncash benefits, such as health insurance, are cheaper to obtain if they are "purchased" through an employer rather than paid for out of after-tax income. As an example, assume that a family's tax rate is 20 percent and that the family wants to buy $100 of health insurance. If the employee takes compensation in the form of

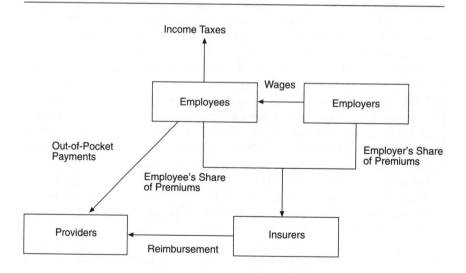

Figure 2–2 Representation of health care services and insurance markets with employer-provided health insurance. Employers and employees typically share premiums. Health insurance premiums are a tax-free benefit to the employee.

wages, the employee must earn $125 in order to have $100 after paying the 20-percent tax (20 percent of $125 is $25). The employee need earn only $100 if compensation is taken in the form of benefits. Or put another way, $100 of compensation in the form of nontaxable benefits will buy more health insurance. The economic importance of this is that present taxation arrangements make health insurance cheaper and encourage more of it to be bought.

It was mentioned above that when economic units are bigger or have a larger share of the market, they may be able to obtain better terms when selling or purchasing services. One type of arrangement that has been increasing in importance is the employer coalition. Employer coalitions are formed by businesses in local markets. Coalition members share information on provider prices, utilization trends, and so on, and they also cooperate with each other in developing benefit designs (e.g., common copayment arrangements). The original purpose of forming coalitions was to develop a sort of countervailing power in the market so that the buyers—the employers—would be able to exert some degree of market influence over price (McLauchlin et al. 1989). Another type of arrangement is the health insurance purchasing coalition (HIPC), which is a coalition of purchasers of insurance designed to garner the benefits associated with group purchasing (Reinhardt 1993). HIPCs have been set up in some states to improve the access of smaller purchasers to health insurance.

2.2.3.3 Medicare

Many individuals are insured by government programs. Medicare is a program of the federal government that covers individuals 65 years old and over, certain disabled groups, and individuals with certain kidney diseases. Medicare has two parts, an institutional portion and a noninstitutional portion. The institutional portion, called *Part A* (or *hospitalization insurance*), covers hospital care, home care, and a small amount of long-term care (limited to skilled nursing facility care). As shown in Figure 2–3, there is no Part A premium. Part A is largely financed by a federal payroll tax paid by both employers and employees. In 1995 this tax amounted to 1.45 percent of taxable earnings from each the employee and employer. The proceeds from this tax go into the Hospital Insurance Trust Fund and form the bulk (87.5 percent of total revenues in 1994) of the fund's revenues. Hospital expenditures, which form most of the trust fund's payments, have greatly outpaced the fund's receipts (from the payroll tax). As the fund is set up, it cannot be supplemented to any great extent by other forms of receipts, such as general taxes (which could be allocated by the legislature), without major changes in legislation. Indeed, projections made in the early 1980s indicated significant deficits in the fund would occur during the 1990s. These gloomy forecasts, which were predicated on projections of rapidly rising hospital costs, led to significant changes in the method by which Medicare reimbursed hospitals.

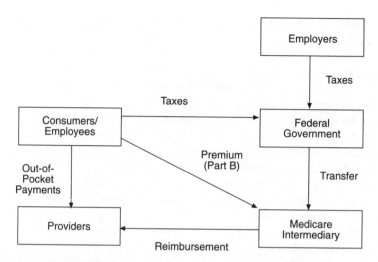

Figure 2–3 Representation of Medicare Parts A and B flows. Consumer and employer taxes include the payroll tax, which is paid into the Hospital Insurance Trust Fund (part of the federal government). Medicare enrollee premiums are only for Part B.

Although Part A Medicare has no premiums, the level of copayments is high. In 1995 there was a deductible of $716, which covered the first 60 days of care, and for anyone needing 61 to 90 days of hospitalization, there was a coinsurance payment of $179 for each day. If someone exceeded 90 days of care during a year, they could draw upon a lifetime reserve totaling 90 days. For many enrollees, the out-of-pocket payments have been considerable, and many individuals have purchased a private form of insurance called *Medigap*, which covers Medicare direct expenses.

Part B coverage is for noninstitutional care, such as physician care, lab and radiology services, and physiotherapy. Enrollment in Part B, called *supplemental medical insurance*, is voluntary and can be purchased with a premium payment ($46.10 monthly in 1995). This premium entitles the holder to partial coverage— there is an annual deductible of $100 of provider charges (billings) and a copayment of 20 percent after that. These direct payments can be insured against by purchasing a Medigap policy from a private insurer.

Unlike Part A, whose revenues come primarily from a single source, Part B revenues come from several sources. The main sources are enrollee premiums and allocations from general taxation. Although Part B expenses have increased considerably, there has been more flexibility in financing them through additional allocations. Nevertheless, there is growth in Part B expenditures, as well as in the Medicare program's share, and the out-of-pocket burden of enrollees.

Medicare now reimburses hospitals on a per case basis, with distinct payments made for each type of case (DRG). The DRG rate is preset and is called *prospective*. The payment system is called a *prospective payment system* (PPS). Currently Medicare Part B pays fees to physicians, with fees determined by a fee schedule predicated on a resource-based relative value system (RBRVS).

2.2.3.4 Medicaid

Medicaid (Figure 2–4) is a joint federal-state program that was introduced in 1966 to cover poor individuals. Federal guidelines set basic minimum criteria for eligibility. Medicaid covers families who receive payments from Aid to Families with Dependent Children (AFDC), a program whose purpose is to provide financial aid where one parent is absent or the prime income earner is unemployed or cannot work. Medicaid also covers the aged poor and the blind. The mandated services covered by the program include inpatient hospital and outpatient care, laboratory and radiology services, physiotherapy, and skilled nursing facility care. States have the option of covering drugs and intermediate care. Eligibility for Medicaid above the basic, federally mandated coverage is determined by state governments, and there is a wide variation. Recently Medicaid coverage has been expanded to include recipients of cash assistance, poor children under the age of 5, and low-income pregnant women. Generally Medicaid-covered services do not have a copayment or deductible, though for some services direct prices can be charged.

The sharing of Medicare expenses between state and federal governments is determined by a formula. States receive a proportion equal to 45 percent of the ratio of state to federal per capita income. However, the state's share can be no less than half of Medicaid expenditures and no more than 83 percent.

Provider reimbursement differs considerably among the states. Hospitals traditionally were paid on the basis of costs that they incurred. This "retrospective" payment system has proved to be inflationary, and many states have moved over to a prospective payment basis. Physician payments are on a fee-for-service basis, but Medicaid agencies have traditionally paid at a discount. Thus Medicare fee levels have been lower than those of other payers. A number of states have moved to a prepaid managed care format (Rotwein et al. 1995).

2.2.3.5 Health Maintenance Organizations

Managed care refers to forms of insurance coverage in which enrollee utilization patterns and provider service patterns are monitored by the insurer or an intermediary with the aim of containing costs. An HMO is one type of managed care organization.

Payment of HMO premiums are on a "capitation" basis. That is, there is a set fee for each enrollee, and the HMO receives a single annual amount for each enrollee whether it provides much or little care. This form of payment puts the HMO

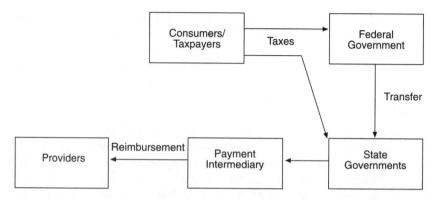

Figure 2–4 Flow of funds for Medicaid program. Federal transfers to state governments are for federal share of the combined state-federal program. Beneficiaries pay no premiums, and direct consumer payments are minimal.

at risk for all expenses incurred when serving enrollees, which incidentally means that the HMO serves as an insurer as well as a provider.

Traditionally, an HMO had one of two forms: either it was a self-contained unit that functioned as insurer and provider or it was an amalgamation of private practice physicians (called an independent practice association) that acted much like an HMO except that the providers were separately reimbursed by the HMO on a fee-for-service basis. Recently, there have sprung up many new forms of HMOs, many owned by traditional insurance companies such as Blue Cross or commercial companies. These new types receive the capitation fee and contract out for services with providers that the HMO enrollees use.

One of the salient features of any HMO is the restriction of access to providers. Whereas under traditional coverage individuals can go to any provider, enrollees in an HMO must use a group of designated providers. This closed panel arrangement allows the HMO to monitor the providers and possibly have some impact on provider behavior. The providers on the panel may be employees of the HMO or contractors; in either case, monitoring providers is more likely to be feasible than if the enrollees' choice of providers is more diffused. Such monitoring can potentially encourage providers to practice in a more conservative, less costly manner.

Since the beginning of the 1980s HMO enrollment has expanded rapidly. In 1994, an estimated 42 million individuals had HMO-type coverage. HMO coverage is offered for enrollees of Medicare and Medicaid, as well as for those who are traditionally covered. A simple flow diagram for HMO coverage is shown in Figure 2–5. HMO receipts would typically include employer contributions as well. It should be noted that, unlike in the case of traditional insurance coverage, there is

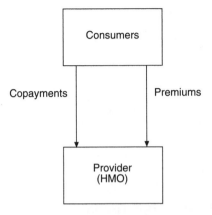

Figure 2–5 Flow of funds for an HMO. Consumers pay premium to the HMO, which is also the provider. Copayment levels vary among plans, and some plans do not require any copayment.

---

typically no pass through from insurer to provider; the insurer is, in essence, the provider. However, there are some types of HMOs that do contract with independent providers.

2.2.3.6 Preferred Provider Organizations

A major drawback of HMO coverage is that enrollees can only choose from a limited panel of providers. In many cases, an enrollee may be attached to or prefer a specific physician. If the physician is not on the provider panel, the enrollee must pay the provider's full price. Preferred provider organizations (PPOs) were designed to expand consumer choice while maintaining many of the monitoring benefits of managed care.

A PPO will contract with certain providers ("preferred providers") who agree to change low prices and submit to utilization monitoring in exchange for being designated as a preferred provider (see Figure 2–6). The PPO will then contract on behalf of these providers with insurance companies to gain their business. The insurers offer their enrollees a dual pricing system—one price for those who use the preferred providers and a higher price for those who use nonpreferred providers. This price differential might take the form of varying copayment rates, for example, a low (or zero) copayment rate for those who visit the preferred group and a higher direct payment for those who use nonpreferred providers. This creates an economic incentive for the consumers to use the preferred group, but it allows partial coverage when the consumers choose a nonpreferred provider.

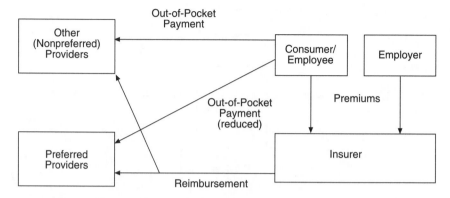

Figure 2-6 Outline of flows in a preferred provider arrangement. The preferred provider organization (PPO), not shown, arranges the preferred reimbursement rate from the preferred providers and conducts reviews of utilization. The PPO could be the preferred provider, the insurer, or an independent organization.

Preferred providers gain from the fact that they will likely get a greater volume of business from the enrollees. Their agreeing to submit to some form of utilization monitoring will, if the monitoring is successful, translate into lower utilization patterns and lower premiums, which in turn translates into savings for the employer and employees.

A PPO can be a separate contractor that receives a fee from the insurer. It can be part of the insurance company itself. Or it can be owned by provider groups and used as a marketing mechanism. In fact, there are many types of PPOs. What distinguishes them from HMOs is their allowance of greater choice of provider. Recently, however, HMOs have been relaxing their closed panel restrictions in favor of coverage that is more akin to PPO coverage. An HMO that allows members to seek care from nonpanel providers for a differential fee is called a point-of-service plan.

PPOs have been growing in popularity in recent years. Between 1988 and 1993, the proportion of all employees who were enrolled in PPOs increased from 11 percent to 30 percent (Gabel et al. 1994). In fact, their popularity has earned them a place in a popular health insurance package now offered by many employers: the "triple option" package. With such a package, the employer offers each employee a choice among types of coverage: traditional coverage, HMO coverage, and PPO coverage. In order to make the three types roughly comparable, the employer can alter the out-of-pocket payments and employee premiums. For example, for traditional care, the least restrictive in terms of consumer choice, the employer might set higher copayments, and enrollees who choose the more restrictive managed care options might be offered lower copayments.

2.2.3.7 The Meaning of "Managed Care"

Managed care is most frequently associated with HMOs and PPOs, because these types of organizations were the first to try to control the utilization of care. In a traditional HMO, providers are typically employers of the HMO and are subject to some degree of regulation. More recently, indemnity insurers have begun to introduce regulatory controls over providers, such as second-opinion requirements for surgery and length-of-stay reviews. Providers transact with indemnity insurers at arm's length, and so indemnity insurers have had to develop such mechanisms to restrain utilization. Also, HMOs have been changing in form. In many cases providers are no longer employees but contract with the HMO to provide care for the members. In this type of arrangement, controlling utilization requires the establishment of contractual mechanisms. For example, providers who serve HMO members often have to obtain permission from the HMO before initiating expensive therapies.

The regulatory function of indemity and contractual HMOs is shown in Figure 2–7. In this diagram, the financial flows are shown as before. The flow of services from the providers to the consumers is also shown. A dotted line from the insurer to the service flow line indicates the care-management function established by the insurer. Under managed care, the service flow is regulated.

In order to set standards for providers, HMOs engage in profiling, which involves collecting comparative data on the treatment patterns of providers. Using this information, the insurers can set benchmarks that can be used to regulate the utilization of care.

2.3 COST OF ACTIVITIES

Having identified productive activities as efforts involving resource inputs whose aim is to create commodities, we now need to find some common measure. The concept of *cost* is often used. In the context of a flow, cost is taken to be the magnitude of the resources devoted to an activity. Several different meanings can be attached to this concept. One definition of cost is the money outlay or expenditure that has been paid to the providers for their services. For example, if an optometrist performs an eye pressure test, the money cost is simply what is paid for the optometrist's services. Money cost is a convenient way to measure the magnitude of an activity, but it is not always a totally valid measure. The same optometrist may do the same test for free; then the money cost would be zero. Yet some activity has taken place, and this activity has used scarce resources.

In the health care sector, many examples exist of free (i.e., zero money cost) services. Clinical teachers in medical schools frequently donate their efforts. Volunteer collectors for such organizations as the American Heart Association, United Way, and March of Dimes donate their efforts. The notion of *opportunity cost*, defined as the value of the most valuable alternative course of action given

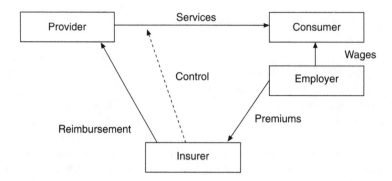

Figure 2–7 The flows of money and services shown in this diagram are consistent with any insurance arrangements. What is added is a control function by which the insurer establishes some form of control over the provider, thus regulating the flow of services from the provider to the consumer.

---

up for the chosen course of action, is used as a measure that does not depend on whether providers are paid in money for their services. Opportunity cost is relevant when a resource has several alternative uses. If used in activity A, the opportunity cost of an input is what that input would have earned if it had been used in alternative activity B, where B is the highest valued alternative employment for that resource. Let us say that an optometrist who performs a refraction for free in a clinic could have obtained a fee of $20 had he or she performed it in the office. By valuing this service at $20, we make it comparable to services performed for a fee. Whenever a service is provided at a price below its alternative value, the money cost will not take into account the portion of cost that is, in effect, subsidized; opportunity cost is a better measure of the true size of the total resources committed to an activity.

Costs can be categorized, among other ways, as direct or indirect. *Direct costs* refer to money expenditures, while *indirect costs* refer to unpaid resource commitments. Though these later are unpaid, they may still have significant opportunity costs.

Table 2–1 shows the estimated value of all direct national health expenditures for one year (1995) in the United States (Burner and Waldo 1995). These expenditures amount to $1,007 billion. If this figure is compared with the total of all final goods and services expected to be produced in the economy during that year (the gross national product [GNP]), the ratio arrived at would be 14.2 percent. That is, 14.2 percent of all final goods and services would be health care services. The ratio of national health expenditures to the GNP is generally considered a critical indicator of resource use in the health care sector. In fact, as seen in Figure 2–8, this ratio has

Table 2–1 U.S. 1995 Estimated Health Care Expenditures (Billions of Dollars)

Type of Care	Total	Direct Patient Payments	Private Insurance	Medicare	Medicaid	Other
			Source of Payment			
Personal care						
Hospital	364.5	8.8	128.4	109.0	48.7	69.6
Physician care	198.0	28.0	96.1	44.5	14.8	14.6
Nursing home care	80.2	25.7	2.0	9.5	39.9	3.1
Other personal care	155.0	112.7	64.3	23.7	28.9	0.3
Total	897.7	175.2	290.8	186.7	132.3	87.6
Other	109.9					
National health expenditures	1,007.6					

Source: S.T. Burner and D.R. Waldo. Dataview: national health expenditure projections, 1994–2005. *Health Care Financing Review* 16 (1995):221–242.

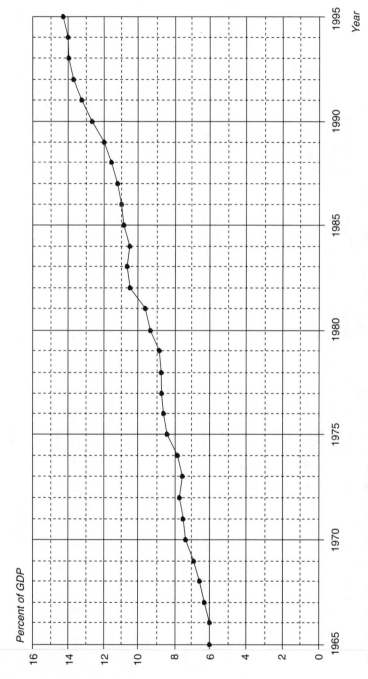

Figure 2–8 Ratio of total national health care expenditures to gross domestic product, 1965 to 1995.

been growing steadily and significantly over the past several decades, a phenomenon that has caused a great deal of concern (Fuchs 1990) and has motivated many inquiries into the cause and appropriateness of this growth. While the increase in the ratio has been impressive, we should caution that the ratio by itself does not tell us enough to be able to judge whether its current level is unwarranted. We need much more information, including information on the benefits these resources yield, before we can reach a considered judgment on appropriateness.

The above data provide us some idea of the direct costs of services provided. They do not, however, provide an indication of the total "burden" of costs—direct and indirect—that fall on all members of society as a result of illness. This total measure comprises what are called the *social costs*. Before examining the social costs, we need to introduce one additional concept: present value. An activity (e.g., being ill) can result in costs incurred (value of lost time) in different time periods. An individual can become ill and miss three years of work, for example. If he/she earns $30,000 a year, one might be tempted to estimate the economic cost of the illness at $90,000. But this would be incorrect, because the costs have not all occurred at the same time. To be valued on an equal footing, costs that occur in different time periods must all be valued as of the same point in time. This is because people usually place different (lower) values on future costs than on present costs. The adjustment factor that brings future costs in line with present costs is called a *discount factor* (this revaluation procedure is discussed in Chapter 14). The result of adjusting a future period cost to the present is called the *present value*, and a discount rate can be applied to costs occurring in different periods in order to put them all on the same footing, that is, valuing them all as of the present period.

Social costs of illness have been measured in the aggregate and for specific groups of illness. These costs include the direct expenditures, mentioned above, and the indirect costs of morbidity and mortality. Studies have been undertaken that measure the costs of all illnesses occurring in a single year. Sometimes the costs of illnesses will occur in future years as well as the one under consideration, and these costs must be factored in appropriately and discounted. One study for 1980 estimated the social costs from all illnesses in the United States to be $455 billion (Rice et al. 1985). This amount was broken out as follows: direct personal health care expenditures, $211 billion; indirect morbidity costs, $67 billion; and indirect mortality costs, $137 billion (present value). It might be noted that in 1980 all expenditures on personal health expenditures amounted to $219 billion, and thus the remainder ($219 billion less $211 billion) was not allocated to any illness but was for services such as preventive care. These results indicate that importance of indirect costs in calculating social costs; overall, indirect and direct costs are roughly of the same magnitude.

These same concepts have been used in innumerable studies of specific diseases. One disease which has received a great deal of current attention is human immunodeficiency virus (HIV) and acquired immunodeficiency syndrome (AIDS). One estimate of the direct costs of HIV/AIDS (for 15 months' worth of treatment) is $119,000 per patient (Hellinger 1993). If an individual with AIDS did not work during a portion of that time due to the AIDS portion of the illness (25 months) but would have otherwise earned $3,000 monthly, the indirect morbidity costs of the illness would be $75,000. (If the individual had worked part time, the opportunity cost would have been less.) The mortality costs would depend on the age of the individual. If the individual was 35 years old at the time of death and would have otherwise worked for 30 more years, he or she would have lost 30 years of earnings. The mortality costs would be the present value of these lost earnings. Because of the relatively young age of the victims, mortality costs for AIDS cases are high. It is estimated that the indirect costs for AIDS cases are three times the direct costs (Scitovsky and Rice 1987).

2.4   ACCOUNTING FOR THE GROWTH OF COSTS

A major confusion in interpreting the growth in health care costs arises from the failure to clearly distinguish between total cost and the components of total cost. If we separate total cost into two components, average cost per unit (called AC) and the number of units (called Q), then total cost is the product of AC and Q. It is a mistake to think that one is containing total cost when only AC is being contained. If Q increases enough, a reduction in AC may not be enough to contain total cost.

If the total cost of a program or activity has increased, it is often desirable to separate this change into components to determine the contribution of each component to the overall change. A useful technique that permits one to account for these relative contributions, provided the growth rate is small, is outlined next here. Let us assume that the total cost of hospital care in 1975 is $12,000 and in 1996 it rises to $12,750. The mere fact that the total cost rose does not tell us by how much unit costs or output contribute to this increase. To determine this we must apply additional information to a formula. Let C represent total cost, Q represent units of output measured in bed days, and K represent unit cost in terms of dollars per bed day. If subscript 1 stands for 1995 and subscript 2 for 1996, the total cost can be broken down as follows:

$$C_1 = K_1 Q_1 \text{ and } C_2 = K_2 Q_2$$

Furthermore, let $K_1 = \$12$, $K_2 = \$12.50$, $Q_1 = 1,000$, and $Q_2 = 1,020$. If we let Δ signify "change in," then $K_2 = K_1 + \Delta K$, where ΔK is $0.50, and $Q_2 = Q_1 + \Delta Q$, where ΔQ is 20 beds. We can now express C_2 as follows:

$$C_2 = (K_1 + \Delta K)(Q_1 + \Delta Q) = C_1 + \Delta C.$$

Multiplying out the terms in parentheses, we obtain

$$C_1 + \Delta C = K_1Q_1 + K_1\Delta Q + \Delta KQ_1 + \Delta K\Delta Q.$$

Since $C_1 = K_1Q_1$, we can subtract the quotient from both sides and maintain the equality of both sides. Furthermore, by dividing both sides by C_1 (or K_1Q_1), we obtain

$$\frac{\Delta C}{C1} = \frac{K1\Delta Q}{K1Q1} + \frac{\Delta KQ1}{K1Q1} + \frac{\Delta K\Delta Q}{K1Q1}$$

Cancelling terms, we have

$$\frac{\Delta C}{C1} = \frac{\Delta Q}{Q1} + \frac{\Delta K}{K1} + \frac{\Delta K\Delta Q}{K1Q1}$$

The expressions $\Delta C/C_1$, $\Delta Q/Q_1$, and $\Delta K/K_1$ are growth rates of the variables C, Q, and K. That is, $\Delta C/C_1$ is 750/12,000, or 0.062, which means that C has increased by .062 (6.2 percent) over its base value. The last equation displayed above allows us to express the growth rate of cost in terms of the growth rates of the two components of cost, K and Q, plus a residual term, $\Delta K\Delta Q/K_1Q_1$. Assuming that ΔK and ΔQ are of relatively small magnitude, this residual term can be approximated by zero. We are then left with this approximation:

$$\frac{\Delta C}{C} = \frac{\Delta Q}{Q} + \frac{\Delta K}{K}$$

This formula shows that the growth rate of total cost is approximately equal to the sum of the unit cost and output growth rates. Applying this formula to the figures in our example, we calculate that unit costs rose by 4.1 percent (0.50/12.00) and output increased by 2 percent. Thus, the 6.25-percent growth in total cost was roughly attributable to a 4.1-percent increase in unit costs and a 2-percent increase in output.

The formula can be used to estimate the components' contributions to growth if, for example, only the growth rates of total costs and unit cost are known. If $\Delta C/C_1$ is 5 percent and $\Delta K/K_1$ is 1 percent, then the difference, 4 percent, can be attributed to $\Delta Q/Q_1$. The formula can also be extended to account for the contribution of separate elements to the overall growth of costs when three or more variables form a product. Total cost can be expressed as the product of costs per bed day, the number of bed days used per capita, and the total population. The overall growth rate of total cost can be approximated by the sum of the growth rates for each variable. Thus, if $\Delta C/C_1$ is 6 percent, $\Delta K/K_1$ is 3 percent, and population growth is

1 percent, we can approximate that per capita utilization rose by 3 percent. This formula is thus a useful way of organizing information about growth in overall costs and its determinants. It must be remembered, however, that this formula allows us to obtain approximations, not precise figures.

The growth formula can be used to analyze hospital cost increases. Overall data for nonfederal short-term general hospitals in the United States can be obtained for the variable total hospital expenditures and its components: total expenditures per patient day, patient days per admission (or average length of stay), and number of admissions. Since the first variable (total expenditures) is the product of the other three, the growth in this variable can be approximately expressed as the sum of the growth rates of the three components. Data for the years 1981–1987 indicate an average growth rate of 9.3 percent for total expenditures (American Hospital Association 1988). As for the components, there was an average annual growth of 11.25 percent for expenditures per patient day, an average annual *decline* of 2.3 percent for average length of stay, and an average annual decline of under 1 percent for admissions. This indicates that the major contributor to growth in hospital costs during this period was hospital expenses per day. Utilization actually declined. Much of the decline in utilization was the result of a shift from inpatient to ambulatory care, especially outpatient surgery.

To understand the growth in hospital expenses per day, it is necessary to decompose this variable further. Cromwell and Pushkin (1989) conducted a study of the growth in the components of hospital expenditures per stay for short-term hospitals during this period. They broke down expenditures per discharge into the following (multiplicative) components: expenditures per employee hour, employee hours per intermediate service (termed "productivity"), and intermediate service per discharge (termed "service intensity"). They also examined the periods 1981–1983 and 1984–1987 separately to take into account the introduction of the prospective payment system (PPS) by Medicare. Their results show a reduced overall growth rate in the 1984–1987 period (14.9 percent before the introduction of PPS and 7.4 percent after). In both periods expenses per employee hour accounted for the bulk of the growth in expenses (10.5 percent before and 5.2 percent after). Hours per service was next in magnitude (2.8 percent before and 1.6 percent after), and services per discharge contributed the least toward growth (0.8 percent before and 0.1 percent after). These results seem to indicate the following: hospital cost inflation fell after the introduction of PPS, and input prices have been the major cause of rising hospital costs.

Note that the use of the term *hours per service* to indicate productivity may be somewhat misleading. In recent years there has been some concern over the role of the growth of high-technology services as a driving force pushing up hospital costs. Increased hours per procedure may be partly explained by a shift toward a more highly trained labor force, thus indicating a higher skill level rather than lower productivity. Indeed, all three component variables might be increasing partially as a result of a greater use of high-technology services: even higher wages might be partially due to the hiring of workers who have more skills. For these reasons, these results do not allow an unambiguous interpretation. Nevertheless, the analysis forms a very useful indicator of the sources of growth in hospital costs.

BIBLIOGRAPHY

Overall Dimensions

Angell, M. 1985. Cost containment and the physician. *JAMA* 253:1203–1207.

Bauerschmidt, A.D. 1969. Sources and uses of healthcare funds in South Carolina. *Business and Economics Review of the University of South Carolina* 3:2–7.

Health Insurance Association of America. 1989. *Source book of health insurance data.* Washington, D.C.: Health Insurance Association of America.

Letsch, S.W., et al. 1988. National Health Expenditures, 1987. *Health Care Financing Review* 10 (winter):109–122.

Levit, K.R., et al. 1989. Health spending and the ability to pay. *Health Care Financing Review* 10 (spring):1–12.

Mullner, R., and Hadley, J. 1984. Interstate variations on the growth of chain-owned proprietary hospitals. *Inquiry* 21:144–151.

Rice, D.P., and Feldman, J.J. 1983. Living longer in the United States. *Milbank Quarterly* 61:362–396.

Sutcliffe, E.M. 1972. The Social Accounting of Health. In *The Economics of Medical Care*, ed. M.M. Hauser. London: George Allen and Unwin.

Costs, Prices, and Expenditures

Anderson, G., and Knickman, J.R. 1984. Patterns of expenditure among high utilizers of medical services. *Medical Care* 22:143–149.

Burner, S.T., and Waldo, D.R. 1995. National health expenditure projections, 1994–2005. *Health Care Financing Review* 16:221–242.

Cromwell, J., and Pushkin, D. 1989. Hospital productivity and intensity trends. *Inquiry* 26:366–380.

Freeland, M.S., et al. 1979. National hospital input price index. *Health Care Financing Review* 1 (summer):37–61.

Fuchs, V.R. 1990. The health sector's share of the gross national product. *Science* 247:534–538.

Ginsburg, D.H. 1978. Medical care services in the consumer price index. *Monthly Labor Review* 101:35–40.

Hellinger, F.J. 1990. Updated forecasts of the costs of medical care for persons with AIDS. *Public Health Reports* 105 (January):1–12.

Hellinger, F.J. 1993. The lifetime cost of treating a person with AIDS. *Journal of the American Medical Association* 270:474–478.

Kelly, J.V., et al. 1989. Duration and cost of AIDS hospitalizations in New York. *Medical Care* 27:1085–1098.

Klarman, H.E. 1972. Increases in the cost of physician and hospital services. *Inquiry* 7:22–36.

Long, S.H., et al. 1984. Medical expenditures for terminal cancer patients during the last year of life. *Inquiry* 22:315–327.

McCall, N. 1984. Utilization and costs of Medicare services by beneficiaries in their last year of life. *Medical Care* 22:329–342.

Pope, G. 1990. Physician inputs, outputs, and productivity; 1976–1986. *Inquiry* 27:151–160.

Rice, D.P., et al. 1985. The economic cost of illness. *Health Care Financing Review* 7 (fall):61–80.

Scitovsky, A.A. 1984. The high cost of dying. *Milbank Quarterly* 62:591–608.

Scitovsky, A.A., and McCall, N. 1977. *Changes in the cost of treatment of selected illness.* Pub. no. HRA 77-3161. Hyattsville, Md.: National Center for Health Services Research.

Scitovsky, A.A., and Rice, D.P. 1987. Estimating the direct and indirect costs of acquired immunodeficiency syndrome in the United States, 1985, 1986, and 1991. *Public Health Reports* 102:5–17.

Sisk, J.E. 1987. The cost of AIDS: A review of the estimates. *Health Affairs* 6 (summer):5–21.

Sloan, F.A., et al. 1985. The teaching hospital's growing surgical caseload. *JAMA* 254:376–382.

Zook, C.J., and Moore, E.D. 1980. High cost users of medical care. *New England Journal of Medicine* 302:996–1002.

New Institutions

de Lissovoy, G., et al. 1987. Preferred provider organizations one year later. *Inquiry* 24:127–135.

Gabel, J., et al. 1986. The emergence and future of preferred provider organizations. *Journal of Health Politics, Policy, and Law* 11:305–321.

Gruber, L.R., et al. 1988. From movement to industry: The growth of HMOs. *Health Affairs* 7 (summer):197–208.

McLauchlin, C.G., et al. 1989. Health care coalitions. *Inquiry* 26:72–83.

Health Insurance

DiCarlo, S., and Gabel, J. 1989. Conventional health insurance: A decade later. *Health Care Financing Review* 10 (spring):77–89.

Gabel, J., et al. 1994. The health insurance picture in 1993. *Health Affairs* 13:325–336.

Reinhardt, U.E. 1993. Reorganizing the financial flows in American health care. *Health Affairs* 12:172–193.

Rotwein, S., et al. 1995. Medicaid and state health care reform. *Health Care Financing Review* 16:105–138.

Rubin, R.M., et al. 1989. Private long-term care insurance. *Medical Care* 27:182–193.

Short, P.F. 1988. Trends in employee health insurance benefits. *Health Affairs* 7 (summer):186–196.

Smeeding, T.M., and Straub, L. 1987. Health care financing among the elderly. *Journal of Health Politics, Policy, and Law* 12:35–52.

PART II

Explanatory Economics

CHAPTER 3

Demand for Medical Care: A Simple Model

3.1 THE CONCEPT OF DEMAND

The purpose of explanatory economics is to predict economic behavior. When analyzing demand behavior, our attention focuses on the quantity demanded by consumers of a specific commodity or service. To perform the analysis, we use a demand model that serves two purposes: It provides a categorization of the separate factors that might cause demand or quantity demanded to increase or decrease, and it provides a specific hypothesis about how economic factors (e.g., price and income) influence demand or quantity demanded.

Models are the devices we use to obtain our results. A model is a representation of reality, not a complete description of it. The purpose of a model, however specified, is to present us with an "If . . . then . . ." type of explanation. In the case of the demand model, the reasoning is of this form: "If factor x increases, then demand or quantity demanded will increase (or decrease, depending on what factor x is)." A good model screens essential causal factors and incorporates them into a logical, coherent system.

Even though every model is conjectural, it should tell us something about movements in real phenomena (e.g., the quantity of medical care demanded). In assessing a model, it is therefore sufficient to examine whether its predictions concerning movements in selected phenomena are realized by comparing the predictions with actual movements in the phenomena as measured by data. In other words, accuracy of prediction is the test of an explanatory model.

This chapter introduces a simple model of the demand for a commodity. Section 3.2 sets forth the model, using an individual's demand for medical care as an example. Section 3.3 takes us behind the scenes and shows how the model of demand can be derived. Several key shortcomings of the simple model when applied to the medical care context are emphasized; these objections are central to the extended analyses of Chapter 4. Section 3.4 examines the factors influencing the market demand for the commodity. Section 3.5 develops the concept of elasticity, a tool used to measure the magnitude of the hypothesized movements, and Section 3.6 presents the demand analysis when insurance is present. Finally, Section 3.7 presents some actual estimates of the demand relationship.

3.2   INDIVIDUAL DEMAND: THE PRICE–QUANTITY RELATION

3.2.1 Demand and Quantity Demanded

We begin our exposition of the price-quantity relation with a specification of the terms of reference and definitions of the variables used. The unit of analysis is the individual consumer. In the present context, we examine the economic behavior of a typical or representative consumer. This behavior involves attaining or attempting to attain commodities. Since our focus is on health care, the commodity *physician care* is used as the major example. Physician care is defined as examinations and treatments administered by physicians to their patients. Physician care is only one of many commodities in the health care sector. Thus, when following the analysis, keep in mind that the relations specified in this chapter can be applied to other health-related commodities as well, including hospital services, pharmaceuticals, dental care, home care, preventive measures, and nutritional services.

Having identified the commodity in our analysis, we must next find an appropriate unit of measurement. Here we encounter a problem that is pervasive in medical care organization analysis: defining and measuring quality differences among units of medical care. Examinations and treatments can vary in thoroughness, in the physician's technical competence, and in the physician's bedside manner, among other factors. Quality differences constitute differences in these characteristics. When analyzing physician care as a commodity, all these variations should be kept in mind. In this chapter, we will abstract from quality differences to avoid complicating our initial entrance into explanatory economics.

Our commodity, physician care, is measured by the number of visits to a physician by the typical consumer. Each visit is taken as identical with all others. Finally, we specify the time span as being one year. Given this time frame, our commodity measure becomes the number of physician visits per year.

With this background, the demand hypothesis used to predict the effect of a change in direct per unit price on the quantity demanded of a commodity can be presented. The hypothesis is that the lower the out-of-pocket price offered to consumers (all other factors held constant), the greater the number of units of that commodity they will demand. A number of conventions or interpretations are related to this hypothesis. By "quantity demanded" we mean the quantity demanded at any specific price, all other causal factors held constant. By "demand" we mean the set of quantities demanded at various prices, all other causal factors held constant. By "out-of-pocket price" we mean the price paid directly by consumers for a particular unit of the commodity. By "all other factors" we mean those variables other than price that influence consumer demand behavior. The economic approach to consumer behavior is to specify an initial relation between out-of-pocket price and quantity demanded and then to introduce other causal factors to see how they affect the basic demand relation.

One such demand relation, assuming all other factors remain unchanged, is illustrated diagrammatically as line d_1 in Figure 3–1. The specific relation shown by this line, or curve, entails that, at a price of \$7 per visit, the consumer would be willing to visit the doctor twice a year; at a price of \$6 per visit, the consumer would be willing to make three visits; and so on. Assuming that the quantities demanded at all other prices trace out a straight-line relation, d_1 represents a particular demand curve at one specific level of demand. The lower-case letter d is used to indicate that we are representing the behavior of a single individual.

The downward slope of the demand curve is explained by the possibility of substitution. The economic approach implies that very few, if any, commodities are absolute musts. Substitutes exist for most commodities; some are almost identical and others are less similar. The longer the time span during which the consumer adapts his or her behavior to any substitutes, the more relevant they become. A sore throat, for example, can be treated by a physician or by resorting to drugs or home remedies. Furthermore, even if the malady is treated by a physician, alternative types of broad-spectrum antibiotics can be used. In recent years use of outpatient treatment instead of hospitalization has been suggested for many types of ailments. In the long term, health foods and other preventive services are substitutes for medical care in maintaining desired health levels. In these as well as other instances, the hypothesized relation applies: the lower the price of any specific alternative, the more it will be demanded.

Other (alternative) hypotheses than the demand relation might be put forward to explain consumer demand behavior. One alternative hypothesis that has received much attention in the medical care literature is that at higher prices individuals will still demand and pay for the same quantity of medical care. This alternative hypothesis would be represented by a vertical demand curve. Similar vertical demand curves have also been hypothesized for other items considered necessities, such as housing, basic foods, and even alcohol.

Having two alternative hypotheses, we are faced with the problem of determining which is the more useful for explaining actual behavior. Debating the issue by itself cannot resolve the controversy, however. The hypothesis chosen should be the one that most closely fits the actual data. The empirical testing of hypotheses is discussed in Section 3.7.

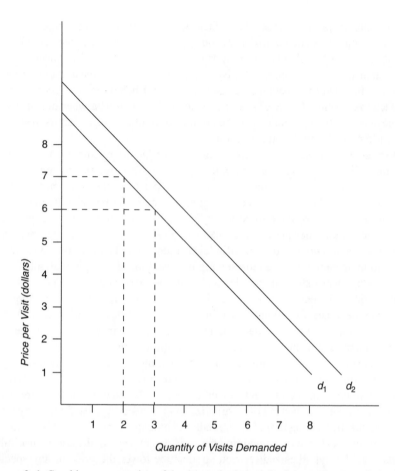

Figure 3–1 Graphic representation of the demand relation, the famous downward-sloping demand curve. Curves d_1 and d_2 show the quantity demanded increasing as the direct price decreases. Each curve represents a separate level of demand. With reference to curve d_1, curve d_2 represents an increase in demand.

Before proceeding with qualifications to our hypothesis, we should emphasize that we are focusing solely on consumer behavior. Our hypothesis relates only to how much the consumer is willing to buy at any price. We are not inquiring at this stage about whether the amount demanded will be supplied or available. (Such an inquiry is relevant to producer behavior, discussed in Chapter 6.) At present, we are merely examining a portion of the total picture of scarcity—that part relating to demand.

3.2.2 Changes in Demand

The effects of factors other than the out-of-pocket price on the economic behavior of consumers are introduced by way of their influence on the basic price-quantity relation. These other factors can be placed into three broad categories: (1) income, (2) prices of other (related) commodities, and (3) tastes. Each category is considered in turn.

3.2.2.1 Income

The income of the consumer is generally assumed to be positively related to demand. That is, if income increases, the quantity demanded at each price will be greater. The basic relation between income and demand can be illustrated with the use of demand curves. In Figure 3–1, curve d_1 can now be interpreted as representing a level of demand at some initial level of income. Let us suppose that, from this initial level, income increases. The hypothesized effect on demand is such that at a price of $7 there will be three visits demanded instead of two, at a price of $6 there will be four visits demanded instead of three, and so on. The new demand level, corresponding to the higher income level, can be represented by the curve d_2. In the diagram the relative position of the two curves summarizes the net influence of income on consumer behavior. A shift in demand from curve d_1 to curve d_2 is called an *increase* in demand.

The same reasoning can be applied in reverse to a fall in income. This decline causes the consumer to demand less of the commodity at each price. The change in the level of demand might, for example, be represented by a shift from d_2 to d_1. This is called a *decrease* in demand.

Income is frequently defined as an individual's earnings in a specific time period. It is a variable used to measure the ability of the individual to afford medical care, but it is only an approximate measure. Another measure of the affordability of medical care is the individual's level of wealth, including bonds, bank deposits, real estate, and other assets, less any debt, such as bank loans and mortgages. It has been proposed that these factors of wealth (or the income flowing from them) be incorporated into the measure of affordability. A third measure is after-tax income. This measure is particularly important to take into account when considering changes in tax rates and their effects on purchasing power. Whatever measure, single or composite, is used, it should be a good approximation of the individual's ability to pay for medical care.

3.2.2.2 Prices of Related Commodities

The demand for a particular commodity is also influenced by the quantities of related commodities consumed. The quantities of these related commodities are, in turn, influenced by their prices. Two classes of commodity relations are of concern to us: complements and substitutes. A complementary commodity is one whose use is generally accompanied by the use of the commodity in question. Examples might include penicillin and syringes, the services of a surgeon and the hospital's surgical services, and the services of a radiologist and x-ray film. The hypothesis relating the demands of complementary commodities is as follows: A fall in the price of a commodity increases the quantity demanded of that commodity, and it also leads to an increase in the demand for commodities that are complements. Similar reasoning, in reverse, applies to an increase in the price of one commodity in a complementary set. As an example of this relation, we can hypothesize that a fall in the out-of-pocket price of the surgical services involved in tonsillectomies will lead to an increase in the quantity of services demanded; it will also increase the demand for hospital room services.

Complements play an important role in medical care demand. The close relation between physician care and hospital care has frequently led to the assertion that much hospital demand is really determined by the quantity of physician services consumed.

The second type of commodity relation is that of substitution. A substitute is a commodity that can replace the original commodity. The hypothesis is that a fall in the price of a commodity increases the quantity demanded and leads to a reduced demand for substitute commodities. This relation can be illustrated using an example of two substitute services, postoperative recuperation time in the hospital versus home care. A rise in the price the patient pays for an additional day of hospital care decreases the quantity of hospital days demanded. At the same time, it increases the demand for home care.

Substitution was also the reason given in Section 3.2.1 for the downward slope of the demand curve for any commodity. For example, quantity of inpatient care demanded is negatively related to patient price because inpatient care can be substituted for home care when the price of inpatient care falls and vice versa. This assumes, of course, that the price of home care remains constant. When the price of home care rises, this leads to additional substitution, which is accounted for in our model by an outward shift in the inpatient care demand curve. The slope of the demand curve of any commodity, as well as how much it shifts when substitute prices change, depends on how similar the patient perceives the substitutes to be. Services such as inpatient and outpatient surgery (e.g., for hernia repair and tonsillectomies) are highly substitutable, as are nursing home care and home care in many instances.

3.2.2.3 Tastes

Consumer tastes is a catchall category covering all other factors that might influence demand. Tastes have sometimes been called *wants*, a term connoting the intensity of desire for particular commodities. The elements that influence the intensity of an individual's desire for medical care include health status, educational background, sex, age, race, and upbringing. Any of these can explain differences in the intensity of desire for medical care among individuals. That is, with other factors (incomes, prices of other commodities, and so on) held constant, these differences can offer explanations as to why one individual's demand curve is d_1 (Figure 3–1) whereas another's is d_2. (The explanation might simply be that the health status of the first individual is lower than that of the second individual.)

Tastes are usually considered to be fixed from the standpoint of economic analysis. Although tastes differ among individuals, they are hypothesized, for most commodities, to be stable over fairly short periods of time. If they are stable, once the factors that underlie tastes are accounted for, differences in demand can be attributed to differences in incomes, prices of other commodities, and factors influencing tastes. However, controversy exists over the stability of individual tastes for medical care. In addition to the dependence of tastes on health, which is itself transitory, physicians potentially can exert considerable influence over tastes for medical care. Changing tastes have played a large role in health economics. Because of this, it is necessary to go behind the scenes to discover the role of tastes in medical care demand.

3.3 DERIVING THE DEMAND RELATIONSHIP

In Section 3.2, the demand for medical care was analyzed as if medical care were an ordinary commodity like carrots or shoes. However, certain characteristics of medical care make it unlike many ordinary commodities. We must pay closer attention to these characteristics to determine if and when standard demand analysis is appropriate for medical care. To do this, we present a theoretical model focusing on the conditions that are required for the demand relation to hold; special attention is paid to whether these conditions are likely to be met in the case of medical care.

The factors influencing a consumer's behavior with regard to the demand for a commodity can be placed under the categories of income, prices, and tastes. Let us assume that a typical individual has a choice of purchasing only two commodities. These two commodities are carrots and physician care (as measured by physician's office visits). In what follows, we will specify the assumptions underlying our model for the demand for these two products.

3.3.1 Tastes

Tastes are essentially desires for products. These desires, or wants, are quantified using an index that we call *utility*. Although it is a hypothetical construct, the concept of utility is very valuable as an instructive device. It is often equated with the notion of satisfaction. The utility of carrots for a hypothetical individual is shown in Table 3–1. The numbers in this table were devised to show an increasing total amount of utility (total utility) as more carrots are consumed, but, more importantly, they were devised so that the increases gradually diminish. The concept used to represent the increases in utility from successive quantities of a commodity is called *marginal utility*. Marginal utility is the change in total utility resulting from a unit change in the commodity. Thus the marginal utility for the first carrot is 6, it is 5 for the second, and so on. This decrease in the size of the utility of successive quantities of a commodity is called *diminishing marginal utility*. Note that, in general, total satisfaction will still increase. This is a key assumption of demand analysis.

The same assumption can be applied to medical care as well, but the circumstances in which the relationship of diminishing marginal utility will hold needs to be explored in greater detail. We therefore list the conditions that must occur:

3.3.1.1 Health Status

The initial health status of the individual (H) is given and known by the individual. That is, the individual knows what medical condition she has.

3.3.1.2 Consumer Information

The relationship between medical care (MC) and health status (H) is also known by the individual. That is, she knows how "productive" medical care will be in influencing her health.

3.3.1.3 Productivity of Medical Care

In general, we assume that the marginal productivity of medical care in influencing health is constant. As more units of medical care (visits) are consumed,

Table 3–1 Relationship between Quantity Consumed of Two Commodities and Utility of (Satisfaction Derived from) the Commodities

Quantity	Medical Care		Carrots	
	Total Utility	Marginal Utility	Total Utility	Marginal Utility
1	22	22	6	6
2	42	20	11	5
3	60	18	15	4
4	76	16	18	3
5	90	14	20	2
6	102	12	21	1

equal additions to health status will result. Obviously, there must be a limit to how healthy an individual can become, and we will show what happens when this assumption is altered. For the moment, we will hold with the assumption of constant productivity.

3.3.1.4 Quality

The quality of medical care is constant. All visits are of the same quality.

3.3.1.5 Other Taste-Influencing Variables

It should be noted that the utility function is dependent on a host of other variables, each of which may influence the individual's intensity of desire for medical care. These variables include the individual's education, upbringing, marital status, and age, among others. For example, it is believed that increasing education increases an individual's desire for good health. Thus we should be aware that in back of any taste function lies a series of formative factors that cause the utility-quantity relation to be what it is. We will assume that there are no other sources of utility other than medical care and carrots.

Given these assumptions, we can hypothesize the type of relations between utility and medical care shown in Table 3–1, where each added visit results in a smaller increment of added utility. Unless the individual is a competitive bodybuilder, the hypothesis is a plausible one.

3.3.2 Income

The second variable in our demand model is the individual's income. We will assume that the income is $10 for the time period.

3.3.3 Prices of Other Commodities

Other variables include the prices charged for medical care and carrots. We will initially set these at $1 per carrots and $4 per physician's office visit. The purpose of our analysis is to predict what happens when the price of medical care changes and, in the process, to make explicit what variables are initially being held constant in the analysis.

3.3.4 Behavioral Assumption: Utility Maximization

Finally, we come to our behavioral assumption, which is what sets the model in motion. Our assumption is that the individual is a utility maximizer (i.e., the individual desires to gain the most satisfaction or benefit from his or her income).

3.3.5 Conclusions

The model's conclusion stems from these assumptions together with assumptions about its price changes. Let us first determine what quantities of medical care and carrots are demanded at these initial prices. In doing this, the critical variable to focus on is the marginal utility per dollar of expenditure, or the ratio of marginal utility to price (MU/P). It is this variable that expresses the satisfaction per dollar of expense for each alternative use. At a price of $1 per carrot, buying a carrot will be the best bet for the first $1 of expenditure, since the first carrot yields 6 units of utility. The next item purchased will not be another carrot, because an additional expenditure here would yield 5 units of utility per $1, whereas a visit to the doctor would yield 5.5 units (22 units/$4). Therefore, the individual makes a visit to the doctor. The individual has now spent a total of $5 and has $5 left. The next items of expenditure will be a carrot and another visit to the doctor (indeed, both have an MU/P ratio of 5). At this point the individual will have used up all income and will have achieved an equal marginal utility per dollar for the last purchases of each commodity. This equality of MU/P in each use indicates that the individual's income cannot be reallocated to obtain more utility.

To show that the individual is maximizing utility, let us assume that, after the second carrot, the individual allocates the remaining $4 to the purchase of carrots instead of medical care. The marginal utility of the third, fourth, fifth, and sixth carrot would be 4, 3, 2, and 1, respectively. The individual would now be getting 1 unit of utility per $1 of expenditure instead of the 5 units obtainable by purchasing medical care. That is, the individual would have been better off with two carrots and two visits than with this alternative set of purchases.

Having shown that there is a utility maximizing "equilibrium" quantity for each commodity, let us now change the Assumption about prices of other commodities and lower the price of medical care to $3. A carrot will still cost $1. This fall in the price of medical care results in an increase in the utility per dollar of medical care for all visits and makes medical care more valuable in dollar terms. Under this altered assumption, the individual will maximize utility by "consuming" three visits and only consume one carrot.

The essential implication of this analysis is that when the price of medical care falls, the quantity demanded increases (assuming all other variables, including other prices as well as incomes and tastes, remain the same). This is thus a derivation of the demand relationship. It should be noted that the model only holds when other variables are held constant. Changing them will shift the demand relationship in one direction or the other, depending on the variable and the degree of change. For example, a more educated person may perceive health as having a greater utility relative to carrots, thus causing a shift in tastes. This will shift the demand for medical care as well.

With regard to one particular loose end, our Assumption about the productivity of medical care, let us consider the probable effect of a more realistic assumption. In particular, let us assume that medical care has diminishing marginal productivity with respect to health. If additional units of health diminished in size with successive visits, this would make the marginal utility of medical care fall more quickly and would reduce the relative desirability of additional units of medical care. There would still be a downward-sloping demand curve, but it would be shifted inward in comparison to the situation where the productivity of medical care was constant.

3.4 MARKET DEMAND

The model developed previously provided a means of analyzing an individual's demand for medical care. To generalize the model to explain market demand, we must make an additional assumption. (By "market" we mean the network of buyers and sellers of a commodity.) The assumption is that the more individuals there are who seek the product, the greater will be the market demand and the quantity demanded in the market at any price.

This is illustrated in Figure 3–2, which shows the demand curves of three individuals: d_b is Mr. B's demand curve, d_k is Ms. K's demand curve, and d_j is Mrs. J's demand curve. At a price of $20 per visit, Mr. B will demand 3 visits, Ms. K will demand 2, and Mrs. J will demand none. At $15 per visit, Mr. B., Ms. K., and Mrs. J will demand 5 visits, 4 visits, and 1 visit, respectively. At $10, the number of visits will be 7, 6, and 4. Using information on individual demand curves and on the number of individuals, we can derive a market demand curve.

Given the three individual demand curves, the market quantity demanded at a given price will be the sum of the quantities demanded by all three individuals at that price. At a price of $20, the quantity demanded in the market will be 5 visits; at $15, the quantity will be 10; and at $10, it will be 17. The market demand curve is shown in Figure 3–2 as D_m.

We can now divide the factors influencing market demand into two categories: (1) factors influencing individual demands only and (2) factors influencing market demand. The former includes prices, incomes, and tastes. If any of these change, individual demands or the quantities demanded will also change. If individual demand curves shift out, market curves, being based on individual curves, will shift out as well. In addition to responding to changes in individual curves, market demand is influenced by changes in the number of participants in the market. For example, an influx of people into an area will cause market demand to increase.

3.5 MEASURING QUANTITY RESPONSIVENESS TO PRICE CHANGES

In the preceding sections, we developed a model that enabled us to predict how a particular factor will affect quantity demanded or demand. Thus, we can predict

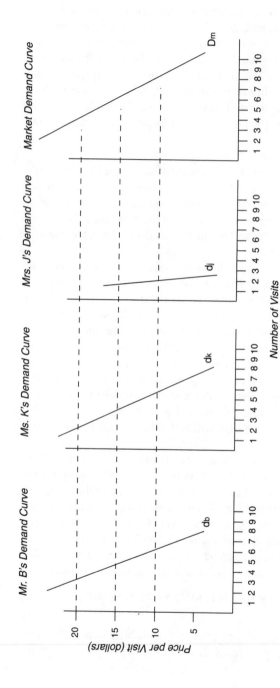

Figure 3–2 Derivation of the market demand curve from individual demand curves. The quantity demanded at each price by all consumers in the market is the sum of the individual quantities demanded. The market demand curve is the horizontal sum of all individual demand curves.

that, when the out-of-pocket price falls, the quantity demanded will rise. We can now ask, by how much will the quantity demanded rise? The answer to this question is likely to play an important role in setting policy.

The concept used to measure quantity responsiveness to out-of-pocket price changes is the concept of *price elasticity of demand.* Price elasticity is designed to measure the responsiveness of demand to a price change at a given point or between two given points on a single demand curve. That is, it attempts to measure responsiveness when the only factor undergoing change and thereby influencing the quantity demanded is price.

The elasticity of demand is designed to measure changes independent of the units of measurement. That is, the measure of elasticity is a measure of relative magnitudes and will not change if cents rather than dollars are used to measure price or units rather than thousands are used to measure quantity. Elasticity is thus a pure measure of the magnitude of change. The formula used for small changes in price is the percentage change in quantity demanded over the percentage change in price. In symbolic terms, this is written

$$E = \frac{\Delta Q/Q}{\Delta P/P}$$

where E is elasticity, Q is the original quantity, P is the original price, and ΔQ and ΔP are changes in Q and P. This formula is known as a *point elasticity formula.* The point elasticity formula is appropriate for very small changes along the demand curve. If the change in price is at all appreciable, an average elasticity measure over the range of the demand curve covered by the change is more appropriate. This measure, known as the *arc elasticity of demand* is written as

$$E = \frac{(Q_2 - Q_1) / (Q_2 + Q_1)}{(P_2 - P_1) / (P_2 + P_1)}$$

where Q_1 and P_1 refer to one price and quantity set and Q_2 and P_2 refer to a second set at another point on the same demand curve. In fact, both the price and quantity changes are expressed in terms of average price and quantity levels, that is, as $(P_1 + P_2)/2$ and $(Q_1 + Q_2)/2$. In the first equation above, the 2s would cancel out, leaving us with the second formula.

An example will help to illustrate the use of this formula. Assume that the Richland County Health Department charges $3.00 per syphilis test and that in May it performed 1,200 tests. In June the County Council decided to raise the charges to $3.25 per test. Only 1,150 people requested tests in June. What is the elasticity of demand?

The elasticity measure of a price change is supposed to be a measure of responsiveness along a demand curve, that is, when all factors other than price remain constant. If other factors have indeed remained constant, we can use the elasticity formula as an approximation of the responsiveness of quantity demanded to price changes. If other factors have changed, we must make some adjustment to take into account the extent to which these other factors influenced the quantity demanded. Assume in our example that these other factors remained constant and that only price influenced quantity. In this case, we can use the elasticity formula directly:

$$E = \frac{(1,150 - 1,200)/(1,150 + 1,200)}{(3.25 - 3)/(3.25 + 3)} = -0.53$$

The elasticity of demand at that point is –0.53. (The minus sign is frequently dropped from discussions, so one will often see the price elasticity quoted as the absolute value, e.g., 0.53. The reader should remember that, in the case of price elasticity, the negative sign, if dropped, is taken for granted.) We thus have a figure indicating the responsiveness of quantity to price.

Price elasticity is related to how total consumer expenditures respond to a change in the out-of-pocket price. For any elasticity measure whose absolute value is less than 1, total out-of-pocket expenditures will increase with a reduction in price; at such points on the demand curve, demand is said to be inelastic. In our example, total expenditures ($P \times Q$) were $3,600.00 before the price change and $3,737.50 after. Receipts from this source rose by $137.50 because of the nature of the responsiveness at that point on the demand curve. An elasticity measure of –0.53 is thought of as relatively unresponsive; that is, a small relative price rise or fall will generate a smaller relative quantity change. If price increases by 1 percent, the quantity will decrease by only about 0.5 percent, and the total amount spent on syphilis tests will increase. With an elasticity of –0.53, a reduction in price will lower total expenditures (i.e., total consumer expenditures in terms of dollars) because the relative increase in quantity purchased will not be sufficient to overcome the relatively greater price decrease. Thus, if the Richland County Health Department wants more revenue and does not care about how many tests are performed, it should raise its price to $3.25.

Demand curves can also have unitary elastic and elastic portions. Where the elasticity measures –1, demand responsiveness is said to be *unitary elastic*. In the case of a small change in price, total expenditures will remain constant. When the demand responsiveness is elastic (i.e., greater than 1 in absolute value), it means that the relative change in quantity consumed exceeds the relative change in price. If there is a small increase in price, the decrease in quantity will be relatively greater, and total expenditures will fall. If there is a small decrease in price, total expenditures will rise.

These relations are shown in Figure 3–3. A straight-line demand curve for vaccinations is shown in Graph A. At a price of $10, no vaccinations are demanded,

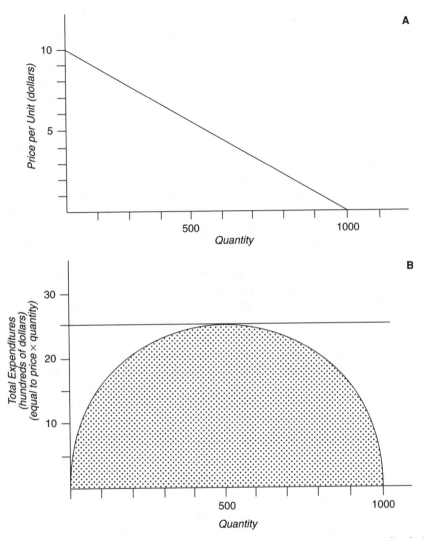

Figure 3–3 Relationship between price, quantity demanded, and total revenue. Graph A shows the basic relation between quantity demanded and price. Graph B shows the relation between total expenditures (which equal price times quantity) and quantity. Graph B is derived from Graph A.

but as the price falls in $1 increments, vaccination demand increases by 100. Thus, at a price of $9, 100 vaccinations will be demanded; at a price of $8, 200 will be demanded; and so on. Graph B shows the total expenditures generated at each level of sales. Thus, if 100 vaccinations are sold, $900 in expenditures is generated, and so on (see Table 3–2 for the actual values). Over a range, total expenditures increase, but eventually the increase levels off to a maximum, and beyond that point total expenditures begin to decline.

There is a connection between the elasticity along a specific segment of the demand curve and the total expenditures specific to relevant points on the curve. At relatively high prices and low quantities on a straight-line demand curve, only a relatively small change in price (in terms of percentage) is needed to induce a relatively large change in the quantity demanded. The lower individual expenditures resulting from the fall in unit prices is therefore more than offset by the large increase in quantity demanded, and so total expenditures will increase. For example, in Table 3–2, for a reduction in price from $9 to $8, the arc elasticity of demand along that segment of the curve is –4.76. Demand is therefore said to be elastic, and if that reduction in price is instituted, total expenditures will increase (in this case, from $900 to $1,600). As we move down the demand curve, the relative price change becomes smaller in relation to the associated quantity change. Thus the absolute value of elasticity falls. But as long as this value in absolute terms is greater than 1 (i.e., we are on the elastic portion of the curve), total expenditures will increase, although not by as much as in higher priced segments. Eventually, the elasticity takes on a value of –1. At this point, price and quantity changes offset each other exactly, and total expenditures stay constant (we are at the top of the total expenditures curve). As prices fall further, we move on to the inelastic portion of the demand curve. Price reductions offset quantity increases, and total expenditures fall. Thus, along any single straight-line demand curve, the elasticity of demand will decrease with successive reductions in price.

Further insight into the concept of elasticity can be gained by examining elasticity for two different demand curves at a single price. Assume that two demand curves in two different markets for physician visits cross at a price of $3, as in

Table 3–2 Price for Vaccinations, Quantity Demanded, and Total Expenditures

Price	Quantity Demanded	Total Expenditures
$10	0	$0
9	100	900
8	200	1,600
7	300	2,100
6	400	2,400
5	500	2,500
4	600	2,400
3	700	2,100
2	800	1,600
1	900	900

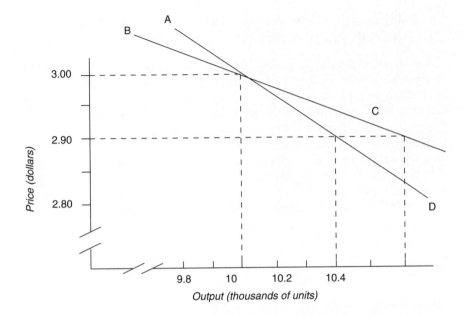

Figure 3–4 Responsiveness of quantity demanded to price for differently sloped demand curves. Curve *BC* shows a greater responsiveness of quantity demanded to price than does curve *AD*.

Figure 3–4. The consumers in Market 2 are more responsive to price reductions than are those in Market 1. Let *AD* be the demand curve in Market 1 and *BC* be the demand curve in Market 2. Now let the price fall by 10 cents. Consumers in Market 1 demand 10,300 visits, whereas those in Market 2 demand 10,500. The arc elasticity in Market 1 is

$$E = \frac{300/20,300}{-.10/5.90} = -.87$$

The arc elasticity in Market 2 is

$$E = \frac{500/20,500}{-.10/5.00} = -1.44$$

As can be seen, demand curve *BC* is for a more responsive group of consumers, and the elasticity for a given quantity will be greater in absolute value than that of a less responsive group.

3.6 INSURANCE, OUT-OF-POCKET PRICE, AND QUANTITY DEMANDED

A major factor in considering the demand for medical care is the role that insurance plays in influencing the out-of-pocket price of medical care. There are a number of different types of insurance arrangements that consumers can obtain, and these will affect the out-of-pocket price and hence the quantity demanded in different ways. We will examine the important alternatives.

In analyzing the effect of alternative insurance arrangements, we initially specify a demand curve in which the consumers have no insurance and hence pay the full price charged by the provider (e.g., a physician). This curve, where full price equals the out-of-pocket price, is labelled D_n, in Figure 3–5. Now let us introduce the first type of insurance arrangement: a copayment arrangement.

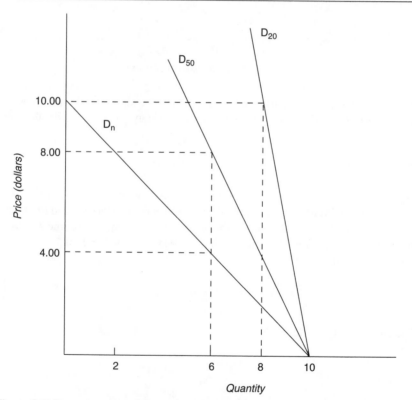

Figure 3–5 Representation of demand curves with no insurance (D_n), with a 50-percent copayment (D_{50}), and with a 20-percent copayment (D_{20}). When there is a copayment, D_n also represents the relation between the quantity demanded and the out-of-pocket price.

A copayment is a payment of the proportion of the charged price that is paid by the patient; the insurance company pays the remainder of the charged price. For example, with a 20-percent copayment and a charged price of $20 per visit, the patient pays the provider 20 percent of the charged price, $4, and the insurance company pays the remainder. In analyzing the impact of a coinsurance contract on demand, we assume that, even though the consumer has purchased an insurance contract, demand behavior is still governed by the demand curve D_n. What changes is that the out-of-pocket price and charged price now differ from one another. At any given charged price, the consumer faces a lower out-of-pocket price and hence will move down the demand curve D_n.

If the coinsurance rate is 50 percent, the demand curve facing the provider is D_{50} (Figure 3–4). Here, at any charged price, the out-of-pocket price is one-half the charged price, and the consumer demands a quantity determined by the out-of-pocket price and the demand curve D_n. In fact, D_n becomes the demand curve relating quantity to out-of-pocket price. Thus, if the provider's charge were $8 per visit (in Figure 3–5), the consumer with a 50-percent coinsurance contract would pay a $4 out-of-pocket price and the quantity demanded would be six visits. If the coinsurance rate was 20 percent, the market demand curve facing the providers would be D_{20}. A charged price of $10 would mean an out-of-pocket price of $2 and a quantity demanded of eight. As the coinsurance rate falls, the market demand curve facing the providers shifts out but the curve D_n continues to represent the relation between quantity demanded and out-of-pocket price.

Next we examine the impact of an indemnity contract. An indemnity contract sets a fixed per unit amount up to which the insurer will pay in the event of a service being used. For example, if an individual has pediatric coverage, an indemnity contract might specify that the insurer will pay up to $4 per visit. If the price is greater than $4, the consumer is responsible for the balance. In Figure 3–6 D_n is again the demand curve with no insurance coverage. Now let the individual purchase an indemnity contract that requires the insurer to reimburse the provider up to $4 per visit. The demand curve facing the provider becomes D_{n+i}, which is the D_n curve raised by $4 at all points. The position of D_{n+i} is such that, at each price charged, the out-of-pocket price will be $4 less than this, and the quantity demanded will reflect this lower out-of-pocket price. In Figure 3–6, a charged price of $8 means an out-of-pocket price of $4 and a quantity demanded of six. An increase in the amount by which the insurer indemnifies the consumer would shift D_{n+i} upward. The curve D_n would remain the same.

Finally, we examine the impact of a deductible. A deductible is a fixed total amount that the insurer deducts from the bill; the consumer must spend up to this amount before coverage begins. Until the consumer spends this amount, he or she pays the full price for each additional unit consumed (the price paid for the next additional unit is called the *marginal out-of-pocket price*). The marginal out-of-

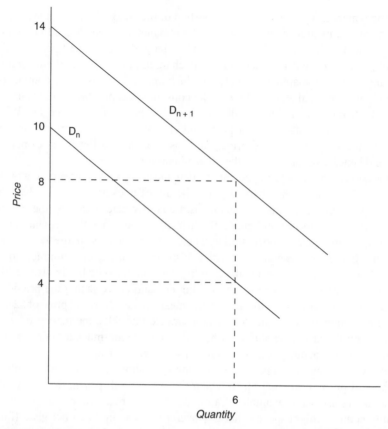

Figure 3–6 Representation of demand curves with no insurance (D_n) and with an indemnity payment of \$4 (D_{n+i}). When there is an indemnity, D_n also represents the relation between the quantity demanded and the out-of-pocket price.

---

pocket price before the deductible is reached is the charged price. If there is no copayment in addition to the deductible, the marginal out-of-pocket price, after the deductible is met, is zero.

To analyze the impact of a deductible on demand, we will slightly reinterpret the demand curve. Assume that the curve shows the value to the consumer of each additional visit (the marginal value). If the patient consumes one visit, the value of the visit is \$9. The second visit has a smaller marginal value, in this case \$8. The two visits together would have a value of \$17. These numbers and the value of additional visits are contained in Table 3–3. The table shows a declining marginal

Table 3–3 Schedule of Value of Additional Medical Visits to Patient and Total (Summed) Value of All Units of Care

Quantity	Value of Additional Unit of Care to Consumer	Total Value of All Care Received up to Given Quantity
1	$9	$9
2	8	17
3	7	24
4	6	30
5	5	35
6	4	39
7	3	42
8	2	44
9	1	45
10	0	45

value for successive visits, which is consistent with what we assumed in deriving the demand hypothesis.

Let us now assume a market price of $8 and a deductible of $32. At this market price, the out-of-pocket marginal price to the consumer will be $8 per visit until (and if) the deductible is met. Thereafter, it will be zero (if there is no copayment as well). In answering the question of how many visits will be demanded, we must look at the consumer's valuation of visits in Table 3–3 and compare these with the marginal out-of-pocket price and the deductible level. At first, we might be tempted to say that only the first two visits are worth at least the marginal out-of-pocket price and so only two will be demanded. One would then conclude that, having spent $16 in total, the consumer did not meet the deductible, and so demand will be at two visits.

But our consumer is truly a logical "economic person" and will look more carefully at all the options. The consumer realizes that he or she could buy the third and fourth units and, in doing so, use up the deductible of $32. Once the deductible is used up, the rest of the visits demanded would be free! Indeed, if the individual consumed nine units, the value to him or her of all of them would be $45, well in excess of the outlay of $32 for the first four units. In general, we can say that, with a deductible, the amount demanded will be determined by the consumer's comparison of the additional value of all extra units with the additional out-of-pocket cost of all extra units. Even if the marginal value of the next visit (third, in this case) is less than its marginal out-of-pocket price, overall it will pay the individual to spend more in order to receive the benefits of the postdeductible units. If, however, the deductible was $100 and the charged price $8, the individual would stop consuming at two units, because there would be no other quantity of consumption at which the total value to the individual exceeded what the individual had to pay.

Frequently, a deductible and a copayment are found together in the same policy. In our example, a $32 deductible is combined with a 20-percent copayment (on units of care after the deductible has been reached). With a charged price of $8, the individual would then pay a marginal out-of-pocket price of $1.60 for each unit consumed after four. The individual would overspend the deductible in this case but would demand only eight visits, because the ninth, costing $1.60, would have a marginal value of only $1.

3.7   ELASTICITY OF DEMAND ESTIMATES

Demand responsiveness can be measured by natural experiments and controlled trials. A natural experiment (in the demand context) occurs when a change in insurance coverage is implemented by an insurer. We can use the results of such a policy action to determine demand responsiveness by conducting before-and-after comparisons of the data. Assuming all else has remained the same (e.g., that an increase in a deductible has not driven the sicker insureds to buy more complete insurance elsewhere), we can use the data to measure the degree of responsiveness. Natural experiments, unfortunately, often do not provide sufficient information. The investigators have no control over insurer policy decisions and are therefore restricted to researching the changes in price and coverage introduced by the insurers.

A more flexible, but also more expensive, approach is to do a controlled experiment. In this approach, study groups are selected randomly (to avoid any bias due to self-selection, such as sicker individuals choosing more complete insurance coverage) and assigned to specific categories (e.g., 20-percent copayment, 40-percent copayment, etc.). Differences in utilization (which are assumed to be caused by differences in demand) can be measured, and thus a measure of demand responsiveness can be obtained.

An example of a natural experiment in the demand field occurred in 1977, when the United Mine Workers introduced a $250 deductible for inpatient services and a 40-percent copayment for physician and outpatient visits up to a maximum family liability of $500. Prior to this, the insureds had no out-of-pocket expenses.

Scheffler (1984) conducted a study of the impact of this cost sharing on hospital admissions, average length of hospital stay, the probability that an insured would have at least one physician visit, and the number of times an insured visited a physician.

According to the analysis, in the five months prior to introduction of the hospital deductible (the comparison period), the hospital admission rate was 6.8 per 1,000 enrollees and the average length of stay per hospitalization was 5.42 days.

The corresponding figures for the five months after introduction (the study period) were 4.8 per 1,000 for admissions and 6.45 days per hospitalization. The longer average length of stay in the study period may have been due to the fact that sicker cases were hospitalized. With regard to physician visits, the study's results indicated that the proportion of the population seeing a doctor at least once fell from 44 percent in the comparison period to 28 percent in the study period, and the average number of visits of those who did see a doctor at least once fell from 2.3 to 1.6.

The results of this experiment, like the results of other such studies, convincingly demonstrate the immediate impact of cost-sharing policies on utilization. But do the reductions in utilization last? Are there bad consequences farther down the line? One study (Scitovsky and McCall 1977) verified that reductions in physician visits did last several years, but several others have raised doubts as to whether longer term impacts occur (see Section 4.2).

By far the best known controlled experiment in this area is the six-site Health Insurance Experiment conducted by the Rand Corporation (Newhouse et al. 1981). In this study, 2,756 families agreed to participate in an experiment in which each family was assigned to one of five groups with different copayment rates. The rates included free care: 25-, 50-, and 95-percent coinsurance; and a deductible with 95-percent coinsurance (all services, such as physician visits and hospitalization, were covered under the single copayment). Those families with greater potential out-of-pocket expenses than their pre-experiment coverage were compensated accordingly. Upper limits were placed on each family's out-of-pocket expenses. The families participated for three to five years.

The results dramatically indicated the differential impact of higher out-of-pocket expenses. For example, those with free care incurred average expenses for all services of $401, whereas those with 25-, 50-, and 95-percent coinsurance incurred expenses of $346, $328, and $254, respectively. Furthermore, these differentials held up over several years. Since the experiment was designed to control for all other intervening factors (e.g., health status, income, etc.), the results have had a considerable impact in health policy circles. The fact is that such controlled results are seldom obtained.

Several questions have been raised concerning the applicability of the study's results. First, the experiments affected only a small portion of all the health care market in each of the six communities studied. If copayments were raised for the entire market or a substantial portion of the market, would providers (doctors) react and generate additional demand, thus changing the results (see Section 4.2.6) (Stoddart and Labelle 1985)? Furthermore, the aged (and presumably the fragile) were omitted from the study. Would their responses be any different?

Despite the unanswered questions, such studies have moved us closer toward developing a quantitative measure of the impact of out-of-pocket price on demand. As seen previously, demand elasticity depends on the starting point on an individual's demand curve, which in turn is affected by the individual's level of insurance. A rough estimate of demand elasticity when consumers have 0 to 25 percent coinsurance is −.2 (Newhouse et al. 1980).

Such an estimate can be used in the following way. If the price for a physician visit is $100, the copayment rate is 10 percent, and initially there are 120 visits, what would be the expected number of visits after the copayment rate is raised to 20 percent? The answer (assuming an elasticity of −.2) is obtained by solving for Q_2 (visits in Period 2), where

$$E = \frac{(Q_2 - Q_1)\,/\,(Q_2 + Q_1)}{(P_2 - P_1)\,/\,(P_2 - P_1)}$$

or

$$-.2 = \frac{(Q_2 - 120)\,/\,(Q_2 + 120)}{(20 - 10)\,/\,(20 + 10)}$$

The result gives a value for Q_2 of 104 visits (rounded to the nearest integer). In this case the total price did not change, although the copayment rate and therefore the out-of-pocket price did. A similar analysis could be done if the charged price and the copayment rate had both been changed.

A number of studies have been conducted analyzing demand in the nursing home market. Nursing home care is a health care service whose demand has distinct characteristics that have an impact on its elasticity of demand. First, there are a significant number of self-pay (uninsured) patients in this market; in 1994, out-of-pocket payments accounted for one third of all nursing home expenditures. For those patients who are not covered by public insurance (primarily through Medicaid), the out-of-pocket price becomes an important variable because private insurance for long-term care is still a minor factor. Second, there are close substitutes for nursing home care. Home health care is, in many instances, a viable alternative to nursing home care. Also, some patients who are hospitalized and could be moved to a skilled nursing care facility "economize" on this skilled nursing home care by remaining in the hospital longer and transferring later or not at all. The existence of close substitutes increases the elasticity of demand for nursing home care.

Lamberton and colleagues (1986) conducted a cross-county study of nursing home demand in South Dakota. In analyzing the relationship between nursing home days and variables such as price, income, and home care visits, they estimated an elasticity of demand for private patients of −.76. They also detected a significant negative relationship between home care visits and nursing home care, which substantiated the hypothesis that the two forms of care are substitutes. These results, which show that nursing home care has greater elasticity of demand than hospital care, were expected. Given the current interest in expanding long-term care insurance, an elasticity of this magnitude indicates that the demand for long-term care would increase substantially if long-term care insurance were to increase (since the out-of-pocket price of long-term care would be lowered).

BIBLIOGRAPHY

Consumer Demand: Analysis and Surveys

Frech, H.E., and Ginsburg, P.B. 1975. Imposed health insurance in monopolistic markets. *Economic Inquiry* 13:55–69.

Ginsburg, P.B., and Manheim, L. 1973. Insurance, copayment and health services utilization. *Journal of Economics and Business* 25:142–153.

Joseph, H. 1971. Empirical research on the demand for health care. *Inquiry* 8:61–71.

Mushkin, S.J. 1974. *Consumer incentives for health care.* New York: Neale Watson Publishers.

Empirical Studies

Alexander, D.L., et al. 1994. Estimates of the demand for ethical pharmaceutical drugs across countries and time. *Applied Economics* 26:821–826.

Beck, R.G. 1974. The effect of co-payments on the poor. *Journal of Human Resources* 9:129–142.

Chiswick, B.R. 1976. The demand for nursing home care. *Journal of Human Resources* 11:295–316.

Davis, K., and Russell, L.B. 1972. The substitution of outpatient care for inpatient care. *Review of Economics and Statistics* 54:109–120.

Freiburg, L., and Scutchfield, F.D. 1976. Insurance and the demand for hospital care. *Inquiry* 13: 54–60.

Gold, M. 1984. The demand for hospital outpatient services. *Health Services Research* 19:384–412.

Hellinger, F. 1977. Substitutability among different types of care under Medicare. *Health Services Research* 12:11–18.

Hershey, J.C., et al. 1975. Making sense out of utilization data. *Medical Care* 13:838–851.

Holtmann, A.G., and Olsen, E.O. 1978. *The economics of the private demand for outpatient health care.* Pub. no. NIH-78-1262. Bethesda, Md.: John E. Fogarty Center of the National Institutes of Health.

Keeler, E.B., and Rolph, J. 1983. How cost spending reduced medical spending of participants in the health insurance experiment. *JAMA* 249:2220–2222.

Lamberton, C.E., et al. 1986. Factors determining the demand for nursing home services. *Quarterly Review of Economics and Business* 26:74–90.

Nelson, A.A., et al. 1984. The effect of a Medicaid drug copayment program on the utilization and cost of prescription services. *Medical Care* 22:724–736.

Newhouse, J.P., et al. 1980. On having your cake and eating it too. *Journal of Econometrics* 13:365–390.

Newhouse, J.P., et al. 1981. Some interim results from a controlled trial of cost sharing in health insurance. *New England Journal of Medicine* 305:1501–1507.

Reeder, C.E., and Nelson, A.A. 1985. The differential impact of a copayment on drug use in a Medicaid population. *Inquiry* 22:396–403.

Scheffler, R.M. 1984. The United Mine Worker's health plan. *Medical Care* 22:247–254.

Scitovsky, A.A., and McCall, N. 1977. Coinsurance and the demand for physician services. *Social Security Bulletin* 40 (May):19–27.

Stoddart, G.L., and Labelle, R.J. 1985. *Privatization in the Canadian health care system.* Ottawa, Ontario: Health and Welfare Canada.

Warner, J., and Hu, T.-W. 1977. Hospitalization insurance and the demand for inpatient care. In *Socioeconomic issues of health*, ed. B.C. Martin. Chicago: American Medical Association.

CHAPTER 4

Demand for Medical Care and Insurance: Additional Topics

4.1 INTRODUCTION

In Chapter 3, the demand for medical care was introduced as if medical care were an ordinary everyday commodity. Some types of medical care *are* ordinary everyday commodities. Pediatric visits, the consumption of aspirin, and visits to a dentist are routine occurrences for many people. However, the circumstances surrounding many types of medical care are quite unlike the circumstances surrounding the use of everyday commodities. As a result, the traditional model must be modified to incorporate special factors. This chapter brings these factors into consideration by showing how they influence the demand relation as developed in Chapter 3.

Section 4.2 presents a series of topics related to the demand for medical care. Section 4.2.1 examines the economic implications of one alleged characteristic of medical care—that it is indispensable for life and health. Section 4.2.2 analyzes the implications for medical care demand when individuals other than direct consumers are concerned with the consumption of medical care by direct consumers. In this context we look at the relationships between private, external, and social demand. Section 4.2.3 examines the influence of quality differences on medical care demand. Section 4.2.4 is concerned with situations when the money paid for medical care is not an adequate reflection of the total resource commitment made by the patient in acquiring medical care. In particular, patients devote a great deal of traveling and waiting time to the obtaining of medical care. This section develops a more general picture of the cost of medical care, including time cost. Section 4.2.5 analyzes the demand for health rather than the demand for medical care. In this analysis, medical care and other resources are viewed as inputs in the production of a more fundamental commodity: health. Finally, Section 4.2.6 discusses the possibility that doctors can influence patient demand under conditions of consumer ignorance.

Section 4.3 examines another characteristic of medical care: the uncertainty of the occurrence of illness. In Section 4.3.1 a model is developed that examines the circumstances under which the presence of this characteristic leads individuals to demand insurance. Section 4.3.2 extends the results of Section 4.3.1 to the market demand for health care insurance. Section 4.3.3 examines an issue that arises once an individual has purchased insurance: With the insurance policy in effect, the out-of-pocket price for insured health care services falls and the quantity demanded increases. This phenomenon—the increase in the postinsurance quantity demanded—is known in insurance circles as *moral hazard*. Finally, Section 4.3.5 uses the concept of elasticity to help explain the responsiveness of consumer demand for insurance to changes in the out-of-pocket price of insurance coverage.

There are potentially a large number of alternative insurance arrangements and types of policies (e.g., deductible and copayment levels, HMOs versus traditional care, etc.). Demand analysis can be used to predict how individuals will respond to prices for various plans, which is the topic of Section 4.4.

Finally, Section 4.5 presents a basic economic model of the labor supply. The labor market is the market in which wages and fringe benefits, such as health insurance, are determined. The labor supply can be modeled along the lines of the basic demand model. This is because, when employees are deciding how much labor to supply, they are in fact demanding income and leisure.

4.2 TOPICS IN THE DEMAND FOR MEDICAL CARE

4.2.1 Implications of Health Care for Life and Health

One of the most widely cited characteristics of the commodity medical care is its ability to improve health. In some instances, if a person does not obtain timely medical care, he or she may die or become permanently ill. Where this condition holds (e.g., after a heart attack or a serious traffic accident), the question of substitutes will have little importance. Presumably the person would be willing to disburse all of his or her wealth to receive lifesaving medical care, and the demand curve would be vertical.

However, such instances amount to a very small portion of the total number of situations that cause individuals to seek medical care. In the vast majority of cases, alternative courses of action are available and individuals have the time to consider the options. In fact, medical care should be viewed as a spectrum of services and products rather than as a commodity only sought and consumed in an emergency. The less a situation calls for immediate action and the greater the relevance of substitutes, the less steeply sloping will be the demand curve for medical care.

For example, dental checkups can be given annually, monthly, or weekly. Few would consider monthly or weekly checkups to be necessary or even reasonable.

Even though most medical problems are not of emergency proportions, a reduction in medical care consumption can lead to a deterioration in health. In such instances, it may be desirable to analyze medical care demand from the longer perspective of a multiperiod analysis. The imposition of a copayment on drugs or physician visits will generally lead to a reduction in the quantity demanded in Period 1. There is nothing in the theory of demand that says which units of medical care will no longer be demanded. Some units may have been unnecessary to begin with, but some may have been highly desirable (from the point of view of their effects on health status). When medical care is desirable, a reduction in its consumption in Period 1 may lead to a decline in health status (e.g., in Periods 2, 3, or 4) and to possible increases in medical care demand in these subsequent periods.

This phenomenon was first examined with regard to the imposition of a $1 copayment for each of the first two doctor's visits and $.50 for each of the first two prescriptions in the California Medicaid program. An original study (Roemer et al. 1975) stated that reductions in doctor's office visits and diagnostic tests after the copayment's introduction were accompanied by increases in hospitalization rates in subsequent periods. Although the data methods of the study were questioned, with no conclusive results (Chen 1976; Dyckman 1976; Hopkins et al. 1976), the study raised the issue of the importance of examining demand-reducing measures in a more general context. A subsequent study based on the national Rand Health Insurance Experiment (Brook et al. 1983) examined the effects of reductions in use due to copayments on subsequent consumer health status and found that they were generally not adverse except for certain groups. In particular, for poor individuals with hypertensive conditions, free care was associated with better blood pressure control and reductions in the risk of early death. Neither group of studies focused on populations who might be particularly susceptible to disease (the poor, elderly, or chronically ill), and so there is a likelihood that, for selected groups, reductions in demand can have considerable impact on subsequent health status and medical care demand (Fein 1981; Relman 1983).

4.2.2 External and Social Demand for Medical Care

In the analysis in Chapter 3, it was assumed that the sum of all individuals' self-regarding demand for medical care was the same as the total societal demand for medical care. Whether this assumption is reasonable has been called into question. For certain social goods, such as medical care and education, it has been asserted that individuals would be willing to pay something to enable others to consume them. This is not true for all commodities. Many individuals would be willing to pay something to help ensure that a heart attack victim could reach a hospital on time; they would not be so generous if a person's car had broken down and he or she "needed" $400 for repairs. Furthermore, people's generosity probably extends only to certain types of medical care. The need for medical care with substantial health implications for the recipients (e.g., inoculations or care for the aged) elicits great concern; someone's desire to undergo cosmetic surgery does not.

To formalize the analysis of this phenomenon, let us focus on the consumption of a single individual, A. The commodity whose demand we are analyzing will now be defined as individual A's consumption of medical care. A's demand for his or her own consumption may be called *private* or *internal demand*.

Assume that the rest of society can be characterized as individual B. B may also have a demand for A's own consumption of medical care. Such a demand can be characterized in the same way as A's own demand. In particular, as the price is lowered, B's demand for A's consumption of medical care will increase. This demand is in addition to A's own demand and can be called an *external demand*, because it comes from a force external to the consumer of the commodity.

If we define society as the sum total of A and B, then society's demand for A's consumption of medical care will depend on the private demand of A and the external demand of B. This total demand can be called *community* or *social demand*. The effect of the external demand is to increase the quantity demanded (of medical care for A) at any given price, assuming that the external demand is greater than zero at that price. (It may well be, as in the case of the external demand for auto repair, that this external demand is zero at a particular price or at all prices.) The old phrase that "society wants everyone to have a decent level of medical care" can be rephrased in terms of this analysis. Society is the sum of all individuals, and the social demand for an individual's consumption of a given commodity is the sum of all private and external demands. The statement that "society wants everyone to have a decent level of medical care" can be interpreted to mean that, at the given price, there is a social demand for a "decent" level of care for each person.

There are a sufficiently large number of manifestations of external demands for medical care to impress on us how real this phenomenon is. Philanthropic giving to organizations such as the American Heart Association, the United Way, the American Cancer Society, and the National Research Foundation is evidence that people are truly committed to enabling others to consume the services of these organizations, including health education and research. The majority of hospitals in the United States began as nonprofit organizations with large charitable components. In recent years these charitable components have decreased because of the growth of government health programs such as Medicare and Medicaid. Such programs themselves may be an expression of external demands expressed through the "political marketplace." Before the introduction of Medicare and Medicaid, physicians contended that a great deal of their medical services were provided as a form of charity.

4.2.3 Influence of Quality on the Demand for Medical Care

In Chapter 3 the analysis of medical care demand was based on the assumption that each unit of the commodity medical care was like any other unit. Of course, this is not always the case. One of the more problematic tasks in analyzing resource allocation in medical care is coming to terms with quality differences.

Quality is not a single attribute but rather a series of attributes, any of which can make the product appear better or worse to the consumer (Congress of the United States 1988). We will assume, in this section, that the consumer is fully aware of how each of these attributes that determine the quality level of a product will affect him or her. Furthermore, we will regard quality as subjective, that is, in terms of how the consumer values these attributes of the commodity.

Two attributes of the commodity medical care will be used in identifying quality: (1) the comfort or luxury of the particular services provided and (2) the level of medical excellence of the services. The former attribute is associated with the doctor's bedside manner, the amenities in a hospital room, whether soft music is piped into the dentist's office, and so on. The latter attribute is associated with the accuracy of a diagnosis, the effectiveness of a treatment in restoring health, the effectiveness of a preventive course of action, and so on. Assuming that these can be accurately assessed, a consumer can make a personal evaluation of the overall quality levels associated with alternative units of medical care and can rank these alternative units according to their quality levels.

How might consumers behave when faced with different overall medical care quality levels? A reasonable hypothesis is that a higher quality level will increase the importance of medical care in relation to other commodities at all levels of medical care consumption. This will result in an outward shift of the demand curve for medical care.

One qualification must be mentioned. If the quality of care is low, the demand may be less. But if low-quality care results in subsequent illness (e.g., if rheumatic fever develops from a failure to check for strep throat, or if a patient with chicken pox contracts Reye's syndrome because he or she was prescribed aspirin), it may lead to a greater demand for care subsequently.

4.2.4 Time and Money Costs

Until now we have measured the resource commitment necessary to obtain a unit of commodity by the per unit out-of-pocket money price of that commodity. Thus, if a unit of medical care costs $5, then $5 was treated as an accurate measure of what a person had to give up (the opportunity cost) to obtain a unit of medical care. Yet the resources devoted to consuming a commodity include more than the money price of the commodity; when obtaining medical care, people have to travel to and from the doctor's office and wait to see the doctor and be examined.

The effort and time expended are personal resources and are part of the totality of resources committed to obtaining medical care.

The value of the time spent by a person travelling and waiting is referred to as the time cost of obtaining medical care. The associated resource commitment is equivalent to the amount that could have been earned if the person had not visited the doctor (assuming the person does forgo income in undertaking this action). If the person does not forgo income, valuable time is still given up. In this case, the opportunity cost of time would be taken to be equivalent to value to the person of the activity given up. This latter magnitude is very difficult to measure, so for our purposes we will assume that all time spent in obtaining health care can be measured in terms of the person's wage rate.

The total cost or total resource commitment made by the person for each unit of health care can be expressed as $(w \times t) + p$, where t is the amount of time involved in obtaining a unit of health care, w is the wage that would have been earned had the person worked during this time, and p is the money price of the commodity.

We can use this expression to substitute total per unit cost for money price in our demand analysis. If we regard the commodity as medical care and the total cost per unit of this commodity as $(w \times t) + p$, we can develop a more general hypothesis about the consumption of medical care. Our new hypothesis is this: As the total per unit cost (time cost plus price) falls, more medical care is demanded. To give an example, if the time required for a visit to the doctor is 1 hour, the wage forgone is $4 per hour, and the money price of a visit is $8, the total per unit cost is $12. If the money price is set at zero by a government program, the total cost falls to $4 per visit. Medical care may still be too costly for some people, even at a zero price. If the government wishes to encourage consumption beyond this point, it might have to take steps that would lower waiting or travel time (e.g., by relocating a clinic to a more populous area).

Framing the analysis of demand in terms of total cost provides additional insight regarding issues of distribution. Even though money costs may be the same for all consumers, total costs may vary because of variations in w and t. For example, w may vary among consumers because some may have their wages docked if they take time off from work, whereas others may not. And t may vary because of variations in distances from care providers. Our generalized demand hypothesis states that, other things being equal, the quantity demanded will vary inversely with the total per unit cost. When medical care is offered for "free," that is, at a zero money price, variations in quantity demanded will be determined by variations in time costs. In particular, individuals who "pay" the lowest time cost will demand the greatest quantities. Perhaps those who pay the lowest time costs and hence demand greatest quantities are not the same as those with the most acute medical conditions. In this case, medical care would be rationed to those who are willing to wait and not to the most ill. This problem arises when a program lowers the direct money price to zero while failing to increase supply sufficiently to meet the increased quantity demanded. An excess demand results and queues may form. This raises the time cost, which becomes the mechanism by which medical care is rationed.

4.2.5 The Demand for Health

Chapter 1 showed that the output of the health care sector can be regarded either as health care or as health. An alternative formulation of consumer behavior in this area has been presented in terms of the demand for health (Grossman 1972). Health care can be regarded as an end in itself, something people want for its intrinsic characteristics, or as a means to an end. For example, better health, by enabling a person to earn more income and purchase other commodities, would function as a means for attaining a higher level of consumer consumption.

In this analysis we assume health to be an end in itself that can be created or produced by the activities individuals undertake. These activities can include receiving medical care, engaging in self-care (exercise and proper diet), and so on. Such activities are substitutes for one another, since each contributes to achieving the desired end. The cost of each alternative activity can be expressed in terms of the resources an individual would have to commit in order to produce one healthy day. Since each activity will normally require time and purchased inputs on the part of the consumer, the cost of one healthy day can be expressed as follows:

$$c = (a \times w) + (b \times p)$$

In this equation, c is the unit cost (cost per one healthy day produced) of the activity; a is the amount of time required to produce one healthy day by engaging in the activity; b is the amount of purchased inputs required in conjunction with a to produce one healthy day; w is the opportunity cost of the individual's time, and thus a measurement of the size of the resource commitment of one unit of time; and p is the price of one unit of purchased input. The cost of one healthy day (c) depend on a, b, w, and p. For each health-producing activity, there will be a different c. If one activity, say self-care, is very productive (i.e., a and b are small), then the cost of producing an extra healthy day through self-care will be low. On the other hand, if self-care is not very effective in producing health, then a may be very high and c in turn will likely be high. Recall that, although the unit price of purchased inputs (p) may be high, the number of units required to produce a healthy day (b) may be low. Thus, purchased input–intensive activities such as medical care are not necessarily more costly than other health-producing activities.

One prediction of this model is that, if the value of c of one type of health-producing activity rises relative to the value of c for another type, individuals will substitute in favor of the lower cost alternative. For example, if waiting time in a doctor's office (a) becomes lengthy, the cost of medical care will rise. Self-care becomes relatively less expensive under these circumstances, and individuals will engage in more self-care activities.

It is unlikely that a and b will remain constant across all levels of an activity. Instead, it is probable that the more of an activity (e.g., physician care or self-care) is engaged in, the more a and b will increase. That is, it will take successively larger doses of personal effort and purchased inputs to yield a unit of health. For this reason, several health-producing activities will be demanded by an individual. For example, the individual will probably demand both medical care and self-care. However, if a factor changes (e.g., there is an increase in the amount of waiting time necessary to obtain medical care), this will cause a shift in demand (e.g., more self-care and less medical care will be demanded).

Viewing the demand for health-related resources in this way allows us to incorporate the full resource commitment of alternative ways of producing health. In such a framework, medical care becomes one of several alternatives, and a broader picture of health-related resources can be obtained. However, while the picture is broader, it is also more complex, and for many purposes such a broad and complex picture is not required.

4.2.6 Consumer Ignorance Regarding the Effect of Medical Care on Health

This section serves as an introduction to the difficult topic of consumer ignorance. Many consumers do not know the effect of medical care on health, and physicians have been regarded as having two main roles: (1) to act in an advisory capacity and inform patients of their level of health and courses of treatment that might improve their health and (2) to undertake treatments their patients have decided upon.

As we saw in Chapter 3, a patient's perceived level of health and the probable effect of medical care on the patient's health can influence the patient's demand for medical care. Since the physician potentially has influence over how the patient views his or her health, as well as the patient's beliefs regarding the efficacy of medical care in altering this level, the physician conceivably can change the patient's demand for medical care by providing pertinent information. For example, telling a patient that he or she has a dangerous but possibly curable neoplasm will almost certainly increase that patient's demand for cancer treatment.

Let H stand for the level of a patient's health (e.g., measured by the number of healthy days), let M represent units of medical care, and let X stand for the number of units of a second commodity, food. To analyze the physician's role as an agent, we make the following assumptions:

- We assume that health creates utility (U) in such a way that, as the patient moves to higher health levels, the additional satisfaction or utility from one additional unit of health, termed the *marginal utility of health* ($\Delta U/\Delta H$), diminishes. (Of course, *total* utility is still increasing with additional health.)
- Other things being equal (lifestyle, environment, etc.), the increment of additional health produced with an additional unit of medical care, termed the *marginal productivity of health* ($\Delta H/\Delta M$), becomes progressively less as the medical care continues. More medical care of course produces more health but at a diminishing rate.
- The patient's health is at an initial level (although he or she may not know what it is).
- Each unit of medical care is purchased at a cost to the patient of C_m.
- The other commodity, X, has a declining marginal utility ($\Delta U/\Delta X$). This commodity has a per unit cost of C_x.
- The patient's income is set.
- The patient knows the values of all relevant variables, such as H, M, C_x, C_m, and, most importantly, $\Delta H/\Delta M$.
- The patient's goal is to maximize utility.

Now, each additional unit of medical care has a marginal utility equal to the product of the additional health produced by the unit of medical care ($\Delta H/\Delta M$) and the marginal utility of health ($\Delta U/\Delta H$), that is, $\Delta U/\Delta H) \times (\Delta H/\Delta M)$. Thus, if one extra doctor's visit produced 3 additional healthy days, and the additional utility for each healthy day is 5 units of utility, then an additional visit will have a marginal utility of 15.

The patient's equilibrium for both commodities (M and X) will be at that point where the marginal utility per penny spent on each commodity is the same. That is, the patient cannot get more utility from switching from buying one more unit of M (thus lowering its marginal utility) and one less unit of X (thus raising its marginal utility). Of course, at the same time the patient, if he or she gets utility from M and X and nothing else, will also use up his or her budget. The expression for this equilibrium condition is

$$\frac{(\Delta U/\Delta H) \times (\Delta H/\Delta M)}{C_m} = \frac{\Delta U/\Delta_x}{C_x}$$

However, the patient may not know H and most certainly will not know the productivity of medical care in improving his or her health. If we assume that the physician knows H and $\Delta H/\Delta M$ and has an awareness of the patient's tastes and other circumstances (prices and income), then, assuming the physician behaves as a "perfect agent," he or she will prescribe and/or provide a quantity of M such that the patient's equilibrium conditions are met.

There are, of course, a number of possible deviations from this ideal. Even if the physician knew H and $\Delta H/\Delta M$ and could infer the patient's values and economic circumstances, the physician's interests may deviate from the patient's. The physician could then provide the patient with estimates of H ("You have a strep throat") and $\Delta H/\Delta M$ ("You'll need one more x-ray to be sure the condition is stabilizing") that were distortions of the truth. In such circumstances, the physician could induce a demand for his or her services. If the physician exaggerated the seriousness of the patient's condition, for instance, this would increase the marginal utility of a unit of medical care ($\Delta U/\Delta M$) and thereby increase the demand for medical care.

But there are limits to such a process. For one thing, with repeated events (e.g., common colds) the patient eventually gains information that can be used to evaluate H and $\Delta H/\Delta M$. In addition, information sharing between patients or between patients and other physicians limits the degree to which a physician can sway the patient with misinformation. The physician may also have moral misgivings about misrepresenting the facts. Finally, the assumption that the physician has perfect information about H and $\Delta H/\Delta M$ is not always realistic. Diagnosis and treatment are often undertaken under conditions of uncertainty. Physicians then experiment to obtain the best treatment. Although a physician can still generate demand, it is impossible to say with certainty how much of the "experimentation" was purposive demand generation and how much was honest experimentation.

4.3   THE DEMAND FOR HEALTH INSURANCE

4.3.1 Individual Demand for Insurance

In Chapter 3 the analysis of demand was based on the condition that the consumer knows with certainty that he or she will maintain a given state of health during the relevant time period. This underlying assumption is not plausible for many medical problems. In the case of these problems, a consumer cannot be certain of the particular period during which the problem will occur (or if any given problem will ever occur). The consumer does know, however, that he or she *might* be sick during a particular period and might have to visit a doctor and even be hospitalized.

In this type of situation, a consumer faces the choice of whether or not to prepare financially for medical contingencies. The consumer can prepare by purchasing insurance. This action entails an increased outlay (the premium) at the outset, followed by reduced outlays should an illness occur. The basic theory of the demand for insurance presents a systematic view of how certain underlying variables—tastes, wealth, price, the likelihood of an illness, and the loss resulting from the illness—can influence the decision to buy insurance. Following is a presentation of the basic assumptions of the model as well as a brief elaboration of their meaning. Such an elaboration can aid the reader in understanding the model and its limitations. The assumptions of the model are as follows:

1. *Consumer Tastes.* To characterize consumer tastes with regard to the alternative situations resulting from an illness, let us assume that when an illness occurs it leads to medical care expenses that constitute a loss in wealth to the individual. To specify what this loss means to the individual, we must introduce a concept to characterize the individual's well-being at alternative levels of wealth—the concept of utility. One hypothetical individual's taste for wealth is presented in the form of an index of utility in Table 4–1. This index shows what level of utility is associated with each specific level of wealth. Thus, a level of wealth of $1,000 is associated with a level of utility of 100, a level of wealth of $990 is associated with a level of utility of 99.8, and so on. The numbers in the utility index are arbitrary. That is, we could have (arbitrarily) picked 389.4 to be the utility level at $1,000. What is important is the change in utility that is associated with a given change in wealth. Our assumption is that the taste function is characterized by diminishing marginal utility. That is, each additional $10 of wealth results in less additional utility than the previous additional $10. For example, at $850 an extra $10 will yield 3 extra units of utility; at $860 an extra $10 will yield 2.8 extra units; and so on.

   If wealth has diminishing marginal utility for an individual, that individual is said to be *risk averse*. The basic idea is that, for a given wealth level, a loss of a given amount is of greater subjective importance (utility) to the person than would be a gain of an equal amount. Utility is the subjective index of the relative importance of wealth.

   It should be noted that we are not saying that additional wealth means less to a rich person than it does to a poor person. This kind of comparison, called *interpersonal comparison*, involves specifying different people's utilities on the same scale. Interpersonal comparison is discussed in Chapter 11, which deals with evaluative economics.

2. *Level of Wealth.* Our second assumption is that our individual initially has a level of wealth of $1,000. We use a wealth rather than income variable because people derive satisfaction from their assets, and health care expenses can potentially affect the level of people's assets, not just their annual income.

3. *Medical Expenses in the Event of Illness.* Our third assumption is that, if the individual becomes sick, he or she will face medical expenses of $100. This financial loss can be broken down into two components: (1) a unit cost

Table 4–1 Relationship between Wealth and Utility

Wealth	Total Utility	Marginal Utility
$800	57.0	4.2
810	61.2	4.0
820	65.2	3.8
830	69.0	3.6
840	72.6	3.4
850	76.0	3.2
860	79.0	3.0
870	81.8	2.8
880	84.4	2.6
890	86.8	2.4
900	89.0	2.2
910	91.0	2.0
920	92.8	1.8
930	94.4	1.6
940	95.8	1.4
950	97.0	1.2
960	98.0	1.0
970	98.8	0.8
980	99.4	0.6
990	99.8	0.4
1000	100.0	0.2

component and (2) a component representing the number of units consumed. We will assume that the unit cost is $10 per visit and that the individual requires ten visits.

4. *Likelihood of Illness.* A fourth assumption concerns the element of uncertainty. We will assume that we can assign probabilities to the various possible health states the individual may experience. Let us say there is a .1 probability the individual will be ill (i.e., of 10 people in similar circumstances, 1 will become ill) and will demand ten units and a .9 probability the individual will remain well and will not have to spend $100 to become better. These are the only two possibilities, so the sum of the probabilities equals 1. (See Section 4.3.3 for a discussion of how probabilities are assigned to alternative health states of individuals.)

5. *Price of Insurance.* The individual can shift the risk of loss on to an insurer but will have to pay a premium to do so. In exchange for this premium, the insurer assumes the risk.

6. *Behavioral Assumption.* The sixth assumption is that the individual wants to maximize his or her utility. Thus the individual will choose that course of action from which he or she can expect to receive the highest level of utility.

The model's conclusions are obtained by determining how, under these assumed conditions, the individual will behave so as to maximize utility. The model predicts that if health insurance is available on the right terms, the individual will buy it to reduce the variability of his or her income (and hence increase utility). To see how this conclusion is derived, let us examine how much wealth and utility the individual would expect to have with and without insurance. Without insurance, the individual has a 90-percent chance of having $1,000 in wealth and a 10-percent chance of having only $900 because of the payout for medical care. The expected value of wealth will be 90 percent of $1,000 plus 10 percent of 900, or $990. This is the sum of the amounts the individual expects to receive under various conditions adjusted for the probabilities that those conditions will arise. If $1,000 is the level of wealth, the utility is 100 units. If $900 is available, the utility is 89 units. But the individual has only a 90-percent chance of having 100 units of utility and a 10-percent chance of having 89 units. The expected value of the utility achieved will be 90 percent of 100 and 10 percent of 89, or 98.9. This is approximately the same utility that 100-percent certainty of having $970 would yield.

If the individual had $970, this wealth would yield about the same utility as the present situation when no insurance is purchased. Let us say that for $20 he or she could buy insurance coverage against the $100 loss. By buying the insurance, the individual would be certain of having $980. This is because the individual's wealth would be reduced by the amount of the premium ($20), and if he or she became ill, the insurer would bear the risk. Certainty of having $980 would yield certainty of receiving 99.4 units of utility, which is a higher expected utility than that in the uncertain situation. Being a utility maximizer, the individual would buy the insurance on these terms. Indeed, he or she would pay up to $30 to avoid the risk of losing wealth because of illness.

Why is the risk of loss so unpleasant that the individual would be willing to pay so much to avoid it? The reason is the diminishing marginal utility of wealth. Even though the individual faces only a 10-percent chance of losing $100, the loss of utility becomes significant at lower levels of wealth. The pain of losing $10 at a level of wealth of $910 is greater than the pain at a level of $1,000. Thus, the individual is willing to pay a premium rather than face the risk of suffering such large losses.

Let us now assume that the individual, if sick, would demand 10 units of care at any price and that medical care is now $15 instead of $10 per unit. In this situation, the individual faces an expected loss of $150 if he or she becomes sick. The individual would have an expected wealth of $985 (10 percent of $850 and 90 percent of $1,000) and an expected utility of 97.6 units (10 percent of 76 and 90 percent of 100). If the individual was certain of having $960, he or she would be certain of receiving 98 units of utility. Therefore, the individual would be willing to pay something over $40 for insurance.

The conclusion is that, as the possible loss increases because of the rising price of medical care, the amount of money the individual is willing to pay to avert the possible loss increases as well, and the individual will be willing to buy additional insurance coverage if terms are right. The size of the financial loss in relation to the individual's wealth and the associated utilities is called the *financial vulnerability factor*. A second factor, which is related to the probability of illness, is referred to as the *risk perception factor* (Berki and Ashcraft 1980). In the preceding example, if the probability of becoming sick increased from 10 to 20 percent, the expected utility in the no insurance situation would fall to 97.8 (80 percent of 100 plus 20 percent of 89). This is associated with a wealth level of close to $960, indicating that the individual would be willing to pay up to about $40 to avoid the risk of a $100 loss.

4.3.2 Extensions and Limitations of the Theory

The theory of insurance demand has the virtue of explicitly organizing some of the variables that are central to the decision to purchase insurance. As presented, however, it has important limitations. The following observations may be of help in understanding what these limitations are.

First, the utility function presented above incorporates a specific degree of risk aversion. But risk aversion can vary by degree. For example, if a consumer's marginal utility was 3.2 at $850, was 2.0 at $860, and decreased rapidly after that, the consumer would be much more risk averse than the individual in the previous example. (Note that the total utility would fall only slightly.) An increasing degree of risk aversion will result in a greater demand for insurance.

Second, the reader may find it strange that the utility function, which is supposed to measure satisfaction, does not include medical care. This is indeed a shortcoming of the model, because well-being can depend on appropriate care. Including medical care, however, creates a much more complicated model that is more difficult to apply, and while it is important to understand that we have abstracted from reality, this should not detract from the value of the model. The present model has the virtue of focusing on the benefits of risk shifting, which is an economic good distinct from medical care.

Third, insurance has the effect of lowering the direct price of medical care. One would expect the demand for medical care to increase under these circumstances, yet in the basic insurance model we have assumed that medical care demand does not change with the lower, postinsurance price. That is, the model implies that if an individual becomes ill, he or she will demand 10 units of medical care with or without insurance. This means that the elasticity of demand for medical care is zero, an unlikely scenario for most types of medical care. Again, such an assumption was necessary to simplify the model. In Section 4.3.4 we show what will happen when this assumption is changed.

Fourth, we have assumed that the individual pays the full amount of the premium. In fact, often an insured's out-of-pocket premium is substantially less than the total premium. The insured might receive insurance through his or her employer, who pays part or all of the premium. This is not to say that the insured receives "free" insurance. The insured, through a bargaining unit or via an employer's policy, negotiates for or receives a total compensation package that includes wages (a direct money component), and benefits (e.g., pension rights and health insurance). The individual pays taxes on the money portion of compensation, and with after-tax wages, directly pays his or her share of premiums. Under the Internal Revenue Code, many nonwage benefits received through the employer, including health insurance, are not taxed. Therefore, insurance has a lower price when purchased through employment benefits than directly by the consumer.

This point is illustrated numerically in Table 4–2. In our example, the marginal tax rate of the individual or family is 20 percent, which means that for each $100 in taxable income the employee receives, he or she pays $20 in taxes and takes home $80. Now if $625 of additional compensation is made in the form of wages and there are no deductible expenses, the individual will pay $125 (20 percent of $625) in taxes, and will have $500 left over to purchase goods or services, including health insurance. If, on the other hand, the $625 in compensation is in the form of employer-provided health insurance, then this compensation is not taxed and $625 in insurance coverage can be received. A dollar's worth of coverage purchased with after-tax wages is thus worth $(1-T)$ times the value of the coverage received via employer benefits, where T is the marginal tax rate. Thus $(1-T) \times \$1$ is sometimes called the price of $1 of employer-provided premiums (Taylor and Wilensky 1983). In terms of our demand model, such tax benefits will lower the cost of health insurance to the individual and thus will increase its demand.

4.3.3 The Market Demand for Insurance

Insurance availability requires the existence of at least one organization willing to accept the risks and pay the costs when they arise. To determine under which

Table 4–2 A Comparison of Health Insurance when Purchased by Employer and Employee

	Purchased by Employee	Purchased by Employer
Compensation	$625	$625
Tax	125	0
After-Tax Money Available for Purchasing Premiums	$500	$625

market conditions this will occur, let us assume an insurance company is being formed to cover the risks of 1,000 people with tastes, incomes, and health experience exactly like those of the representative individual in Section 4.3.1. We can now give a more definite meaning to the "probabilities" assigned to the alternative health states. Assume that the insurance company can be almost certain that 100 of the 1,000 insureds will become ill and require medical care during the month. Because pooling a large number of risks yields a considerable degree of certainty, it becomes possible to assign a risk to each insured and evaluate his or her expected loss experience in terms of the group.

The insurance company knows that, in a group of 1,000 insureds, 100 will most likely become ill and will require 10 physician's office visits each. At a price of $10 a visit, the expected medical expenses will be $10,000 for the group. The actuarially fair rate, the expected loss per individual insured, is $10. If each insured pays a premium of $10, the expected losses of the group will just be covered. According to the analysis in Section 4.3, every insured would be willing to pay a premium equal to the actuarially fair rate to reduce the risk of large losses. Indeed, with diminishing marginal utility, they would be willing to pay somewhat more.

The insurance company cannot charge the actuarially fair rate, because resources are necessary to administer an insurance business and some level of profit or surplus must be earned. The insurance company must charge more to cover these administrative costs and profits. The additional fee charged by the insurance company is called the *loading fee*. The premium each individual pays is thus made up of two components: the fee for benefits received and the loading fee. In our example, let us assume that the insurer has administrative expenses of $750 in total and desires a profit of $250; the total load is thus $1,000. The insurance company must charge premiums of $11,000, of which $10,000 will be paid out in benefits. With premiums spread over 1,000 insureds, if all pay the same rate, the premium rate will be $11 per insured.

Strictly speaking, the price of insurance is the loading fee, not the premium. In this case, the price of insurance is $1 per insuree. This price can be expressed in several ways, including as a ratio of benefits to premiums ($11/$10 or 1.1), as a cost per policy ($1), or as a ratio of the loading fee to benefits (0.10). The reason the loading fee is the price of insurance is that the product is insurance, the protection from risk, not the provision of medical care. The gains the consumer received from insurance coverage are the utility gains from the risk reduction. And the price of this risk reduction is the loading fee. It is the level of this fee that will determine whether or not the individual will purchase insurance.

The overall market demand will thus depend on the various factors that influence individual demand and the number of individuals in the market. If all individual have exactly the same tastes, incomes, sickness profiles, and so on, then they will have the same demand for insurance. In actuality, this is unlikely to be the case. Individuals will differ by illness level, wealth, and degree of risk aversion. Their gains from risk reduction will thus differ, and so as the price of *insurance* (the loading fee) increases, some individuals will drop their coverage and market demand will fall off.

4.3.4 Insurance and Moral Hazard

Once an individual has purchased medical insurance, the direct price he or she pays for medical care decreases. If the individual has purchased full insurance, this price is zero. However, as was shown in Chapter 3, when the direct price of medical care decreases, for any reason (including the result of buying insurance), the quantity demanded will increase (i.e., the absolute value of the elasticity of demand is greater than zero). This phenomenon—the existence of an elasticity of demand for medical care—is known in the insurance industry as *moral hazard.* The term suggests that individuals "shirk" their responsibilities and consume recklessly when they are insured. From the point of view of economics, they are simply behaving in accordance with the principle expressed by the downward-sloping demand curve.

The existence of moral hazard has been used to explain why individuals only partially insure against health care risks, that is, why they accept copayments and deductibles rather than full insurance coverage (Feldstein and Friedman 1977; Friedman 1974). Such analyses are more complicated than the basic insurance models, but the essentials can be presented in a simple fashion. Let us assume that an individual has the same utility function as in the model discussed in Section 4.3.1. Other basic assumptions of the model are as follows:

- The probability of being sick is 0.2 and of being well is 0.8 (1 − 0.2). That is, out of each 100 insureds, 20 will get sick.
- If an insured gets sick, he or she will pay $5 for each unit of medical care demanded.
- The individual's initial level of wealth is $1,000.

We also initially ignore, as in our previous model, utility received directly from medical care and health. We now distinguish three situations: in Situation 1, the individual has no insurance but pays the market price ($5.00) per unit of medical care used; in Situation 2, the individual is fully insured and pays a zero price for medical care; and in Situation 3, the individual has a 10-percent copayment and thus faces a direct price of $.50 per unit of medical care.

Because demand varies with price, the quantity of medical care demanded will vary in the three situations. We assume that in Situation 1, where the direct price is $5.00, 10 units of medical care will be demanded. In Situation 2, where the price is 0, 30 units will be demanded. In Situation 3, where the price is $.50, 12 units will be demanded. We now wish to focus on the demand for insurance in these three situations. To simplify the analysis, let us specify a loading fee of zero (no load), which means that the premium rate will equal the expected loss to the individual.

Let us first consider Situations 1 and 2. We will compare the expected utilities to determine which provides the highest utility level (and hence which is preferred). If the expected utility in Situation 1 (called $E(U)_1$) is greater than that in Situation 2 ($E(U)_2$), then the individual will not buy insurance, since having no insurance yields a higher expected utility than having full insurance. In fact, in Situation 1 the individual faces a 20-percent chance of becoming sick, paying the full $50 in medical costs, and having $950 left over. The utility of $950 in wealth is 97 (see Table 4–1). On the other hand, the individual has an 80-percent chance of not getting sick, in which case the level of wealth remains at $1,000 and the utility is 100. The $E(U)$ for this situation is 99.4 (80 percent of 100 plus 20 percent of 97). The $E(U)$ in Situation 2 is equal to the original level of wealth minus the premium ($30). This amounts to 98.8. Since no insurance has greater expected utility than full insurance, the individual will demand no insurance under these conditions.

Let us now bring Situation 3 into the picture. First note that the premium is less than under full insurance, where 30 units of medical care were demanded. In Situation 3, 12 units are demanded, but because of the 10-percent copayment, the insurance company pays only $4.50 per unit, or $54.00 in total. The individual, having a 20-percent probability of becoming sick, will pay a premium of $10.80. (This premium is paid regardless of whether the individual is sick or not.) In addition, if the individual is sick, he or she pays a copayment of $.50 per unit, or $6.00 overall. The $E(U)$ for this situation is roughly 99.6 [20 percent of (1,000 – 10.80 – 6.00) plus 80 percent of (1,000 – 10.80)]. This is greater than the expected utility of not buying insurance. Now the individual probably will buy insurance.

However, this may not be the preferred option. Other copayment rates will have other expected utilities. What is important to note is that the individual will, in some circumstances, prefer insurance with a copayment to that with full coverage (or no coverage) if the moral hazard is great enough.

One shortcoming of this model should be mentioned. Medical care has utility, as does insurance. We have ignored this. In fact, the extra units of medical care consumed in Situations 2 and 3 yield extra utility in their own right. It may well be that the marginal utility of these units would make the full coverage option preferable to one of lesser coverage. While this may be the case, the point of this discussion is that, if the conditions are right, insurance with copayment may be preferred to all other options.

4.3.5 Consumer Responsiveness to the Price of Health Insurance

In Chapter 3 we discussed the concept of the elasticity of demand for medical care, which is a measure of how responsive the quantity of medical care is to out-of-pocket price changes. In a similar vein, one can estimate an elasticity of demand for health insurance in order to determine how consumers will respond to changes in the price of insurance. The formula can be written as follows:

$$Ed = \frac{(\text{PREM}_2 - \text{PREM}_1) / (P_2 - P_1)}{(\text{PREM}_2 + \text{PREM}_1) / (P_2 + P_1)}$$

where Ed is the elasticity of demand for insurance coverage, PREM is the dollar amount of premiums demanded (with subscripts 1 and 2 referring to Situations 1 and 2), and P is the price of insurance (with subscripts 1 and 2 referring to Situations 1 and 2). Note that the price of insurance is the loading fee, as discussed in the previous section. Let us say that the loading fee increases from $80 per policy to $100 and that as a result consumers reduce their premiums from $1,050 to $950. Then the elasticity of demand is

$$\frac{(1,050 - 950)/2,000}{(1.00 - 0.80)/1.80}$$

or –0.45.

It is very important to know the magnitude of this variable for policy purposes. The exemption from income tax of health insurance benefits is equivalent to a reduction in the price of health insurance. This exemption has the effect of increasing the demand for health insurance benefits, such as reductions in the copayment. Lower copayments increase the quantity of medical care demanded. In the immediate post–World War II era, when the government was trying to encourage the consumption of medical care, this increase in demand was not regarded as a problem. In current times, with the concern over medical care costs, the issue has grown in importance.

Several studies have been undertaken to establish the responsiveness of the demand for insurance to changes in the price of insurance. Taylor and Wilensky (1983) examined how premiums increase as the variable tax rate (1 – marginal tax rate) falls. (This variable was taken to be a proxy for the after-tax price of employer-provided health insurance.) They found the elasticity to be –0.2. In other studies, the value has ranged from –0.2 to –1. There is considerable uncertainty, then, as to the value of this variable. If we accept –0.2 as the correct figure, then an individual in the 20-percent marginal tax bracket who received $1,000 in employer-provided premiums has been able to buy $1 in premiums for 80 cents. If the government would eliminate this subsidy, the price would rise to $1. The quantity of insurance demanded (premiums) would fall to about $955.

Such a reduction in benefits would mean higher copayments and would subsequently translate into less medical care demanded and, with an inelastic demand for medical care, into lower medical expenditures. The reader should be aware of the interaction between insurance and medical care markets. What happens in one market influences what happens in the other.

4.4   CHOICE OF HEALTH PLAN

Many employers provide their employees with a selection of health plans and allow the employees to make their own decisions about the types of coverage and service they will obtain. The plans with more complete coverage will cost more, and so the insurer will charge a higher premium. Often the employer will pay a fixed contribution toward the premium regardless of the plan chosen, and the employee will pay out of pocket the difference between the premium and the employer's contribution. The employee, in such cases, has a choice among alternative types of health care coverage. From an economic standpoint, we are concerned with discovering what factors influence consumer demand for alternative plans.

Which economic determinants influence the choice of health plan is a topic of considerable importance. If individuals or families with specific characteristics (e.g., sick people, young couples with families) prefer one type of plan over another on economic grounds, their selection is termed *biased*. *Biased selection* thus means that these individuals or families with these characteristics will demand one particular plan systematically. Often the basis for the selection of a plan is economic. In such cases, the selection is a manifestation of demand behavior.

The economic significance of this lies in the fact that, as a result of these selections, different health plans will have different populations with different experiences of health care utilization. One plan (e.g., a traditional plan) may appear to be high cost relative to another (e.g., an HMO). Some of this difference may be due to the enrollment of families with different characteristics in the plan (e.g., older people may tend to enroll in the traditional plan). Any comparison of the cost of the two plans that *did not account for these differences* would yield biased results. Thus, we must be aware of these factors and of their causes.

To demonstrate the concept of biased selection, we will apply our insurance demand model to two alternative situations. In both, there is an employer with 2,000 employees. Each employee has one chance in five (i.e., a probability of .2) of becoming sick. However, the employees can be divided into two groups of 1,000 each. Those in the "unhealthy" group will require $200 in medical care if they become sick; those in the "healthy" group will require only $100 of medical care. Individuals in both groups have an initial wealth level of $1,000 and the utility function shown in Table 4–1.

The insurance plan in Situation 1 is a "high-option" plan, in that it covers all expenses in the event of illness. We will assume, for simplicity's sake, that the insurance company has no loading fee. The premium is thus equal to the expected loss for the employee. The total payout will be $40,000 ($200 × .2 × 1,000) for the unhealthy employees and $20,000 for the healthy employees. On average the payout is $30 per employee. We will assume that all insureds pay according to *community rating*; that is, each pays the same premium regardless of his or her experience. The full premium is $30. The employer's contribution is assumed to be $20 per employee and the employee's is $10. It should be remembered that the employer's $20 contribution is employee compensation, and normally there would be tax advantages in receiving compensation in this way. We will ignore these benefits to keep our example uncomplicated.

With our assumptions specified, we now examine the demand for the high-option plan. This is done using the utility model of insurance demand that we introduced in previous sections. According to this model, individuals will demand an insurance plan if the expected utility associated with the plan greater than the expected utility in the absence of the plan. Consider first the unhealthy group. The expected loss for a person in this group if he or she became sick and had no insurance would be $200. The person would be left with $800 in wealth (yielding a utility of 57.1). However, 80 percent of the individuals in this group will remain healthy, and each will be left with $1,000 and have an associated utility level of 100. The average expected utility for the entire group would be 91.4 (80 percent of 100 and 20 percent of 57.1). Similarly, the average expected utility of the healthy group would be 97.8 (20 percent of the utility of $900 and 80 percent of the utility of $1,000), since their costs are only $100.

To determine the situation of these groups when they have insurance, we must know the premium. In this case it is $30. This amount is treated as a reduction in employee's wealth even though some of it may be employer paid, because more nonwage benefits would mean less wages (and so, in the absence of tax considerations, we can regard them as equivalent). The premium rate is the average loss over all employees, since there is a single community rate for the entire group. If each employee incurs a premium cost of $30, he or she will be left with wealth of $970 and have a utility level of 98.8. Since utility with insurance for both groups is greater than utility with no insurance, both groups would demand insurance coverage.

Let us now introduce Situation 2, in which there is a low-option plan with the following characteristics. First, there is a limit on the benefits of $100 (thus the plan is similar to an indemnity policy). That is, if anyone becomes sick, the insurance company would cover the first $100 of expenses, but beyond that the individual would be responsible. The premium of such a plan would be lower, because the insurance company's payout would be limited to only $100 per episode of illness. In fact, it would be $20 (.2 × $100).

Our utility model can again shed light on the choice of plan. First of all, the unhealthy group members, if they joined such a plan, would pay the $20 premium plus the excess of illness expenses ($200) over covered expenses ($100), or $100 per illness. Their wealth would be $880 if they were sick and $980 if they were well, and their expected utility would be 96.4 (20 percent of 84.4 and 80 percent of 99.4). Utility theory predicts that these individuals would be better off joining the high-option plan (where the expected utility is 98.8) and so would choose the high-option plan. The healthy group, on the other hand, would spend $20 on premiums for the low-option plan and would have no additional out-of-pocket expenses. They would retain $980 whether or not they were sick, and their expected utility would be 99.4. This is greater than under the high-option plan, and so they would choose the low-option plan.

Our model thus shows that the characteristics of a group partially dictate the choice of plan. An unhealthy group uses more care and will demand higher coverage. There are a number of reasons why one group might consist of high-cost users: the individuals might be older, have special health problems, be more likely to have children, and so on. If, for whatever reason, the group members have higher expected costs, then they will *systematically* select a plan with a higher degree of coverage.

Of course, when biased selection occurs, the rejection of the high-option plan by the healthy group would leave relatively more unhealthy people in that plan, and so the average cost of that plan would increase. This results in a very important implication for the functioning of the insurance market, an implication that is discussed in Chapter 6.

There is a very important issue that the model throws light on. As shown above, different benefit plans will attract different types of insureds. For example, a high-option plan will attract individuals who are less healthy and tend to use more care. In a previous section, we established that individuals with more complete coverage will demand more medical care (because of lower out-of-pocket costs) whatever their health status. If we review actual data comparing plans and notice that individuals in the higher option plan use more care than in the lower option plan, what can we conclude? In fact it could be both the lower out-of-pocket price and the difference in health status that contributed to differences in utilization. This confounding of causal factors in health care demand has been a source of bias in many studies comparing utilization between plans. For example, a number of studies have compared utilization between enrollees in HMOs and conventional insurance plans. The general conclusion has been that hospital utilization under HMO coverage is lower than under conventional coverage (Luft 1978; Miller and

Luft 1995). But the issue has been somewhat clouded by the lack of clear evidence that the groups being compared were similar in terms of health status.

4.5   DEMAND FOR HEALTH PROMOTION AND DISEASE PREVENTION

The basic model of demand under uncertainty can be extended to explain the behavior of individuals who might potentially engage in the prevention of illness and the promotion of health. Individuals can shift risks or retain them. They can also act to reduce them through smoking cessation, weight control, exercise, reducing their intake of alcohol, and so on. To show how health-promoting activities fit into the choice framework, we set up a model with the following assumptions.

Let us imagine a utility-maximizing individual with the same utility function shown in Table 4–1 and a level of wealth of $1,000. The individual has a choice of engaging in preventive activities or not. With no prevention, the individual has a 25-percent chance of becoming ill. If she is ill, she will incur costs of $100. If she engages in preventive activities, she will reduce the probability of becoming ill to 5 percent. However, the preventive activities carry an out-of-pocket cost of $10.

The predictions of the model are as follows. In order to determine whether the individual will engage in preventive activities, we compare the expected utility with and without prevention. Without prevention, the expected utility will be 97.27 (.25 × 89 + .75 × 100). With prevention, the expected utility will be 99.1 (0.05 × 86.8 + .95 × 99.8). The value 86.8 is the utility when an individual has spent $10 on prevention plus $100 on health care. We conclude in this case that the individual will engage in preventive activities.

Illness prevention and health promotion activities entail present costs and only uncertain future benefits (Kenkel 1994; Russell 1984; Scheffler and Paringer 1980). The higher the costs and the lower the value of the benefits, the less likely a person is to engage in these activities. Our model can combine the option of risk reduction with the options risk shifting and risk assumption. The individual will select the option that will yield the maximum utility gain per dollar of expenditure. Which option this is will depend on the individual's tastes and the risks and costs of the various alternatives.

4.6   LABOR SUPPLY

4.6.1   Individuals

The economic analysis of the supply of labor focuses on the quantity of labor individuals are willing to supply in order to earn income. The general framework used in this analysis is the consumer demand model. One main assumption of this model is that each consumer has a demand for income (usable to obtain goods) and for leisure time. The model examines how individuals alter their willingness to work in response to changes in labor compensation, such as wages. The end result of the analysis is a supply of labor curve, one relating the quantity of labor supplied to the wage rate.

The unit of observation in this model is the individual consumer (although some analysts have used the household as the observation unit, because in many cases data are collected at the household rather than the individual level), and the dependent variable is the number of hours an individual is willing to work. The assumptions in our analysis are as follows.

Imagine a utility-maximizing individual who has a utility function that encompasses two distinct goods: income (usable to purchase selected goods and services) and leisure time. As more is obtained of each good, the individual moves to higher levels of utility.

The amounts of the two goods that will yield the same level of utility are shown in Table 4–3. If the individual has no income, he will be willing to take 60 hours in leisure. This combination of income and leisure will yield the same utility as will $100 per week and 50 hours of leisure, $200 and 42 hours, and so on. Note that, whereas income increases in equal increments, leisure hours are reduced in successively smaller increments. This indicates a diminishing relative valuation placed on income. The individual will give up 10 hours of leisure to get the first $100 in income but only 8 additional hours of leisure to get the next $100.

The individual has a total of 60 available waking hours per week. If 50 hours are spent on leisure, then 10 hours will be spent working. Finally, the individual can work for a wage of $15 per hour for up to 60 hours. Total income equals the product of wages and hours worked.

The conclusions of the model are as follows. The individual will increase work time hours from zero as long as the value of lost leisure is less than the wage rate. For example, at the point when the individual has full leisure, he is willing to give

Table 4–3 Income and Leisure Time Combinations at the Same Level of Utility

Income per Week	Leisure Hours per Week (out of a total of 60 available hours)	Work Hours per Week (leisure + work = 60 hours)
0	60	0
$100	50	10
$200	42	18
$300	36	24
$400	32	28
$500	30	30

up 10 hours of leisure for $100, a unit value of $10 per hour. However, he is willing to give up only an additional 8 hours of leisure for an extra $100 in income. This implies a marginal value of leisure of $12.50 per hour at that point. The next 10-hour reduction in leisure is worth $16.67 per hour. Thus the individual must be compensated at increasingly higher wages to induce him to give up more leisure (i.e., to work more).

If the wage is $15 per hour, the individual will give up 18 hours of leisure. Beyond that, the value of lost leisure is greater than the wage rate. Therefore, the individual will choose to work 18 hours at the wage rate of $15. If the wage rate increases, say, to $20, then the individual would be willing to give up 6 more hours of leisure and work for a total of 24 hours per week.

The positive relationship between wages and labor time measures what is called the *substitution effect of income for leisure*. Figure 4–1 shows how the quantity of labor changes as the wage rate increases (curve Supply₁). There is also an income effect, which may offset the substitution effect. As the wage rate increases, the total income that the individual can receive will increase, and the individual can purchase more goods and services. As income increases, the individual will want to spend more leisure time consuming goods and services and hence will want to work less. It is possible that this income effect can more than offset the substitution effect, resulting in a backward-bending labor portion of the supply curve, especially at higher wage rates and income levels. However, statistical studies have shown than this is not a common event.

Supply curves for labor can have varying slopes. If an individual does not have a strong willingness to work more as wages increase, then the curve will be steeply sloped (Supply₂ in Figure 4–1). An individual more willing to work for small increases will have a curve like Supply₂. In Figure 4–1, an increase in wages from $10 to $12 will, depending on the labor supply curve, increase the labor supply to 11 hours (Supply₂) or 15 hours (Supply₁).

4.6.2 Health Insurance Benefits and Labor Supply

The most common way of financing health insurance in the United States is through the payment of health insurance premiums for individuals in the workplace. Health insurance coverage is a component of total worker compensation, which consists of wages plus fringe benefits. From the viewpoint of the individual worker, the amount of total compensation is what influences labor supply. However, economists have modeled labor supply decisions using wage rates as the base price. We will follow that tradition.

In Figure 4–2 we present two labor supply curves, one for the case where fringe benefits exist and one for the case where there are none. Let us begin our analysis

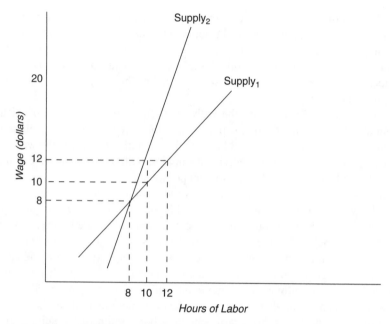

Figure 4–1 Alternative labor supply curves. Curve Supply₁ shows a positive relation between the wage rate and labor hours. Curve Supply₂ shows a curve with a similar direction but a steeper slope, which means that an increase in the wage rate from $8 to $10 will induce a smaller increase in the number of labor hours supplied.

by focusing on the situation without fringe benefits. Curve Supply₁ relates the quantity of labor supplied to money wages. At a wage of $10, a total of 10 units of labor are supplied, at a wage of $15, 15 units of labor are supplied, and so on.

Let us now introduce the fringe benefits of $5 per worker (an amount independent of hours worked). We will assume each worker places a value of $5 on these benefits. It is certainly possible, of course, for a worker to place a lower value than $5 on these benefits, and indeed fringe benefits may be worth very little to some workers. Under our assumption, however, total compensation is $10 when the wage is $5, it is $15 when the wage is $10, and so on. Put another way, the curve that relates the wage rate to the quantity of labor supplied will shift downward and to the right (Supply₂). At a wage of $5 (plus $5 worth of fringe benefits), the supply of labor will be the same as it would be at a wage of $10 without fringe benefits. An additional $5 increase in benefits, wages held constant, will further shift the supply curve downward and to the right. (Of course, if the workers place a lower value on these benefits than their face value, the shift will be less than $5.)

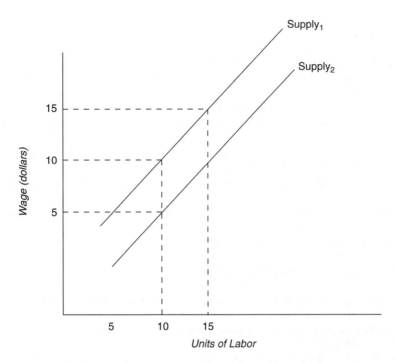

Figure 4–2 Labor supply curves with and without a benefits package. Curve Supply$_1$ shows the relation between the wage rate and units (hours) of labor supplied when there are no benefits. We make the assumption that workers place a $1 value on each dollar of benefits. If we introduce a $5 benefits package, curve Supply$_2$ indicates the new quantity supplied at each wage rate. The reason why the curve shifts is as follows. The $5 wage rate now represents $10 in compensation and will induce the same amount of labor as will a $10 wage rate with no benefits. This is true for all wage rates. If, however, $1 in benefits is worth less to the worker than $1 in wages, the shift in the curve will be less.

4.6.3 Market Supply of Labor

The market labor supply is composed of the labor supply curves of all the individuals in the market. As with the demand curve, the labor supply curve of each individual comprises the summed quantity for that individual at each wage rate. An increase in the number of individuals in the market will cause the supply curve to shift to the right.

BIBLIOGRAPHY

Utilization and Subsequent Health Implications

Brook, R.H., et al. 1983. Does free care improve adults' health? *New England Journal of Medicine* 309:1426–1434.

Chen, M.K. 1976. Penny-wise and pound foolish: Another look at the data. *Medical Care* 14:958–963.

————. 1976. More about penny-wise and pound foolish: A statistical point of view. *Medical Care* 14:964–968.

Congress of the United States. *The quality of medical care*. Washington, D.C.: Office of Technology Assessment, Congress of the United States, 1988.

Dyckman, Z.Y. 1976. Comment on "Copayments for ambulatory care: Penny-wise and pound foolish." *Medical Care* 14:274–276.

Dyckman, Z.Y., and McMenamin, P. 1976. Copayments for ambulatory care: Son of thrupence. *Medical Care* 14:968–969.

Fein, R. 1981. Effects of cost sharing in health insurance. *New England Journal of Medicine* 305:1526–1528.

Hopkins, C.E., et al. 1975. Copayments for ambulatory care: Penny-wise and pound foolish. *Medical Care* 13:457–466.

Hopkins, C.E., et al. 1976. Rebuttal to "Comment on 'Copayments for ambulatory care: Penny-wise and pound foolish.'" *Medical Care* 14:277.

Keeler, E.B., et al. 1985. How free care reduced hypertension in the health insurance experiment. *JAMA* 254:1926–1931.

Relman, A. 1983. The Rand Health Insurance Study: Is cost sharing dangerous to your health? *New England Journal of Medicine* 309:1453.

Roemer, M.I., and Hopkins, C.E. 1976. Response to M.K. Chen. *Medical Care* 144:963–964.

Stoddart, G., and Labelle, R.J. 1985. *Privatization in the Canadian health care system*. Ottawa, Canada: Health and Welfare Canada.

Demand for Health

Grossman, M. 1972. On the concept of health capital and the demand for health. *Journal of Political Economy* 80:223–255.

————. 1972. *The demand for health*. New York: National Bureau of Economic Research.

————. 1982. The demand for health after a decade. *Journal of Health Economics* 1:1–4.

Hay, J.W., et al. 1982. The demand for dental health. *Social Science and Medicine* 16:1285–1289.

Lairson, D., et al. 1984. Estimates of the demand for health: Males in the pre-retirement years. *Social Science and Medicine* 19:741–747.

Wagstaff, A. 1986. The demand for health: Theory and applications. *Journal of Epidemiology and Community Health* 40:1–11.

Warner, K.E., and Murt, H.A. 1984. Economic incentives for health. *Annual Review for Public Health* 5:107–133.

Wedig, G.J. 1988. Health status and the demand for health. *Journal of Health Economics* 7:151–163.

Williams, A. 1985. The nature, meaning and measurement of health and illness: An economic viewpoint. *Social Science and Medicine* 20:1023–1027.

The Demand for Insurance

Anderson, G., and Knickman, J. 1984. Adverse selection under a voucher system: Grouping Medicare recipients by level of expenditure. *Inquiry* 21:135–143.

Berki, S.E., and Ashcraft, M. 1980. HMO enrolment: Who joins what and why: A review of the literature. *Milbank Memorial Fund Quarterly* 58:588–632.

Berki, S.E., et al. 1977. Enrollment choice in a multi-HMO setting. *Medical Care* 15:95–114.

Chernick, H.A. 1987. Tax policy toward health insurance and the demand for medical services. *Journal of Health Economics* 6:1–25.

Feldman, R., et al. 1989. *Employer based health insurance.* Pub. no. PHS-89-3434. Rockville, Md.: U.S. Department of Health and Human Services, National Center for Health Services Research and Health Care Technology.

Feldstein, M., and Friedman, B. 1977. Tax subsidies, the rational demand for insurance and the health care crisis. *Journal of Public Economics* 7:155–178.

Friedman, B. 1974. Risk aversion and the consumer choice of health insurance option. *Review of Economics and Statistics* 56:209–214.

Hemenway, D. 1990. Propitious selection. *Quarterly Journal of Economics* 104:1063–1069.

———. 1992. Propitious selection in insurance. *Journal of Risk and Uncertainty* 5:247–251.

Huang, L.F., et al. 1989. Demand for medigap insurance by the elderly. *Applied Economics* 21:1325–1339.

Jensen, G.R., et al. 1984. Corporate-benefit policies and health insurance costs. *Journal of Health Economics* 3:275–296.

Marquis, M.S., and Long, S.H. 1995. Worker demand for health insurance in the non-group market. *Journal of Health Economics* 14:47–63.

Miller, R.H., and Luft, H.S. 1995. Estimating health expenditure growth under managed competition. *Journal of the American Medical Association* 273:656–662.

Pauly, M. 1986. Taxation, health insurance, and market failure in the medical economy. *Journal of Economic Literature* 26:629–675.

Taylor, A., and Wilensky, G.R. 1983. The effect of tax policies on expenditures for private health insurance. In *Market reforms in health care,* ed. J.A. Meyer. Washington, D.C.: American Enterprise Institute for Policy Research.

Thomas, K. 1994–1995. Are subsidies enough to encourage the uninsured to purchase health insurance? An analysis of underlying behavior. *Inquiry* 31:415–424.

Supplier-induced Demand

Feldstein, M.S. 1974. Econometric studies in health economics. In *Frontiers in quantitative economics,* ed. M. Intriligator and D. Kendrick. Amsterdam: North-Holland Publishing Company.

Grylten, J., et al. 1995. Supplier inducement in a public health care system. *Journal of Health Economics* 14:207–229.

Pauly, M.V. 1980. *Doctors and their workshops.* Chicago: University of Chicago Press.

Schaafsma, J. 1994. A new test for supplier-inducement and application to the Canadian market for dental care. *Journal of Health Economics* 13:407–431.

Time Costs

Acton, J.P. 1973. *Demand for health among the urban poor.* Pub. no. R-1151-OEO/NYC. New York: Rand Institute.

Culyer, A.J., and Cullis, J.G. 1976. Some economics of waiting lists in the NHS. *Journal of Social Policy* 5:239–264.

Economics of Disease Prevention and Health Promotion

Jones, L., and Bakler, M.R. 1986. The application of health economics to health promotion. *Community Medicine* 8:224–229.

Kenkel, D.S. 1994. The demand for preventive medical care. *Applied Economics* 26:313–325.

Russell, L.B. 1984. The economics of prevention. *Health Policy* 4:85–100.

Scheffler, R.M., and Paringer, L. 1980. A review of the economic evidence on prevention. *Medical Care* 18:473–484.

Shepard, R.J. 1987. The economics of prevention: A critique. *Health Policy* 7:49–56.

CHAPTER 5

Behavior of Health Care Costs

5.1 INTRODUCTION

The present chapter focuses on the economic behavior of health care providers. We first examine how the resource commitment made by individual suppliers varies with the amount of production undertaken by these suppliers. We then focus on the individual providing unit. The measure that we use to weigh the magnitude of the resource commitment of each providing unit is the cost to the unit of resource services. We examine how these costs vary as the size of operations of the providing unit varies.

Before embarking on the analysis of costs, we consider, in Section 5.2, the relation between inputs (resources) and outputs (the input-output or production relation). The presentation is in purely "physical" terms and is designed to provide a brief summary of the role of production in determining cost. In Section 5.3 we explore the basic cost-output relation and examine three alternative ways of looking at this relation. Using the cost-output relation as our basic reference point, we examine, in Section 5.4, the various factors that affect this relation, such as changing technology, the quality of care given, the incentives offered to providers, and the size of the production unit.

In Section 5.5 we examine the impact of one particular organizational factor on a unit's operating costs: the relatedness of the types of services produced together in the same unit. Producing services of different types in the same unit may give rise to economies and diseconomies of scope. In Section 5.6 we examine the impact of operating scale on a unit's costs. Finally, in Section 5.7, we investigate the empirical estimation of cost curves in relation to physician practices, hospitals, nursing homes, and health insurance companies.

5.2   PRODUCTION: THE INPUT-OUTPUT RELATION

5.2.1 Basic Relation

The economic analysis of production involves the specification of alternative combinations of inputs that yield varying levels of outputs. The production process itself, its organization, and the technology used lie in the realm of administrative practice and medicine. The production process has considerable impact on economic variables and can be influenced by economic factors as well (see Section 6.6).

The production process is partially determined by the technology used. Roughly defined, technology is a way of doing things. The production process in medical care is determined by what things are done to the patients as well as the way they are done. In this sense, there are many "technologies" even for the same illness. To bring out the essential characteristics of the production (input-output) relation, we focus initially on one technology and later introduce complicating factors and determine how they affect this relation.

The simplest production process can be illustrated by the imaginary cast of a solo private practice physician who treats patients all with the same disease—the common cold. Treatment involves an examination, diagnostic tests, and a prescription of two aspirins and a glass of water. Two simplifying assumptions should be noted. First, the patients' conditions are homogeneous (the patients have equally severe cases of a single disease). Second, the treatment provided is of the same quality (all patients receive the same examination and the same tests and listen to the same banter by the physician).

The process involves the use of various resources. These resources can be divided into two groups: fixed and variable inputs. Fixed inputs are those whose use is restricted to their current function for the time period under consideration. Given their specialized nature, the high costs of transferring them to other uses, or other contractual arrangements, fixed factors cannot be used elsewhere in the economy during the current period of production. Furthermore, the producer cannot increase the quantity during this period, which we will assume to be one month. In our example, fixed factors include physician office space, test equipment, and physician time.

Office space and equipment are rented annually, let us say, and so their use for a one-year period is fixed. As for physician time, we assume that the doctor has by choice decided to remain in his or her present position for at least the next month and will work 40 hours per week. Physician time is therefore a fixed factor. Whether or not a factor is fixed depends on the time period under consideration. If the time period was five years, office space, equipment, and even physician time might vary. The variable factor of production is nursing time. This input can be purchased in varying quantities by the physician. It will be assumed that one or more nurses perform all tasks that the doctor does not.

The production process consists of three types of tasks performed by the available resources. The first are the administrative tasks of setting appointments, keeping records, moving patients through the office, and billing patients. The second type are technical tasks, such as the testing of blood with the rented equipment. These tasks are performed by the nurses. Finally, there is the examination itself, which is performed by the physician. For simplicity's sake, we will assume no patient can be processed without the involvement of a nurse. Generally, of course, the doctor is able to process some patients with no help, but we will assume this is not the case. We will also assume that, within the current ranges of resource use considered, the doctor can treat all patients who ask for an appointment; his or her time limitations do not create a "capacity" problem.

We now inquire into the number of patients who can be treated at different levels of variable input. The specification of this production relation will be made under the condition that, whatever the level of variable input used in conjunction with the fixed inputs, the maximum number of patients possible are being served. This condition, discussed further at the end of this section, will only hold if the human resources (nurses) have incentives to produce as much as possible. Under this condition, a production function that expresses how output will vary when inputs are changed in quantity can be specified. In specifying this function, let us use L to refer to the nurses' input, which is measured by hours worked. All other factors, which in our example are fixed, will be called F. Output, called Q, is measured by patient visits (each visit is assumed to be identical in nature). The production function can be written $Q = Q (L, F)$, which means that Q depends on L and F.

The production function is a summary of what goes into the process and what comes out. With F fixed, only L can vary. By varying L, we are in fact specifying different combinations of L and F. With few nursing hours, a single nurse will perform all the nonexamination tasks and consequently cannot afford to specialize. Few patients will thus be treated. In Table 5–1 we present this by showing only one patient treated as a result of the first eight hours of nursing input. When more patients are treated, the single nurse can begin to perform some tasks for several patients together. This concentration of tasks allows additional output to be produced with fewer additional resources. Indeed, in our example, only seven additional nursing hours are required to process a second patient.

The additional production yielded by the use of one extra unit of variable input is called the *marginal product*. It can be expressed symbolically as $\Delta Q/\Delta L$. As can be seen in Table 5–1, at the lowest level of output (one visit), an extra nursing hour adds one-eighth of a visit to the level of output. At a level of two visits, the additional output of an extra nursing hour is one-seventh of a visit. This fraction repre-

Table 5–1 Relations between Cost and Output

Total Nursing Hours (L)	Total Visits (Q)	Marginal Product (ΔQ/ΔL)	Total Fixed Cost (TFC)	Total Variable Cost (TVC)	Total Cost (TC = TFC + TVC)	Average Fixed Cost (AFC = TFC/Q)	Average Variable Cost (AVC = TVC/Q)	Average Total Cost (ATC = TC/Q)	Marginal Cost (ΔTC/ΔQ)
8	1	1/8	100	16	116	100.0	16.0	116.0	16
15	2	1/7	100	30	130	50.0	15.0	65.0	14
20	3	1/5	100	40	140	33.3	13.3	46.7	10
24	4	1/4	100	48	148	25.0	12.0	37.0	8
30	5	1/6	100	60	160	20.0	12.0	32.0	12
38	6	1/8	100	76	176	16.7	12.7	29.3	16
50	7	1/12	100	100	200	14.3	14.3	28.6	24
64	8	1/14	100	128	228	12.5	16.0	28.5	28
100	9	1/30	100	200	300	11.1	22.2	33.3	72
140	10	1/40	100	280	380	10.0	28.0	38.0	80

sents the marginal product. This tendency toward an increasing marginal product, created initially by the gains that the concentration of tasks allows, is reinforced by gains from the specialization of tasks as output continues to grow. As more patients are processed and more nursing hours and more nurses are used, some tasks can be divided among the nurses, resulting in gains from specialization.

But such gains cannot be reaped forever. Eventually, overroutinization will lead to boredom. In addition, the fixed amount of equipment in the office becomes heavily taxed and nurses have to wait to perform lab tests. This changes the relation between additional output and additional input; to produce successively more units of output at these higher levels of output requires successively larger doses of nursing hours. Putting the argument in terms of marginal productivity, at higher levels of output the marginal productivity of nurses' efforts begins to decline. Thus, in our example, at a level of output of four visits, the marginal product is one-fourth of a visit; at a level of output of five visits, the marginal product falls to one-sixth of a visit; and for six visits the marginal product is lower still, one-eighth of a visit per nursing hour added. Production has reached the stage of diminishing marginal productivity. It should be noted that total output is constantly rising; the assumed relation in our production function stipulates that additional increases of output are harder and harder to come by as the size of output rises.

The figures used in our example were invented to illustrate the principle we are hypothesizing—that marginal productivity eventually diminishes. Other equally illuminating examples could have been chosen to elucidate this principle.

5.2.2 Shifts in the Relation

We have now defined a production function and specified in general terms the most important property we would expect such a function to possess: the marginal product will eventually decline when the size of output increases. This relation was specified on the basis of restrictive underlying conditions. We can now examine how the productive relation will be affected by changes in these conditions. These changes will be examined using the basic production (input-output) relation specified in Table 5–1 as a point of reference. A change in any of these underlying conditions will be regarded as causing one of two possible results: it will increase or decrease the amount of output obtained from given amounts of input. Either result will be regarded as a shift in the production relation. An upward shift means that at each level of input more output can be produced; a downward shift means that less output can be produced. Looking at an upward shift in marginal terms, at any level of input, more additional output can be produced with an additional unit of the variable input. Expressed in output terms, at any level of output, less additional input is required to produce one extra unit of output. Stating the same thing in marginal terms, we would say that the marginal product is greater at any level of output. Thus, at a level of output of eight visits, the original production relation was such that an extra nursing hour employed led to an increase in output of one-fourteenth of a visit. With an upward shift in the production function, an extra nursing hour might now produce one-tenth of a visit. Of course, the assumption that marginal productivity is diminishing still holds, but the entire relation is such that now more can be obtained at any level of output.

We will now examine how changes in some of the underlying conditions affect the production relation. The possible changes include a change in the case mix, in the severity of illness of patients, in the quality of care, in technology, in the amount of capital (F) that the employer uses, and in the underlying incentive structure.

First, a change in the case mix would occur if the physician was confronted with a number of rheumatic fever cases in addition to patients with colds. More resources would need to be expended on each of these cases, shifting the production relation downward. The same type of downward shift would occur if the physician merely had to treat some patients with especially severe colds. These cases would require more resources and would thus shift the production relation downward.

Second, the result of a change in the quality of care will depend on the precise meaning attached to *quality*. If greater thoroughness in performing an examination is an aspect of higher quality care, then the effect of providing higher quality care is to shift the production relation downward, since more resources would be required for each examination. Similarly, if more extensive patient education is an aspect of higher quality care, then the production relation will again be pushed downward.

Third, high quality is frequently associated with high technology—in other words, highly trained specialists and sophisticated equipment. Offering the benefits of advances in technology thus usually entails an increase in capital, both human and physical. More input is required to produce a single unit of output (measured as a visit), and therefore the measured relation between input and output will shift downward. However, note that more resource-intensive visits are qualitatively different than less resource-intensive ones. We cannot say that medical resources are less productive in any of these instances. Instead, a given amount of resources will produce a lower quantity of care, but this medical care is likely to be of a higher quality.

Of course, sometimes the introduction of a new piece of equipment can increase the quantity of output without changing the quality. As an example, if a computerized blood counter replaces a Kolter counter, more tests of the same quality can be processed with the same amount of variable input (technician time). The production relation shifts upward in this case.

A final factor influencing the production relation is the "management" incentive system. Our production relation was derived using the assumption that the maximum output would be obtained at any given level of resource use. Incentives enter the picture when we consider the benefits that accrue to management (the doctor, in our example) as a result of the way resources are used. If management is rewarded for keeping production costs low, then management will have an incentive to use as few resources per unit of output as possible. However, incentives can be structured in such a way as to encourage use of inputs. If, for example, the management receives a fixed rate of compensation that is positively related to its costs, then it will have an incentive to use more resources to perform each task. Even though the analysis of production lies in the realm of production management and medicine, the production relation cannot be analyzed in total isolation from the economic incentives that exist within the organization.

5.2.3 Substitution among Inputs

The analysis of the previous section was based on the assumption that one variable input existed. In fact, there may be several variable inputs, and they may be substitutable for each other, at least to some degree. Let us suppose that there are two variable inputs, physician time (P) and nurse practitioner time (N), in addition to the fixed inputs (F). The production function is now expressed as $Q = Q(P, N, F)$. Substitutability among inputs is often analyzed by assuming the level of output (Q) is held constant and then examining, for example, how much nurse practitioner time must be added to the process to offset a unit of physician time. We will call this the *marginal rate of substitution of nurse practitioners for physicians.*

The replacement of physicians, although possible in certain situations, may have limited feasibility. For example, if a given number of patients are being treated in an ambulatory setting, and initially there are ten physicians and one nurse practitioner, the tasks of the physicians may be such that a nurse practitioner could be substituted for a physician with no adverse effects on the quantity or quality of output. However, additional substitution may prove to be more difficult, and two nurses might be required to replace the next physician. Eventually, no additional substitution may be feasible if the quality and quantity of output are to be maintained. Nevertheless, within a given range, substitution is possible.

A number of areas have been identified in health care where substitution makes sense. One study examined the use of paraprofessional surgical assistants as substitutes for physicians or surgeons in the role of assistant to the operating surgeon. The study found that trained assistants could replace physicians in this assisting role with no adverse effects on the operating surgeon's time, particularly in less complex operations (Lewit et al. 1980).

Another example of the substitutability of inputs is the use of drugs in the care of mental patients. To some extent, increased utilization of drugs reduces the amount of effort required of psychiatric hospital attendants. Also, physician assistants and nurse practitioners can perform many of the tasks that doctors traditionally perform (Reinhardt 1972), and dental technicians can perform simple tasks, such as cleaning teeth and doing easy repairs.

Frequently, substitution is feasible and even economical, but barriers exist to limit it. For example, licensing laws may limit the degree to which nurse practitioners can substitute for doctors. In such cases, one must separate what is feasible from what is legally or institutionally permitted.

5.2.4 Volume–Outcome Relation

The production function has been specified as a relation between the volume of services provided and the quantity of inputs. As noted, there is also a relation between the quality and volume of services. This relation has usually been specified for specific surgical procedures.

In discussing the relation between volume and outcome, the focus can be on the volume of services that are provided by individual providers (surgeons or surgical teams) or the service volume of a health care organization (Garnick et al. 1989). Surgeons individually or as part of a team can maintain their skills better when they perform more of the same types of procedures during a specified time period. If they do only a few operations of a given type within a given time frame, they may get out of practice and the quality of their work may deteriorate. We would therefore expect a positive relationship between the volume of a given procedure for a given practitioner or team and outcomes of the care provided.

A positive relation between volume and outcome may also hold for an institution, but for different reasons. An institution with an especially large volume of certain procedures may hire specialized personnel and acquire specialized equipment. For example, in the area of rehabilitation, an institution with specialized personnel and equipment can return patients to normal functioning sooner. Thus, the relation between volume and outcome can work separately for the surgical (or treatment) team and for the institution where the treatment occurs.

There is a confounding factor that can make it difficult to interpret an observed relation between outcome and volume. If a surgical team is known to be more skilled, then the team will be sought out by patients. We would then observe a positive relation between outcomes and volume, but the high volume may not be the cause of the team's maintenance of its skills. Thus, a policy that encourages larger volumes for surgical teams regardless of their skill levels may not be successful in improving the overall levels of outcome. Determining the causes of the observed relationship is important for policy reasons, though it may be difficult in practice to uncover the real causes.

5.3 SHORT-RUN COST–OUTPUT RELATIONS

5.3.1 Production and Cost

Section 5.2.3 focused on the relation between output and alternative combinations of inputs. In specifying the production relation, the inputs were presented as separate entities that work together. The next step in our analysis is to present a measure of the commitment of resources by the provider in producing the output. One such measure, which places all inputs on a single scale measured in money terms, is cost. To a provider, cost means the value of inputs used in the production process. However, this value is not always well approximated by money outlays.

Therefore, a broader view of cost, one that measures what the provider gives up by using all the resources committed to production, not just the ones paid for, is used in this section. Of control importance is the concept of opportunity cost, which is defined as the value that the provider gave up by not committing the resources to the next highest valued use. Another way of putting it is that the cost of resources is measured by the amount for which those resources could be sold in the market. This concept is particularly important when measuring the value of resources that are not paid (e.g., resources that the producer owns) and hence that appear to be free. If the owner of these unpaid resources is giving up some return on them, then there is a cost associated with them, and this cost must be estimated by calculating the probable market value of the resources.

Since we are concerned with the functioning of an organization, the cost of resource use will be considered from the organization's point of view. Any organization can undertake a resource commitment that does not appear in its paid out costs. Nevertheless, if the organization commits its resources to a particular use, they are part of the organization's costs and should be counted as such. On the other hand, an economic unit outside the organization may make a resource commitment that allows the organization to function. For example, a person may give blood to a blood donor clinic, a benefactor may endow a hospital with an operating room, or a doctor may volunteer teaching time at a medical school. In these instances, resources are used to undertake activities, but they are not part of the resource commitment of the institution. Rather, they are part of the total resource commitment required to undertake the activity. In this chapter we are concerned with the operations of health care organizations and so focus on the resource commitment made by these organizations in their activities. This leaves out the question of the total (or social) resource commitment made to perform any activity, including the commitment of donors, volunteers, benefactors, and government agencies. For a discussion of the broader social viewpoint, see Section 10.3.3.

In the analysis that follows, the definitions presented are placed in a time frame of one month. Given this time frame, we can divide production costs into fixed costs and variable costs. Fixed costs are defined as those that do not change with output within the relevant time frame. Variable costs, on the other hand, increase as output increases. In the physician's practice example, the fixed costs are those that do not vary during the month; they are the costs of the fixed factors, including space and equipment rental costs and the cost of physician time. We will assume the rental values to be $50 during the period. We will also assume that the physician could have earned $50 working in a clinic rather than in a private practice; this amount measures the opportunity cost the physician faced when making the decision whether to continue to practice privately. Given that the decision to practice privately has been made, the forgoing of other ways of using work time becomes a "sunk" cost, relevant more to the past than to the present. Nevertheless, it is still a cost and is classified as a fixed cost. The total fixed costs are thus $100. (The cost curve of a company incorporates the return that the owners could normally get on their assets, including their time, the buildings they own, etc. This normal return is called *normal profit*. Any return above normal profit is called *economic profit*.)

Variable costs are costs of variable inputs. In our example, the only variable input is nursing hours. Assume that the price of nursing services is $2 per hour. Thus, 8 hours of services cost $16. We can now specify the relation between the cost to the provider and the level of output. This relation depends on the quantities of resources used (determined by the production relationship) and the money paid for, or the opportunity cost imputed to, these resource services. The relation can be viewed in three different ways. First, we can examine costs from the point of view of the total resource commitment required to maintain production at any specific level of output. In this case, we determine how total costs vary with output. Second, we can look at the average value of resource commitment, that is, the value of the resource commitment required to produce a single unit of output. The value of this average resource commitment is called *average cost*. The third way of viewing costs is to examine the value of additional resources that must be committed to the production process to produce an additional unit of output. This value is called the *marginal cost*. We will now discuss how each of these alternative measures varies as the level of output changes.

5.3.2 Total Cost

Total cost (*TC*) is the sum of all costs incurred in producing a given level of output; total variable cost (*TVC*) is the total cost of variable inputs for any level of output; total fixed cost (*TFC*) is the total cost of all fixed factors. Total cost is the sum of the total variable cost and the total fixed cost. We now look at these types of cost with regard to the data contained in Table 5–1. The total fixed cost is $100 whatever the level of output. Therefore, this cost, plotted on the graph in Figure 5–1, is represented by a straight horizontal line (*TFC*) at the $100 level.

The behavior of the total variable cost depends on two factors: (1) the relation between output and variable inputs, specified in Section 5.2, and (2) the unit cost of these variable resources. Figure 5–1 contains a total variable cost curve that reflects the data in our example.

The total cost curve (*TC*) is the vertical sum of the two curves *TVC* and *TFC* at each output level (see Table 5–1, Column 6). The level of the *TC* curve is determined by the fixed cost; its shape is determined by the production function and the variation of output with variable inputs. Given the fixed per unit price of the variable input ($2 an hour), the production function relation, translated into a cost-output relation, entails that the addition to total costs of the extra resource commit-

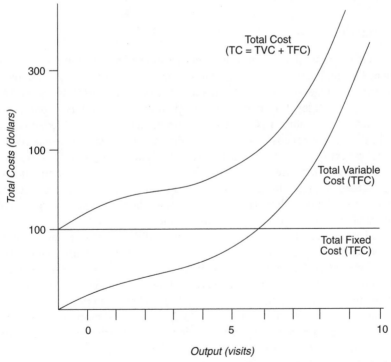

Figure 5–1 The relation between the total fixed cost, total variable cost, total cost, and level of output. At each production level, one total cost can be divided between the fixed and variable costs. The fixed cost does not vary with output. This graph is based on data from Table 5–1.

ment levels off as output increases. Thus, the total variable cost is $16 at a scale of one visit, $30 at a scale of two visits, $40 at a scale of three visits, and $48 at a level of four visits. This levelling off of cost is shown diagrammatically by the flattening of the section between 0 and 4 of curve *TVC* in Figure 5–1. If additional resources had been increasingly more productive beyond this scale of input, the *TVC* curve would have continued levelling off. At the extreme, if higher levels of production could be undertaken with the same resources, then *TVC* would be horizontal. But, beyond four units of output, diminishing marginal productivity begins to set in, and in terms of costs this means that successively greater resource commitments are needed to attain successively higher levels of output. In Table 5–1, the total variable cost rises to 60, 76, 100, 128, 200, and so on, and the total cost also rises rapidly. As seen on the curve, beyond a scale of 4, *TVC* is curving upward; at the extreme, it would become almost vertical. Thus a considerable commitment in resources in required to move to a higher output level. The shape of *TC* is similar to that of *TVC*, except that *TC* is higher by $100.

5.3.3 Marginal Cost

Implicit in the total variable cost-output relation is the marginal cost-output relation. The marginal cost at any level of output is the additional cost required to move one unit higher on the output scale. It is thus defined as $\Delta TC/\Delta Q$. Since *TFC* is constant over all levels of output, the marginal fixed cost would be zero at any value, since the additional fixed resource commitment is zero at all levels of output. Thus, the marginal cost is simply the addition to total variable cost needed to produce one extra unit of output. In Table 5–1 the marginal cost (*MC*) is shown in Column 10. As can be seen, the extra cost of moving to one unit of output from zero is $16, to two units from one is $14, and so on. Until we have reached four units of output, *MC* is falling. However, because of the diminishing marginal productivity of variable inputs, coupled with the fact that the additional variable inputs used are all paid the same wage, producing additional units of output eventually requires successively greater resource commitment. This is reflected in rising marginal cost after the fourth visit; the fifth visit costs $12 extra; the sixth, $16 extra; and so on. The marginal cost curve is shown in Figure 5–2. Note that beyond an output of 4, marginal costs cease falling and begin to rise.

The concept of marginal cost is central to the analysis of most economic decisions. For the most part, the types of decisions that concern economists involve determining the consequences of employing additional (or fewer) resources for a particular purpose. For example, we might be concerned with the implications of placing additional surgeon-training facilities in either Boston or Boise; we might analyze the consequences of adding one or more paramedics to an existing medi-

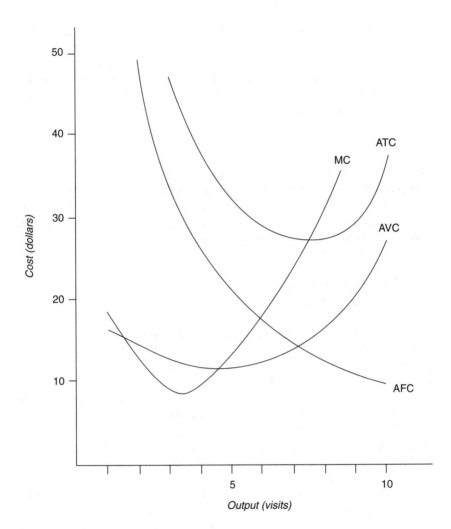

Figure 5–2 Relation between cost and output. The average cost is shown in total (*ATC*) and as separated into the two components of the total: fixed cost (*AFC*) and variable cost (*AVC*). Marginal cost (*MC*) is the addition to total cost of the next unit produced. There is a unique relation between *MC* and both *AVC* and *ATC*: when *MC* is below *ATC* (or *AVC*), the average cost is falling; when *MC* is greater than *ATC* (or *AVC*), the average cost is increasing; and when *MC* equals *ATC* (or *AVC*), the average cost is constant, that is, it has reached its minimum point.

cal practice; or we might be interested in the consequences of decreasing the number of obstetrics beds in a particular region of the country or a particular hospital. In these instances, as in most other cases of resource allocation, the allocation decision concerns whether to expand a particular facility or service or increase the available quantity of trained personnel. The concept used to measure the added resource commitment is the marginal cost.

5.3.4 Average Cost

The third way of looking at costs is to average the costs required to obtain a given level of output. The average total cost (ATC) is the total cost per unit of output and is defined for any level of output. It equals TC/Q. It measures the value of the average resource commitment required to sustain a given scale of output. However, because it is useful in making comparisons, this variable has been frequently used in empirical studies.

The behavior of the average total cost depends on the behavior of the average fixed cost (TFC/Q) and the average variable cost (TVC/Q). The average fixed cost is lower at successively higher levels of output because the $100 in fixed cost is spread out over more output. Thus, at one visit, the average fixed cost is $100; at two visits, it is $50, and so on. The average variable cost initially falls at successively greater levels of output. At one unit of output, it is $16; at two, it is $15; at three, it is $13.30; and so on. The fall in average variable cost is made possible by the increasing productivity of additional variable inputs at low output levels.

Another way of viewing this relation is to consider that the marginal cost is initially below the average cost, which brings down the average as output increases. The marginal cost for the first visit is $16, and the average variable cost is $16. For the second visit, the marginal cost is $14. This brings down the average variable cost of the two visits to $15 (i.e., $30/2). The falling average variable and the average fixed costs together ensure that average total cost (which is the sum of the two) will also fall as output expands. Eventually, after four visits, the marginal cost increases as output expands. Expanding output from four to five visits costs an extra $12; expanding to six visits costs another $16; and the marginal cost at seven is $24. However, as long as the marginal cost is lower than the average total cost, a further expansion of output will continue to reduce the average total cost.

For example, in Table 5–1 we can see that at five units of output, the total cost is $160 and the average total cost is thus $32. An expansion of output by one unit to a level of output of six would cost an additional $16. The ATC at six units of output decreases to $29.33 because the MC of the sixth unit of output is lower than the ATC, and so expanding output brings down the average. With a rising MC, this situation will not continue indefinitely. At some level of output, the MC will just equal the ATC and at a still higher level it will exceed it. The ATC must then begin to rise. In our example, the level where the *MC* equals the *ATC* is eight visits. As seen in Table 5–1, an expansion from seven to eight visits will cost an extra $28. With an *ATC* of $28.57 at the level of seven visits, expansion to eight visits leaves the *ATC* at about the same level. An expansion to nine visits has an *MC* of $72. This is above the *ATC* at eight visits. The *ATC* increases to $33.33 at nine visits.

The average cost curves are shown in Figure 5–2 in juxtaposition to the *MC* curve. These curves are based on the data presented in Table 5–1 but have been smoothed out. The average fixed cost (*AFC*) curve declines over all levels of output. The average variable cost (*AVC*) curve declines until four visits. At five visits, the *MC* just equals the *AVC*, and so the *AVC* curve bottoms out. For output levels higher than five, the *MC* is above the *AVC*, and so the *AVC* increases with expansion of output. The *AVC* curve is thus U-shaped, indicating that at lower levels of output the *AVC* falls as output expands. The *AVC* curve then bottoms (where *MC* = *AVC*) and begins to rise. The *ATC* curve (remember, *ATC* = *AVC* + *AFC*) is also U-shaped. It is located above and slightly to the right of the *AVC* curve and also bottoms out where the rising *MC* cuts it.

The *ATC*, as already noted, has a fixed and a variable component. The relative sizes of these two components will determine at which level of output the *ATC* curve will begin to slope upward. The fixed cost component (*AFC*) always falls as output increases, because the same costs are spread over a greater output. The variable cost component (*AVC*) follows the rules of productivity and begins to rise, because eventually higher marginal costs will raise the average. The larger the fixed cost component, the greater the range over which the average total cost will fall. Hospitals have been identified as having large fixed cost components. If this is indeed true, then hospitals should experience a diminishing average total cost over a wide range of potential output levels.

The fixed cost component is related to the use of capital equipment. A heavy investment in capital equipment will create a large fixed cost. However, such equipment may permit additional procedures to be undertaken with a small additional commitment of resources up to high levels of output. In such a situation, although the fixed cost would be high, the marginal cost would be low, and the average total cost would fall over a wide range of output levels. In a related phenomenon, called *indivisibility*, expensive equipment, available in a large dose, cannot be divided into smaller units. It is operated at low levels of output at a high *ATC* and operated at high levels at a low *ATC*.

This section has identified three related cost-output measures: total cost, average cost, and marginal cost. Their shapes are dependent largely on the production relation. As shown in Section 5.2, the production relation is subject to shifts caused by a variety of conditions. These same conditions can cause a cost curve to change its positions, as discussed below.

5.4   COST CURVE POSITION

The position of a cost curve is determined by the same factors that influence the production relation. These factors include the case mix and the severity of cases treated, the quality of care provided, the technology used, the amount of fixed factors employed in the production process, and the incentive system under which the provider is operating. Each factor will be considered separately.

Given fixed inputs and fixed costs, a change in the case mix toward more complicated cases and an increase in the average severity level will increase the variable resources required per unit of output and will thus increase marginal and average costs at all output levels. The positions of both the *ATC* and *MC* curves will now be higher. The shifts in position are shown in Figure 5–3. Here, *ATC*₁ and *MC*₁ are the average total cost and marginal cost relations before the change to a more complex case mix. This change results in a shift to *ATC*₂ and *MC*₂.

An increase in quality, if this entails more thorough examinations or treatments, will similarly shift the cost curves upward. The adoption of a technology that uses

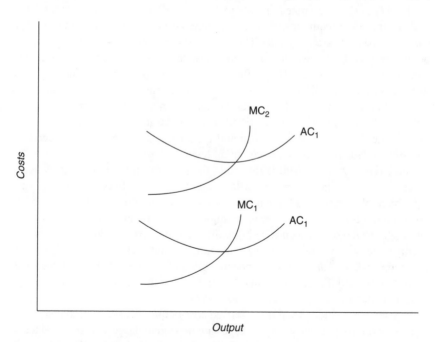

Figure 5–3 Diagrammatic representation of a shift in average and marginal cost curves. Curves ATC_1 and MC_1 indicate the initial relation between costs and output. Curves ATC_2 and MC_2 represent an upward shift in costs at every level of output.

more resources per case will have a similar effect. Many recent technological innovations have been associated with a large capital investment for equipment as well as a larger flow of variable expenditures for the services of the highly trained personnel needed to operate this equipment. Examples of such technological innovations include open-heart surgery, a procedure that intrigued economists in the 1960s; critical care units (CCUs) or intensive care units (ICUs), which are high-cost monitoring and life support units; computed tomography (CT) scanning; and magnetic resonance imaging (MRI), a revolutionary and somewhat costly advance on x-rays and laparoscopic surgery that allows one to perform surgery through a small incision. All these examples require a heavy investment in equipment, and the effect of introducing any of them would be to shift both the fixed and variable components of the ATC upward, thus increasing in the ATC for all levels of output. However, it should be remembered that an increase in the quality of services provided may accompany the introduction of new technology. One physician visit or one hospital stay is not always the same as another.

All technological innovations in medical care are not of this resource-using type, however. Innovations in pharmaceuticals have reduced the length of hospitalization required for some illnesses. Two notable examples are tuberculosis treatment and mental illness treatment. Furthermore, new laboratory equipment has allowed many tasks to be automated. This has led to falling average costs over broad ranges of output because of the low variable costs associated with the use of this equipment.

The effect of incentives that encourage resource use is to raise the level of average cost associated with any single level of output. Assuming that a single least-cost position is associated with each output level, we can identify a least-cost average cost curve. Incentives to use resources will encourage the provider to choose a position above this curve. It has been questioned whether a cost curve that measures the cost output relation when given resources are not used to maximize output (i.e., a more-than-least-cost curve) is a meaningful concept. This is because more than one such average cost point may exist at any output level. There can only be one least-cost point, however, and in the least-cost case, a cost curve that supposedly represents a unique relation between cost and output can be uniquely determined. Once a provider chooses to use more than the least amount of resources to achieve a given output level (with no change in quality), he or she can use these excessive resources to varying degrees. There is no longer a unique cost curve (Zuckerman et al. 1994).

Another factor that might cause cost curves to shift is the price the provider pays for hired resources. In our example, if the physician had to pay $3 per nursing hour instead of $2, both the marginal and the average cost curves would shift upward. Conversely, if the price fell to $1, the curves would shift downward. A final factor that can influence the position of the average cost curves appears when two or more types of variable input exist. When these inputs can be substituted for each other, at least to some degree, then a substitution of a less costly for a more costly input can lower the cost curves, although other factors may push it the other way. For example, if a paramedic is substituted for a physician but takes much longer to do the same task, the total or average cost may not shift downward as a result of the substitution. Also, keep in mind that the quality of the product may become lower as a result of the substitution, and even though the output may cost less to produce, it might not be exactly comparable.

5.5 ECONOMIES OF SCOPE

We have proceeded with the discussion of costs as if a health care institution had a single type of output. Although this assumption helps to clarify certain relations between costs and output, it is generally false in the case of larger certain institutions, notably hospitals. Hospitals are multiproduct firms that offer a large number of separate product lines, such as clinical laboratory services, emergency department services, physical therapy, and intensive care (Berry 1973; Goldfarb et al. 1980).

The product line dimension of output should be distinguished from the case mix dimension. Case mix refers to the complexity of the types of diseases being treated. A hospital that treats a large number of different diseases has a different case mix than one that specializes in a few. If, as is sometimes done, severity is included as a dimension of case mix, then case mix indexes can be developed (Hornbrook and Monheit 1985). Each hospital also has a number of services or product lines. In fact, two hospitals can have very similar case mix measures but very different service scopes. As a consequence, the relation between cost and scope offers itself as a possibly fruitful topic of investigation.

Economies of scope are savings derived from producing different products jointly in the same production unit rather than producing them individually in separate production units. Let X_1 stand for one output (e.g., family planning services) and X_2 stand for a second output (e.g., pediatric services). Let $C(X_1)$ stand for the total cost of producing X_1, $C(X_2)$ stand for the total cost of producing X_2 in a separate setting, and $C(X_1, X_2)$ stand for the cost of jointly producing X_1 and X_2 in the same production unit. Economies of scope arise when the cost of jointly producing specific quantities of the two services ($C(X_1, X_2)$) is less than the sum of the costs of producing each service separately ($C(X_1) + C(X_2)$). In our example, economies of scope would exist if a clinic could jointly produce given quantities of family planning services and pediatric services more cheaply than the same quantities produced in sharply separated units or departments.

Economies of scope might arise when some of the tasks involved in providing two district services are complementary. For example, if family planning and pediatric services require a common core of testing capabilities, then providing the two types of services in separate units would cause duplication. Savings could be achieved by combining the two services into a single unit that caters to both groups of patients. Of course, it is also possible to have diseconomies of scope. This would occur when two types of output are best produced in separate units. For example, if psychiatric patients are treated with one regimen and home health service patients with a different one, combining the psychiatric and home health services in a single unit may be more costly than keeping them separate.

In one study of the economies of scope in health care, Cowing and Holtman (1983) estimated economies of scale and scope for 138 short-term hospitals in New York State. They divided hospital output into five diagnostic categories (actually representing different case mixes rather than service scopes): medical-surgical, maternity, pediatric, other inpatient care, and emergency department care. For four of the services (pediatric care being the exception), marginal cost fell over low ranges of output and then became constant. These results indicate substantial economies of scale in these services and suggest that merging services produced on a small scale into larger units could yield considerable savings. However, with regard to the existence of economies of scope, the findings were generally negative. These findings, if they hold up in repeated trials, indicate that, on cost grounds alone, hospitals should specialize rather than become multiproduct organizations. One must be careful not to overgeneralize, because, even though economies of scope may not be widespread, specific services may have production conditions that, when combined, yield scope economies.

5.6   LONG-RUN COST CURVES

In deriving the cost curves in Section 5.4, the assumption was made that some of the inputs were fixed. Suppose we take a longer perspective and allow enough time for the providing unit to change its "fixed" factors—to expand or contract its physical plant to buy and sell equipment, and hire and fire physicians. For planning periods of sufficient length, such changes are certainly possible. An analysis of relevant issues is called a *long-run analysis.*

Indeed, the factors that are considered fixed from the perspective of the short term are no longer fixed; they, too, can vary. From the longer planning perspective, all resources are variable. Suppose a hospital board is planning to build a new facility from scratch. The board can choose either a 60-, 120-, or 250-bed facility, entailing a capital outlay of $2 million, $3 million, or $3.5 million, respectively. Associated with each size are the given annual capital cost of depreciation and the interest on the financial capital. During the planning period—up until the size decision is made—these capital costs can be varied (in three different levels) and thus are variable.

Associated with each facility under consideration is an average cost curve (either ATC_1, ATC_2, or ATC_3 in Figure 5–4), which includes capital costs (remember that, in the long run, there are no fixed costs). Now assume that each facility is least costly for a given range of output. For fewer than 1,000 annual admissions, ATC_1 is the least costly; for over 3,000 admissions, ATC_3 is the least costly. Depending on which level of output is chosen, one plant size will be the least costly. The dashed curve in Figure 5–4 represents the least cost that can be produced at any given output level (assuming we can choose the size of the facility). This is called the *long-run average cost (LRAC) curve*. It is made up of the minimum cost points at each output level. The *LRAC* is usually hypothesized, if it were represented in a smooth fashion, to be U-shaped. Such a shape would be generated by falling long-run average costs (economies of scale) at low levels of output, followed by constant and finally increasing costs (diseconomies of scale).

Before discussing such costs, it is necessary to specify whether the entity in question is a single operating unit (e.g., an individual hospital, nursing home, or ambulatory care clinic) or an entire system (e.g., a corporate chain). A single oper-

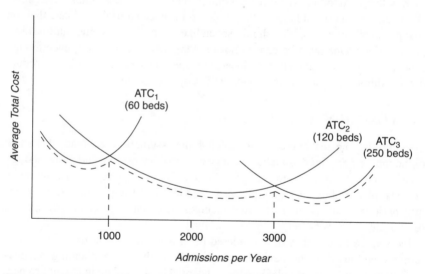

Figure 5–4 Relation between short- and long-run average cost curves. Short-run curves (ATC_1, ATC_2, and ATC_3) are shown for three plant sizes (expressed in terms of bed size). The long-run average cost curve (*LRAC*) is derived from these curves (shown as the dashed line). The *LRAC* is the minimum cost point at each level of output. At 1,000 and 3,000 admissions, the *LRAC* becomes associated with the different cost curves (different plant sizes), because it becomes more economical to produce successively greater outputs with larger-sized plants.

ating entity may be subject to eventual diseconomies because the gains from specialization in certain tasks eventually run out. Also, a single hospital unit may be able to expand only by the addition of diverse units (e.g., a CAT scanning unit or a physiotherapy department), and such units may be costly to manage in a single unit. For these reasons, the long-run cost curve of the single operating unit may exhibit diseconomies of scale.

A multiplant system, such as a multihospital corporation, may exhibit economies of scale as it expands by acquiring additional distinct operating units. Certain functions, such as purchasing, may be run more efficiently on a scale that exceeds that of an individual operating unit. Furthermore, a multiunit system can develop standardized procedures in patient records, accounting, and the like and can make comparisons between units. For these reasons, as a system expands, it may exhibit economies of scale, at least up to a point.

5.7 EMPIRICAL ESTIMATION OF COST CURVES

5.7.1 Background

Average or per unit cost is a convenient and accessible summary of a producer's performance. To obtain the average cost at any level of output, divide total cost by quantity. Given the convenience of this measure of performance, it is natural that analysts would use it to compare providers who produce roughly the same product but at different levels of output. Our simple, unqualified, short-run hypothesis would lead us to expect a U-shaped relation between average cost and output. However, interproducer comparisons are fraught with complications.

Quality, case mix, and technology differences among producing units may make comparisons difficult. For this reason as well as others cited in Section 5.4, producers may be operating on different cost curves, as shown in Figure 5–5, where ATC_1, ATC_2, and ATC_3 are average short-run cost curves of three producers. As compared to Producer 1, Producer 2 is producing a higher quality product or serving patients with a more severe case mix but is using the same amounts of fixed inputs. Therefore, Producer 2's cost curve (ATC_2) is above ATC_1 at all levels of output. To identify the shape of the short-run cost curve, one must control for factors that shift the curve. Assume, for example, that Producer 1's cost-output point is at x and Producer 2's is at v. Without knowing how the quality of services and other factors differed, one would not know if points x and v are on the same curve or on different curves.

In estimating long-run cost curves, one encounters even greater difficulties. Let us say that Producer 3 has a more capital-intensive operation than Producers 1 or 2 because Producer 3 has invested more heavily in capital equipment to gain economies from automation. Let us also assume that the quality and case mix of Pro-

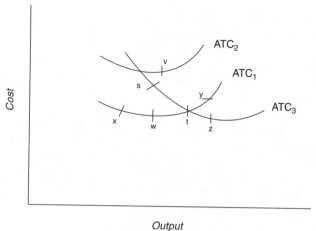

Output

Figure 5–5 Identifying points on the *ATC* curve. When data are gathered from producers on their average total costs at various output levels, care must be taken in interpreting these points. Data points collected from different producers may be on similar *ATC* curves (such as *x*, *w*, *y*, and *t*) or on different *ATC* curves (such as *v* and *y*). The key to determining which is more likely is to identify extraneous circumstances (other than output) that might have caused producers to operate on different curves. These circumstances, if identified, would lead us to conclude whether pairs such as *x* and *z* are on different or similar curves. The circumstances that shift the cost curve (or lead to different cost curves) include differences in input prices, quality of output, and capital equipment.

---

ducer 3 are similar to those of Producer 1. The true long-run cost curve for the industry (assuming that these are the only two scales of operations available) is ATC_1 up to point *t* in Figure 5–5 and ATC_3 for scales of output above and beyond point *t*. But when we start to estimate this curve, we do not know this. Among the data that are usually available for making such comparisons, we have only one observation for each producer. These observations tell us, for example, that Producer 1 is producing at 1,000 units of output with an ATC of $50; Producer 2 is producing at 1,200 units with an ATC of $80; and so on. (We may, of course, also have some information on some of the operating characteristics of each producer.) With this information, we have only one point on each producer's cost curve, which is not enough to tell us where on its cost curve each producer is operating.

If, for example, Producer 1 is producing at point *x* and Producer 3 at point *z*, then both are on the long-run cost curve, and an estimation of a long-run cost curve with points such as these will give us a reasonably accurate picture of what the long-run cost curve looks like. But there is no reason why we should be so lucky. Producer 1 could well be producing at a high-capacity level, such as point *y*, and

Producer 3 could be at a low-capacity level, such as point *s*. While both are on their short-run curves, neither is on its long-run curve. We would have no way of knowing this, and if we assumed that we were estimating a long-run curve, we would end up with biased results.

In fact, where on its cost curve each producer is producing depends on supply. It also depends on the producer's goals or objectives as well as the conditions underlying costs and revenues, which is the topic of Chapter 6. Following are brief summaries of empirical evidence on producer cost curves for several health-related activities. When reviewing this material, keep in mind the difficulties in identifying actual cost-output relations.

5.7.2 Group Practices

Group medical practices have occasionally been held up as institutions that should yield considerable economies of scale and thus help raise output while moderating increases in total costs. Since a fairly large number of group practices are in operation, it might seem that the proposition that average costs are falling would be easy to test. However, because of the considerable variation in the types of group practices, difficulties in output measurements, and problems associated with gathering appropriate data, only tentative answers have been obtained. The first statistical analysis was done using data collected on solo and group practices in the field of internal medicine (Bailey 1968). Because the study compared practices in the same field, it circumvented problems associated with the inclusion of different production techniques used by different types of practices. The data collected showed that the average volume of services provided per physician, adjusted for the type of visit (e.g., routine visit, annual examination, or complete examination), was greater for solo practices than for group practices. Although the sample size was small, it cast some doubt on the existence of economies of scale.

There are several reasons why this finding may not be so surprising. First, the technology generally used in internal medicine is such that the gains from task specialization and the use of capital-intensive techniques may be achieved at a low level of output. For the tasks involved in operating an internal medicine practice, the *ATC* curve may reach a lower point at a scale of output supportable by one practitioner. Second, an incentive factor may be at work when several practitioners combine forces. This factor, which has a tendency to shift the *ATC* curve upward when the group is formed, in situations where members of the practice share revenues and costs. When this sharing occurs, the revenues that any single member of the group generates are shared and the costs that he or she incurs are borne by all the members. Because of reduced burden, the individual physician can make a heavier use of nurses' time and of equipment while feeling less impact than in a solo practice. It is hypothesized that, under cost-sharing arrangements, each physician in the group will generate more costs than in a solo practice and the cost curve for the group will be higher. Furthermore, the larger the group, the higher will be the cost curve (assuming that offsetting factors do not exist; see Scheffler 1975).

Another study analyzed interpractice variations in the relation between staff salary costs with scale of output (measured by office visits) for a sample of single-specialty practices, although not all of the same specialty (Newhouse 1973). The presence of cost sharing was found to shift the cost curve upward for group practices. Furthermore, after adjusting for this incentive factor, the cost curve was found to exhibit economies of scale, indicating that such economies do exist among practices with no cost sharing and also among practices with some cost sharing. Because of the small sample, the inattention paid to case mix, and technology differences among practices due to specialty differences, the results are not conclusive.

5.7.3 Hospital Marginal Costs

The importance of the topic of hospital marginal cost is related to the objective of reimbursing hospitals for the extra resource costs they incur when their volumes change. If a hospital is being reimbursed at the level of costs in 1995 and its admissions have increased by 5 percent, its additional costs may be greater than, equal to, or less than 5 percent. If the hospital is reimbursed an additional 5 percent (ignoring inflation) to cover the volume differential and actual costs had gone up by 3 percent, the hospital would incur a windfall gain. On the other hand, the hospital would lose out if its costs had increased by 10 percent.

Marginal cost variation is often measured using the ratio of marginal to average costs (M/A). Recall that if M is greater than A (or $M/A > 1$), then the average cost will increase (Section 5.3). For example, beginning from an initial output level of 1,000 admissions and an average cost of $200 per case, if output expands by 5 percent (50 admissions) and M is $220, then M/A is 1.1. Expansion has raised the average cost, and if the hospital was reimbursed for the additional cases at $200 per case, it would incur a loss. If the hospital was reimbursed on the basis of its prior year's costs plus the marginal cost of its additional cases, it would be fully reimbursed.

This problem has arisen in a number of instances. During the early 1970s, when price controls were set on hospital revenues, allowable revenues were set at the previous year's revenue levels, plus an inflation factor, plus a volume adjustment based on estimates of M/A (Lipscomb et al. 1978). In the Finger Lakes region of New York State, a regional reimbursement experiment was set up: hospitals were reimbursed based on a base year cost, plus an inflation factor, plus a volume adjustment that assumed that the value of *M/A* was .4 for inpatient care and .6 for outpatient care (Farnand et al. 1986). And, currently, under Medicare regulations, hospitals are given extra reimbursement for cases in a particular diagnostic group whose length of stay or costs are outside diagnostic limits (outliers). The additional reimbursement is based on an *M/A* value of .6 for the extra days.

One way of estimating hospital marginal cost is to take short-term (e.g., monthly) values of operating costs and volume for a given hospital over a period (2 to 3 years) and find the average variation in costs with a given variation in output. Another way is to relate variation in costs and outputs across hospitals. The former method will probably give a more accurate estimate than the latter of short-run marginal cost, but there are difficulties even with it. Among these are that the cost levels of inputs must be adjusted for (assuming they have changed) and that capital equipment and operating techniques must remain the same throughout the study period (otherwise the hospital will have moved from one short-run cost curve to another).

In addition, the marginal cost will depend on the measure of output (e.g., whether it is length of stay or admissions). It will vary with the amount of the volume adjustment (e.g., 2 or 5 percent) and the relative permanence of the adjustment as estimated by the hospital administrator. For a volume increase that is small or short lived, the administrator may decide to tax existing resources for a time rather than immediately expand and thereby raise marginal cost. The estimate of *M* under these circumstances would appear to be lower than if the administrator responded more automatically.

For the preceding reasons, there is no accepted measure of the true short-run value of *M/A* (Lave and Lave 1984). Estimates range from .2 to .6, but remember that the value will vary depending on a number of factors (Friedman and Pauly 1983).

5.7.4 Hospital Economies of Scale

A large number of studies have investigated the possible existence of economies of scale in hospitals, with very mixed results (Berki 1972; Frech and Mobley 1995). Early studies identified economies of scale but subsequent studies have uncovered no evidence (Lave and Lave 1984) or conflicting evidence (Frech and Mobley 1995). There is an explanation for the differences in findings.

As discussed earlier, the typical hospital is an organization with a complex case mix and a large number of different services. Each service has its own cost-output relation, which may exhibit economies of scale. The scope of services is greater for larger hospitals (Berry 1973), but these hospitals may have more varied cast types, so some services (e.g., cobalt therapy) that are devoted to specific case types may be operated at low capacity and high cost. A multiproduct hospital can be quite large yet have a number of services with considerable excess capacity (Finkler 1979b). As a result, it might exhibit a higher average cost than many smaller hospitals.

One study (Hornbrook and Monheit 1985) that incorporated both case mix and service scope variables to investigate economies of scale found no such economies at the hospital level. But a number of studies of individual services, such as open-heart surgery facilities, *CT* scanner units, therapeutic radiology facilities, and hospital laundries, have found evidence of economies of scale (Finkler 1979a; Gregory 1976–1977; McGregor and Pelletier 1978; Okunade 1993; Schwartz and Joskow 1980). This suggests that the economies of scale that do occur in hospitals are offset by diseconomies of scale.

5.7.5 Nursing Home Costs

A number of studies have been undertaken in the nursing home area with a view to determining the effect on costs of operating variables such as volume of operations, product quality, case mix, and organizational characteristics (e.g., for-profit or nonprofit status and membership in a chain) (Bishop 1980). The relevant variable for such studies is average cost, which is the most appropriate variable for a comparison of costs in different facilities. There is no agreement as to whether total costs (which include fixed costs such as administrative costs, interest, and depreciation) or only variable costs should be used. Using just variable costs would be appropriate when focusing on short-term operations, whereas including capital and other fixed costs would be appropriate when dealing with long-term issues. For example, one might want to find out whether a large-scale plant is more efficient than a small-scale plant. Asking which is the most efficient implies that time would be allowed to develop a plant of the appropriate size.

Studies that have examined the relationship between average cost and various causal variables have uncovered some interesting relationships. There is disagreement as to the relationship between average cost and scale of operations (Bishop 1980; McKay 1988). The fact that a nursing home is a member of a chain does not appear to influence its costs (Ullman 1986). On the other hand, for-profit nursing homes have been identified as having a lower average cost that nonprofit nursing homes (Ullman 1984).

As with all cost studies in the health care area, such studies have had to deal with difficulties in measuring and netting out the impact of patient case mix and the level of quality, two factors that influence the level of care and hence nursing home costs. For example, it has proved extremely hard to identify patient characteristics associated with specific levels of care. Patients differ considerably with regard to health status, and their different needs should translate into differences in the level of care or resource intensity. Several case mix classifications (for long-term care patients) that try to take into account resource use differences have been developed (see Chapter 7). These measures are far from perfect, but even allowing for their shortcomings, their inclusion in the cost analysis may not be sufficient to account for differences in average cost that are related to level-of-care differences. A nursing home that offers "high-quality" care as measured by resource-intensive processes (rehabilitation, nursing care) may provide more care to all patients regardless of their health status. Similarly, in a low-quality nursing home, all patients may receive fewer services than in the high-quality home, adjusting for health status. One must therefore find a quality measure that is independent of case mix or case severity in order to control for the influence of each factor on cost of care. As will be seen in the following chapter, most measures of case mix do not adequately distinguish between case mix and severity, and so it has been very difficult to identify each factor's specific impact on cost.

Average cost is not the only relevant cost measure in nursing home analysis. Marginal cost is also important when forecasting resource use or when assessing nursing home profitability. A New York study analyzed the marginal cost of nursing homes, adjusting for variables such as SNF/ICF days, average level of service in the institution, patient characteristics, input prices, and for-profit or nonprofit status. The marginal cost for the healthiest patients was $51 per patient day. For the least healthy patients the marginal variable cost was $60. These rates can be compared with the reimbursement rate of $72, indicating a profit for patients at all levels.

5.7.6 Health Insurance Costs

Theoretically, health insurance administrative costs are potentially influenced by the scale of a firm's operations. Additionally, a very important factor affecting these costs is the ratio of group policies to all policies that an insurance company sells. Per policy, individual policies are more expensive to sell. Also, employers perform many of the functions for group policies that insurers perform for individual policies. This fact may influence public policy, because if individual and group policies have significantly different costs, the government may act to encourage holders of individual policies to obtain group policies.

One study examined health insurance administrative costs for a cross section of insurance companies that offer health insurance. The study found that both factors have a significant impact on these costs (Blair et al. 1975b). An unexpected finding of their study was that mutual (nonprofit) companies had lower administrative costs than stock (for-profit) companies. As will be seen in Chapter 6, one might have expected the opposite to occur.

BIBLIOGRAPHY

Production of Medical Care

Cromwell, J. 1974. Hospital productivity trends in short-term general non-teaching hospitals. *Inquiry* 11:181–187.

Goldfarb, M., et al. 1980. Behavior of the multi-product firm. *Medical Care* 18:185–201.

Lewit, E.M. et al. 1980. A comparison of surgical assisting in a prepaid group practice. *Medical Care* 18:916–929.

Nyman, J.A., and Bricker, D.L. 1989. Profit incentives and technical efficiency in the production of nursing home care. *Review of Economics and Statistics* 71:586–593.

Reinhardt, U. 1972. A production function for physicians' services. *Review of Economics and Statistics* 54:55–66.

————. 1973a. Manpower substitution and productivity in medical practice. *Health Services Research* 7:200–277.

————. 1973b. Proposed changes in the organization of health care delivery. *Milbank Memorial Fund Quarterly* 51:169–222.

Ruchlin, H.S., and Leveson, I. 1974. Measuring hospital productivity. *Health Services Research* 9:308–323.

Scheffler, R.M. 1975. Further consideration of the economics of group practice. *Journal of Human Resources* 10:258–263.

Outcome–Volume Relation

Bunker, J.P., et al. 1982. Should surgery be regionalized? *Surgical Clinics of North America* 62:657–668.

Garnick, D., et al. 1989. Surgeon volume vs. hospital volume: Which matters more? *JAMA* 262:547–548.

Luft, H.S. 1980. The relationship between surgical volume and mortality: An exploration of causal factors and alternative models. *Medical Care* 18:940–959.

Luft, H.S., and Hunt, S.S. 1986. Evaluating individual hospital quality through outcome statistics. *JAMA* 255:2780–2784.

Luft, H.S., et al. 1987. The volume–outcome relationship: Practice makes perfect or selective referral patterns? *Health Services Research* 22:157–182.

Luft, H.S., et al. 1990. *Hospital volume, physician volume, and patient outcomes*. Ann Arbor, Mich.: Health Administration Press Perspectives.

Costs: Hospitals

Barer, M. 1982. Case mix adjustment in hospital cost analysis. *Journal of Health Economics* 1:53–80.

Bays, C. 1980. Specification error in the estimation of hospital cost functions. *Review of Economics and Statistics* 62:302–305.

Berki, S. 1972. *Hospital economics*. Lexington, Mass.: D.C. Heath.

Berry, R.E. 1973. On grouping hospitals for economic analysis. *Inquiry* 10:5–12.

Cowing, T.G., and Holtmann, A.G. 1983. Multiproduct short-run hospital cost functions. *Southern Economic Journal* 49:637–653.

Evans, R.G. 1981. Behavioural cost functions for hospitals. *Canadian Journal of Economics* 4:198–215.

Feldstein, P. 1961. *An empirical investigation of the marginal cost of hospital services.* Chicago: University of Chicago Graduate Program in Hospital Administration.

Finkler, S.A. 1979a. Cost effectiveness of regionalization: The heart surgery example. *Inquiry* 16:264–270.

————. 1979b. On the shape of the hospital industry long run average cost function. *Health Services Research* 14:281–289.

Fraser, R.D. 1971. *Canadian hospital costs and efficiency.* Ottawa, Ontario: Economic Council of Canada.

Frech, H.E., and Mobley, L.E. 1995. Resolving the impasse on hospital scale economies. *Applied Economics* 27:286–296.

Friedman, B., and Pauly, M.V. 1983. A new approach to hospital cost functions and some issues in revenue regulation. *Health Care Financing Review*, 4:105–114.

Gregory, D.D. 1976–1977. Some evidence on the economic aspects of hospital cooperative ventures. *Journal of Economics and Business* 29:59–64.

Hadley, J., and Zuckerman, S. 1994. The role of efficiency measurement in hospital rate setting. *Journal of Health Economics* 13:335–340.

Horn, S.D., et al. 1985. Severity of illness within DRGs: Impact on prospective payment. *American Journal of Public Health* 75:1195–1199.

Hornbrook, M.C., and Monheit, A.C. 1985. The contribution of case mix severity to the hospital cost–output relation. *Inquiry* 22:259–271.

Kralewski, J.E., et al. 1984. Effects of contract management on hospital performance. *Health Services Research* 19:479–498.

Lave, J., and Lave, L.B. 1984. Hospital cost functions. *Annual Review of Public Health* 5:193–213.

Lee, M.L., and Wallace, R.L. 1972. Problems in estimating multi-product hospital cost functions. *Western Economic Journal* 11:350–363.

Lipscomb, J., et al. 1978. The use of marginal cost estimates in hospital cost-containment policy. In *Hospital cost containment*, ed. M. Zubkoff et al. New York: Watson Publishing International.

McGregor, M., and Pelletier, G. 1978. Planning of specialized health facilities: Size vs. cost and effectiveness in heart surgery. *New England Journal of Medicine* 299:179–181.

Newhouse, J.P. 1994. Frontier estimation: How useful a tool for health economics? *Journal of Health Economics* 13:335–340.

Schwartz, W., and Joskow, P. 1980. Duplicated hospital facilities. *New England Journal of Medicine* 303:1449–1457.

Sloan, F.A., et al. 1985. The teaching hospital's growing surgical caseload. *JAMA* 254:376–382.

Zuckerman, S., et al. 1994. Measuring hospital efficiency with frontier cost functions. *Journal of Health Economics* 13:335–340.

Costs: Medical Practice

Bailey, R.M. 1968. A comparison of internists in solo and fee-for-service group practice. *Bulletin of the New York Academy of Medicine* 44 (2nd series):1293–1303.

————. 1970. Economies of scale in medical practice. In *Empirical studies in health economics*, ed. H. Klarman. Baltimore: Johns Hopkins University Press.

Dunn, D.L., et al. 1995. Economies of scope in physicians' work: The performance of multiple surgery. *Inquiry* 32:87–101.

Frech, H.E., and Ginsburg, P.B. 1974. Optimal scale in medical practice. *Journal of Business* 47:23–36.

Hillson, S.D., et al. 1992. Economies of scope and payment for physician services. *Medical Care* 30:822–831.

Newhouse, J.P. 1973. The economics of group practice. *Journal of Human Resources* 8:37–56.

Rossiter, L.F. 1984. Prospects for medical group practice under competition. *Medical Care* 22:84–92.

Costs: Long-Term Care

Bekele, G., and Holtmann, A.G. 1987. A cost function for nursing homes: Toward a system of diagnostic reimbursement groupings. *Eastern Economic Journal* 13:115–122.

Bishop, C.E. 1980. Nursing home cost studies and reimbursement issues. *Health Care Financing Review* 1:47–65.

———. 1983. Nursing home cost studies. *Health Services Research* 18:382–386.

Chattopadhyay, S., and Hefley, D. 1994. Are for-profit nursing homes more efficient? *Eastern Economic Journal* 20:171–186.

Kass, D.I. 1987. Economies of scale and scope in the provision of nursing home services. *Journal of Health Economics* 6:129–146.

McKay, N.L. 1988. An econometric analysis of costs and scale economies in the nursing home industry. *Journal of Human Resources* 23:58–75.

Nyman, J.A. 1988a. Improving the quality of nursing home outcome. *Medical Care* 26:1158–1171.

———. 1988b. The marginal cost of nursing home care. *Journal of Health Economics* 7:393–412.

Nyman, J.A., and Conner, R.A. 1994. Do case mix adjusted nursing home reimbursements actually reflect costs? *Journal of Health Economics* 13:145–162.

Okunade, A.A. 1993. Production cost structure of U.S. hospital pharmacies: Time series, cross sectional bed size evidence. *Journal of Applied Econometrics* 8:277–294.

Schlenker, R.E., and Shaughnessy, P.W. 1984. Case mix, quality, and cost relationships in Colorado nursing homes. *Health Care Financing Review* 6:61–71.

Schlenker, R.E., et al. 1985. Estimating patient level nursing home costs. *Health Services Research* 20:103–128.

Ullman, S.G. 1984. Cost analysis and facility reimbursement in the long-term health care industry. *Health Services Research* 19:83–102.

———. 1986. Chain ownership and long-term health care facility performance. *Journal of Applied Gerontology* 5:51–63.

Vitaliano, D.F., and Toren, M. 1994. Cost and efficiency in nursing homes. *Journal of Health Economics* 13:281–300.

Costs: Other Areas

Blair, R.D., et al. 1975a. Blue Cross-Blue Shield administrative costs. *Economic Inquiry* 13:237–251.

Blair, R.D., et al. 1975b. Economies of scale in the administration of health insurance. *Review of Economics and Statistics* 57:185–189.

Hay, J.W., and Mandes, G. 1984. Home health care cost-function analysis. *Health Care Financing Review* 5:111–116.

CHAPTER 6

Behavior of Supply

6.1 INTRODUCTION

This chapter is concerned with the determinants of the quantity and quality of output of various health-related products. Our approach is to consider the behavior of the organizations supplying these products. It provides hypotheses about what causes suppliers to produce particular quantities and qualities of output. These hypotheses are formulated in terms of models of supplier behavior, and they incorporate the key causes of such behavior. The goal is to isolate the direction in which individual factors cause supply to move, while keeping in mind other factors that may also be influencing supply movements.

In presenting the hypotheses about supply behavior, a distinction is made between the supply of a single producer and supply of all producers in the market (i.e., individual versus market supply). It should be pointed out that, like in our analyses of demand, our focus is on the behavior of a group of market participants in isolation—in this case, suppliers.

In this chapter no single model of supplier behavior is presented as uniquely appropriate. The subject is complex, and our models offer suggestions rather than definitive answers. In particular, health care providers differ with regard to type of organization. Some organizations, such as proprietary hospitals and nursing homes and physician practices, are profit-seeking institutions. Others, such as voluntary hospitals, the Red Cross, independent blood banks, and philanthropic organizations (e.g., the March of Dimes and the American Heart Association), are nonprofit. This means that their "owners" (or, more appropriately, governors or trustees) can neither appropriate for themselves any profits that the organization might make nor sell the rights to the assets of the organization for personal gain. Separate hypotheses are discussed for both types of organizations.

We start off by developing a basic model of an individual profit-seeking supplier, then develop a model of the market supply behavior of a group of such firms. Because for-profit and nonprofit organizations differ radically, the following three sections focus on the effects that the nonprofit organizational form has on the behavior of the nonprofit organization. Much disagreement exists over the analysis of nonprofit agency behavior. As a result, several alternative hypotheses about nonprofit agency behavior need to be presented.

In Section 6.4, the nonprofit agency is examined as if it were an output-maximizing agency. In the next section, we extend this analysis to incorporate the role of the agency in producing quality as well as quantity output, and we look at the organizational structure of the voluntary hospital, a peculiar type of nonprofit organization. In Section 6.6, we develop a model in which the nonprofit agency is regarded as an instrument used to the benefit of its managers. In Section 6.7, another key economic variable, the method of financing the organization's activities (which can influence the output of the organization), is introduced. Reimbursement plans for doctors, hospitals, HMOs, and nursing homes are analyzed with regard to the manner in which they influence the economic behavior of the various suppliers. In Section 6.8, we present a model of provider supply when the providers are acting as agents of an HMO, and in Section 6.9, we present a model of the demand for labor (a model similar to that of a firm's supply). Finally in Section 6.10, we present a model of the supply of an insurer.

6.2   A MODEL OF SUPPLY BEHAVIOR: AN INDIVIDUAL FOR-PROFIT COMPANY

6.2.1 The Basic Model

The assumptions of our initial supply model fall into three categories: (1) revenue assumptions, (2) cost assumptions, and (3) assumptions about the objectives of the organization. In our analysis we will use the example of a laboratory (ABC Labs) that is owned by a pathologist and produces blood tests of a given level of quality.

We will assume that ABC Labs' revenues can come from two sources: (1) reimbursement for patient services (termed *patient* or *earned revenues*) and (2) other sources (philanthropic or government grants, endowment funds, and other non-patient-related sources). We will initially assume that all revenues are from reimbursement (i.e., non-patient-related revenues are zero). This assumption will be altered later in the analysis.

With regard to patient revenues, we make the assumption that ABC Labs is a "price taker," that is, a supplier that has no influence on the price of its output. This may be because the price is set by an independent administrative agency or because the lab is operating in a competitive situation in which the best price it can get for its product is the price prevailing in the market. The charging of high prices by one supplier in a highly competitive market will drive consumers to lower priced competitors, and lower prices will therefore not enable the higher priced supplier to achieve its goal. (The setting of price by market forces is discussed in Chapter 7.)

We will assume that ABC Labs receives $12 for each test performed. Its marginal revenue (*MR*), defined as the addition to total revenue (*TR*) for one additional unit of output produced and sold ($\Delta TR/\Delta Q$), is $12. Total and marginal revenues for output levels from 0 to 10 are shown in Table 6–1, Columns 11 and 12.

As for cost, we will assume that there are both fixed and variable costs. Our assumption regarding fixed costs is that the lab spends $7 monthly on equipment rental and mortgage payments. In addition, we will assume that the pathologist-owner could earn a total of $5 if she worked elsewhere. This sum is at the same time a fixed cost and opportunity cost. That is, it incorporates a "normal" return on the investment of the owner's assets and efforts. The pathologist, once committed to work in the lab, gives up $5 per period. The total fixed costa are thus $12, and, being fixed, they do not vary as output changes. The total fixed costs are shown in Column 2 in Table 6–1; the associated average fixed costs are shown in Column 5.

Variable inputs are assumed to be employed in a least-cost manner (the total minimum variable cost for operating the lab at different levels of output are as shown in Column 3). Average variable cost initially falls and subsequently rises, (Column 6), and marginal cost eventually rises (Column 8). Total cost, the sum of fixed and variable costs, are shown in Columns 4 and 7 (total and average values, respectively). Therefore, the cost curves are shaped as hypothesized in Chapter 5 (see Figure 6–1). Whereas in Table 6–1 the values jump in discrete steps, the curves are drawn as smooth functions for geometric convenience.

These dollar figures are approximated in Graph A of Figure 6–1 for total values and Graph B for marginal revenue (*MR*), marginal cost (*MC*), average variable cost (*AVC*), and average total cost (*ATC*). Note that the *TR* curve rises at a rate of $12 per blood test, and that *MR* is constant at $12. These are two different ways of saying the same thing: the revenue per unit of output sold is fixed at $12. This is a concrete expression of our assumption that ABC Labs is a price taker.

Finally, since ABC Labs is a for-profit company, it seems reasonable to assume that is main objective is maximize profits (total revenues minus total costs).

We are now in a position to examine the conclusions of our model and answer the question that underlies our analysis: What will the quantity of output be? Our task is to present a hypothesis that will enable us to predict which quantity will be chosen and how this quantity will vary when some of the underlying variables in our model—prices and costs—themselves vary.

Referring to Table 6–1, we can now derive from our model a specific quantity of output that achieves ABC Labs' profit-maximizing objective: Profits are at a

Table 6–1 Illustrative Data on Relation between Revenue, Costs, Profit, and Output

Quantity of Tests	Total Fixed Costs (TFC)	Total Variable Costs (TVC)	Total Costs (TC)	Average Fixed Costs (TFC/Q)	Average Variable Costs (TVC/Q)	Average Total Costs (TC/Q)	Marginal Costs (ΔTC/ΔQ)	Total Earned Revenue (P x Q)	Total Grants	Total Revenue	Marginal Revenue (ΔTR/ΔQ)	Profits (TR-TC)
0	12	0.00	12.00									
1	12	6.75	18.75	12.00	6.75	18.75	6.75	12	0	12	12	-6.75
2	12	10.50	22.50	6.00	5.25	11.25	3.75	24	0	24	12	1.50
3	12	13.25	25.25	4.00	4.42	8.42	2.75	36	0	36	12	10.75
4	12	17.00	29.00	3.00	4.25	7.25	3.75	48	0	48	12	19.00
5	12	23.75	35.75	2.40	4.75	7.15	6.75	60	0	60	12	24.25
6	12	35.50	47.50	2.00	5.92	7.92	11.75	72	0	72	12	24.50
7	12	54.25	66.25	1.71	7.75	9.46	18.75	84	0	84	12	17.75
8	12	82.00	94.00	1.50	10.25	11.75	27.75	96	0	96	12	2.00
9	12	120.75	132.75	1.33	13.42	14.75	38.75	108	0	108	12	-24.75
10	12	172.50	184.50	1.20	17.25	18.45	51.75	120	0	120	12	-64.50

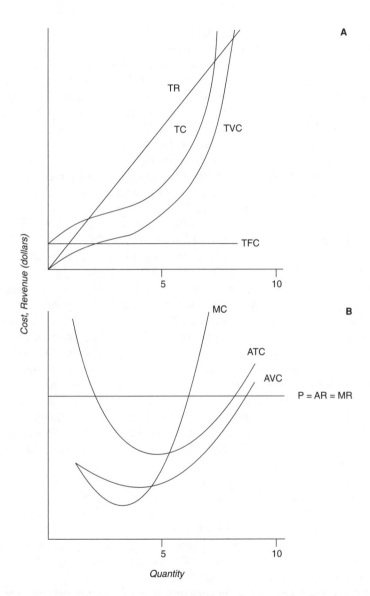

Figure 6–1 Supply relation for a profit-maximizing firm in terms of total costs and revenues (Graph A) and average and marginal costs and revenues (Graph B). In Graph A, the supplier produces where total profits, equal to the difference between total revenues (*TR*) and total costs (*TC*), are at a maximum. In Graph B, the same conclusion can be derived in terms of marginal costs and revenues. Here the profit-maximizing point is where *MR* = *MC*. In the diagram, since the price per unit is constant, price and *MR* are the same.

maximum at six units of output (here they amount to $24.50). The reasoning used to obtain this conclusion can best be presented in marginal terms. Say that ABC Labs was initially supplying four units of output. Profits here, given the assumed revenue and cost conditions, equal $19.00. If ABC Labs produces and sells one more test, additional revenue will be $12.00 (i.e., MR = $12.00), and the additional costs of production (MC) will be $6.75. The additional profit obtained by expanding output from four to five tests will be $5.25, bringing total profits to a new level of $24.25. ABC Labs, being profit maximizers, would expand production to at least five units. In fact, they will move beyond this amount because profits can be further increased by doing so. The best ABC Labs can do at the given price and cost conditions is to produce six units of output. Expanding beyond six units still results in positive profits for a while, but these profits would be less than the profit at six units of output. According to our model, a profit-maximizing firm will continue to expand production as long as MR exceeds MC. If we were dealing with smooth, continuous changes, our conclusion would be that a profit-maximizing firm will expand output up to the point at which MR = MC, as long as MC is rising with output. At this point the firm is maximizing its profits, and so the quantity where MC = MR is the supply position the firm should be aiming for.

This conclusion is shown diagrammatically in Figure 6–1. In Graph A, profits at each level of output are shown as the vertical distance between total revenues and total costs at that level of output. Since profits are defined as TR − TC, then where this vertical distance is at a maximum, profits are also at a maximum. This profit-maximizing point occurs at six units of output (allowing for small variations because we are dealing with continuous curves). In Graph B, the same conclusion is shown, but in terms of marginal costs and revenues. Here the point where MR = MC is the profit-maximizing quantity, that is, the quantity that will be supplied. A movement in quantity supplied in either direction would detract from total profits and so would not be consistent with the profit-maximizing objective.

The first conclusion of our model, then, is that, given revenue (i.e., price) and cost conditions and given the profit-maximizing objective, a profit-maximizing firm will produce at the quantity where MC = MR. Using this information, we can now derive a supply curve or schedule that shows what the quantity supplied will be at different prices. This analysis is shown diagrammatically in Figure 6–2. If the price rises from $12 to $19, the lab will add to its profits by expanding output to a seventh unit, because, even though the cost of this unit is higher, the higher extra revenue will make it profitable to expand output. The same reasoning applies to additional price increases: Higher prices will bring forth greater quantities supplied until MC = MR. It also applies to price declines, with one major exception: Eventually the price could become so low that the owners of the firm would be better off, from the point of view of profits (or losses), to shut down operations and produce nothing. For all prices below this level (represented by point j in Figure 6–2), the quantity supplied by the firm would be zero.

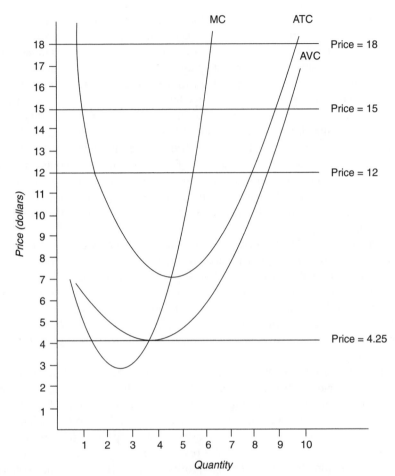

Figure 6–2 Profit-maximizing supply points at alternative prices. At each price above $4.25, the firm will maximize profits by supplying at the quantity where price = *MC*. If the price is at $4.25, the firm will just be meeting its variable costs. At any price below this, the firm's least unprofitable supply point will result in larger losses than if the firm shut down operations; therefore, the firm will not supply at any price below $4.25. For prices above $4.25, the firm's supply curve and its *MC* curve are the same.

The critical price below which the firm will shut down depends on the variable costs of the firm. Recall that fixed costs are the same thing as "already committed" costs, while variable costs are those that can be avoided by not hiring the variable factors; total costs are the sum of the two at each output level. If the price falls sufficiently, it is possible that even at its best level of output (from the profitability standpoint) the firm will be incurring a loss. The criterion the firm would use in deciding whether to continue operating under such unfavorable circumstances is not whether the firm is incurring a loss, but whether it is minimizing its losses. The importance of variable costs comes into play here. As long as the firm's revenues are exceeding its total variable costs, the firm will be adding to a surplus. In this case $TR - TVC$ will be positive. Even though total profits $(TR - (TVC + TFC))$ may be negative, signifying a loss, the loss is less than it would be if the firm shut down entirely. For if the firm shuts down, both TR and TVC are zero and the losses would equal TFC. In sum, as long as the firm is meeting its variable costs and adding something to cover some or all of its fixed costs, the firm should continue to operate; in this case, its supply curve is traced out by the MC curve. The quantity supplied will be where price equals marginal cost. Should the price fall so low that at no level of output could the firm meet all its variable costs, then it should shut down.

We can now present a complete analysis of the firm's supply behavior using the curves in Figure 6–2. If the price is equal to or greater than the lowest point on the AVC curve (point j), then at some level of output all variable costs will be covered and the firm will produce some output. If the price is lower than this critical minimum price, the firm will shut down operations. If the price is above the critical minimum level, the firm will produce output at the quantity where $MR = MC$ (i.e., where price $= MC$). The MC curve of the firm, then, is its supply curve, relating price to output.

In the context of this analysis, we can make some sense of the assumption that the costs of a for-profit firm are at a minimum. It was shown in Chapter 5 that the producer has a choice of producing a given quantity of output at the lowest possible cost or above the lowest possible cost. By choosing the lowest possible cost method of production, the firm can achieve its greatest profits, since profits are defined as the difference between total revenues and total costs. If costs were above the minimum, they would cut into profits, which is contrary to the assumed goal of the firm.

It should be noted that the supply relationship focuses on the behavior of suppliers in isolation. That is, the term *quantity supplied* refers to a distinct schedule—that of supplier responsiveness to price. As in the chapter on demand, where we studied how demanders would respond to price while ignoring suppliers, in this chapter we focus on supplier behavior in isolation from demanders. Before putting the separate forces, supply and demand, together, it is essential to understand how each operates on its own.

6.2.2 Nonpatient Revenues

Let us now introduce a new element into our analysis, nonpatient revenues. We will focus on a particular form of unearned revenue, a grant or subsidy, that is unrelated to output. Such a grant might be received from a donor or foundation. Our analytical task is to determine how it might affect the provider's supply.

The economic significance of a grant unrelated to output is that it provides a set amount of money whether output expands or contracts. Such a grant can be treated analytically in one of two ways, either as a fixed addition to revenue or as a fixed reduction from total costs (a negative fixed cost). While the rationale for the first option seems clear-cut, the rationale for the second requires some explanation. A fixed subsidy in a sense reduces by a fixed amount the total costs that the provider must meet at each output level. Operationally, it will have the same impact on profits. We can therefore treat it as a reduction in total costs.

Let us say that ABC Labs received a fixed subsidy of $5. This would increase nonpatient revenues in Table 6–1 by $5 at each and every level of output. Profits would also increase by $5 at each level of output. In Figure 6–1, the increase would appear as an upward parallel shift in the *TR* curve.

What is important from a supply standpoint is that neither patient revenues (including *MR*) nor variable costs are affected. Thus, while profits are higher by $5 at every output level, the maximum profitability level of output remains—at six units. The fixed subsidy does not affect the most profitable level of output; it only affects the level of profits at that and every other level of output.

This conclusion would not hold if the subsidy was related to output. For then, as output expanded, the marginal revenue would be the additional revenue from patient sources plus the additional (output-related) grant revenues. When estimating the most profitable output level, the firm would have to consider both sources of additional revenue and relate them to marginal cost.

The conclusion, then, is that a grant that is not output related will not influence the supply decisions of a profit-maximizing firm; the firm's supply position will still be where marginal patient revenue equals marginal cost.

6.2.3 Shifts in the Supply Curve

In this section, we consider what happens to the supply curve of the firm when factors that influence the position of the *MC* curve change. In general, as shown in Figure 6–3, any factor that causes the *MC* curve to shift upward from MC_1 to MC_2 will amount to a leftward shift in the supply schedule of the firm (a decrease in supply). The quantity supplied at any price will be reduced from Q_1 to Q_2. Such shifts might occur because of higher input prices or a higher quality of product being produced, to cite two of the factors discussed in Section 5.4 that might cause the firm's cost curve to shift. In the case of the production of a higher quality product, for example, the net result is that a lower quantity will be produced by the firm at any given price. The same reasoning in reverse holds for downward shifts in the *MC* curve. For example, an increase in the capacity of the firm to produce output, caused by additional capital expansion, will cause the *MC* and thus the

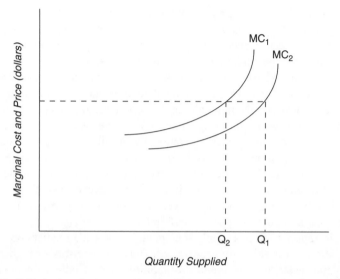

Figure 6–3 Shifts in the supply curve for a profit-maximizing supplier. An upward shift in the *MC* curve of a profit-maximizing firm will mean a lower quantity supplied at any price. In this figure, a shift from MC_1 to MC_2 means a decrease in supply level indicated by the dotted line, the quantity supplied decreases from Q_1 to Q_2.

supply curve to shift to the right, indicating a willingness on the part of the firm to supply more output at any given price. Such expansion is likely when the firm is operating on the downward-sloping part of its long-run average cost curve. An expansion in output would allow it to move to a lower point on the *LRAC* curve (i.e., to a lower cost short-run curve).

6.3 MARKET SUPPLY

We now demonstrate how the analysis of individual supply movements can be extended to form a hypothesis about movements in product supply in a specific market. To do this, we will add two new assumptions concerning individual supply behavior:

- There is a set number of suppliers in the market.
- There are no agreements on the part of suppliers to restrict supply.

In the present model, two groups of factors influence market supply: the number of suppliers and the factors that influence individual supplier behavior. In other words, the market supply schedule can be obtained once we know the number of suppliers and their individual supply schedules. Let us assume the market consists of three suppliers: ABC Labs, XYZ Labs, and GHI Labs (see Figure 6–4). Each has a given supply schedule. XYZ Labs supplies 5 tests at $1.00, 10 tests at $1.50, 15 at $2.00, and so on. GHI Labs supplies 3, 6, and 9 tests at these prices, respectively, and ABC Labs supplies 6, 9, and 12 tests. Given these schedules and the fact that these three labs are the only ones in the market, the market supply curve is the sum of these individual supply curves at each price. At $1.00, the market supply of tests is 14 (5 + 3 + 6); at $1.50, 25 tests are supplied, and at $2.00, 36 tests are supplied. The market supply curve is shown as the horizontal sum of all individual supply curves. Given a particular price, our model predicts the quantity that will be supplied in the market.

The market supply curve will shift outward (to the right) (1) if, given the number of producers, any factors cause the individual supply curves to shift outward, and (2) if the number of suppliers increases. In either case, more will be supplied at any given price. Our model has enabled us to classify these influences and separate their effects on supply. The same type of analysis applies to reductions in supply.

With regard to the number of suppliers, just as profits are the motivating force behind the expansion (or contraction) of output by an individual firm, so are they a driving force behind the expansion of the market—the entry of new firms into the market. At any particular time, there are a number of prospective suppliers capable of acquiring the techniques and equipment needed to supply a product (e.g., blood tests). If profits are high in the market, they will be motivated to enter it as suppliers and thus will shift the supply curve to the right. Of course, in real life existing firms, protective of their high profits, may act to keep potential suppliers out, but this type of behavior is ruled out of the model.

6.4 SUPPLY BEHAVIOR OF NONPROFIT AGENCIES: THE OUTPUT MAXIMIZATION HYPOTHESIS

Nonprofit suppliers abound in the health care field. One reason appears to be the existence of external demands for health care products and services (discussed in Section 4.2.2). To satisfy these external demands, individuals may form nonprofit agencies whose purpose is to provide products and services to those perceived to be needy, usually on a less-than-cost basis. Health-related philanthropies, such as the American Heart Association, give away educational services that are financed by donors who want others to consume the services. The Red Cross blood program exists because there is sufficient concern on the part of blood donors about the health of those requiring transfusions. Voluntary hospitals were, until recently, providing free and subsidized hospital care to the needy in substantial amounts; this care was financed largely through philanthropic donations, which can be re-

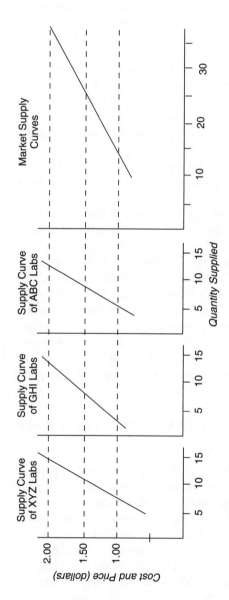

Figure 6–4 Derivation of the market supply curve from individual supply curves. The market supply curve shows the quantity supplied by all firms supplying the product to the market at each price. It is obtained by summing individual suppliers' quantities at each price.

garded as payments to satisfy the donors' external demands for the care of the needy. Public health departments attempt to satisfy external demands for health care through government-provided services.

There are, no doubt, other reasons for the formation of nonprofit agencies. For example, these agencies may be formed as "captives" of other nonprofit groups. During the 1930s and 1940s, Blue Cross plans began under the auspices of nonprofit hospitals to ensure that hospitals were paid. The scope of our inquiry does not encompass the conditions under which health service agencies become organized on a voluntary basis (see Culyer 1971). Rather, we will treat the existence of this type of organization as a given and restrict our attention to the supply behavior of these agencies once they are formed.

To ensure that the services offered by a nonprofit agency are provided in a reasonable manner, a board of trustees is formed. The members of a board of trustees cannot gain direct financial benefit from the organization either in the form of profits or of proceeds from the sale of the enterprise. Furthermore, they are frequently banned from garnering indirect gains, such as might occur if a board member's law firm provided legal services to the organization. The board of trustees is primarily responsible for setting organizational policies, but many of their responsibilities are delegated to a full-time, salaried administrative staff. The actual responsibilities of each (the trustees and the staff), including the making of supply decisions, vary from organization to organization.

Several approaches can be taken in forming hypotheses about the supply behavior of nonprofit agencies. One approach is to regard the trustees as being in charge. Following this approach, we would hypothesize goals the trustees are likely to pursue and then develop a model of the organization that incorporates these goals. Another approach is to regard the salaried executives as the people who maintain control, make hypotheses about their goals, and develop a model of organizational supply based on *these* goals. No doubt the supply behavior of a real nonprofit firm is influenced by trustees and staff, but to keep our analysis simple we will pursue each approach separately. We begin with the trustee dominance model. We will assume that the trustees' objective is to maximize the output of the agency, that is, to carry out their mandate to the fullest extent possible.

Now, let us imagine a nonprofit lab initially financed by a public-spirited benefactor. Cost and revenue conditions are the same as in the ABC Labs example, with the exception that the pathologist is under contract and receives an explicit payment of $5 per month for his services. From the point of view of the lab, once the contractual commitment is made, this is a fixed cost, and so the total fixed costs of the laboratory are $12. The quality of the product is the same as in the previous example and is constant. Revenues are $12 per test, but now the reimbursement may be made by a third party. (Reimbursement may be collected through individual donations or from a united agency.) The major difference between the two examples is that the nonprofit lab seeks to maximize output rather than profits.

According to our model, since revenues come only from reimbursement for services, output will be expanded to the point where the firm breaks even, that is, where $TR = TC$. In Table 6–1, given a price of $12, output will be expanded to eight units. In Graph A of Figure 6–1, the break-even point at eight units of output is shown in total terms. In Graph B, the lab's operating point is where price per unit equals average total cost. The lab just covers costs for all units when it operates at this level.

Given our assumptions, output for a for-profit firm will be lower than that for a nonprofit firm that behaves as we have hypothesized (i.e., maximizes output). The supply curve for an output-maximizing firm is its ATC curve for prices above the minimum point on the curve. If the revenues do not total at least this minimum amount, the firm runs a deficit and must raise the funds from nonpatient sources. For the moment we will assume that nonpatient revenues are zero and that the firm has no reserves to meet a deficit. If it does not meet all its obligations, it will go out of business.

As long as price is above the minimum point on the ATC curve, the supply curve of the nonprofit agency that maximizes output is the ATC curve. As price rises, so will supply. Any factor that shifts the ATC curve downward (lower unit costs at any level of output) will cause output to increase at any price.

The response of an output-maximizing nonprofit firm to a fixed subsidy is very different from that of a profit-maximizing firm. Recall that a fixed subsidy will not influence a profit-maximizer's supply (Section 6.2.2). Let us assume that a donor gives our nonprofit lab a $25.00 subsidy unrelated to output. Analytically, we can treat this as an overall increase in total revenues or as an overall reduction in total costs (and a reduction in average fixed costs of $25.00/$Q$). In the former case, the analysis in Table 6–1 would be altered to show TR and profits higher at every level of output by $25. Whereas, formerly, the output-maximizing output level was eight, with the subsidy an output level of nine will shown an overall (operating and nonoperating) profit of $2.25 ($25.00 − $22.75). The lab would be in the red at an output level of 10, but it could now meet all its costs at a level of nine, and this is where it would maximize output (subject to the fact that it must break even).

Graphically, if the fixed subsidy is treated as a reduction in fixed costs, it would appear as a downward shift in AFC and also ATC (because AFC is part of ATC). It will appear as an outward shift in the firm's supply curve, which is identical to the ATC curve. The conclusion in either case is the same: a non-output-related grant will shift the supply curve of the output-maximizing firm and thus will lead to increased output. In this respect, the output-maximizing firm is very unlike the profit-maximizing firm.

The market supply analysis in the case of nonprofit organizations is somewhat more complicated than in the case of for-profit organizations. If we make the assumption that each separate nonprofit supplier has a vested interest in providing output to the needy, the market supply curve will be made up of the sum of what all the individual suppliers would be willing to supply at each price or reimbursement rate. That is, the market supply curve is the sum of the individual producers' supply curves for prices above the minimum *ATC*.

Individual nonprofit suppliers might act competitively if the trustees developed some sense of identification with the organizations of which they were board members. However, if this sense of identification did not develop, trustees would not care which organization supplied the output to the needy as long as it was supplied by someone. In this situation, market supply would consist of a far more complicated set of arrangements, since trustees would pull their organizations out of the market when other organizations supplying the same product appeared. We will assume that in our example organizational pride develops to the point that the standard market supply model is appropriate.

6.5 SUPPLY DECISIONS INVOLVING QUALITY

Until now we have assumed that quality of output was held constant and thus did not enter the supply decision. In fact, quality is an extremely important supply variable for suppliers. In particular, it has frequently been asserted that hospitals seek to supply output of the highest quality. In this section, a model is developed to incorporate quality of care into the supply picture.

To understand the bias of nonprofit hospitals toward high-quality supply, it is necessary to examine their unusual management structure. Like other nonprofit firms, a nonprofit hospital includes a board of trustees and a group of salaried administrators. However, doctors have a special relationship to the hospital: They are in charge of the medical activities of the hospital, and yet for the most part they are unsalaried staff members. Because their services are so crucial (indeed the hospital's activities revolve around them), doctors have enormous influence over hospital supply decisions, and hospital supply policies are set by an informal arrangement between doctors, trustees, and administrators. This type of arrangement has been termed a "management triangle," and hospital activities are the result of directives (sometimes conflicting) issued by two lines of authority, medical and administrative. In particular, the medical influence in the decision-making process has been held to be responsible for the bias toward quality in hospital objectives, since doctors benefit considerably from high-quality inputs.

A supply model that is based on the preceding analysis but incorporates the bias toward quality can be developed. Assume a given level of reimbursement, say $200 per patient day (see Figure 6–5). *ATC* curves are drawn for three different levels of quality of service; each higher level is produced with more resources. ATC_1 represents an *ATC* curve for a specific level of output and level of quality. ATC_2 and ATC_3 are similar curves for successively higher levels of quality.

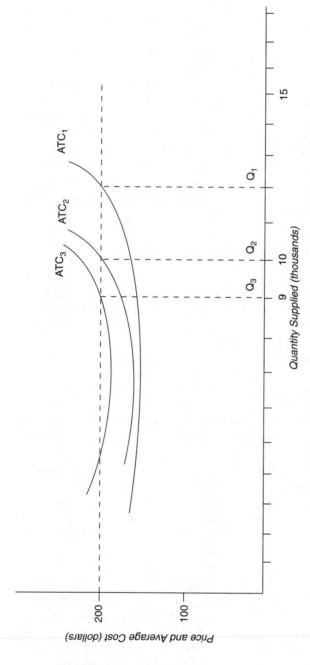

Figure 6–5 Representation of alternative quantities and qualities supplied by a nonprofit supplier. The *ATC* curves represent relations between *ATC* and output at various quality levels. *ATC*$_3$ represents the highest quality level, *ATC*$_2$ the intermediate level, and *ATC*$_1$ the lowest level. A nonprofit producer who maximizes the quantity of output (given the quality level) will produce where the unit reimbursement rate or price equals *ATC*. For the lowest quality level, the output will be 12. Higher quality levels entail a reduction in the maximum output levels achievable given the reimbursement rate.

An output-maximizing hospital will choose Q_1 (12,000) units of output at Quality Level 1, Q_2 (10,000) units at Quality Level 2, and Q_3 (9,000) units at Quality Level 3. Indeed, a trade-off between quality and quantity of care typically occurs. Such a trade-off is shown in Figure 6–6, with quality of care represented on the vertical axis and the quantity on the horizontal. Curve XY shows the maximum output that can be achieved for each level of quality given the reimbursement rate of $200 and thus reflects the constraints or the choices facing the hospital. The actual combination of quality and quantity supplied will depend on the hospital's policies. A highly quality oriented hospital will choose a quality level close to Qu_3,

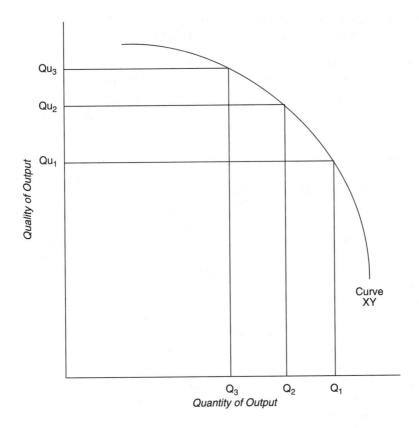

Figure 6–6 Representation of the trade-off between quality and quantity. Based on Figure 6–5, for any given reimbursement rate, a higher quality level can be achieved only with a lower quantity of output. The curve shows alternative levels of quantity and quality that can be achieved at a given reimbursement rate.

whereas an output-oriented hospital will choose a level closer to Qu_1. If the assertion that hospitals are quality oriented is correct, it might be expected that Qu_3 would be more frequently observed. That is, of the various output combinations that a nonprofit hospital can choose, it will tend to provide care of a higher quality level. By itself, however, this does not mean that we will observe such high-quality care in the market. For it must be remembered that we are currently examining only the supply side of the market. The quality of care actually produced will be determined by what the suppliers are willing to supply and what the consumers are willing to take. Determining what output actually is produced and utilized requires that we examine the market in its entirety.

✳ 6.6   SUPPLY BEHAVIOR OF NONPROFIT AGENCIES: THE ADMINISTRATOR AS AGENT MODEL

An alternative theory of resource allocation and product supply in nonprofit agencies focuses on the behavior of the executive or administrator of the organization. The underlying assumption is that the administrator, even though just an agent of the trustees, has considerable control over the organization's resources. This seems a plausible assumption given that trustees of a nonprofit agency typically can devote only a small portion of their time to trustee-related activities, whereas the administrator is usually a full-time employee. As part of this approach, a comparative analysis can be done that examines how the same administrator would behave if operating at the same agency as a profit-seeking enterprise and as a nonprofit enterprise. The differences in behavior, which are due solely to the different incentive structures that the two types of organizations create, create differences in the use of the agency's resources and in the agency's output.

The theory can be viewed as simply an extension of the basic demand hypothesis presented in Chapter 3. This hypothesis was that the lower the direct cost of a commodity or other benefit to an individual, the more the commodity will be demanded. The extension of the hypothesis involves identifying the commodities that are desired by the administrator of an agency as well as their relative prices or costs under varying institutional circumstances. Since we are focusing on the administrator's behavior, we will identify two types of benefits that can be obtained in the context of the job. First, there are the pecuniary benefits, including especially the administrator's salary. In addition, if the administrator is a part or full owner of the agency, the pecuniary benefits will encompass the profits that accrue. The second type, sometimes called *on-the-job benefits*, are nonpecuniary. These include high-grade office furniture, a relaxed work atmosphere, "business" trips to exotic places, and so on. Both types of benefits are wanted by the administrator, but because their supply is limited, the administrator cannot have everything he or she would like.

Before developing the hypothesis about how much of each type of benefit will be demanded, we will look at the implications for resource use of obtaining the two types. First, when a smaller amount of resources are used to obtain a given output, an opportunity to increase profits is created. Nonpecuniary benefits also require the commitment of resources. Better office equipment, more liberal working conditions, and other on-the-job benefits are obtained from the expansion of the total resource commitment and result in an increase in costs and a contraction of profits. In a nonprofit enterprise this reduction in profits does not detract from the manager's pecuniary benefits since he or she will not be rewarded on the basis of the profits the enterprise earns.

The hypothesis as to how the administrator will behave under these alternative incentive structures is based on the constraints facing the administrators in the two different environments. In a nonprofit environment, since the administrator cannot convert profits into pecuniary, take-home benefits, they must be converted into organizational resources if any benefit is to be obtained. On the other hand, the use of these extra resources in a for-profit organization will detract from profits and hence from pecuniary or take-home benefits, assuming these are related. The personal costs of on-the-job benefits are lower for the administrator of the nonprofit agency, and we thus hypothesize that more will be demanded.

The implications of this hypothesis for nonprofit resource allocation are considerable. The hypothesis implies that the nonprofit agency will use more resources to get a given job done and so its costs will be higher. The absence of incentives for efficiency has been the target of investigation, including its effect on nonprofit agency operating costs, particularly in the case of nonprofit health insurers (Frech 1976), nursing homes (Borjas et al. 1983; Frech 1985), and dialysis units (Lowrie and Hampers 1981). Similar analyses comparing nonprofit and for-profit hospital behavior have not been as conclusive for several reasons. First, to compare operating costs between nonprofit and for-profit hospitals, variables such as case mix, case severity, and quality must be adjusted for. Assertions have been made that nonprofit hospitals have a more complex case mix because for-profit hospitals engage in "cream skimming" by encouraging the admission of low-cost cases. Evidence on this score seems mixed (Bays 1977a, 1979b; Renn et al. 1985; Schweitzer and Rafferty 1976). Even more difficult to determine is whether quality differentials exist by ownership category. Nonprofit managers do have an incentive to produce quality care (which will show up in higher costs). The role of quality in pushing costs higher has yet to be fully explored.

Another difference that has been uncovered when comparing nonprofit and for-profit hospital behavior lies in the pricing area. Charges are the prices set by the hospital for its services. Two California studies found that for-profit hospitals had higher charges (relative to costs) for ancillary (lab, radiology, pharmacy) services (Eskoz and Peddecord 1985; Pattison and Katz 1983). Generally, markups (charge to cost ratios) for ancillary services were found to be higher than basic room charges. For-profit hospitals also provided more (high-profit) ancillary services per patient than nonprofits in the studies and were more profitable, although cost levels were similar. One possible explanation of this finding is that nonprofit managers (or trustees) can gain nonpecuniary benefits from encouraging the use of hospital services by keeping patient charges low (which may result in lower profits) as well as by providing more free care to indigents.

However, relying solely on the incentives identified in the administrator as agent model to explain cost and price differences between for-profit and nonprofit hospitals would be a mistake. The incentive differences are but one factor operating to influence costs (and possible cost differences) in the two types of organizations. The reimbursement system is another major influence on cost and supply behavior. Indeed, the absence of cost differences between nonprofit and for-profit hospitals that was uncovered by the investigators in California may have been partly due to the reimbursement system, which, at the time of the studies, encouraged cost inflation in all types of hospitals. It is to this factor that we now turn.

6.7   PROVIDER REIMBURSEMENT

6.7.1 Overview

In this section we use the marginal revenue–marginal cost (MR/MC) framework to predict the effect of different kinds of provider reimbursement systems on the quantity of services supplied. We begin with a general description of how the MR/MC approach can be applied to predict the effects of different provider reimbursement schemes on provider behavior. We then apply this approach to a number of different settings: hospitals, nursing homes, and health maintenance organizations.

There are two components to a payment system: the payment basis and the payment rate. For example, a payment for inpatient care can be made on the basis of individual services supplied (ward days of care, lab tests, x-rays, or drugs provided), days of care, or cases treated. If payment is made on a per service basis, then there will be a positive MR (equal to the payment rate) for each service provided. If the payment basis is days of care, then there will be a positive MR for each day of care, but if any additional services are supplied during the day, these will not be specifically reimbursed for (their MR will be zero). The same holds if a hospital is funded on a per case basis. The MR for each case will be positive, but the MR for additional services provided or additional days during a stay will be zero.

If supply decisions depend on profits, the relationship between the MR and MC is of relevance. If the MR is zero, then the supplier will operate at a loss of MC for each additional unit of service produced. If the hospital is paid on a per case basis, for example, it will have a zero *MR* for additional days and services and so will not have any incentive to supply above a minimum level of services for each day. In comparison, payment based on services would encourage additional services to be provided as long as the *MR* exceeds the *MC* for each service.

The second factor that is important in supply analysis is the rate of payment. A higher rate entails a greater *MR*. As has been shown in previous sections of this chapter, the quantity of services supplied by a for-profit provider will increase as the rate of payment increases. This will hold true even if profits are not the sole objective of the supplier. All that needs to be true is that profits are one of the supplier's objectives.

The relationship between the rate and basis of payment should be noted. Even if the rate increases, the basis can be such that *MR* is zero. If a hospital is paid on a per case basis, the *MR* per additional service and per additional day will be zero and no additional services per day or additional days per case will be supplied.

Below we survey the effect of alternative payment systems on provider supply behavior. When reviewing the supply analyses, the reader should keep one qualification in mind: Each analysis narrowly focuses on the reaction of a supplier to specific incentives. A complete analysis would examine how the relevant portions of the entire system are affected. A discussion on how to conduct more complete analyses will come later, in Chapters 7 and 8.

6.7.2 Physician Reimbursement

There are four major types of physician reimbursement: fee-for-service, per case, per capita, and salary reimbursement.

6.7.2.1 Fee-for-Service Reimbursement

The fee-for-service method of reimbursement is similar to a piece-rate method. The physician is paid a specific sum by a third party for each individual service he or she provides to the patient. The services are broken down into units, such as a complete physical exam, a follow-up visit, a tonsillectomy, and so on.

There are several ways in which the fees can be set by the third party. One, which most closely corresponds to the assumption in this chapter of an absence of control by the provider over the fee, is the relative value scale (Havighurst and Kissam 1979; Hsiao and Stason 1979). In this method, each category of service is assigned a relative value in accordance with some criterion (e.g., the number of minutes required to perform the procedure). For example, in the frequently used California Relative Value Scale (surgical component), a single coronary bypass operation would have an index number of 25. This relative value can be converted to fees by applying a conversion factor. If the conversion factor for surgery was

$50 per point on the relative value scale, the surgeon would be reimbursed $1,250 for the bypass operation. A recent version of this mode of payment will be discussed below.

A second type of fee setting does not really correspond to the assumption that fees are beyond the control of the individual provider. This method is referred to as the UCR (usual, customary, and reasonable) form of reimbursement. *Usual* refers to the usual or typical fee charged by the billing physician, *customary* refers to fees charged by all physicians in the community, and *reasonable* refers to allowances for particular circumstances (Epstein and Bluenthal 1993). Suppose Dr. Welby performed 100 varicose vein injections and charged an average of $100. Her usual fee for the procedure would then be $100. The customary fee would be derived from the frequency distribution of the fees charged by all doctors in the community for the procedure (e.g., the doctors in the 10th percentile might charge an average of $55, those in the 20th percentile might charge $63, and so on). The insurer then decides which percentile to use to set an allowable maximum fee. If the reimburser used the 70th percentile, then the associated charge might be $87. Dr. Welby would then be reimbursed her usual fee or the customer fee, whichever was lower (in her case, the customary fee, since her usual fee is $100).

The reason why the provider is not a mere price taker in this approach is that the provider's fee partly determines the customary fee prevailing in the market. If all doctors (or even some) raise their fees, the customary fee will increase as well. Each doctor thus exerts some degree of influence over the market's fees. When there are many doctors in the market, the degree of influence may be small, and for analytical purposes the doctors might take the customary fee as a given fee. (Note that the fee in this case is also beyond the control of the insurer.)

The profit-maximizing model is a useful starting point for analyzing the effects of a fee-for-service payment system. Since the physician is paid a fixed rate per unit of service provided, the number of units produced will depend on what the reimbursement rate is and on the physician's marginal costs for the specific service. If the marginal cost schedule slopes upward steeply, only a slight addition to supply will result from an increase in the fee (Phelps 1976). Another important factor is the composition of fees. If surgical fees are high relative to general checkup fees—that is, surgical operations yield considerable profits relative to checkups—then surgeons will have an incentive to operate more. Physicians, on the other hand, will not have an incentive to perform checkups (which might be marginally profitable, if at all). Indeed, fee-for-service reimbursement is believed to encourage doctors to provide more medical care. As we have just seen, however, the degree of encouragement, if any, will depend on the relation between the fee and the service's marginal cost. Some analysts have taken the argument one step further and claimed that fee-for-service reimbursement encourages many unnecessary practices (Klarman 1963). In the context of the present analysis, we can only say whether additional services are likely to be offered; we cannot determine whether they would be necessary.

The fee schedule is a potentially powerful tool that third parties can use to influence both the type of practices performed and where they are performed. For example, tonsillectomies are thought to be unnecessary in many instances. If a third party wanted to discourage this procedure, it could lower the amount of reimbursement. Also, if a third party wanted to encourage certain procedures to be performed on an outpatient rather than an inpatient basis, it could reimburse physicians differentially for the same procedure. For example, the South Carolina Preferred Personal Care Plan reimbursed physicians $675 for a colonoscopy performed in an outpatient setting and $515 for the same procedure performed in a hospital.

The profit-maximizing hypothesis can be altered to take into account alternative possible behavior patterns of the physician-owners of the medical practices. A more complete analysis might recognize that physicians desire leisure as well as income (see Section 6.7.3). As their profits (incomes) rise, physicians may want to engage in activities that require more leisure time. They will then be forced to trade some profits for additional leisure time. This will cause their supply curves to slope more positively (i.e., output will respond less to fee increase), and if the fee increase is sufficiently high, their supply curves may even become vertical and then slope backward. It should be stressed that this result is not inconsistent with the assumption that the physicians are profit maximizers (Feldstein 1970; Sloan 1975).

6.7.2.2 Per Case Reimbursement

The second type of physician reimbursement is payment per case. In this type of reimbursement, the physician is paid a fixed amount for each type of case treated, much like the DRG system. In fact, the DRG system is among the systems proposed as a basis for per case reimbursement (Mitchell 1985). In per case reimbursement, the physician bears the cost of any services he or she provides and is paid a sum for the entire case. If the physician reduces the number of services, more money will be left over as profit. The profit-maximizing physician thus has an incentive to attract cases where the fee exceeds the marginal cost while referring elsewhere those cases that are unprofitable. At the same time, incentives exist to reduce the number of services per case.

Per case reimbursement for physicians is not widely being considered at this time, in part because studies have indicated that there are wide variations in services for a single case type (DRG), which would result in difficulties in establishing rates or fees and would give providers greater leeway to select cases with potentially low costs and to refer potentially high-cost cases.

6.7.2.3 Per Capita and Salary Reimbursement

The incentives for physicians who are paid on a per capita or a salary basis are decidedly different than the incentives in fee-for-service reimbursement. In both cases, there is no incentive for physicians to provide any more than the basic minimum level of services. Indeed, it might be argued that the physicians have an incentive to perform even less than that. In any event, considerable evidence exists regarding the impact that the payment system has on physician practices. Reference has been made to the large difference in surgical operations in the United States and England, and the difference in general payment patterns is considered one underlying factor. In England, surgeons were traditionally paid on a salary basis, while in the United States the usual payment basis is fee for service (Aaron and Schwartz 1984), although the fee schedule has been changed considerably since the introduction of the Resource-Based Relative Value Scale (RBRVS). (See Section 6.7.3 for a description of the RBRVS.) In the United States, several reimbursement experiments have been undertaken (Eisenberg and Williams 1981; Myers and Schroeder 1981). In one, primary care physicians were given financial responsibility for the entire health care expenditures of their patients; they shared in any surpluses of premiums over total medical care costs (including hospitalization costs, laboratory, and x-ray fees, etc.) as well as in any deficits. The incentive was for them to reduce the expenditures paid out so that the surpluses would be greater. This experiment was based on the view of the physician as "gatekeeper" to the health care system, someone who has the ability to control a good deal of the patient's cost. The results showed a considerable reduction in overall expenses relative to a fee-for-service comparison group (Moore 1979). Another study examined how physician prescribing behavior was affected by an ambulatory care center's introduction of monetary incentives to generate additional business. The findings showed there was a substantial increase in x-rays (Hemenway et al. 1990).

6.7.3 A Resource-Based Relative Value Scale

Medicare adopted a variant of the UCR system called *customary, prevailing, and reasonable* (CPR), but it had regulated these fees since 1984. Recently, a new fee schedule has been adopted to replace the old fee system. The new schedule has fixed fees that are based on resource use measures. This system, called RBRVS, attempts to classify the costs that would be incurred by physicians operating in a competitive environment. Based on the classification, a questionnaire was developed to capture the costs incurred in the classification scheme. The questionnaire was applied to national samples of physicians in 18 specialties to develop a relative cost schedule for physician procedures or services. The cost categories include costs related to actual work done by a physician, costs of operating practices, and the "amortized" cost of physician training (an annual amount derived from averaging training expenses over the period of a standard career). A fee schedule was developed that reflected these costs.

The national survey interviewed a sample of physicians about the time, mental effort and judgment, physical effort, technical skill, and stress associated with each procedure. These elements were combined into work indexes. For example, an office visit for internal medicine had a work index of 100, whereas a resection for rectal carcinoma had an index value of 445. To these work indexes were added practice cost factors and the opportunity cost of training. Practice costs were determined by specialty based on a survey of costs and revenues by physicians in each specialty.

The results of the calculations indicate the value of the services relative to each other, not their value in dollars. The relative valuations must then be assigned a dollar value in order to be translated into a fee schedule. For example, if the dollar value assigned to the schedule was $1 per index point, then the physician would receive $445 for a resection for rectal carcinoma (which was given an index value of 445 points).

Table 6–2 presents simulated fees for selected office visits under the old Medicare system and under the RBRVS. These numbers, which reflect the direction the RBRVS is taking, show that surgical fees would be cut substantially under the RBRVS, whereas evaluation and management fees would increase substantially (Hsiao et al. 1988, 885).

The effects of such changes can be analyzed in terms of the supply analysis presented in this chapter. An increase in the fee for a procedure should increase the quantity supplied of that procedure, and a reduction should reduce the quantity supplied. Thus, for those procedures whose fees are increased, quantity supplied will increase. This is shown in Figure 6–7, where S_1 is a supply curve for a single profit-maximizing physician (ignore S_2 for the moment). Initially the fee for an office visit is $40, and at this level the physician will be willing to supply 210 office visits. An increase in the fee to $100 will result in a supply of 500 visits.

Table 6–2 Simulated Charges for Selected Procedures According to Medicare and Simulated RBRVS, 1986

Procedure	Mean Medicare Charge (dollars)	RBRV Fee (dollars)	Ratio of Medicare Fee to RBRV Fee
Extended Office Visit—Medical	37	130	0.27
Coronary Bypass Surgery	4,663	2,871	1.62
Interpretation of Chest Film	20	22	0.91

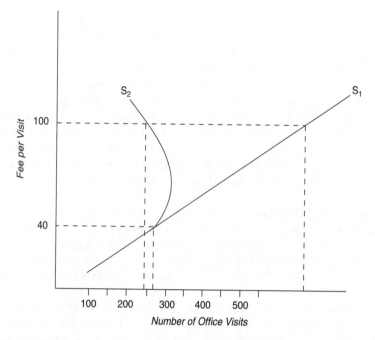

Figure 6–7 Supply curves for physician services are shown under two sets of assumptions. Curve S_1 shows a situation where higher fees result in more labor (and less leisure). Curve S_2 shows a case where higher fees result in physician's taking more leisure time and cutting back on work.

According to this analysis, a fee increase will increase the quantity of procedures and a fee reduction will reduce the quantity. The RBRVS, according to this analysis, will have substantial supply effects in favor of primary care and away from more intensive and invasive procedures.

We should note that this discussion is restricted to the issue of supply. The number of services actually provided will depend on the quantity of services *demanded*.

There are some other qualifications that should be kept in mind. The first is the appropriateness of this analysis for dealing with labor supply issues. After all, the physician's labor is a key factor in the supply of physician visits. Individual physicians have limitations on their work time, and the supply model needs to be modified to take this into account.

As shown in Section 4.6.1, at lower income and wage levels, the propensity to substitute leisure for work may be strong enough to more than offset the income effect. An upward-sloping supply curve would result. However, at higher wage levels, the income effect may more than offset the substitution effect, and a backward-bending supply curve would result. In Figure 6–7, the supply curve of S_2 begins to bend back just beyond 200 office visits. Up to the fee of \$40, the physician behaves as in curve S_1. If the fee rises above \$40 per visit, the physician's supply will increase in smaller amounts and eventually begin to decrease. If this is the way physicians behave, then raising fees above the maximum point will cause physicians to cut back on the number of services they are willing to provide. An increase in primary care fees, then, may not necessarily cause an increase in the quantity of primary care supplied. However, there is little evidence to support the contention of a backward sloping supply curve of labor.

6.7.4 Hospital Reimbursement

Until the early 1980s, hospitals were reimbursed on a retrospective basis. That is, a third party would reimburse a hospital for the expenses it had already incurred (if reimbursement was on a cost basis) or the charges it had already billed (if reimbursement was on a charge basis). There are numerous variations of retrospective reimbursement. The third party can pay on a cost-plus basis, which means it can reimburse the hospital for its allowable costs plus a specified amount (say, 2 percent of costs). In another method of reimbursement, the third party pays the hospital whichever is lower, costs or charges. There is also considerable variation in how costs are defined. Allowable costs could exclude costs not directly related to patient care (e.g., teaching costs). Whatever the arrangement, retrospective reimbursement has one overriding effect on supply and on costs: It encourages an organization to expand. Increases in both the scope and quality of services tend to occur, and if the provider is a maximizer of anything (e.g., profits or perquisites) retrospective reimbursement can lead to higher costs, more services, and higher quality services.

In response to this recognized bias in retrospective reimbursement, a number of prospective reimbursement plans have been introduced. Prospective reimbursement involves setting the basis of reimbursement before the reimbursement period. As a result, this sort of payment scheme puts the provider "at risk" for any excesses of cost over revenue. There are many different bases for setting the rate of prospective payments and an infinite number of rate levels. We will examine several of the alternatives and their hypothesized effects on cost and quantity.

To help classify the effects of different types of reimbursement, we will use the following formula to break out the components of total cost:

$$\frac{\text{Total}}{\text{Cost}} = \frac{\text{Cost per}}{\text{Service}} \times \frac{\text{Services per}}{\text{Patient Day}} \times \frac{\text{Days of Stay}}{\text{per Admission}} \times \frac{\text{Number of}}{\text{Admissions}}$$

Let us now explore the likely effect of three types of prospective reimbursement—per service, per diem (per day), and per admission—on an output-maximizing hospital.

In per service reimbursement, the hospital will receive a fixed amount for each service performed (e.g., an operation, an x-ray, or kidney dialysis). This amount is set in advance (e.g., $45 for a specific lab test, $300 for a complete CT scan, etc.). In response to this type of reimbursement, an output-maximizing hospital will expand its services as long as the reimbursed rate at least covers the cost of provision. The expansion may be achieved by increasing the number of services per patient per day, the number of days a patient stays (so more services can be provided), and the number of admissions (if this is feasible).

If per diem reimbursement is the method of payment used, a per diem rate is set by multiplying the cost per service by the number of services per patient day. There will be no incentive to expand the number of services per patient day because the hospital will receive no extra revenue for doing so. However, the hospital will receive added revenue from having more patient days. As long as the added reimbursement covers the added costs, the hospital will expand the number of patient days by increasing patient length of stay and, if possible, admissions. Since the cost to the hospital of adding an extra day to an admitted patient's stay is usually quite low (all the expensive services having been provided early in the patient's visit), the hospital will usually benefit considerably by increasing the average length of stay.

The third prospective payment method, per admission reimbursement, will reward the hospital only for adding more patients. Consequently the hospital will cut back on length of stay and services per patient and attempt to draw in more patients, as long as it does not run a deficit by doing so. The hospital will also encourage the readmission of patients and interhospital transfers of patients, since this will mean additional payment (Morrissey et al. 1988).

When evaluating types of hospital reimbursement, several things have to be kept in mind. First, one must distinguish between an all-payer system and a multipayer system. In an all-payer system, each payer pays the same rate. For example, assume that Medicare, Blue Cross, and commercial insurers each have one-third of the overall caseload of 300 cases in a hospital and that the case mixes and severities of the patient groups are identical (so there is no objective basis for differential payments). Assume, further, that the regulatory authority in the state has determined that the hospital's allowable revenues should be $900,000. This means that each insurer "should" pay $300,000, and this is what it would pay in an all-payer system.

A multipayer system is more like a free-for-all, with each payer setting up its payment rules unilaterally or based on market principles. Let us say that, in the preceding example, the regulatory agency only regulates Medicare and Blue Cross rates and that it allows each to pay $270,000. The commercial group rates are unregulated. In this instance, the hospital must charge the commercials more to cover its deficit. Whether or not it collects all its bills is another issue. What is significant here is that the hospital is no longer a price taker, and so a more complex model that can incorporate the reaction by the hospital to the regulated rate is needed.

A second important fact to keep in mind is that other parts of the health care system may be affected by the reimbursement type and level. For example, if a system penalizes a hospital for keeping patients hospitalized for more than a specified time, this will most certainly reduce length of stay. It may have other effects as well. For instance, if home health care or nursing home care are reimbursed separately, the hospital may open up a nursing home or begin a home health care program to which it could discharge its patients.

A considerable number of experiments with prospective reimbursement have been conducted at the state level (Bauer 1977; Carter et al. 1994). Most of these have occurred in multipayer systems, and so their effects are harder to identify than they would be in an all-payer system. One such experiment, conducted by the New York State legislature, set per diem rates for Medicare- and Blue Cross–reimbursed patients according to a pre-established formula beginning in 1970. In testing for the effect of this type of reimbursement, a comparison was made between length of stay and occupancy rates after 1970 in New York State and those in several comparison states, where prospective per diem rates were not in force (Ohio and the New England states). Between 1970 and 1974, New York showed a slight increase in the average length of stay and no net change in the occupancy rate (i.e., the average percentage of beds filled). Both of these indicators of hospital supply decreased considerably in the control states during the same period of time. This suggests that the reimbursement mechanism had its expected effect (Berry 1976).

6.7.5 Diagnosis-Related Groups

In 1983 the federal government introduced a new prospective payment system (PPS) for Medicare hospital patients. In this system, reimbursement for all Medicare discharges is on a per diagnosis basis. Here, we review how diagnoses are grouped into separate DRGs and how rates are set for each DRG. We then use the quantity-maximizing model to examine the effects of DRGs on the supply system.

The DRG system is one of many possible ways of classifying patients according to common elements (Hornbrook 1982). There is the presumption that, if the classification system is to be used for reimbursement purposes, all cases in each group must be similar with regard to resource use. Based on several patient characteristics (the major diagnostic group, the presence of comorbid diagnoses, the presence of a surgical procedure, and discharge status), an algorithm was developed to assign individual cases to groupings that exhibit common resource-use tendencies (as measured by length of stay) (Fetter et al. 1980). The component characteristics of one set of DRGs is shown in Figure 6–8. As can be seen, DRGs for breast disorders were developed based on the major diagnostic groups the disorders fell into and on factors such as the need for surgery, the patient's age, and the presence of complicating diagnoses. The criteria were selected so that cases in each category would use similar amounts of resources and thus could be reimbursed with a single rate. There are 495 categories in the DRG classification system. A sample list of DRGs, along with their relative weights, is presented in Table 6–3.

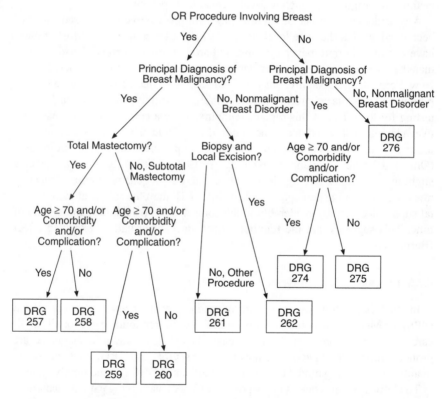

Figure 6–8 Derivation of diagnosis-related groups (DRGs) for breast disorders. Among the criteria used to separate the various DRGs are the use of operating room (OR) procedures, the principal diagnosis, the type of OR procedure (if used), the age of the patient, and complications and/or comorbidity.

Table 6-3 Relative Weights for Selected Diagnosis-Related Groups (DRGs) (1995)

DRG	Description	1995 Relative Weight (average = 1.0000)
39	Surgical lens procedure	0.5055
60	Tonsillectomy, age 0–17	0.2724
70	Otitis media, age 0–17	0.5812
103	Heart transplant	13.5495
211	Hip and femur procedures, age >17 without complications	1.2990
302	Kidney transplant	4.1394
371	Cesarean section, no complications	0.6340
373	Vaginal delivery	0.3387
481	Bone marrow transplant	15.3076

Based on cross-hospital studies, an average cost for each DRG was estimated. Factors in the calculation included the lengths of stay (within the DRG) in routine and special care, per diem costs in routine and special care, and the estimated per case cost of ancillary services (laboratory, radiology, drugs, medical supplies, anesthesia, and other services) (Pettengill and Vertrees 1982). Each DRG was then assigned a relative weight intended to approximate the relative amount of resources used by an average case in the group. For example, a cardiac arrest (DRG 129) has an assigned weight of 1.1959 and a coronary bypass (DRG 106) has an assigned weight of 5.6791. This means that, in comparison to an "average" diagnostic group (with a weight set equal to 1), a typical case of DRG 129 uses 1.1959 times the amount of resources and a case of DRG 106 uses 5.6791 times the amount.

Using these weights and the frequency of types of cases, a hospital can develop a case mix–adjusted admissions measure. This measure would presumably be a better approximation of the resources required to serve the hospital's patient population than mere admissions or patient days (which have traditionally been used). For example, let us say that both Aiken and Bethesda General Hospital treated 200 patients in 1990, with an average length of stay of 6 days. Both would have a measured output of 1,200 patient days. Let us say, however, that of Aiken's 200 cases, half were inguinal hernia cases (DRG 162, with a weight equal to .50) and half were complicated peptic ulcer cases (DRG 176, with a weight equal to 1.00). Then Aiken's case mix–adjusted measure of admissions would be equal to 150 (.50 × 100 + 1.00 × 100). Bethesda's case mix included 100 cases of DRG 106, bypass surgery, with a weight equal to 5.50, and 100 kidney transplants (DRG 302, with a weight equal to 3.84). Bethesda's adjusted output would equal 934 (5.50 × 100 + 3.84 × 100).

With the hospital's output being measured in terms of case-weighted admissions, a reimbursement rate (called a *standardized amount*) must be set for each single point (relative weight = 1.00). Originally, this rate had national, regional, and hospital-specific components. In 1989 Medicare went to a national rate, although the rate for each hospital is affected by its location (urban or rural), the number of residents per bed (for teaching hospitals), and the number of low-income patients treated (Russell 1989). For example, in 1996 the national standardized amount for hospitals in large urban areas was 3,839. An urban hospital with no teaching facilities would be reimbursed 1,300 for a vaginal delivery (0.338 points times 3,839 per point). These amounts are also adjusted for geographic locations and the share of low income cases.

If the hospital was a teaching hospital, it would be entitled to an "indirect" teaching adjustment to pay for additional services (lab tests, x-rays, etc.) consumed in the process of teaching interns and residents. This additional amount is based on the hospital's intern-resident per bed ratio (Lave 1984). The indirect teaching adjustment equals about a 7 percent increase in the basic rate for each .1 interns and residents per bed. A large teaching hospital with a ratio of .4 residents per bed would have a 28-percent increase added to its basic rate. This hospital, if it was in a large urban area, would receive $4,913 per point.

As an example, let us say that a typical teaching hospital, Denver City Hospital, with 200 beds and .4 residents per bed, had 24,000 admissions last year, one-quarter of which were Medicare patients. Assume, further, that one-half (3,000) of the Medicare cases fell into DRG 39 lens surgery, with a weight equal to 0.5055 and one-half into DRG 211 hip procedures, with a weight equal to 1.2990. Since this hospital is in a large urban area, it was reimbursed at a rate of $4,913.00 per point (after the adjustment for its intern-resident population). Denver's receipts for its 6,000 Medicare patients would be about $26.6 million (3,000 cases) with a weight equal to .5055 and 3,000 with a weight equal to 1.2990.

Medicare also reimburses the hospitals for certain additional costs that fall outside of the basic case-mix formula: outlier-related costs, and direct medical education costs. An *outlier* is a case whose costs or length of stay is sufficiently high that it falls outside certain predetermined limits. There are two kinds of outliers—day and cost outliers. A day outlier for a specific DRG is a case whose length of stay exceeds a preset number of days (e.g., 24 days); all days in excess of this trim point are called *outlying days*. For example, if the preset number of days for DRG 103 is 24 and a case has a stay of 32 days, then 8 of these days will be deemed outlying days. There are similar criteria for cost outliers (e.g., costs in excess of $28,000 for a case). Outlier rules were developed to reimburse hospitals for cases that used an unusual high amount of resources. Rates for reimbursing hospitals for outlying portions of cases are set by Congress. For day outliers, this rate is currently 60 percent of the average per diem rate for the specific DRG. Outlier payments cover about 5 percent of total per case reimbursement, and their importance will vary depending on the degree of complexity of the hospital's cases.

We can use the output-maximizing model to predict the likely effects of implementing DRGs. The DRG system replaced the old inflationary cost-based (retrospective) reimbursement system used by Medicare. Furthermore, this system reimburses hospitals on a per case basis. The simple one-product, output-maximizing model predicts that, in order to maximize its output, a hospital will produce at minimum costs. Indeed, under the DRG system, the hospital is at risk for any expenses incurred above the given reimbursement rate for that particular DRG. Thus it will strive to economize, unlike a hospital reimbursed on a retrospective basis, which has an incentive to balloon its costs. The most notable prediction with regard to DRG-based funding is that the average length of stay will fall (Donaldson 1991; Donaldson and Magnussen 1992; Muller 1993). However, this prediction must be regarded as a partial view, because in order to assess patient care, we must know where the patient was discharged (home, nursing home, etc.). A reduction in quality of care is also consistent with an attempt to reduce services per case. The possibility of quality reductions due to premature discharging of patients and reductions in services has received a good deal of attention (Fitzgerald et al. 1987, 1988; Morrisey et al. 1988). However, it should be noted that, to the extent that services under the prior, cost-based system were excessive, a reduction in unnecessary services can also raise the quality of care (Lave 1989).

Overall, the model predicts a tendency for hospitals to try to increase the number of admissions. Recognizing this, Medicare regulations make provision for professional review of admissions to determine necessity of care. While the presence of a regulation will not change the incentive for hospitals to increase their caseload, it may place constraints on how they do it. At the individual DRG level, those cases with the highest rates relative to costs will be sought after by hospitals (e.g., surgical cases) (Omenn and Conrad 1984). How can hospitals influence their case mix? They appear to have a considerable amount of control over who is hospitalized, as indicated by large areawide variations in hospitalizations by type of case (Wennberg et al. 1984). If specialists and facilities in a region are more readily available than elsewhere, patients under the care of these specialists are hospitalized at a higher rate. By expanding in certain areas (e.g., ophthalmology) and "recruiting" physicians, hospitals can encourage a greater supply in these areas (Goldfarb et al. 1980). In many cases hospitals have the discretion to "upcode" their case mix measures by reassigning diagnoses so that those with higher weights appear as the primary diagnoses. Also, hospitals can be more thorough in recording secondary or additional diagnoses, thus increasing the likelihood that cases will fall into DRG categories with higher weights.

The Medicare payment system is, of course, a system only for Medicare patients. Not being an all-payer system, there may be additional responses to the PPS rate level and structure by the hospital itself; that is, these rates may affect hospital policies with regard to non-Medicare patients. With low Medicare rates, hospitals may shift services toward non-Medicare patients, or they may shift costs to these patients.

DRGs also have systemwide ramifications. Shorter lengths of stay may not mean lower systemwide costs. If nursing home and home care product lines are financially viable, an output-maximizing hospital can expand into these areas and accept its own discharged patients. Since each form of care is separately reimbursed for, increased output in these other forms of care may be encouraged. Additionally, the reimbursement rate covers only the inpatient portion of care. The hospital could provide certain services that have traditionally been included in the inpatient portion of the stay, such as lab tests, on an outpatient (preadmission) basis, thereby garnering additional reimbursement for these services.

Finally, DRGs are not as clean cut as one would like in a case-mix measure. A number of studies have shown substantial within-group variation in case severity and resource use (Horn and Sharkey 1983). For example, some hospitals might include cases of greater severity in certain DRGs than other hospitals; the system would not reward them for doing this. This has led some commentators to predict that some hospitals might try to avoid more costly cases (e.g., by eliminating specific services). While attempts are being made to modify DRGs for severity, the DRG system as it stands is already quite complex. Additional modifications would increase the complexity, something the administrators of the system would like to avoid.

The Medicare Prospective Payment System (PPS) is overseen by a government commission called the Prospective Payment Assessment Commission. This commission, which is based in Washington, D.C., conducts studies focused on the system and recommends changes in such factors as the payment rate, DRG weights, and outlier policy. It issues a report annually to the Secretary of the Department of Health and Human Services, which is responsible for the Medicare system.

6.7.6 Nursing Home Reimbursement

Because there is such wide variability in nursing home lengths of stay, it is not feasible to reimburse nursing homes on a per case basis. They are therefore funded on a per diem basis. Medicaid state agencies, being the largest third party payers of nursing homes, have traditionally paid nursing homes in two different ways: with a flat per diem (per day) rate or with a facility-specific rate. Facility-specific rates are largely retrospective and consequently result in high costs. In flat rate reimbursement, a single rate is paid to all nursing homes regardless of patient characteristics, quality levels, and so on. Often a separate rate will be paid by level of facility—SNF or ICF. One virtue of the flat rate is that, at least in the case of for-profit nursing homes, facilities have an incentive to maximize profits and minimize costs. This may lead to some problems, however. Nursing homes might seek to attract patients who are healthier or who need less care (and hence cost less to treat), or they might compromise on quality (which would also lower costs and increase profits). As long as nursing homes seek profits to some degree (they might also have other objectives), they will tend to lower costs when such a payment mechanism is in place. It is primarily to balance the incentive to select patients with fewer needs that case mix measures have been introduced (Schlenker 1986). The primary purpose of case mix reimbursement in long-term care is to relate reimbursement rates to required levels of care and help ensure patients receive appropriate care.

One case mix measure that has been developed is called *Resource Utilization Groups* (RUGs) (Fries and Cooney 1985). This measure has now been superseded by RUGs II (Micheletti and Shala 1986) and RUGs III (Fries et al. 1994). The RUGs case mix measure is based on a set of five hierarchical groups related to levels and types of services (rehabilitation, extensive services, special care, clinically complex cases, impaired cognition, behavioral problems, and reduced physical functioning) and, within these hierarchical groups, scores on the activities of daily living (ADL) scale. The ADL scale assigns numerical scores according to the degree of physical functioning an individual can attain in each of six categories: bathing, dressing, toileting, feeding, transferring between locations, and continence (Katz et al. 1963). RUGs III uses four of these categories: eating, transferring, bed mobility, and toileting. Based on the points assigned to each of these, in combination with the six hierarchical groups, the patient is assigned to 1 of 44 RUGs III categories. The categories are assigned weights according to their relative costs (see, e.g., Schlenker et al. 1985), and reimbursement is made in accordance with these relative weights.

Such a system overcomes the first disadvantage mentioned above—that case mix selection creates a bias in favor of light-care patients. Indeed, if the weights of each category are in line with the relative costs of treating patients, then the selection bias should be removed. This does not mean that other selection biases do not exist. Indeed, three other types of biases that result from a RUGs type of payment system have been identified (Butler and Schlenker 1989). The first of these is a bias against patient rehabilitation. If a patient improves, he or she moves into another payment category and the nursing home loses revenue. Particularly if the case mix reimbursement system is oriented toward patient condition rather than services, the nursing home will incur higher costs by rehabilitating patients. An incentive not to rehabilitate would therefore be present (Smits 1984). To counteract this, a reimbursement program might pay nursing homes on the basis of outcomes or to pay at the higher reimbursement level for a limited period even when the patient improves. A second bias in such a system involves the provision of unnecessary care. If the reimbursement system pays more for certain services (e.g., rehabilitation), then this might give the nursing home an incentive to provide such services, sometimes unnecessarily. As for the third bias, the nursing home has a motive to misreport patient status, thus acquiring a higher reimbursement rate.

The best way to eliminate these biases may be to adopt regulations and institute a monitoring system. New York state, which adopted the RUGs II system, had a regulatory system to monitor the quality of care in nursing homes (Micheletti and Shlala 1986). Such a monitoring system was developed because the reimbursement system was not sufficient to achieve all of the public policy goals of the nursing home system.

6.7.7 Health Maintenance Organizations

The major characteristics of a HMO from a supply standpoint are that it is responsible, simultaneously, for two types of two services—health insurance and health care. Health insurance coverage is sold to customers on a per capita basis. The medical care itself is provided, or contracted for, by the HMO directly. The HMO assumes all the financial risk for providing this care. At the same time, its physicians act as "gatekeepers" and therefore have some degree of control over the patients' utilization of care.

In discussing the supply incentives inherent in such an organization, we must recognize that an HMO can make a number of different types of arrangements with the physicians that it contracts with and the hospitals to which it sends its patients.

The per capita funding formula provides an incentive for any for-profit HMO to minimize costs (all other factors being held constant). A HMO can reduce its costs by lowering the use of services by existing patients, encouraging the enrollment of members who are at low risk, and disenrolling high-risk patients. Lower cost enrollees would include younger members, nonsmokers, individuals who exercise, and so on. In order to encourage healthy enrollees to select it, the HMO can design a product with this end in mind. It might, for example, have more pediatricians and fewer gerontologists on staff, specialize in sports medicine, and open more branches in the suburbs and few or no branches in the inner city (Enthoven 1988; Hellinger 1995; Luft 1986). Indeed, the likelihood of a HMO's encouraging self-selection and thus having an enrollee mix that does not reflect the demographics of the general population has resulted in the development of adjustment formulas to compensate for potential differences in enrollee risk and the cost of utilization (Anderson et al. 1986). These formulas are used to calculate higher payment rates for higher risk individuals, thus inducing HMOs to enroll these individuals.

One such adjustment formula, Medicare's average adjusted per capita cost (AAPCC) formula, is used to determine the rates at which Medicare pays HMOs. The rates are based on Medicare's own current payment rates for hospital and physician services in the fee-for-service system. Separate AAPCCs are calculated for separate groups of patients (factors used in constructing the groups include sex, age bracket, county, welfare status, and institutionalization). For example, the monthly AAPCC for noninstitutionalized females aged 70–74 who were not on welfare in Washington County, Oregon, was $62 for hospital services and $30 for medical services. The Medicare rate to be paid to the HMOs for these individuals would be 95 percent of the AAPCC of $92. The rationale behind this payment rate is that, for those individuals who do shift from fee-for-service coverage to HMO coverage, Medicare will save 5 percent of its average cost. The HMO would benefit if it could provide coverage at a cost lower than this.

One criticism of this payment system is that it does not pinpoint risk categories accurately enough and HMO cream skimming is still a distinct possibility even with the AAPCC adjustments. For example, the AAPCC does not take into account the amount of prior health services used, which is a good indicator of future utilization of services. If an HMO could use this information to supply a product with characteristics that appeal to low-risk individuals, then it could obtain a large share of low-cost users even allowing for AAPCC adjustments. The result could be costly to Medicare, whose 95 percent rule was designed to achieve savings for the program.

Assume that there are 100 individuals in Washington County who are enrolled in Medicare and who have the characteristics specified above (70–74 years old, female, noninstitutionalized, nonwelfare). If they were in the fee-for-service program, Medicare would pay on average $92.00 a month for each. For each such individual attracted by an HMO, the HMO will receive 95 percent of the AAPCC, or $87.40 monthly. If the HMO is successful, through careful design of product characteristics, in drawing 10 very healthy, low-risk females from this group of 100, its average costs for these members will likely be below the $87.40 rate. The total cost to Medicare will be $87.40 times 10. The fee-for-service sector will now be left with a higher cost pool, having lost 10 lower-than-average-cost members, and its costs will rise. It is thus possible that this payment scheme could end up costing Medicare more money.

The cause of this problem is an inappropriate choice of member characteristics. Medicare could experiment with other population characteristics (e.g., smoking habits, weight, etc.) to fine-tune the categories. Indeed, in recent years a number of studies have been undertaken that attempt to adjust the Medicare population and other populations for additional factors. Among the most promising adjustment factors are previous usage of health care and selected health status measures

(Giacomini et al. 1995). In addition, it has been suggested that payment methods might blend prospective with actual costs in order to reduce an HMO's risk, because traditional risk adjustment does not resolve a large portion of the variance in costs (Newhouse 1994).

6.7.8   Provider Supply under Managed Care

6.7.8.1 Agency Theory and Incentive Contracts

The quantity and quality of services that an HMO supplies to its members are determined to a large extent by the health care providers that the HMO contracts with. The HMO is reliant on these providers to assess the HMO members' conditions and to provide appropriate levels of care. The manner in which the HMO compensates these providers will affect their supply behavior.

The HMO management does not usually know its members' health status, nor what treatments are appropriate. The providers have the best information about these matters, and so there is an "information asymmetry" between the two groups. Consequently, it is possible for the providers to act strictly in their own interest. In order to encourage the providers to act in the interest of the HMO, the HMO management can design a compensation scheme for the providers. Models that examine such compensation schemes are called *agency models*. The two contracting bodies in such models are the *principals* (in this case, the HMOs) and their *agents* (in this case, the providers). We will set out such a model in this section to examine how alternative compensation schemes influence the supply behavior of providers.

The principal, or HMO, contracts with its members (on a per capita payment basis) to provide them with care.

- *HMO objectives.* We assume that the HMO's objectives are to maximize profits. However, we also assume that there is a minimum profit level that is acceptable to the HMO; in our example, this will be $500,000. Profits are equal to total revenue minus total cost.
- *HMO revenues.* The HMO's revenues depend on the capitation rate applied to its members and the number of members who join the HMO. In our model, we will hold the capitation rate constant.
- *HMO costs.* The HMO's costs include those that are incurred in treating the HMO members who become patients.
- *HMO/provider interaction.* In many respects, the HMO is dependent on its agents, the providers of care (doctors, physical therapists, hospitals, etc.), for the achievement of its profit targets. Providers can influence HMO profits by varying their levels of effort. If providers function at very low effort levels, patients will be dissatisfied with the heath care they receive and will switch to

other health plans. As a result, HMO profits will be low. As physician efforts increase, quality of care will improve and more members will join. However, additional physician effort means more lab tests, more procedures, and so on. While this will bring in more members to the HMO, it will also increase costs. Eventually, the additional effort will work against profitability, and profits will fall. Graph A of Figure 6–9 shows the relationship between the HMO's profits and the effort of the agents. At some effort level (E_3), profits

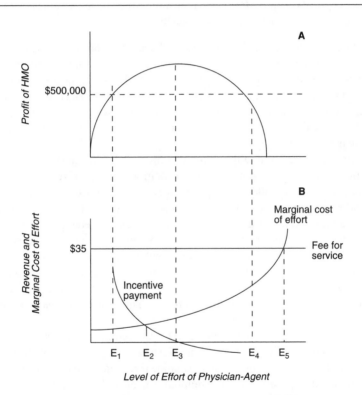

Level of Effort of Physician-Agent

Figure 6–9 Optimal compensation of health care providers by a HMO. Graph A, the top diagram, shows the relationship between the providers' average effort and the HMO's profits. The minimum acceptable profit level for the HMO is $500,000. Graph B indicates each physician's level of effort under alternative payment schemes. The marginal cost of additional effort is the same under all payment schemes. Under a straight salary payment scheme, the provider will supply the minimum level of effort acceptable to the HMO, E_1. Under a fee-for-service scheme, at the assumed wage of $35 the provider will supply up to E_5, but only E_4 is acceptable. Under a profit incentive arrangement, E_2 will be provided. This is slightly less than the HMO's maximum profit because the incentive scheme is not "perfect."

will be at a maximum level. At other effort levels (E_1 and E_4), profits will be at minimally acceptable levels.

HMO profits, then, are directly tied to the efforts of its contracting physicians. The physicians know how much effort they are providing and how much is required to treat their patients. The HMO cannot directly observe this effort. This is another way of saying that there is an information asymmetry between the principal and its agents. While the HMO cannot directly observe physician efforts, it can observe its profits. This performance indicator will come in useful when the HMO sets compensation policies for the physicians.

- *Physician objectives.* We turn now to the assumptions about the behavior of the physicians. The objective of each physician is to maximize net income (profits), which is equal to revenues from the HMO minus the personal costs of supplying care (or exerting effort). With a rising marginal cost curve for effort, the maximization point (which indicates what level of effort will be chosen by the physician) occurs where the marginal revenue equals the marginal cost for the physician.
- *Physician costs.* We will assume that all provider revenues come from the HMO (i.e., that each provider has no additional source of revenue). The relationship between alternative payment schemes that the HMO can institute and physician revenues will be discussed below. The physician costs in this model are the opportunity costs to the physician of engaging in productive practices. The physician places a value on his or her time, and this value is based on alternative uses of the time spent on care. We assume that the marginal cost to the physician of time spent on patient care increases as more time is spent. Put another way, as more time is taken away from leisure activities, the value of the last unit of time increases. This rising marginal cost curve of effort is shown in Graph B of Figure 6–9.
- *Physician revenues.* The proposition being established in this section is that the level of effort selected by the physician will be influenced by the basis and level of reimbursement. We will examine three alternative forms of compensation: salary, fee-for-service reimbursement, and incentive compensation based on the HMO's profits.

If the physician is paid a straight salary, any additional effort by the physician results in costs but yields no extra revenue. There is a minimum acceptable level of effort that the physician must put in—the level that corresponds to the minimum profit target of the HMO (level E_1). The physician will provide this level but no more.

We will now assume the physician is paid a fee of $35 per service. Extra effort on the part of the physician will result in extra services provided. These extra services result in marginal revenues of $35 per service (see the straight line at $35 in Figure 6–9). The physician would maximize net income at a level of effort of E_5. However, because the HMO's profits are below those that are acceptable to the HMO, the doctor will reduce his or her effort level to E_4. If the fee falls below $35, then the physician will choose an effort level below E_5. If the fee level increases, then the effort level will also increase. It is quite possible, therefore, to have a low effort level under fee-for-service reimbursement if the fee levels are low enough.

The HMO can set a contract that provides specific incentives. Recall that the HMO does not know how much effort is provided by the physician. The HMO only has a proxy for this—mainly HMO performance (in this case, HMO profits). The HMO can pay the physician a fixed percentage of HMO profits. The marginal revenue curve for the physician will appear like that in any demand situation—it will decline to a level of zero as profits increase to their maximum. However, in these circumstances the physician will not choose the level of effort that corresponds to maximum HMO profits but will choose instead level E_2, where the marginal revenue and marginal cost curves intersect. This will provide the HMO with lower than maximum profits but more profits than under a salary compensation scheme.

There are numerous other compensation schemes that can be selected, some of which are more complicated but may motivate the physician to supply an effort close to optimal level from the point of view of the HMO.

6.7.8.2 Management of Provider Behavior

In addition to setting contracts, insurers can engage in the direct management of provider supply behavior with the objective of influencing utilization patterns. The direct management of providers is an activity that is most closely associated with HMOs, because of their close association with physicians. However, in recent years the management of care has become widespread under all types of payment arrangements. Most of these practices have been focused on the use of inpatient care, primarily because of the expensiveness of this mode of care.

There are a number of different measures that insurers can use to influence providers' supply of hospital care (Scheffler et al. 1991). They include overall case management, preadmission management (e.g., second opinions and preadmission testing), concurrent management (e.g., concurrent review and discharge planning), and posthospital review (e.g., retrospective review and claims denials). Figure 6–10 indicates where the measures are applied. Each measure involves the setting of standards and the review of patients in accordance with these standards.

Many of the regulations set by HMOs carry financial penalties, such as nonpayment for a claim. For example, if a second opinion is required for surgery, payment might be denied if the surgeon operated without a confirming opinion. Prob-

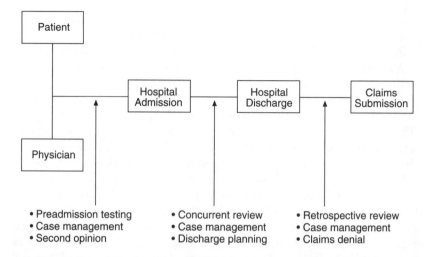

Figure 6–10 Techniques for managing provider behavior. Provider behavior can be regulated before, during, or after hospital admission. Prior to hospitalization, insurers can require providers to seek permission; during hospitalization, insurers can monitor length of stay; and following hospitalization, insurers can conduct reviews and deny claims.

ably for this reason, the private regulation of providers has been quite successful in containing utilization and costs. One study indicated savings of about 7 percent overall (Feldstein et al. 1988; Wickzier et al. 1989), although the savings will depend on the type of program and types of penalties imposed (Scheffler et al. 1991).

6.8   DEMAND FOR LABOR

6.8.1 Demand for Labor by the Individual Firm

In this section we develop an analysis of the demand for a specific resource by an individual provider. The provider could be a health care–producing entity, such as a hospital, laboratory, or physician's office, or it could be a non-health-care producer. We will focus on health care providers but the analysis can be applied to either type of institution. The dependent variable of interest is the demand for labor input. The input can be expressed in time units such as hours or days. The labor demand curve or function that we want to describe is defined as the quantity of labor units that a firm will demand at any given price or wage.

In economic terms, this demand is a derived demand. That is, the firm usually does not demand labor or any other input for itself. Rather, an input is demanded because of the revenue or output it can generate for the firm. In short, the value of an input is derived from the usefulness of the input in achieving some objective. In traditional economic analysis, this objective is profits. While health care firms may indeed have other objectives than profits, the profit maximization hypothesis is a good one to stay with in analyzing the demand for labor and other inputs.

To help with the analysis, we will use the example of a commercial laboratory that provides blood tests. The time frame for our analysis will be a single day. We define the firm's product (or output) as the number of blood tests produced per day. The firm has a series of inputs, which include capital equipment, materials and supplies, fixed management time, and variable labor time. Indeed, labor units, in the form of lab technician time, are assumed to be the only variable input (although in reality reagents will vary with the number of blood tests).

- *Production function.* With inputs and outputs defined, we hypothesize the relationship between them (the production function). Table 6–4 specifies the relationship for the range of variable inputs from one to seven lab technician days. With one lab technician, the lab can produce 50 blood tests; with two lab technicians, it can produce 110 tests; and so on. This relationship at first exhibits increasing marginal productivity, followed by decreasing marginal productivity (the third technician produces 50 extra tests, the fourth produces 40, and so on).
- *Revenue derived from worker production.* The firm's valuation of technician time rests, not on the number of lab tests per se, but on the revenue derived from these lab tests. We make the assumption that each lab test has a fixed price of $3. Therefore, for each extra lab test produced, the firm brings in $3 in extra revenue. The total revenue from all lab tests at each level of input is shown in the fourth column of Table 6–4 (one technician brings in $150 in revenues, two bring in $330, etc.). The fifth column shows the *marginal value product* (*MVP*) obtained when the firm adds successive technicians. The *MVP* is defined as the additional revenue obtained from hiring one more unit of input. As with the marginal productivity, this variable at first increases but then decreases. (The first technician has an *MVP* of $150, the second has an *MVP* of $180, and the MVP of the third is back down to $150). The MVP curve is shown in Figure 6–11.
- *Labor.* The *MVP* is the additional revenue each additional worker yields. We require two additional assumptions to derive a prediction about the demand for labor. The first concerns the cost to the firm of labor units. We make the assumption that each lab technician earns $80 per week. Since each lab technician earns the same amount, the marginal cost of the input is $80.
- *Firm's objectives.* The firm is assumed to have a goal of profit maximization. Profits, as we have defined them, are equal to revenue minus cost. The point

Table 6—4 The Demand for Labor by a Commercial Lab

Number of Lab Technicians	Number of Lab Tests (total product)	Additional Tests per Technician (marginal product)	Total Revenue From All Units of Production (price of product x number of units)	Additional Revenue from Addition of One Lab Technician (marginal value product)	Wage Rate
1	50	50	$150	$150	$80
2	110	60	330	180	80
3	160	50	480	150	80
4	200	40	600	120	80
5	230	30	690	90	80
6	250	20	750	60	80
7	260	10	780	30	80

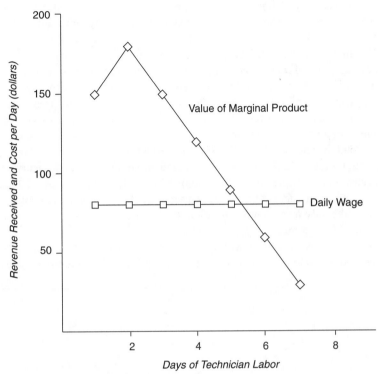

Figure 6–11 Demand Curve for Labor. The demand curve for labor is based on the additional revenue generated by each additional labor unit (days of technician labor), called the value of the marginal product (VMP). Provider profitability is determined by comparing the VMP with the price paid for labor.

at which maximum profits are attained occurs when the revenue gained from adding an additional worker equals the additional cost.

The conclusions of our model are as follows. On profitability grounds, the firm would hire the first worker, as the marginal revenue ($150) exceeds marginal cost ($80). Indeed, the firm would continue to hire workers as long as it was profitable to do so. In our example, the firm would hire up to five workers for reasons of profitability. It would reduce its profits by hiring a sixth worker. Given the assumptions in our model, the firm's demand for labor is equal to five workers.

The demand curve was defined as the quantity of inputs a firm demands at a specific price. If the price of a unit of input changes, so will the quantity demanded. For example, a fall in the wage rate paid by the firm to $50 will increase the quantity of labor demanded to six units. And an increase in the wage rate will reduce the quantity of labor demanded. The quantity demanded will be traced out by the MVP curve, as this curve shows what the additional revenue will be for any given wage rate. Therefore, the MVP curve is the demand curve for the input.

The demand curve will shift outward if labor becomes more productive (yielding more output and revenue) or output prices increase. Labor can become more productive if the firm increases its degree of mechanization. For example, if the firm buys more capital equipment, each worker will be able to produce more. Also, if the price per lab test increases, then each worker will also yield more revenue (though not more output).

To extend the analysis, let us introduce the effects of benefits as a form of compensation. Figure 6–12 shows a firm's demand curve for labor at alternative daily wage rates. For example, at a wage rate of $40, the firm will demand 200 labor days. The demand curve for this rate (curve D_n) is based on the assumption that wages are the only form of compensation; that is, the firm does not offer benefits such as health insurance.

Suppose, however, the firm agrees to provide $10 worth of fringe benefits per day. This adds $10 to the total labor compensation for each worker, but it does not

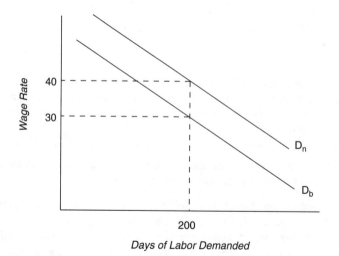

Figure 6–12 The effect of fringe benefits on the demand for labor. Curve D_n shows the demand for labor when the firm does not pay benefits. At a wage rate of $40 per day, the firm demands 200 labor days. In this case, the total wage is the same as total compensation. If health insurance benefits worth $10 per day are instituted, the demand curve relating the wage rate to the quantity of labor will fall by $10 at every quantity. This is because the firm, although still demanding 200 units at an average compensation cost of $40, is now providing each worker only $30 in wages as part of its $40 compensation package.

add anything to the value of the output (the marginal value product). Therefore, the firm will still only be willing to pay $40 in total compensation for the 200th labor day—$30 in wages and $10 in fringe benefits. Thus, under the new benefits agreement, the firm would be willing to hire 200 workers at a wage rate of $30 rather than $40 ($30 in wages plus $10 in benefits is equivalent to $40 in wages with no benefits), and there is a new demand curve for labor. This curve, D_b, is the curve D_n shifted downward by exactly $10 at every quantity of labor. Any further increase in benefits would shift the demand curve down further. Furthermore, D_b, like the original demand curve, will shift in response to factors such as the price of output and the productivity of labor.

We will now introduce taxes on corporate profits as a complicating factor. Let us say that the firm pays a 10-percent profits tax. If an extra worker brings in $120 in revenues and costs the firm $100, then the before-tax profits will be $20 and the after-tax profits will be $18 ($20 × (1 − .10)). If both wages and insurance premiums were deductible expenses, then it would not matter to the firm whether it paid out its compensation in the form of wages or insurance benefits. Under current tax law, insurance premiums are not taxed as employee income. Thus this form of compensation is preferred by the employee. This explains, in part, why benefits are so popular a form of compensation.

6.8.2 Market Demand for Labor

The market demand for labor or other inputs can be derived in the same way as other types of market demand. Assume we know the number of firm's demanding labor in a certain market and the demand curve for each. We can then add together the quantities demanded for labor at each wage rate to derive a market demand curve for labor. We retain the supposition that the price of the service or product is fixed. Often, if firms expand output, the price of the output will fall. Bringing in this phenomenon would complicate our analysis. The market demand for labor (or other inputs) is thus a downward-sloping demand curve that shifts with changes in variables such as the number of firms demanding labor and the productivity of each worker.

6.9 SUPPLY OF HEALTH INSURANCE

6.9.1 Supply Model

The economic behavior of insurers is a topic that has received a great deal of interest in recent years. The product of insurers is the assumption of risks initially borne by consumers, including the risk of heavy medical costs.

An insurer has the choice of accepting or not accepting risks on behalf of consumers, and there are a number of factors that will induce any insurer not to accept certain risks. Our model must take into account this fact. It also must take into account the fact that the owners of the insurance companies (the shareholders) are ordinary consumers and householders and that they react to risk like everyone else.

The assumptions of our supplier model are as follows.

6.9.1.1. Risk Function and Losses

There is a small group of 1,000 individuals who are seeking insurance coverage for medical expenses. They all face the same set of risks, which can be summarized by a risk function. We will suppose there are three possible states of health, all of which carry a price tag. The risk function can be expressed as follows: each person has a 1/4 probability (a one in four chance) of incurring a $600 loss due to medical expenses, a 1/2 probability of incurring a $700 loss, and a 1/4 probability of incurring a $800 loss.

Two summary statistics can be used to describe the risk function for an individual and for a group of individuals: the mean (μ) loss and the variance. The mean loss is the expected loss weighted for the probability of each loss occurring. For each individual, the expected loss is $700. However, because we are dealing in probabilities, in any given round of insuring, the actual value of losses the insurer experiences may vary, sometimes considerably.

The variance is an expression of the degree of dispersion of the mean value of losses experienced by a group of insureds in a given time period. The variance is expressed as

$$\frac{\Sigma(X-\mu)^2}{N}$$

where X is each individual observation, μ is the mean loss, Σ is the sign for summation, and N is the number of individuals. Insurers estimate the variance based on the loss experience of insureds in previous periods. If these losses are evenly distributed on each side of a true mean value (called *normally distributed*), then the expression above can be used to estimate the percentage of times that the mean value of losses (for the entire insured group) will fall within a certain range. The actual expression used is the square root of this function and is called the *standard deviation*. In a normally distributed population, the sample mean will fall within one standard deviation of either side of the true mean 68 percent of the time, within two standard deviations 95 percent of the time, and within three standard deviations 99 percent of the time.

For insurance purposes, the important thing to note is that in the equation

$$\sqrt{[(\Sigma(X-\mu)^2)/N]},$$

which is used to analyze the loss experience of a group of insureds, N represents the size of the group that is insured. As we add additional insureds (increasing N) who have the same expected experience, the standard deviation will fall. This means that the insurer is less likely to experience a loss for the insured group that is above the true mean of the group. In other words, the insurer's risk of large losses, which is measured by the variance, is reduced as the size of the insurance pool increases.

In our simple example, we assume that the probability of a loss of $600 or $800 is 1/4. If the size of the insured group increased, say, to 10,000, the risk function would be narrower around the mean. The probability of a loss of $600 or $800 might then be 3/16. There would still be some probability of a large total loss during any given time period, but as the insured group increases in size, the risk of this happening declines.

6.9.1.2. Insurer's Tastes and Objectives

The insurer is in business to earn profits for its shareholders and in fact is a utility-maximizing entity. Its tastes reflect those of its shareholders. We assume that this group of shareholders is risk averse and that increases in wealth have for the group diminishing marginal utility. The insurance company's utility function is shown in Table 6–5. Note that the insurer's wealth (and hence utility) depends on the revenues collected by the insurer and on the insurer's costs, including its payout. Uncertainty enters the model through the risk function.

The insurer has an initial fund of $200,000. This is called a contingency reserve. Since an insurer faces some risks itself when it takes over the risks of the insureds, it needs to have some backup capital in case it incurs losses.

6.9.1.3. Insurer Revenues or Premiums

The insurer's revenues are the premiums it receives from the insureds. There are two basic ways in which premiums can be set: through experience rating or through community rating. *Experience rating* involves the setting of premiums for individuals or groups according to their risk of loss. Healthy, low-risk individuals

---

Table 6–5 Utility Function of the Insurer

Wealth (thousands of dollars)	Utility
0	0
100	40
200	70
300	90
400	100

will be charged lower premiums than unhealthy, high-risk individuals. In *community rating*, a single rate is set for the entire insured population based on the average experience of that population. High-risk individuals and low-risk individuals all pay the same rate regardless of their expected loss.

We will initially assume that the insurer sets its premiums using experience rating and that the insurer receives a premium of $800 per enrollee, or $800,000 in total. Each individual pays the same rate because all individuals have the same risks of loss (according to our assumptions).

6.9.1.4. Insurer Costs

The calculation of expected costs involves two components: a probability function of losses and the insurer's administrative expenses (see Table 6–6). The administrative expenses are incurred in the selling of insurance policies and the administration of claims. We will initially assume that these are fixed according to the number of insureds, not their loss experience. For the 1,000 insureds, we will assume that administrative expenses are $100,000. We will later assume that the marginal cost curve associated with adding additional insureds is upward sloping. This assumption is for convenience's sake only, since there is some evidence it is not realistic.

6.9.1.5. Losses from Medical Care

In our example, there are three possible scenarios, each with an attached probability of occurrence. In the first scenario, the group incurs $600,000 in medical care expenses, which the insurer would have to pay if it accepted the risk. In the second scenario, the group incurs $700,000 in medical expenses, and in the third scenario, it incurs $800,000. As shown in Table 6–6, the probabilities associated with the three scenarios are 1/4, 1/2, and 1/4, respectively (i.e., there is a 25 percent chance of the group incurring $600,000 in expenses, etc.).

The losses in our analysis are determined by the price of medical care and the quantity of medical care consumed by the insureds. Both of these are assumed to be related strictly to the level of health of the individuals. This is a convenient assumption, and it makes our model much more manageable. However, this assumption covers up a wealth of events that lie at the core of health insurance.

Table 6–6 Basic Insurance Supply Data

Premium (thousands)	Probability of Loss	Amount of Loss (thousands)	Administrative Costs (thousands)	Net Effect on Reserves (thousands)	Postoperating Reserves (thousands)
$800	1/4	$600	$100	$100	$300
800	1/2	700	100	0	200
800	1/4	800	100	−100	100

Insurers play a very active role in setting the price of medical care; sophisticated bargaining arrangements (many covered in subsequent chapters) exist under ordinary insurance arrangements as well as under preferred provider and managed care arrangements. The reader should keep these in mind when using the current model. Second, utilization of care is also subject to a host of forces, including the famous moral hazard phenomenon and direct insurer-provider relationships under managed care. The reader should also keep these in mind when using the model.

6.9.2 Predictions of the Supply Model

Having specified the assumptions of the model, we now turn to the model's conclusions. First, since the insurer is a utility maximizer, we need to compare the expected utility of accepting the risk with that of not accepting it. If the company does not accept the risk, it will be left with its wealth of $200,000 and a utility level of 80. If it does accept the risk, at the premium rate of $800 three levels of wealth are possible (see Table 6–6). Associated with each of these levels is a probability and a utility level. For example, there is a 1/4 chance of earning $100,000 on the contract, thus having $300 in post contract reserves, and a utility level of 100. In total, the expected utility at that given price is 70 ($(1/4 \times 100) + (1/2 \times 70) + (1/4 \times 40)$). This is less than the 80 units of utility obtained if the insurer refused to accept the risk. Therefore, the insurer will not accept the risk (i.e., it will choose not to be a supplier of insurance to this group).

Let us now see what the effect will be of an increase in premium rates. If the premium rate was $900, then the postcontract levels of wealth for the three scenarios would be $400,000, $300,000, and $100,000, and the expected utility would be 87.5 ($(1/4 \times 100) + (1/2 \times 90) + (1/4 \times 70)$). This is greater than the expected utility of not accepting the risk, and so the insurer would supply insurance coverage at that premium rate. Our first conclusion, then, is that the willingness to supply insurance (accept risks) is greater when the premium rate is greater.

We can also draw conclusions about the effect of changes in other variables on the supply schedule of the insurer. Increases in the supply schedule (more risks accepted at a given premium rate) will be induced by the following: a less risk averse utility function on the part of the insurer, a greater initial level of reserves, a reduction in administrative costs, and a drop in the losses experienced by the insureds. In addition, there are some elements of our analysis that need to be elaborated on.

First, we initially assumed that experience rating was the method used to set rates but that all consumers had the same risk function. If all consumers do not have the same risk function, the analysis becomes more complex. Let us now assume that there are two groups, one high risk and the other low risk. With experience rating, a premium would be set that reflected each group's loss experience. The insurer would then have to decide for each group whether to supply insurance, a decision that would be based on the premium rate, marginal costs, and so on, for that particular group.

Use of community rating would create a different situation. Again, there would be two groups, each with its own marginal costs. But now there would be a single premium rate, which would fall somewhere between those of the high-risk and low-risk groups. The for-profit insurer in our example would develop criteria to distinguish between high-risk and low-risk individuals and would refuse to insure the latter (i.e., it would engage in so-called preferred risk selection). In fact, community rating began and evolved as a method in the nonprofit sector, where firms follow different objectives. A nonprofit firm may have as an objective increasing the availability of insurance coverage for higher risk groups. If it did have this objective, its behavior would differ from the behavior of a for-profit firm.

Additionally, we saw in Chapter 5 that there are economies of scale in the administration of health insurance. Therefore, at any given premium level, there is a greater likelihood that larger insurers will be able to profitably accept risks than smaller ones. There is an economic advantage to being large because of the economies of scale.

Second, insurers can lower their costs (and increase their profits) by reducing the insureds' utilization of insured health care services and by lowering the amounts they reimburse the providers of care. Indemnity insurers have developed a number of utilization-reducing instruments, including preadmission review and rules requiring second opinions for surgery. Indeed, HMOs were developed as a means of controlling the intensity of medical care provided to patients. However, even indemnity insurers have become active in the managed care arena and have resorted to utilization-reducing mechanisms.

Third, whereas previously insurers had played a passive role in the setting of prices, they have become increasingly active in contracting with providers and pushing for favorable terms. For example, in a preferred provider arrangement, insurers seek specified prices from providers. Insurers have sought to gain a market advantage over providers so they can either pass the lower prices on to consumers or else can capture the gains for themselves.

Finally, if insurers are risk averse, they will benefit from the reduction in risk that results from having a larger insurance pool. As the pool increases, the variance falls and the percentage of high- and low-value losses falls. Insurers in particular benefit from the lower number of large losses, and they have a strong incentive to increase the size of the risk pool.

BIBLIOGRAPHY

Resource Availability and Supply

Goldfarb, M., et al. 1980. Behavior of the multi-product firm. *Medical Care* 19:185–201.

Hornbrook, M., and Goldfarb, M. 1983. A partial test of a hospital behavior model. *Social Science and Medicine* 17:667–680.

Nonprofit Organization Behavior

Culyer, A.J. 1971. Medical care and the economics of giving. *Economica* 38:295–303.

Harris, J.F. 1977. The internal organization of hospitals. *Bell Journal of Economics* 8:647–682.

Lee, M.L. 1971. A conspicuous production theory of hospital behavior. *Southern Economic Journal* 38:48–58.

McGuire, A. 1985. The theory of the hospital: a review of the models. *Social Science and Medicine* 20:1177–1184.

Pauly, M., and Redisch, M. 1973. The not-for-profit hospital as a physicians' cooperative. *American Economic Review* 63:87–100.

Per Capita Reimbursement

Anderson, G.F., and Knickman, J. 1984. Adverse selection under a voucher system: grouping Medicare recipients by level of expenditure. *Inquiry* 21:135–143.

Anderson, G., et al. 1986. Paying for HMO care: issues and options in setting capitation rates. *Milbank Quarterly* 64:548–565.

Anderson, G.F., et al. 1990. Setting payment rates for capitated systems: a comparison of various alternatives. *Inquiry* 27:225–233.

Beebe, J.A. 1992. Outlier pools for Medicare HMO payments. *Health Care Financing Review* 14:59–63.

Ellwood, P. 1972. Models for organizing health services and implications for legislative proposals. *Milbank Quarterly* 50:73–100.

Enthoven, A. 1988. *Theory and practice of managed competition in health care finance*. Amsterdam, The Netherlands: North-Holland.

Giacomini, M., et al. 1995. Risk adjusting community rated health plan premiums. *Annual Review of Public Health* 16:401–430.

Hellinger, F.J. 1995. Selection bias in HMOs and PPOs: a review of the evidence. *Inquiry* 32:135–142.

Hornbrook, M.C. 1984. Examination of the AAPCC methodology in an HMO prospective payment demonstration experiment. *Group Health Journal* 5(Spring):13–21.

Hornbrook, M.C., and Berki, S.E. 1985. Practice mode and payment method. *Medical Care* 23:484–511.

Hornbrook, M.C., and Goodman, M.J. 1991. Health plan case mix: definition, measurement, use. *Advances in Health Economics and Health Services Research* 12:111–148.

———. 1995. Assessing relative health plan risk with the RAND-36 Health Survey. *Inquiry* 32:56–74.

Klarman, H.E. 1963. The effect of prepaid group practice on hospital use. *Public Health Reports* 78:955–965.

Luft, H.S. 1978a. How do health-maintenance organizations achieve their "savings?" *New England Journal of Medicine* 298:1336–1343.

———. 1978b. Why do HMOs seem to provide more health maintenance services? *Milbank Quarterly* 56:140–168.

———. 1981. *Health maintenance organizations*. New York: John Wiley.

———. 1986. Compensating for biased selction in health insurance. *Milbank Quarterly* 64:566–591.

———. 1995. Potential methods to reduce risk selection and its effects. *Inquiry* 32:23–32.

Manton, K.G., and Stallard, E. 1992. Analysis of underwriting factor for AAPCC. *Health Care Financing Review* 14:117–132.

Newhouse, J.P., et al. Adjusting capitation rates using objective health measures and prior utilization. *Health Care Financing Review* 10:41–54.

van de Ven, W.P.M.M., et al. 1994. Risk adjusted capitation. *Health Affairs* 13:120–126.

Reimbursement and Supply: Physicians

Aaron, H., and Schwartz, W.B. 1984. *The painful prescription.* Washington, D.C.: Brookings Institution.

Burney, I.L., et al. 1978. Geographic variation in physicians' fees. *JAMA* 240:1368–1371.

Eisenberg, J.M., and Williams, S.V. 1981. Cost containment and changing physicians' practice behavior. *JAMA* 246:2195–2201.

Epstein, A.M., and Blumenthal, D. 1993. Physician payment reform: past and future. *Milbank Quarterly* 71:193–215.

Feldstein, M. 1970. The rising price of physicians' services. *Review of Economics and Statistics* 52:121–133.

Gabel, J.R., and Redisch, M.A. 1979. Alternative physician payment mechanisms. *Milbank Quarterly* 57:38–59.

Havighurst, C.C., and Kissam, P. 1979. The antitrust implications of relative value studies in medicine. *Journal of Health Politics, Policy and Law* 4:48.

Hemenway, D., et al. 1990. Physicians' responses to financial incentives. *New England Journal of Medicine* 322:1059–1063.

Holahan, J. 1989. The potential effects of an RBRVS-based payment system on health care costs and hospitals. *Frontiers of Health Services Management* 6:3–37.

Hornbrook, M.C. 1983. Allocative medicine: efficiency, disease severity and the payment mechanism. *Annals of the AAPSS* 468:12–29.

Hsiao, W.C., and Stason, W.B. 1979. Toward developing a relative value scale for medical and surgical services. *Health Care Financing Review* 1:23–39.

Hsiao, W.C., et al. 1987. The resource based relative value scale. *JAMA* 258:799–802.

Hsiao, W.C., et al. 1988a. Results and policy implications of the resource based relative value study. *New England Journal of Medicine* 319:881–888.

Hsiao, W.C., et al. 1988b. Resource based relative values: an overview. *JAMA* 260:2347–2353.

Hsiao, W.C., et al. 1988c. Estimating physicians' work for a resource based relative value scale. *New England Journal of Medicine* 319:835–841.

Levy, J.M., et al. 1990. Impact of the Medicare fee schedule on payments to physicians. *JAMA* 264:717–722.

Lowenstein, S.R., et al. 1985. Prospective payment for physician services. *JAMA* 254:2632–2637.

Mitchell, J.B. 1985. Physician DRG's. *New England Journal of Medicine* 313:670–675.

Monsma, G. 1970. Marginal revenue and the demand for physicians' services. In *Empirical studies in health economics,* ed. H.F. Klarman. Baltimore: Johns Hopkins University Press.

Moore, S. 1979. Cost containment through risk sharing of primary-care physicians. *New England Journal of Medicine* 300:1359–1362.

Myers, L.P., and Schroeder, S.A. 1981. Physician use of services for the hospitalized patient. *Milbank Quarterly* 59:481–507.

Phelps, C.E. 1976. Public sector medicine. In *New directions in public health care*, ed. C.M. Lindsay. San Francisco: Institute for Contemporary Studies.

Schreiber, G.I., et al. 1976. Physician fee patterns under Medicare: a descriptive analysis. *New England Journal of Medicine* 294:1089–1093.

Showstack, J.A., et al. Fee-for-service payment: analysis of current methods and their development. *Inquiry* 16:230–246.

Sisk, J., et al. 1987. Analysis of methods to reform Medicare payment for physician services. *Inquiry* 24:36–47.

Sloan, F.A. 1975. Physician supply behavior in the short run. *Industrial and Labor Relations Review* 28:549–569.

Sloan, F.A., and Hay, J.W. 1986. Medicare pricing mechanisms for physician services. *Medical Care Review* 43:59–100.

Stano, M., et al. 1983. Fee or use? What's responsible for rising health care costs? *Michigan Medicine* 82:228–234.

Wilensky, G.R., and Rossiter, L.F. 1986. Alternative units of payment for physician services. *Medical Care Review* 43:133–156.

Reimbursement and Supply: Nursing Homes

Adams, E.K., and Schlenker, R.E. 1986. Case-mix reimbursement for nursing home services. *Health Care Financing Review* 8:35–45.

Butler, P.A., and Schlenker, R.E. 1989. Case-mix reimbursement for nursing homes. *Milbank Quarterly* 67:103–136.

Fries, B.E., and Cooney, L.M. 1985. Resource utilization groups. *Medical Care* 23:110–122.

Fries, B.E., et al. 1994. Refining a case mix measure for nursing homes: resource utilization groups (RUG-III). *Medical Care* 32:668–685.

Holahan, J., and Cohen, J. 1987. Nursing home reimbursement. *Milbank Quarterly* 65:112–147.

Katz, S., et al. 1963. Studies of illness in the aged. *JAMA* 185:914–919.

Micheletti, J., and Shlala, T.J. 1986. RUGs II: implications for management and quality in long-term care. *Quality Review Bulletin* 12:236–242.

Rosko, M.D., et al. 1987. Prospective payment based on case-mix: will it work in nursing homes? *Journal of Health Politics, Policy and Law* 12:683–701.

Schlenker, R.E. 1986. Case mix reimbursement for nursing homes. *Journal of Health Politics, Policy and Law* 11:445–461.

Schlenker, R.E., et al. 1985. Estimating patient level nursing home costs. *Health Services Research* 20:103–128.

Smits, H.L. 1984. Incentives in case-mix measures for long-term care. *Health Care Financing Review* 6:53–59.

Reimbursement and Supply: Hospitals

Bauer, K. 1977. Hospital rate setting—this way to salvation? *Milbank Quarterly* 55:117–118.

Berry, R.E. 1976. Prospective reimbursement and cost containment. *Inquiry* 13:288–301.

Dowling, W.L. 1974. Prospective reimbursement of hospitals. *Inquiry* 11:163–180.

Eby, C.L., and Cohodes, D.R. 1985. What do we know about rate setting. *Journal of Health Politics, Policy and Law* 10:299–323.

Foster, R.W. 1982. Cost-based reimbursement and prospective payment: reassessing the incentives. *Journal of Health Politics, Policy and Law* 7:407–420.

Horn, S.D., and Sharkey, P.D. 1983. Measuring severity of illness to predict patient resource use within DRGs. *Inquiry* 20:314–321.

Hornbrook, M. 1982. Hospital case mix: its definition, measurement, and use. Parts 1 and 2. *Medical Care Review* 39:1–43, 73–123.

Zuckerman, S., et al. 1984. Physician practice patterns under hospital rate-setting programs. *JAMA* 252:2589–2592.

Diagnosis-Related Groups and Case Mix

Anderson, G., and Ginsburg, P.B. 1983. Prospective capital payment to hospitals. *Health Affairs* 2: 52–63.

Aronow, D. 1988. Severity of illness measurement. *Medical Care Review* 45:339–366.

Broyles, W.W., and Rosko, M.D. 1985. A qualitative assessment of the Medicare prospective payment system. *Social Science and Medicine* 20:1185–1190.

Carter, G.M., et al. 1994. Use of diagnosis-related groups by non–Medicare payers. *Health Care Financing Review* 16:127–158.

Conrad, D.A. 1984. Returns on equity to not-for-profit hospitals. *Health Services Research* 19:41–63.

Donaldson, C. 1991. Minding our Ps and Qs: financial incentives for efficient hospital behavior. *Health Policy* 17:51–76.

Donaldson, C., and Magnusson, J. 1992. DRGs: The road to hospital efficiency. *Health Policy* 21: 47–64.

Ellis, R.P., and McGuire, T.G. 1986. Provider behavior under prospective reimbursement. *Journal of Health Economics* 5:129–151.

———. 1988. Insurance Principles and the Design of Prospective Payment Systems. *Journal of Health Economics* 7:215–237.

Ellis, R.P., and Ruhm, C.J. 1988. Incentives to transfer patients under alternative reimbursement mechanisms. *Journal of Public Economics* 37:381–394.

Fetter, R.B., et al. 1980. Case mix definition by diagnosis-related groups. *Medical Care* 18(suppl 2): 1–53.

Fitzgerald, J.F., et al. 1987. Changing patterns of hip fracture before and after implementation of the prospective payment system. *JAMA* 258:218–221.

Fitzgerald, J.F., et al. 1988. The care of elderly patients with hip fracture. *New England Journal of Medicine* 319:1392–1397.

Hsiao, W.C., and Dunn, D.L. 1987. The impact of DRG payments on New Jersey hospitals. *Inquiry* 24:212–220.

Lave, J.R. 1984. Hospital reimbursement under Medicare. *Milbank Quarterly* 62:251–268.

———. 1985. *The Medicare adjustment for the indirect costs of medical education.* Washington, D.C.: Association of American Medical Colleges.

———. 1989. The effect of the Medicare prospective payment system. *Annual Review of Public Health* 10:141–161.

Long, M.J., et al. 1987. The effects of PPS on hospital product and productivity. *Medical Care* 25:528–538.

McCarthy, C. 1988. DRGs—five years later. *New England Journal of Medicine* 318:1683–1686.

Morrisey, M., et al. 1988. Medicare prospective payment and post-hospital transfers to subacute care. *Medical Care* 26:685–698.

Muller, A. 1993. Medicare prospective payment reforms and hospital utilization. *Medical Care* 31:296–308.

Mullin, R.L. 1985. Diagnosis-related groups and severity. *JAMA* 253:1208–1210.

Neumann, B.R., and Kelly, J.V. 1984. *Prospective reimbursement for hospital capital costs.* Chicago: Healthcare Financial Management Association.

Omenn, G.S., and Conrad, D.A. 1984. Implications of DRG's for clinicians. *New England Journal of Medicine* 311:1314–1317.

Pettengill, J., and Vertrees, J. 1982. Reliability and validity in hospital case-mix measurement. *Health Care Financing Review* 4:101–128.

Russell, L. 1989. *Medicare's new hospital payment system.* Washington, D.C.: Brookings Institution.

Sloan, F.A., et al. 1988. Cost of capital to the hospital sector. *Journal of Health Economics* 7:25–45.

Vladeck, B.C. 1984. Medicare hospital payment by diagnosis-related group. *Annals of Internal Medicine* 100:576–591.

———. 1988. Hospital prospective payment and the quality of care. *New England Journal of Medicine* 319:1411–1413.

Wennberg, J.E., et al. 1984. Will payment based on diagnosis-related groups control hospital costs? *New England Journal of Medicine* 311:295–300.

Young, D.W., and Saltman, R.B. 1982. Medical practice, case mix, and cost containment. *JAMA* 247:801–805.

Other Case-Mix Classification Systems

Kelly, W.P., et al. 1990. The classification of resource use in ambulatory surgery. *Journal of Ambulatory Care Management* 13:55–63.

Optenberg, S.A., et al. 1990. A specialty-based ambulatory workload classification system. *Journal of Ambulatory Care Management* 13:29–38.

Starfield, B., et al. 1991. Ambulatory care groups: a categorization of diagnoses for research and management. *Health Services Research* 26:53–74.

Steinman, M.G., et al. 1994. A case-mix classification system for medical rehabilitation. *Medical Care* 32:366–379.

Tenan, P.M., et al. 1988. PACs: classifying ambulatory care patients and services for clinical and financial management. *Journal of Ambulatory Care Management* 11:36–53.

Weiner, J.P., et al. 1991. Development and application of a population-oriented measure of ambulatory care-mix. *Medical Care* 29:452–472.

For-Profit and Nonprofit Comparisons

Bays, C. 1979a. Case-mix differences between nonprofit and for-profit hospitals. *Inquiry* 14:17–21.

———. 1979b. Cost comparisons of for-profit and nonprofit hospitals. *Social Science and Medicine* 13C:219–225.

Borjas, G.J., et al. 1983. Property rights and wages: the case of nursing homes. *Journal of Human Resources* 17:231–246.

Clarkson, K.W. 1972. Some implications of property rights in hospital management. *Journal of Law and Economics* 15:363–384.

Eskoz, R., and Peddecord, K.M. 1985. The relationship of hospital ownership and service composition to hospital charges. *Health Care Financing Review* 6:51–58.

Frech, H.E. 1976. The property rights theory of the firm: empirical results from a natural experiment. *Journal of Political Economy* 84:143–152.

———. 1985. The property rights theory of the firm: some evidence from the U.S. nursing home industry. *Zeitschrift fur die Gestamte Staatswissenschaft* 141:146–166.

Lewin, L.S., et al. 1981. Investor-owneds and nonprofits differ in economic performance. *Hospitals*, 1 July, 52–58.

Lowrie, E.G., and Hampers, C.L. 1981. The success of Medicare's end-stage renal disease program. *New England Journal of Medicine* 305:434–438.

Pattison, R.V., and Katz, H.M. 1983. Investor-owned and not-for-profit hospitals. *New England Journal of Medicine* 309:347–353.

Relman, A.S. 1980. The new medical-industrial complex. *New England Journal of Medicine* 303:963–970.

Renn, S.C., et al. 1985. The effects of ownership and system affiliation on the economic performance of hospitals. *Inquiry* 22:19–236.

Ruchlin, H.S., et al. 1976. A comparison of for-profit investor-owned chains and nonprofit hospitals. *Inquiry* 10:13–23.

Schweitzer, S.O., and Rafferty, J. 1976. Variations in hospital product: a comparative analysis of proprietary and voluntary hospitals. *Inquiry* 13:158–166.

Provider Supply under Managed Care Contracting

Debrock, A., and Arnould, R.J. 1992. Utilization control in HMOs. *Quarterly Review of Economics and Business* 32 (3):31–53.

Feldstein, P.J., et al. 1988. The effects of utilization review programs on health care use and expenditures. *New England Journal of Medicine* 318:1310–1314.

Hillman, A.L. 1987. Financial incentives for physicians in HMOs. *New England Journal of Medicine* 317:1743–1748.

Hillman, A.L., et al. 1989. How do financial incentives affect physicians' clinical decisions and the financial performance of health maintenance organizations? *New England Journal of Medicine* 321:86–92.

Pauly, M.V., et al. 1990. Managing physician incentives in managed care. *Medical Care* 28:1013–1024.

Robinson, J.C. 1993. Payment mechanisms, nonprice incentives, and organizational innovations in health care. *Inquiry* 30:328–332.

Scheffler, R.M., et al. 1991. The impact of Blue Cross and Blue Shield plan utilization management programs, 1980–1988. *Inquiry* 28:276–287.

Wickizer, T.M., et al. 1989. Does utilization review reduce unnecessary hospital care and contain costs? *Medical Care* 27:632–647.

CHAPTER 7

Competitive Markets

7.1 INTRODUCTION

In Chapters 3 through 6 a number of hypotheses about the behavior of demanding and supplying units were developed. These hypotheses that dealt with demand behavior and supply behavior were examined in isolation. As a result, although we developed a way of predicting what quantity would be demanded (supplied) at any price, our model did not incorporate the behavior of the supplying (demanding) units and thus could not tell us whether the same quantity would be both demanded and supplied.

Beginning with this chapter, our focus shifts to models in which demanders and suppliers interact. The setting in which this interaction occurs is called a *market*. A market in economics should not be thought of as a physical location; rather, the term *market* denotes the web of interactions between those who have commercial relationships or the potential to have such relationships with other buyers and sellers of similar commodities. For example, we can think of a market for psychiatric services as consisting of a group of consumers and a group of providers who have the potential to enter into commercial relations with all members of the other group. Central to the analysis of the functioning of a market is the price that the buyer pays and the seller receives. In Chapters 3 and 6 this price was taken as given for both groups; variations in price were beyond the control of any one buyer or seller. Yet, as a consequence of the related interactions of these groups, prices are set; as a result of some change in demand or supply behavior, prices change.

The market analyses that we will examine consist of three categories of concepts.

- *Phenomena to be explained.* These are objective events, such as changes in the price or the quantity of medical care utilized. The phenomenon of interest might be a rise in prices, and our model would be used to explain why the phenomenon has occurred.

- *Economic forces.* There are the degrees of willingness of demanders to purchase at specific prices and the propensities of providers to supply at specific prices. The economic "forces" influencing these phenomena have been referred to as *demand* and *supply.*
- *Factors influencing forces.* The strength of these forces can be increased or decreased by individual factors, such as incomes and tastes on the demand side and input prices on the supply side. Demand can be increased, for example, by higher consumer incomes and supply can be decreased by higher input costs. As a consequence of changes in causal factors, demand or supply will change, as will price and quantity. Our models should be able to predict such causal chains of events.

In this chapter, one particular market model is developed and used to explain the outcome of price and quantity in the medical care market. This is the competitive market model, which treats the market as an interactive mechanism with many suppliers competing for consumer business. Such a model is helpful in explaining a broad range of phenomena. It offers hypotheses to explain rising prices; increasing or decreasing utilization; shortages in commodities such as doctors' services, nursing services, and blood; and surpluses in commodities such as hospital beds. Thus it is a valuable starting point for any analysis of markets. The competitive market model is presented in Section 7.2, and the predictions of the model are discussed in Section 7.3. Although the competitive model is able to generate a large number of predictions, not all the predictions are borne out of actual events. Indeed, several events are either at odds with or fail to corroborate the predictions of the competitive model. Since accurate prediction is the bottom line of explanatory economics, Section 7.4 is devoted to a discussion of corroborating evidence relating to the competitive hypothesis. Section 7.5 discusses a recent application of the competitive hypothesis in the health care field, in particular, the use of the model to explain selective contracting, and Sections 7.6 and 7.7 introduce the application of the competitive model in analyzing the markets for labor and health care insurance.

7.2   THE COMPETITIVE MODEL: ASSUMPTIONS

In our exposition of the competitive model, we will use a market for physician services as our example. The product is physician visits, which we will assume to be of a constant quality, each involving the same accuracy of diagnosis, effectiveness of treatment, and personal attentiveness.

- *Individual demand.* Our initial demand assumption is that each consumer has a normal demand curve, as set out in Chapter 3. This includes the stipulation that consumers are fully informed about the nature of the services they require and the benefits that they can obtain. This stipulation implies that physicians cannot *directly* influence consumer demand for medical care.
- *Market demand.* We further assume that there are many consumers in the market and that they are competing for physician services. This assumption rules out the possibility that buyers are large enough or can join together to have any influence over price. The market demand curve (*D*) in our model is shown in Figure 7–1. Here conditions are assumed to be such that, at a price of $2.50 per visit, the quantity demanded is 500 visits: at $2.40, the quantity demanded is 600 units; at $2.00 the quantity demanded is 1,000 units; and so on. Curve *D* traces out this relationship. Any change in the underlying causal factors (tastes, for example) will shift demand. These causal factors are listed in the diagram for the purpose of reminding the reader of the underlying assumptions of the model.
- *Individual supply.* Our supply assumptions can similarly be separated into assumptions about individual suppliers and about the supplier group. Individually, each supplier has an upward-sloping marginal cost curve. Assuming supplier profit maximization and no supplier influence over price (a market assumption), the marginal cost curve is the supply curve.
- *Market supply.* With regard to the supply group, we assume there are many suppliers, they do not collude with each other to influence prices, and none is large enough by itself to influence price.

Consumers are assumed to be aware of the price offers of alternative suppliers and so can compare prices when making purchase decisions. Because of consumer knowledge, any supplier charging a higher price than what would prevail in a competitive situation will sell no units. Charging a lower price will mean forgoing some intramarginal profits. And so, in such a market, each supplier will take the price as given and supply where price equals *MC*. The market supply will be the summed individual suppliers' marginal cost curves. Market supply is shown in Figure 7–1 as curve *S*, with 700 units supplied at $1.70, 800 at $1. 80, 1,000 at $2.00, and so on. The factors influencing the position of the supply curve are also shown.

Under these conditions of supply and demand, bargaining occurs between consumers and producers. An equilibrium is reached when the quantity demanded equals the quantity supplied. The next section is devoted to the predictions of the model. That is, it presents what we would expect the market outcome to be (in terms of prices and quantities) if such conditions were approximated in reality.

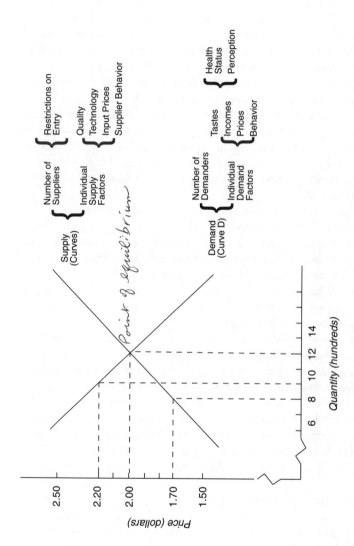

Figure 7–1 Representation of the interaction of market forces. The phenomena, price and quantity, are influenced by the forces of supply and demand. These forces, in turn, are affected by a number of individual causal factors (listed in the diagram). The positions of the supply and demand curves have been set based on the assumption that the causal forces are at given levels. Changes in the magnitude of any of these causal factors will cause a shift in supply or demand (or both).

7.3   THE COMPETITIVE MODEL: PREDICTIONS

7.3.1   Overview

Six important groups of conclusions can be drawn from the competitive model regarding how resources are allocated in the health care sector. These conclusions are presented next. Keep in mind that these conclusions are presented as possible explanations whose usefulness is determined by how well they conform to actual experience.

7.3.2   Market Price

In a competitive market a single price will emerge that clears the market. Competitive bidding will lower the price if a surplus of output exists (i.e., if there is unsold output or excess capacity) and will raise the price in the case of a shortage. Only when buyers are satisfied with the quantities they purchase at the established price and sellers are making maximum profits will market equilibrium be established (i.e., quantity supplied equals quantity demanded). In our example, equilibrium will be reached at a price of $2.00 and a supply of 1,000 visits.

If the price is higher, say, $2.10, then 900 units of service will be demanded, whereas the suppliers will be prepared to supply 1,100. To eliminate this excess capacity, physicians will lower prices and the amounts supplied. The quantity demanded will increase at the same time. The process goes on until both groups are simultaneously satisfied. The quantity supplied will just equal the quantity that consumers demand. The same process will occur in reverse if the price is below $2.00, in which case prices will be driven up to the equilibrium point.

It can be shown that the end result of this process is a single price charged by all producers. If any single physician charged more than the equilibrium price per visit, then his or her patients, who we assume to possess full knowledge of prices charged by other physicians, would obtain medical care elsewhere. The physician would be forced to bring his or her price down to the price other doctors are charging. On the other hand, if a doctor sets fees below the equilibrium level, patients will flock to this physician, creating an overload of work. Given a rising *MC* schedule for this physician, the profits gained from the sale of each additional unit will decline. The physician with such an *MC* schedule would have been better off profitwise to accept the highest price, which is the market price. That a single market-clearing price will emerge is thus one conclusion of the competitive model.

7.3.3   Price and Quantity Movements Caused by Demand Shifts

Additional conclusions based on the competitive model can be drawn regarding price and quantity movements when there is a change in any of the factors that influence demand. This set of conclusions is illustrated in Figure 7–2. Assume D_1 to be the demand curve consistent with given initial values of underlying causal factors of demand. Let S be the supply curve, which remains stable because all supply shift factors are assumed constant. The equilibrium price for these conditions is P_1 ($2.00), and the equilibrium quantity for the market is Q_1 (1,000 visits). If any of the initial conditions that influence demand change, causing an increase in demand to D_2, for example, there will be a new equilibrium price ($2.10) and quantity (1,200 units). The willingness of consumers to buy more at each price allows the producers to increase profits by producing more output (up to 1,200 units). Such a shift in demand can be caused by higher consumer incomes or a greater degree of illness in the population. Or it can be caused by an increase in the amount of health insurance purchased, which also causes demand to shift out (see Section 3.6). In either case the result is the same—higher prices and quantities. The opposite situation, lower prices and quantities, would be the consequence of factors shifting demand downward.

If the quantity utilized is to increase, additional quantity must be available. *Utilization* refers to the actual quantity traded in the market. This should not be con-

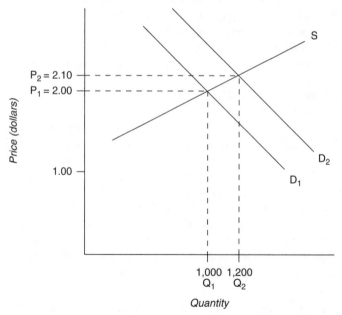

Figure 7–2 Representation of shift in demand with stable supply. An initial set of supply and demand forces, characterized by D_1 and S, will produce given price and output levels. An increase in demand to D_2, with a stable S, will cause price and output to increase.

fused with the amount demanded, because when there is disequilibrium, more (or less) might be demanded than is supplied. Nor should it be confused with the quantity offered by the supplier, because at any one price more (or less) might be supplied than consumers are willing to take at that price. Disequilibrium situations occur when the price does not adjust to allow the quantity demanded and the quantity supplied to equalize.

7.3.4 Price and Quantity Movements Caused by Supply Shifts

Another set of conclusions based on the model concern changes in factors that cause the supply to shift. What occurs if there is an increase in supply is shown in Figure 7–3. In this example, the commodity becomes less scarce and the supply

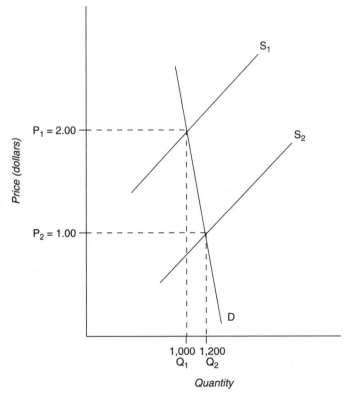

Figure 7–3 Representation of shifting supply with stable demand. Beginning with an initial demand and supply levels D and S_1 and resulting price and output levels, an increase in supply to S_2 will cause output to increase and price to fall.

shifts from S_1 to S_2. If the demand remains the same, the supply increases relative to the demand and the price falls. As a result, a new lower price ($1.00) and a higher level of utilization (1,200 units) are predicted. Of course, a factor that causes a reduction in supply will have the opposite effect on the price and the quantity utilized.

Changes in supply can occur because of changes in circumstances that are beyond the control of supplying firms (and to which they react) or because of changes that the present or potential suppliers themselves initiate. For example, if hospitals or public health departments decide to hire paramedics, they will enter the market and bid for the existing supply of paramedics. This will raise the price of paramedics that all market participants have to pay, because the supply will initially remain relatively stable while the demand will increase. An increase in the price of paramedic services (or for that matter of any input) will shift the supply curve of all producers who use this input to the left. Thus, the market supply curve will shift leftward as well and the price of physician services will increase.

Provider-initiated changes in supply will be undertaken by for-profit suppliers when these changes have the potential to add to profits. Three types of situations are discussed below:

1. a change in input combinations brought about by existing suppliers
2. an increase in the capital stock of existing suppliers
3. entry into the market by new suppliers

An example of the first situation, a change in input combinations, might occur if physicians were to hire paramedics or nurse practitioners to perform, at a lower cost, services previously performed by the physicians themselves. Such a change might be the result of the passage of a law allowing such substitution to occur. The effect would be to shift the average total cost curve downward and the marginal cost curve to the right. In a competitive market, one supplier making such a change would not cause a large shift in the market supply curve. Prices would remain about the same and that one supplier would reap an increase in profits. However, if all suppliers made a change, the market supply curve would shift to the right considerably and the price of medical care would then fall. Consumers would reap the benefits from such actions. The net profit position of each provider after all suppliers have acted may not be any greater than before, because the price of output has fallen, but it is important to note that the providers make their decisions to undertake cost-reducing activities based on pre-existing prices. Providers do not collude with their cosuppliers, and they do not always anticipate that prices will fall as a consequence of their concerted actions. The end result of their actions, however, is lower prices and greater utilization.

The same process occurs when existing suppliers invest in plant and equipment. Additions to capital are often made in anticipation of additions to profits because of lower unit costs. If these investments cut costs, and if they are sufficiently widespread in the industry, the net effect will be to lower prices and raise utilization. As a result, after these effects have worked themselves out, profits may be no greater than before (they may even be less). These effects are presented in a before-after manner here. In actuality, they take a considerable time to occur. The potential for profits must first be realized, planning for the additions and financing them must occur, and the additional capital equipment and plant must then be constructed and put into use. As a result, the increase in supply and the fall in price may take months and even years. For this reason, the analysis of provider behavior involving capital additions, with resulting shifts in average and marginal cost curves, has been referred to as *long-run analysis*. (It is generally difficult to decide when a change in supply conditions is long run and when it is short run. Short-run changes are usually taken to be changes in quantity supplied that occur without changes in capital equipment.)

The third type of variation in supply occurs when new (profit-seeking) suppliers enter an industry or a market in response to high profits. Such a movement results in an increase in supply and a consequent fall in price and increase in utilization. In this instance, since the cost conditions of existing suppliers remain the same, the profit levels must fall for all existing suppliers.

The conditions that determine how easily potential providers can actually enter the industry and place their products on the market are referred to as *conditions of entry*. These conditions depend on existing productive techniques as well as on legal impediments. In some industries, extensive capital requirements preclude many firms from entering because of the large financial commitment necessary to undertake the capital investment and commence production. Such requirements may exist for some types of medical care, such as intensive surgery, although the financial impediments are not nearly as great as they are, for example, in the automobile industry. For many types of medical care, financial impediments are not relevant to entry. More relevant are the legal impediments, such as the licensing requirements for medical personnel and facilities. Licensing regulations frequently amount to restrictions placed on potential entrants into an industry.

7.3.5 Simultaneous Demand and Supply Shifts

In addition to creating movements in either demand or supply alone, where the effects are readily predictable, underlying factors may cause shifts in both demand and supply at the same time. We must be careful at this stage of the analysis to specify that we are referring to separate factors causing changes in demand and supply. That is, an increase in the number of ill people occurring at the same time as an influx of physicians into the market will cause both demand and supply curves to shift; the increase in the illness level will cause demand to increase, and the increase in the number of physicians will cause supply to increase. In Figure 7–4, this is shown as a shift in demand from D_1 to D_2 and, at the same time, a shift in supply from S_1 to S_2. Although quantity increases, the net effect on price is ambiguous and will depend on how much each curve shifts, that is, on the changes in the values of the causal variables and the degree to which they cause demand and supply to shift. In the specific case illustrated in Figure 7–4, price will fall. But if we do not know the extent to which both curves are shifted, our model fails us as a predictive device.

A second type of simultaneous shift may occur when the same factor that causes demand to shift independently causes supply to shift. An increase in quality, for example, will cause supply to decrease and demand to increase. When demand increases and supply decreases, price will increase, but quantity will increase, fall, or remain the same depending on the extent of the shifts. (Another type of simultaneous shift that does *not* belong in this category is when the factors affecting supply and demand are not independent, such as when physicians can induce consumer demand. This phenomenon is discussed in Section 9.2.1.)

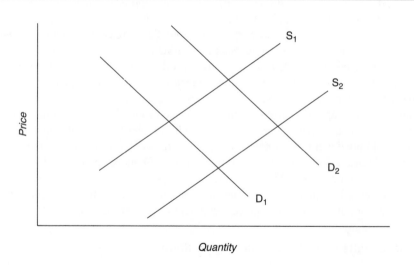

Quantity

Figure 7–4 Representation of the simultaneous shifting of demand and supply curves. Beginning with initial demand and supply levels D_1 and S_1 and resulting price and output levels, a simultaneous shift in demand and supply curves (to D_2 and S_2) will have an ambiguous effect on price and will increase output. The extent of both shifts determines the effects on price and quantity. Some directional shifts, such as a decrease in demand and a simultaneous increase in supply, will lower the price but have an ambiguous effect on quantity traded.

7.3.6 Shortages

Our predictions so far have been concerned with what happens to the equilibrium price when one or several factors change. Not all situations are such that the quantity demanded is the quantity supplied. The medical care market often experiences shortages. A shortage occurs when the quantity demanded exceeds the quantity supplied at the current price. Our model shows that in a competitive market with free bidding, a shortage will cause the price to rise. Then the suppliers will offer more services and the consumers will reduce their demand, making the shortage disappear. That is the theory, although persistent shortages have been observed in the blood market, the market for nurses, the physician services market, and, in some countries, the hospital market. A slight modification of the competitive model allows us to predict why these shortages occur and how they can be eliminated.

Refer to our example in Figure 7–1. Assume that, because of a government regulation, the price cannot rise above $1.70 per visit. Perhaps the regulation is passed and enforced to help low-income consumers, who may go without medical services if the price is $2.00. The consequences of the passage of the regulation can be determined using the competitive model. At $1.70, consumers will be more willing to visit their physicians, and according to our figures 1,300 will call for appointments. But at this price it would be unprofitable for physicians to see 1,300 patients. Indeed, they will reduce quantity supplied and will see only 700 patients. A queue will form of untreated patients; in this case, 600 patients who want treatment will be untreated. Some shortages are the result of such price ceilings. In a competitive market, a shortage can only persist if the price is somehow administered to remain below the market-clearing price. This will usually be done by an official or semiofficial agency that can overrule the price market forces set.

A shortage can also occur when insurance is purchased or when a government program "guaranteeing" medical care is instituted. In such situations, the consumers may face a zero money price, which will mean a high quantity demanded (e.g., 10,000 units, as shown in Figure 7–5). The reimbursed price to the provider may be only $20 per unit, and at this price 7,000 units are provided. In our example, it would take a price of $100 to bring forth a supply of 10,000 units. At the administered reimbursement rate of $20, there is a shortage of 3,000 units.

The situation requires a mechanism to ration the 7,000 available units, assuming that the quality produced remains the same. One tactic is to make the prospective patients wait in line; those who are willing to pay the "time costs" will receive the service (Buchanan 1965; Culyer and Cullis 1976; Sloan and Lorant 1976). Another possibility is for the providers to lower the quality of their product, for example, by reducing the time devoted to providing the service. This action would reduce demand, since the commodity would not have the same worth as before,

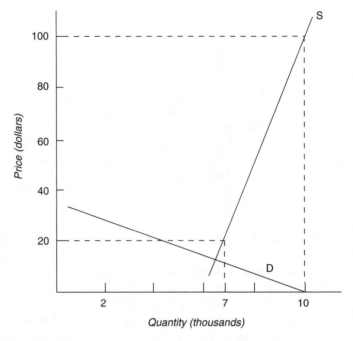

Figure 7–5 Representation of supply and demand forces using the example of full-service coverage by a third party. Full-service (zero out-of-pocket price) coverage with a reimbursement rate of $20 will lead to a quantity demanded of 10,000 and a quantity supplied of 7,000. To reach a quantity supplied of 10,000, the reimbursement rate would have to be $100 (curve S).

and it would increase supply. As a result, the shortage would be reduced and perhaps even eliminated.

7.3.7 Surpluses

The usual definition of a surplus is an excess of quantity supplied over quantity demanded at a given price. For a surplus to persist, some factor must keep quantity supplied above quantity demanded. If the price in the market was kept permanently above the equilibrium price, a surplus would persist: Suppliers would be willing to provide more units than consumers would be willing to purchase. In Figure 7–1, if the suppliers' reimbursed price and the consumers' out-of-pocket price were both $2.10 and could not be lowered, a surplus would appear. In this case, suppliers would be willing to supply more units at that price than demanders would want, and the suppliers would find themselves with excess capacity.

For a surplus to persist, something must prevent the market price from falling, because in a normal competitive situation an excess supply would induce suppliers to lower their prices to induce demanders to buy more. If the government pegged or supported an above-equilibrium price in the market, a surplus would occur. In the case of health care, where insurance exists, a surplus can occur if the reimbursement rate suppliers receive induces a greater quantity supplied than the quantity demanded by consumers at the price they have to pay out of pocket. In Figure 7–1, if the reimbursement rate was $2.50 and the out-of-pocket price was $1.50, a surplus would exist.

In recent years there has been much talk of a "physician surplus" (Schwartz and Mendelson, 1990). In discussions of this topic one hears talk of falling physicians' fees and incomes (although this not always borne out by the data). To the extent that the fees and incomes of doctors are falling, this situation is not a surplus in the technical sense. Falling fees are characteristic of prices responding to a shift supply en route to a new equilibrium point. For a surplus to develop, the market cannot be allowed to move to a new equilibrium; it must remain in *dis*equilibrium.

The surplus in hospital beds is more likely a case of permanent disequilibrium. High hospital reimbursement rates have induced a large quantity supplied; at given out-of-pocket prices, there has not been enough quantity demanded to clear the market.

7.3.8 Multimarket Analyses

The competitive model is well suited to making predictions about the effect of supply and/or demand changes in one market on price and quantity in a related market. Let us take an example of two substitute services, inpatient and outpatient surgical care. Because of the development of quicker acting anesthetics, outpatient surgery has become more feasible. Further, the total cost of outpatient surgery is much less than inpatient surgery for most cases, and outpatient surgery for many procedures is now covered.

Analytically, the impact of moving from no outpatient coverage for a procedure (e.g., tonsillectomy) to outpatient coverage is shown in Figure 7–6. The pre-outpatient-coverage market for inpatient procedures is characterized in Graph A. Here S is the inpatient supply curve and D_{n+i} is the inpatient demand curve. In Graph B, D_n is the demand curve for outpatient tonsillectomies (without insurance) and S is the supply curve. Note that the demand function for *inpatient* care is dependent on the out-of-pocket price for *outpatient* surgery because the two are substitutes.

An increase in outpatient coverage will shift the market curve for outpatient care outward (to D'_n in Graph B) and simultaneously lower the direct price of outpatient care. This will result in an inward shift in the D_{n+i} curve for inpatient care to D'_{n+i}. The inpatient price will fall and the quantity of inpatient procedures will be reduced. Note also that the outpatient procedures will be increased.

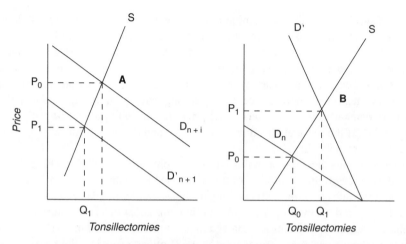

Figure 7–6 Representation of multimarket analysis. Demand curves in inpatient and outpatient markets are related (the services are substitutes). When the out of pocket price in the outpatient market falls (because of an increase in insurance coverage), the demand curve in the inpatient market shifts inward and price and quantity fall.

Similar types of analyses can be conducted for other types of substitute procedures or for complements, such as inpatient surgery and surgeons' services. In some cases, it is not clear whether two services are substitutes or complements. For example, it is not clear whether nursing home care replaces hospital care or is used in conjunction with it. The same holds for home health care and hospital care. In these instances, the model cannot provide unambiguous conclusions.

7.4   EVIDENCE FOR AND AGAINST THE COMPETITIVE MODEL

7.4.1   Overview

There has been some use of the competitive model in explaining resource allocation trends in medical care markets. In the physician services market, the phenomenon of rapidly rising physician fees, both before and after the watershed year of 1966, when Medicare and Medicaid were instituted (see Section 11.2), was explained using the competitive model by hypothesizing that the rapid increase in medical care insurance caused demand shifts (see Section 3.6) and consequent rising prices. In this market, the length of time required to train new physicians means a slow supply response, even in a competitive market, and prices would be expected to rise (Garbarino 1959; Newhouse and Phelps 1977). In the hospital care market, the same type of explanation can be made for rising hospital costs, with one modification. Although insurance was increasing during this time period, hospital input prices, notably employee wages, were also rapidly rising. This latter phenomenon would shift the supply curve inward. Couple this with a rapidly outward shifting demand curve for hospital care, and the net effect would be a larger price increase. Whether utilization would increase or decrease would depend on the magnitude of both shifts. As seen in Chapter 2, hospital utilization increased. Our "after the fact" explanation would state that the supply and demand shifts were such that the increase in utilization was likely to occur. (An application of the competitive model to the hospital field is found in Ro [1977].)

The competitive model has also been used to explain the persisting queues and unmet demands that have resulted from the institution of the National Health Service (NHS) in Great Britain in 1946. The NHS is characterized by a zero money price paid by consumers, per capita remuneration for general practitioners, and salaried remuneration for surgeons. The competitive model applied to this type of health care system would predict large increases in quantity demanded following the lowering of the price to zero. Supply decisions passed into the hands of the central government and large increases in supply did not materialize. As a result, persistent shortages occurred, particularly in hospital care (Culyer and Cullis 1976).

Although the competitive model is a useful device for explaining price and quantity movements and uncovering the causes of shortages of medical care, much attention has focused on the shortcomings of the model. Evidence of the existence of shortcomings might be gotten in three ways. First, we might examine data on market outcomes, such as profits and prices. If such outcomes are not what we would expect in a competitive market (i.e., not what the competitive model predicts would happen), we can infer that the model does not explain what we have observed and seek alternative models to better explain the data. Secondly, we might observe some conditions and characteristics of a market, such as consumer ignorance or product quality level differences. If the observed characteristics are at odds with the competitive model's assumptions, we should consider seeking a different model that incorporates realistic assumptions. Third, we might observe direct actions on the part of providers that suggest the prevalence of noncompetitive practices. These might include constraints on certain activities usually thought of as competitive, such as free entry. We turn to some of the evidence that the competitive model has serious flaws as a model of the health care market.

7.4.2 Excessive Profits

Studies made of the profits accruing from medical practice have shown these profits to be persistent and considerable. These profits, which are the net incomes of the physicians operating the practices, must be adjusted for the costs incurred in medical training, including fees paid and earnings forgone while practicing medicine or during internship and residency. Even after adjusting for these costs, the net present value of medical practice indicates the existence of persistently high profits (i.e., earnings in excess of normal returns) (Lindsay 1976; Sloan 1976). Generally, the competitive model predicts that such excess profits would eventually be bid away by new providers entering the industry to take advantage of the high returns. This has not occurred in medical practice.

7.4.3 Fee Differences among Patients

The competitive model predicts that one price will prevail in the market for all suppliers and demanders. Before the spread of health insurance, physician pricing was characterized by a sliding scale of fees, with high-income patients paying higher prices than low-income patients. This phenomenon has led economists to reject the competitive model as inappropriate for the physician services market and to substitute a monopoly model (Kessell 1958; Newhouse 1970; Ruffin and Leigh 1973; Wu and Masson 1974; see Chapter 8).

7.4.4 Quality of Care

The competitive model assumes a homogeneous service is being bought and sold and that competition is based on price. Yet product quality is a major element of a hospital's output, and health insurance companies often offer different types of policies in terms of coverage (viewed as differences in the quality of the policy as well as differences in service).

When a supplier can vary its quality, it can attract consumers on the basis of its quality. It follows that some "brand loyalty" may ensue, and buyers will not switch brands easily (because of a slight increase in price, for example). This phenomenon is called *product differentiation*, and it implies that each supplier then faces a downward-sloping demand curve, not a horizontal one (as is the case in perfect competition), and can choose to compete with other providers on the basis of price or product quality. The competitive model is not equipped to handle this feature of the health care market, which requires a somewhat more complex model (Chapter 8).

7.4.5 Restricting Competitive Behavior

Additional evidence of anticompetitive control mechanisms is found by examining the behavior of physicians when confronted with potentially competitive colleagues. Two practices have been restricted by physician associations: the advertising of physician fees and the participation by physicians in prepayment group practices. In an ideal world, such as that set out in the model in Section 7.2, advertising is unnecessary because consumers know all about physicians' fees. But in the real world considerable consumer ignorance exists, and advertising would reduce ignorance about alternative physician prices (and perhaps qualifications). Coupled with fee cutting (price reductions), advertising would result in more business for the fee-cutting advertiser but in generally lower prices and profits in the industry.

Advertising bans have been enforced by state medical societies (Kessell 1958), and although such bans are no longer legally enforceable, their existence in the past was evidence that physicians were able to intervene in the market on behalf of themselves and eliminate some degree of competition in the market. Bans on advertising (and other competitive practices) have been used as evidence of the availability of mechanisms to restrict competition (see Chapters 8 and 14).

7.4.6 Consumer Ignorance and Supplier-Induced Demand

The competitive model operates under the assumption that consumers possess a considerable degree of information about their condition, the products they need, and the outcomes of using the products. In fact, consumers appear to operate under a considerable degree of ignorance in this area, which has led some commentators to view physicians as essentially agents acting on behalf of consumers (Feldstein 1974). If physicians do behave as agents for their patients, the implicit assumption that suppliers and demanders are acting independently must be rejected. Demanders are subject to direct supplier influence.

Nor can we assume that, if they do act as agents for their patient, physicians always behave in the patients' best interests. Once the patients are prone to manipulation, the possibility exists that physicians can use their influence to further their own interests. Consumer demands can be shifted by the suppliers through the provision of biased information.

Demand shifting can be detected in market outcome statistics in some circumstances. According to the competitive theory, an increase in the per capita supply of physicians results in an increase in market supply. With everything else held constant, this should bring down the price of health care. Yet it has been alleged that the relationship between physician per capita supply and price is exactly opposite to that predicted by the model; that is, the more physicians per capita in an area, the higher the observed price (Evans 1974; Fuchs and Kramer 1972; Kushman 1976). The reason why this phenomenon is alleged rather than demonstrated is that a number of intervening factors exist that may cause demand to rise at the same time as physician supply increases.

Let us make a simple comparison of two hypothetical medical markets, one in a small town and one in a large metropolitan center with several medical schools. The large city may have more doctors per capita than the small town, and the price for a visit to a physician may be greater. This "raw" relationship by itself does not mean that the higher supply has caused the higher price. Many other intervening variables must also be taken into account, among them insurance, the health status of the two populations, and the quality of care provided. The third factor, the quality of care, is especially important in making comparisons, mainly because it is such a difficult variable to measure and thus may be ignored. It may well be that the quality of care in the city is higher than in the town. If all factors other than the quality of care were adjusted for, we might still observe a positive relationship between physician density and price. Until quality has been adjusted for, however, we cannot be certain that the higher price is not due to the fact that better quality service is being provided.

This type of confounding relationship has caused controversy regarding the observed relationship between price and physician density (Sloan and Feldman 1978). Some commentators have proceeded as if it were true and have constructed alternative models to explain such a relationship (see Chapter 9).

7.5 COMPETITIVE BIDDING

The competitive market has often been held up as an ideal, a standard in the light of which other allocative arrangements might be judged. One mechanism that has been put forward as potentially providing a competitive-style outcome for public programs is competitive bidding. Competitive bidding occurs when a purchaser (e.g., a government agency) requests bids from alternative competing providers and allocates the right to treat patients based on the bids. The object of this practice is to have the patients treated for the least cost.

One approach to developing a model of the competitive bidding process is to examine the behavior of an individual supplier who is facing a single paying agency and who is competing with other providers for the right to provide the services. In constructing such a model, it is essential to recognize that the bids are made under conditions of risk. When they submit their bids, the bidders do not know for certain whether or not they will be selected as providers. Their behavior can be modelled in a manner similar to that of consumers who are faced with risky medical expenses (Section 4.3.1).

The bidder faces two possible outcomes: (1) the bid is accepted, or (2) the bid is rejected. To simplify matters, let us assume that no losses are associated with an unsuccessful bid (i.e., the bidder is no worse off than if he or she did not bid). What the bidder must do is compare the outcomes of the various bids to assess which will prove the most satisfactory.

Our simplified model is presented in numerical form in Table 7-1. We make the following assumptions. First, a request is put out calling for providers to bid for the right to serve a given number of patients in a public program. The bids are to be

Table 7–1 Hypothetical Bidding Data

Option	Bid Price	Probability of Acceptance	Profits (if bid accepted)	Wealth Level (if bid accepted)	Utility Levels	
					Risk Averter	Risk Taker
A	$100	.2	$800	$1,000	126	2,000
B	95	.4	400	600	122	800
C	90	.6	200	400	118	400
D	85	.8	100	300	110	200
E	80	.9	50	250	100	100

expressed in per capita terms for a certain set of services (physician care, hospital care, and drugs). Second, five options (labeled A through E) are open to the bidder: bids of $100, $95, $90, $85, and $80. Third, as the bidder lowers his or her bid, the probability of having the bid accepted increases. At a bid of $100, there is a 20-percent chance of the bid being accepted. This rises to 90 percent with a bid of $80. Fourth, the bidder's profits, if the bid is accepted, are equal to the revenues less the costs of serving the designated number of patients. Given the number of patients (Q) and the costs per patient (C), the higher the accepted bid, the higher will be the profits [equal to $(B \times Q) - (C \times Q)$]. Fifth, we translate the postprofit situation of the bidder into a wealth level. We assume that, without a contract, the bidder's wealth would be $200. A successful bid thus adds to the successful bidder's wealth level by the level of the bidder's profits.

The bidder is thus faced with a trade-off between profits (and hence wealth) and the probability of a successful bid. The individual bidder can increase the likelihood of success, but only by lowering the bid and thus lowering the profits. Given the range of alternatives, which option will the bidder choose? As set up now, our model is incomplete; it does not incorporate the objectives of the bidders or the bidding rules set up by the contracting agency.

With regard to bidder's objectives, let us assume first that the bidder is extremely risk averse. He or she puts a high personal value on small gains and successively lower additional values on larger gains (i.e., wealth, for the bidder, has a diminishing marginal utility). Under this assumption, reflected in Column 6 of Table 7–1, the bidder will choose the option that maximizes his or her *expected* utility, measured as the product of the probability of success (P_s) and the utility associated with the wealth level of that option. In our example, the risk averse bidder will choose Option E, which yields an expected utility of 90. Option D, for example, would yield an expected utility of 88. Although the profits for this option are greater, the bidder prefers to select a very safe but relatively unprofitable option.

A risk taker, whose tastes might be like those summarized in Column 7, considers high levels of wealth to be of the utmost importance, which is shown by the sharply increasing utilities of wealth. To this bidder, substantial profits are so important that they overshadow the very small chances of attaining them. To the risk taker, Option E has an expected utility of 90, whereas Option A has an expected utility of 400. Option A is the one to be selected by the risk-taking bidder.

Competitive bidding does not automatically lead to a low-price bid. Much of the outcome depends on the bidders' costs and goals. But there are several other factors as well. First, an increase in the number of bidders will reduce the probability of any single bidder being successful. Depending on the bidders' utility schedules, a larger number of competitive bidders may cause each bidder to reduce his or her bid. Second, there are a number of selection and reimbursement methods that a contracting agency can resort to. These may influence the bidding strategies of the bidders (Christianson et al. 1984). One method is to reimburse each winning bidder (more than one provider in an area may be chosen as a winner) at the level of the bid he or she submitted. Thus, if Bidder 1 submitted a bid of $95, Bidder 2, $90, and Bidder 3, $85, and if Bidders 2 and 3 are selected as providers, then Bidder 2 would be reimbursed at $90 and Bidder 3 at $85. This method tends to encourage bidding providers to gamble and seek a higher price, since there is a potential reward to them for doing so (they are reimbursed at the price they bid if their bid is accepted). An alternative method will check this tendency to gamble. If the set of rules entailed that all winning bidders would be reimbursed at the rate bid by the lowest winning bidder, there would be no benefit to a winner making a higher bid if he or she deems that some other winner will bid lower. Indeed, raising the bid merely reduces the chances of being successful.

Competitive bidding rules may lead to a competitive market–type outcome. Whether it does will depend on a number of factors, including the number of bidders, their attitudes toward risk, and the bidding rules set up by the agency. In 1982 the California legislative assembly passed a law allowing selective contracting by third-party payers with hospitals and doctors. Previously, third-party payers in California could not exclude any providers from the group they were obligated to reimburse for services provided. The new legislation permitted private insurers and Medicaid to request bids from providers for treating their insureds. They could then select the providers that they would pay for based on these bids. Theory indicates that the more competitive the market, the more successful will be the bidding process in driving down price. Evaluations of this program bear this out; prices were lower in areas where the competition among hospitals was greater (Johns et al. 1985; Johns 1989; Melnick and Zwanzinger 1988; Robinson and Luft 1988).

7.6   LABOR MARKETS

7.6.1   Introduction

This section presents a brief outline of the workings of a competitive labor market. Labor market analysis has a number of uses in health economics. The labor market model can be used to explain price and resource movements of nurses, doctors, and other health professionals. This is very important when conducting manpower planning activities. In addition, much health care is financed through fringe benefits, and this form of health care finance can have a significant influence on the labor market of all individuals who obtain insurance through the workplace.

The competitive labor market model is a theoretical construct that may not be replicated in actual labor markets. Nevertheless, it is a very useful device for organizing our attempts to understand the broad array of variables that influence a labor market. Furthermore, it should not be totally discounted as a predictive device either. The model should be judged against actual events to determine its predictive worth.

7.6.2 Assumptions of the Competitive Labor Market Model

The basic assumptions of the competitive labor market are based on previously developed models of labor demand (Section 6.8) and labor supply (Section 4.6). We will use the example of a private, for-profit market for lab technicians in order to illustrate how the model can be used.

7.6.2.1 The Demand for Labor

We assume that there is a market demand curve for labor (lab technicians), which is the demand curve for the totality of individual laboratories participating in the labor market (D_1 in Figure 7–7). This curve, which shows the relationship between the wage rate and the number of labor days demanded, is downward sloping, and it will shift if any of the underlying variables that affect the labs that are hiring lab technicians change. These variables include the price of lab tests, the productivity of the lab technicians, and the number of labs participating in the market.

7.6.2.2 The Supply of Labor

The supply of labor for lab technicians is shown as curve S_1 in Figure 7–7. We assume that as the wage rate increases, the quantity supplied of workers increases. As was shown in Section 4.6, this assumes that the income effect is not sufficiently strong to create a backward-bending labor supply curve. As well, this curve will shift if the number of persons in the market increases or underlying variables, such as tastes, change.

7.6.2.3 Equilibrium

We assume that the quantity demanded will equal the quantity supplied.

7.6.3 Predictions of the Model

The first prediction of the model is that there will be a single equilibrium wage set at $20. Bargaining among demanders and suppliers of labor will result in this

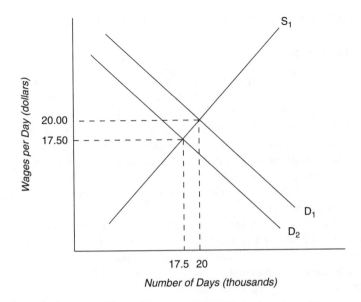

Figure 7–7 Graph of a labor market. The demand for labor is shown as Curve D_1, and the supply curve is shown as curve S_1. Equilibrium occurs at a wage rate of $20 per day and a quantity of 20,000 labor days. If fringe benefits worth $5 a day are introduced, the demand curve shifts down uniformly by $5 (to D_2). The new equilibrium will be at a quantity of 17,500 days and a wage rate of $17.50.

---

single equilibrium price at the equilibrium quantity of 20,000 labor days. Additionally, the equilibrium quantity and price will change with any changes in the related factors. With regard to shifts in demand, increases in the price of the product or the number of firms in the market will result in increased wage rates and increased labor days. Increases in the supply of labor will result in lower wages and higher quantities of labor.

Our model can be of help in analyzing the effect of using health insurance benefits as a form of compensation. Let us say that, for each worker, the labs pay a $5 health insurance premium per labor day. The effect of this is to shift the demand curve uniformly down by $5, to curve D_{21}. We will assume that there is no effect on supply. The prediction in this case is that the wage rate will fall to $17.50 and the quantity of labor days will be reduced to 17,500. This result is useful in explaining changes in health finance methods.

7.7   THE COMPETITIVE HEALTH INSURANCE MARKET

7.7.1 Background

Many commentators argue against using a competitive model to predict price and quantity movements in health insurance. However, the competitive market model is a useful learning device in that it explicitly categorizes the various elements that affect price and quantity. As for how realistic its predictions are, that issue is best left for empirical studies to decide. In this section, we will develop a competitive market model for health insurance. There are numerous such models that can be devised, each with its own special set of assumptions. Once one of these models is understood, single assumptions can be altered to see what difference the change makes.

The economic actors in our basic model are individual consumers on the demand side and individual insurers on the supply side. The product is, in essence, the shifting or transference of risk. Individual demanders face the risk of financial losses associated with medical care consumption. They can induce insurers to accept these risks by paying a premium. By insuring large numbers of consumers, individual insurers can significantly reduce their risks, because the variance of losses falls as the number of individuals accepted in a risk pool increases. In a competitive insurance market, such as the one we are analyzing, the premium will be set by competitive forces. The purpose of the model is to predict the direction of change in the shifting of risks and the adjustment of premiums.

7.7.2 Assumptions of the Model

The model we are developing is similar in form to the models for other health care services; there are demand and supply forces as well as underlying factors. The assumptions of our model include demand, supply, and equilibrium assumptions. The basic demand and supply models were developed in Chapters 4 and 6, respectively, and therefore they are only summarized here.

The product is an insurance policy—a shifting of risk from the consumer to the insurer. All insurers' products are the same, at least in the sense that all insurers offer the same quality of service and are perceived to have the same degree of financial stability.

With regard to the demand for insurance, any individual's willingness to shift his or her risk increases when the premium paid falls. Also affecting demand are the individual's degree of risk averseness, whether the individual is a utility maximizer, the individual's possible states of health, the distribution of risks over the alternative states of health, and the losses associated with the states of health. For example, the individual's willingness to shift his or her risk will increase if the individual becomes less risk averse, the risk of illness falls, the severity of possible states of health falls, or the amount of medical resources needed for treating the individual falls.

Assumptions about the interaction of consumers with the market include these: there are a given number of consumers in the market; all consumers have the same risk function; consumers have different tastes (different degrees of risk aversion) but are similar in all other respects, including health status, degree of risk, and level of wealth; and all consumers know the premiums charged by the different insurers.

The assumption that individuals have different tastes relating to risk (but not differences in the degree of risk itself) has a particular implication: The risk premiums that the different individuals will be willing to pay in order to shift their risks will vary. In the market, there will be a downward-sloping demand curve relating the premium rate to the number of people who transfer their risks to insurers. And, of course, this curve will shift when factors such as the risk functions of the individuals, the amount of wealth of the individuals, the cost of medical care (and hence the size of the loss), and the number of individuals in the market change.

As regards supply, the willingness of an insurer to accept risks will increase when the premium rate increases. (See Chapter 6 for an account of the basic model of supply.) Our assumptions are as follows: Each supplier has given tastes represented by a utility function indicating the relationship between wealth and utility (the relationship is one of risk aversion); each is a utility maximizer; each has a given wealth level; the marginal administrative cost per additional insured increases with the number of insureds; the expected loss is the same for all insureds (since the risk experience is the same for each individual); and the insurer knows what the insureds' risk experience is.

As for the insurance market, we assume that there are a given number of suppliers and that they know what other suppliers' premium rates are.

In general, the market supply of insurance policies (transference of risk) will increase with the premium rates. The supply-premium relation will shift if changes occur in factors such as the degree of risk aversion of the suppliers, the suppliers' level of wealth, their risk functions, and their expected losses (the cost of medical care and amount of utilization). We also assume that insurers can charge different premiums for different individuals depending on their risks (i.e., they can use experience rating).

Equilibrium in the market will occur where the quantity of risks that the consumers want to shift equals the quantity of risks that the suppliers are willing to accept.

7.7.3 Predictions of the Model

7.7.3.1 Premium Rates

Given the desire for risk coverage on the part of consumers and the willingness to accept risks on the part of insurers, exchanges of risks will take place between the two groups. The premium rates are free to fluctuate, although both insurers and consumers know what rates others are charging. However, the series of exchanges will lead to a single premium rate being set in the market. The reason for this is that on the demand side all risks are the same and on the supply side the cost of accepting risks will be equalized. If one supplier charges a higher premium, for whatever reason, the knowledge of the consumers and suppliers about this will result in competitive bids and equalized prices. In equilibrium, only one premium will be charged throughout the market.

7.7.3.2 Individual Risks Shifted and Not Shifted

At the equilibrium premium rate, there will be a given number of risks that will be shifted. All consumers will have had the option of shifting their risks at that premium rate, and every supplier will have had the opportunity of accepting these risks. Not all consumers will shift their risks. There is a cost (the premium) of shifting a risk, and some risk-averse consumers will not be willing to pay this cost. As a consequence, they will retain the risks themselves, which is a perfectly rational decision.

7.7.3.3 Changes in Premium Rates

Our model provides a tool with which to analyze fluctuations in health insurance premium rates. The equilibrium rate will change whenever a supply- or demand-shifting factor changes. On the demand side, an increase in the number of consumers, their degree of risk aversion, or their level of wealth will cause demand to shift outward and the premium rate to increase. Similarly, an increase in insurance administrative costs, the number of insurers, or their degree of risk aversion (in response, for example, to an economy-wide recession) will cause an increase in the premium rate.

Each of the above changes causes a shift in either demand or supply but not both. However, some factors *will* cause a shift in both, and these have important implications. An increase in the degree of risks facing individuals or in the amount of losses (which would be associated with higher costs of medical care or more utilization of medical care) would cause the demand for health insurance to shift and would also cause the insurers to request a higher premium rate (a reduction in supply). Premium rates would increase, although the quantity of risks actually exchanged could go up or down.

7.7.3.4 Interactions among Dependent Variables

There are instances where several dependent variables interact with one another. For example, there is the well-known correlation between health status and family wealth. A poor individual, who will have difficulty paying for insurance, is likely to have poorer health than others—and thus will need insurance more. It is hard to determine how these factors (lack of means to buy insurance and greater need for insurance) will interact and which, if either, will predominate in determining the individual's demand for insurance.

7.7.4 Changing the Model's Assumptions

The above model is a very simple one, and some of the assumptions are unrealistic. Now that the model has been set out and its predictions specified, we can examine what happens to premiums and insurance coverage when specific assumptions are changed.

7.7.4.1 Groups and Individuals

Initially we assumed that all consumers were individuals, but in actuality many consumers purchase insurance in groups, through employment or associations, rather than as individuals. The costs to the insurer of selling and administering insurance for a group are lower than for the same individual separately. Premium rates will thus be higher for individuals, and as a result fewer single buyers will transfer their risks than will group members.

Another factor pushing the health insurance system toward group insurance is the income tax treatment of health insurance premiums. When employees obtain fringe benefits in the form of employer-purchased health insurance, the benefits are not subject to income taxation. As a result, the net price of health insurance coverage is lower when it is obtained through employment. This encourages employees to purchase health insurance. Since the same deduction is not available to individuals who directly purchase health insurance from insurers, they do not have as much reason to purchase health insurance.

7.7.4.2 Heterogeneous Risks

In the model as first described, we assumed that everyone had the same risk. If individuals have different risks (because they differ in health status), there will be differences in premiums. Let us assume that there are two groups, one consisting of healthy individuals and one consisting of unhealthy individuals. If all other assumptions of our model are the same, there will be two separate premiums, one for the healthy and one for the unhealthy. Depending on their demand functions, individuals in each group will choose to insure or not to insure. However, as long as the unhealthy group is not *too* unhealthy, there will be some of this group who are more risk averse and who purchase insurance.

7.7.4.3 Community Rating

Under community-rated premium setting, all consumers pay the same premium regardless of their risk function, their tastes, and the costs of administering their insurance. This form of pricing has been very common among Blue Cross and Blue Shield plans. The impact of community rating is quite considerable.

With community rating the single rate will be set at a level that reflects the average risk among all insureds. If everyone had the same risk function, this would not pose a problem. Some would insure and some not, depending on their tastes for risk. However, let us assume that there is a healthy and an unhealthy group. These two groups will have different loss rates. Let us also assume that there is one premium rate set independently in the market by an insurance commission.

The insurers will compete for risk coverage but not on the basis of price, which is fixed. Individuals in the higher risk group will be induced to purchase coverage at beneficial premium rates, but those in the lower risk groups will not. The price that they will pay will reflect average risk ratings, which are above their ratings. Of course, some healthy individuals may insure if they are sufficiently risk averse. But at a higher premium, more will not insure.

This scenario would last one period. Premium rates are set based on experience, and as a proportion of healthy people drop out of the market, the percentage of high-cost insureds in the market would increase. A spiral that results in the drying up of the market may occur.

This spiral may be dampened by an important factor. If individuals receive their health insurance through a group, all individuals in the group, healthy and otherwise, receive tax benefits that make the purchase of health care insurance a better deal. Healthy individuals may still remain in the market as a consequence.

BIBLIOGRAPHY

On the Competitive Market Model

Buchanan, J.M. 1965. *The inconsistencies of the National Health Service*. Occasional paper 7. London: Institute of Economic Affairs.

Christianson, J.B., and McClure, W. 1979. Competition in the delivery of medical care. *New England Journal of Medicine* 301:812–818.

Culyer, A.J., and Cullis, J.G. 1976. Some economics of hospital waiting lists in the NHS. *Social Policy* 5:239–264.

Evans, R.G. 1974. Supplier induced demand. In *The economics of health and medical care*, ed. M. Pearlman. London: MacMillan.

Feldstein, M.S. 1970. The rising price of physicians' services. *Review of Economics and Statistics* 52:121–133.

———. 1974. Econometric studies in health economics. In *Frontiers in quantitative economics*, ed. M. Intriligator and S. Kendrick. Amsterdam, The Netherlands: North-Holland.

Frank, R.G., and Welch, W.P. 1985. The competitive effects of HMOs: A review of the evidence. *Inquiry* 22:148–161.

Friedman, M. 1962. *Capitalism and freedom*. Chicago: University of Chicago Press.

Fuchs, V.R., and Kramer, M. 1972. *Determinants of expenditures for physicians' services in the United States, 1948–1968*. Publication no. HSM 73-3013. Washington, D.C.: National Center for Health Services Research.

Garbarino, J.W. 1959. Price behavior and productivity in the medical market. *Industrial and Labor Relations Review* 13:3–15.

Greene, V.L., et al. 1993. Do community-based long-term care services reduce nursing home use? *Journal of Human Resources* 28:297–317.

Hay, J.W., and Leahy, M.J. 1984. Competition among health plans. *Southern Economic Journal* 50:831–846.

Kessell, R. 1958. Price discrimination in medicine. *Journal of Law and Economics* 1:20–53.

Lindsay, C.M. 1976. More real returns to medical education. *Journal of Human Resources* 11:127–129.

Mwabu, G., et al. 1993. Quality of medical care and choice of treatment in Kenya. *Journal of Human Resources* 28:838–862.

Newhouse, J.P. 1970. A model of physician pricing. *Southern Economic Journal* 37:147–183.

———. 1977. Policy options and the impact of national health insurance revisited. *International Journal of Health Services* 7:503–509.

Pauly, M.V., and Langwell, K.M. 1983. Research on competition in the market for health services. *Inquiry* 20:142–161.

Rizzo, J.A., and Zeckhauser, R.J. 1992. Advertising and the price, quantity, and quality of primary care physicians' services. *Journal of Human Resources* 28:387–421.

Ro, K.K. 1977. Anatomy of hospital cost inflation. *Hospitals and Health Services Administration* 22:78–88.

Salkever, D. 1975. Hospital wage inflation. *Quarterly Review of Economics and Business* 15:33–84.

———. 1978. Competition among hospitals. In *Competition in the health care sector*, ed, W. Greenberg. Washington, D.C.: Federal Trade Commission, Bureau of Economics.

Schwartz, W.B., and Mendelson, D.N. 1990. No evidence of an emerging physician surplus. *JAMA* 263:557–560.

Sloan, F.A. 1976. Real returns to medical education. *Journal of Human Resources* 11:118–126.

Sloan, F.A., and Feldman, R. 1978. Competition among physicians. In *Competition in the health care sector*, ed. W. Greenberg. Washington, D.C.: Federal Trade Commission, Bureau of Economics.

Sloan, F.A., and Lorant, J.H. 1976. The allocation of physicians' services. *Quarterly Review of Economics and Business* 16:86–103.

Wu, W.S., and Masson, R. 1974. Price discrimination for physicians' services. *Journal of Human Resources* 9:63–79.

Zwanzinger, J., et al. 1990. Measures of hospital market structure: A review of the alternatives and a proposed approach. *Socio-Economic Planning Sciences* 24:81–95.

Insurance Markets

Abraham, K.S. 1985. Efficiency and fairness in insurance risk classification. *Virginia Law Review* 71:403–451.

Pauly, M.V. 1986. Taxation, health insurance, and market failure in the medical economy. *Journal of Economic Literature* 25:629–675.

———. 1989. Competition in health insurance markets. *Law and Contemporary Problems* 51:237–271.

Labor Markets

Holtman, A.G., and Idson, T.L. 1993. Wage determination of registered nurses in proprietary and nonprofit nursing homes. *Journal of Human Resources* 28:55–79.

Kreuger, A.B., and Reinhardt, U.E. 1994. Economics of employer versus individual mandates. *Health Affairs* 13:34–54.

Competitive Bidding

Brown, E.R., et al. 1985. Competing for medical business. *Inquiry* 22:237–250.

Christianson, J.B. 1984. Provider participation in competitive bidding for indigent patients. *Inquiry* 21:161–177.

———. 1985. The challenge of competitive bidding. *Health Care Management Review* 10 (2):39–54.

Christianson, J.B., et al. 1983. The Arizona experiment: Competitive bidding for indigent medical care. *Health Affairs* 2:87–103.

Christianson, J.B., et al. 1984. A comparison of existing and alternative competitive bidding systems for indigent medical care. *Social Science and Medicine* 18:599–604.

Dranove, D., et al. 1992. Is hospital competition wasteful? *Rand Journal of Economics* 23:247–262.

Freeland, M.S., et al. 1987. Selective contracting for hospital care based on volume, quality, and price. *Journal of Health Politics, Policy and Law* 12:409–426.

Johns, L. 1989. Selective contracting in California: An update. *Inquiry* 26:345–353.

Johns, L., et al. 1985. Selective contracting in California: Early effects and policy implications. *Inquiry* 22:24–32.

Keijser, G.M., and Kirkman-Liff, B.L. 1992. Competitive bidding for health insurance contracts. *Health Policy* 21:35–46.

Kirkman-Liff, B.L., et al. 1985. An analysis of competitive bidding by providers for indigent medical care contracts. *Health Services Research* 20:549–577.

McCall, N., et al. 1985. Evaluating the Arizona health care cost containment system. *Health Care Financing Review* 7:77–88.

Melia, E.P., et al. 1983. Competition in the health care marketplace. *New England Journal of Medicine* 308:788–792.

Melnick, G.A., and Zwanzinger, J. 1988. Hospital behavior under competition and cost containment policies. *JAMA* 260:2669–2681.

Melnick, G.A., et al. 1992. The effects of market structure and bargaining position on hospital prices. *Journal of Health Economics* 11:217–233.

Robinson, J.C., and Luft, H.S. 1988. Competition, regulation, and hospital costs, 1982 to 1986. *JAMA* 260:2676–2681.

Robinson, J.C., and Phibbs, C.S. 1989. An evaluation of selective contracting in California. *Journal of Health Economics* 8:437–455.

Zwanzinger, J., and Melnyck, G.A. 1988. The effects of hospital competition and the Medicare PPS program on hospital cost behavior in Ontario. *Journal of Health Economics* 7:301–320.

CHAPTER 8

Market Power
in Health Care

8.1 INTRODUCTION

Market power refers to the ability of one participant in a market to influence the terms on which he or she makes an exchange. Market power can be wielded by both buyers and sellers. For example, a heart surgeon can be in a position to influence the fee that patients or insurers pay. Similarly, an insurance company or government health insurance program can be in a position to influence the rate at which it reimburses providers for supplying services to its members.

Essential ingredients of market power are the availability of viable substitutes for the service and the ease with which buyers and sellers can weigh these alternatives. A hospital may be the only hospital for hundreds of miles, in which case it possesses some degree of market power (i.e., it has some leeway in setting prices and other terms for the services it provides). On the other hand, a large number of HMOs may be vying to become providers for a firm's employees; in this case, the HMOs have little or no market power, although the firm may possess some.

Market power is important because, if possessed by buyers or sellers, it might allow them to wield influence over the use of resources to their benefit and to the detriment of the other bargaining parties. In this chapter we develop the analysis of how market power influences the market outcomes (i.e., prices, quantities, and quality). Our analysis is "explanatory" in the sense that we are asking how one set of factors (related to market power) influences specific phenomena. Discussion of the desirability (or lack of it) of market power must wait until we discuss yardsticks with which to gauge actual market conduct.

We will examine several models that explain resource allocation when either buyers or sellers possess some degree of market power. In Section 8.2 we look at two models of the behavior of the ultimate wielder of market power—the monopolist—that offer predictions about how monopolistic suppliers and demanders set price and quantity. All suppliers and demanders would benefit if they possessed market power, and so a pertinent question is, how does one obtain it? In Section 8.3 we consider the determinants of market power. Section 8.3.1 contains a general discussion of market power, and Section 8.3.2 focuses on how providers in one market that possesses many of the preconditions of a competitive market, the physician services market, were nevertheless able to develop and maintain a considerable degree of market power and use it to bolster their incomes.

The monopolistic model and the competitive model are two polar extremes of models of market power. In many (perhaps most) markets, market power and competition are mixed to varying degrees. In Section 8.4 we discuss several models of incomplete market power that elucidate how product quality can be an important outcome in provider competition.

8.2 MONOPOLISTIC MARKETS

8.2.1 Simple Monopoly

A supplier has a monopoly in a market when it is the sole source of supply in that market. In a monopolistic market, the demanders do not have any close substitutes for the service. Of course, some substitutability usually exists. For example, in health care an alternative to treatment usually exists, even if that alternative is to do nothing.

We will develop the monopoly model in the context of a supposed monopolistic market, the market for pediatric ambulatory services. We assume that in this market there is a single group practice. The product is defined as quality-constant pediatric visits. The simple monopoly model consists of demand, cost, and behavioral assumptions.

8.2.1.1 Demand

With regard to demand, we assume that the pediatric group faces a single market demand curve (see Table 8–1 and Figure 8–1). Note that there is a price ($10) at which patients will abstain from making any visits. As discussed in Section 3.5, as one moves down the demand curve, one moves through elastic, unit elastic, and inelastic portions of the demand curve, and the total revenue (*TR*) will increase, level off, and decrease. The marginal revenue (*MR*) is falling throughout, although it is positive when it is associated with the elastic portion of the demand curve and zero relative to the unit elastic point on the demand curve. For the provider, the *MR* represents the additional *TR* that it will receive by lowering the price enough to sell one more visit. Note that as the provider lowers its price, it sells more units, but all of them are sold at the new, lower price. The *MR* is the net change in *TR* and is equal to the difference in the two *TRs* at the two quantity levels.

Table 8-1 Revenue and Cost in a Hypothetical Monopolistic Market

Price	Units of Output	Total Revenue (TR)	Marginal Revenue (MR)	Total Cost (TC)	Marginal Cost (MC)	Profits (TR – TC)
$10	0	0		3		-3
9	1	9	9	4	1	5
8	2	16	7	6	2	10
7	3	21	5	9	3	12
6	4	24	3	13	4	11
5	5	25	1	18	5	7
4	5	24	-1	24	6	0
3	7	21	-3	31	7	-10

The monopolist has the ability to set price at any level it wishes. This ability represents the ultimate degree in market power. (Of course, the price it sets will influence the quantity demanded, something the monopolist will want to keep in mind when setting the price.)

8.2.1.2 Cost

Our cost assumptions are that the total fixed cost (*TFC*) is $3 and that the total variable cost (*TVC*) is increasing in such a way that marginal cost (*MC*) increases as output expands (see Table 8–1, Column 6). The total cost (*TC*) is the sum of *TVC* and *TFC*.

8.2.1.3 Objectives

Profits (Column 7) are equal to *TR – TC* and initially increase and then decrease as output expands. But we cannot tell what price will be charged and what output (and profit) levels will be attained until we know what objectives the provider is pursuing. We will initially assume that the provider's objective is to maximize profits.

Our analysis of the model is as follows. First, the price will be set at that point on the demand curve at which *MR* comes closest to (or equals) *MC* (without *MC* exceeding *MR*). Let us assume that the monopolist initially set its price at $10 per visit. It would have no buyers at such a price (see Table 8–1), and its losses would be confined to its fixed costs, since it would have no variable costs at zero output. If price was lowered to $9, one visit would be sold and the *MR* would be $9. One additional visit would cost only $1 extra (*MC* = $1) and would add $8 to the previous output level's profits. Total profit would therefore be $5. This is certainly better than not operating at all but not as good as lowering the price to $8, selling two units in total, and deriving an additional $7 in revenue in the process (*MR* =

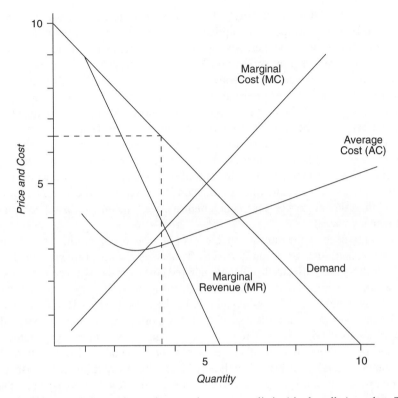

Figure 8–1 Equilibrium price and output in a monopolistic (single seller) market. The monopolist faces a given demand curve for the service, and from this curve is derived its marginal revenue curve. The monopolist's cost conditions are presented in marginal (*MC*) and average (*AC*) terms. The profit-maximizing monopolist will set price and quantity such that its *MR* = *MC*. Equilibrium price is between $6 and $7, and equilibrium quantity is between $3 and $4. (This graph is based on data in Table 8–1.)

$7). For then it would cost the pediatricians only $2 more to provide this added visit, and they would be adding another $5 (*MR* – *MC*) to the previous profit level, making the profits $10 in total. Indeed, the practice would lower its price to $7, selling three visits. It would stop there, because beyond this level of output *MC* begins to rise steeply, *TC* increases more than *TR* increases, and as a result *MR* – *MC* becomes negative. Any further increase in output would detract from total profits.

The above analysis is shown graphically in Figure 8–1, which has smoothed out revenue and cost functions. Here we see that the *MR* and *MC* curves intersect (meaning $MR = MC$) at a quantity of between 3 and 4 (because of our smoothed-out values). This corresponds to a price on the demand curve of between $6 and $7. Profitability cannot be increased by raising or lowering the price.

Let us now see what the model implies. First, the provider will set the price at that point on the demand curve above which the MR and MC curves intersect. Because MC is positive, MR must also be positive (since $MR = MC$) at the profit-maximizing point. It should be noted that MR is positive only at those quantities that correspond to the *elastic* portion of the demand curve. Therefore, a monopolist will set the price only on the elastic portion of its demand curve. Indeed, if the price was set on the inelastic portion of the curve, say at $3, MR would be negative, meaning that a reduction in output coming from a price increase would raise total revenues. At the same time a reduction in output would reduce TC. Profits would therefore always be greater at a higher price (one on the elastic portion of the demand curve).

In addition, since the most profitable level of output is determined by MR and MC alone, and since MC is unaffected by fixed costs, the profit-maximizing price will similarly be unaffected by changes in fixed costs. Let us say that fixed costs in our example increase to $5. Profits would be lower by $2 at every level of output. But the maximum profit level would still be the same (at $Q = 3$), only now the provider would be earning less profit. This important result implies that if the provider's fixed costs increase (e.g., because of an increase in mortgage rates), it cannot do anything about it. If it tries to pass on these added fixed costs to the consumer by raising the price, it will only be moving away from the profit-maximizing position; in raising price it will sell less, and MR will decrease more than MC. This, of course, is not true for an increase in variable costs (i.e., MC).

In a similar vein, if the profit-maximizing monopolist received a fixed subsidy (i.e., one unrelated to output) of $2 to treat poor patients, TR would be increased at every level of output by $2, but MR would not be affected. The monopolist's profit-maximizing price will not change, and unless the granting agency enforces the terms of the subsidy, nothing will change. That is, the profit-maximizing monopolist will not lower the price to induce people to demand more.

One outcome of the monopoly model is that the firm could be persistently earning excess profits. Since the AC curve incorporates all the monopolist's costs, including opportunity costs (see Section 5.3.1), the monopolist's profits in this analysis are equal to $TR - TC$ or, using average terms, the product of the unit margin ($P - AC$) and output (Q). These profits are true economic profits. That is, they are profits over and above all the costs required to operate the enterprise, including a normal return for the owner's efforts and capital. Furthermore, nothing in the model will allow the monopolist's profits to be bid away. There are no potential entrants into the market who can charge a lower price. As a result, the monopolist can earn above-normal profits that persist over time. Recall that, in the competitive market model, entry is inexpensive and any excess profits will attract new entrants, who will expand supply and lower price and profits.

8.2.2 Buyer's Market Power

Market power can also exist on the buyer's side. Let us assume that there is a single buyer of nursing services, a hospital in a small city. For this single buyer, we set out an economic model to predict pricing and output decisions.

8.2.2.1 Supplier Costs

With respect to the supply side of the market, we assume there are a number of nurses available to be hired by the hospital (their supply curve is drawn in Figure 8–2). At a wage of $2 weekly, two nurses will supply their services; if the wage is increased to $3, three nurses will supply their services; and so on. With respect to the demand side of the market, the successive marginal values that the single hospital places on nurses is also shown in Figure 8–2.

8.2.2.2 Revenues

Let us assume (1) that additional nurses allow the hospital to treat more patients but the marginal productivity of these extra nurses diminishes and (2) that the price received for each extra patient by the hospital is constant. The hospital's value curve has been derived from the estimated additional revenue that the hospital estimates the additional nurses will bring in. The marginal revenue (equal to the price of output times the marginal output yielded by an extra nursing unit) is $9 for the first nurse, $8 for the second, $7 for the third, and so on. Note that the total value to the hospital of three nurses is $24 ($9 + $8 + $7).

8.2.2.3 Behavioral Assumption

Finally, we will assume that the hospital wishes to maximize profits.

8.2.2.4 Implications

The implications of our model are that the profit-maximizing hospital will hire additional nurses as long as the marginal cost of doing so is less than the additional revenue. But the *MC* of nurses to the hospital is not the nurses' supply curve, *S*. Since *S* is sloped up, each successive nurse wants an extra dollar of pay. Assuming that the hospital must pay all nurses the same wage, by hiring the second nurse it must pay a higher wage to the first as well. As a result, the *MC* curve is more steeply sloped than the supply curve (see Figure 8–2). For example, the *MC* of the second nurse is $3 but that of the third nurse is $5 ($9 – $4). The profit-maximizing hospital will hire three nurses (between 3 and 4 in Figure 8–2), for then the hospital's added revenue will equal its *MC* for hiring nurses. At such a level of

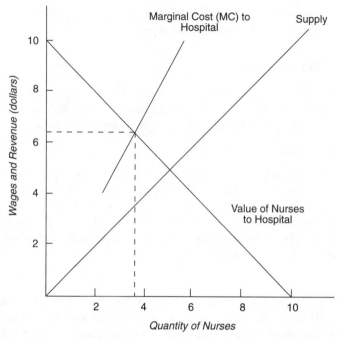

Figure 8–2 The equilibrium wage and number of nurses hired in a monopsonistic (single-buyer) market. The firm's marginal cost for hiring additional nurses is derived from the schedule of nurses in the market. The value of an additional nurse is based on the amount of output that the hospital can produce with nurses (productivity) and the price of the output (in short, the amount of revenue brought in by hiring an additional nurse). The profit-maximizing hospital will continue to hire nurses up to the point where the *MC* equals the additional revenue from hiring another nurse.

hiring, it will pay a wage of $3, since that is the wage at which three nurses will supply their services.

In a monopsonistic (single-buyer) market, fewer nurses would be hired than in a competitive market. In a competitive market, competitive forces would drive the wage up to the level where supply equals demand; more nurses would be hired and wages would be higher. However, a monopsonistic buyer can prevent more nurses from being hired, thus maintaining its profits. At the same time as it depresses wages, it creates a restriction in supply. Substantial buying power may be characteristic of buyers of health insurance in markets where there are not only several large businesses but a large number of HMOs and traditional insurance companies. It may also be characteristic of some preferred provider organizations. An insurer (that is also a PPO) can offer lower premiums if it can get its enrollees to agree to go to designated lower cost providers. The insurer would then negotiate with the providers for lower rates. If the insurer had a substantial enrollment and could negotiate for rates that would be *lower* than in a competitive market, it would possess monopsonistic power (Pauly 1987, 1988).

8.2.3 Price Discrimination

Under some conditions a monopolist can further increase its profits by charging different prices to different buyers. This is called *price discrimination*. Price discrimination can be practiced only when the product or service in the lower price market cannot be resold in the higher price market. In addition, the demand elasticities in the two markets have to be different to make the practice worthwhile.

Let us assume that a pediatric practice can separate its patients into two distinct markets according to patient income. Assume further that demand elasticity is influenced by income so that each market will have different demand curves. Thus, one of the preconditions for price discrimination is met. The product sold is patient visits. These can hardly be sold in one market and resold in the other, so the other precondition is met as well. The demand curves for the two separate markets, "rich" and "poor," are shown in Figure 8–3, Graphs A and B. Our cost assumption is that the *MC* eventually rises, as shown in Graph C. Note that there is one *MC* for the entire operation; production is not separated. Our behavioral assumption is that the pediatric practice seeks to maximize its profits.

Given these assumptions, we can use the monopolistic model to elucidate the monopolist's pricing policy. In doing so, we must rely on the equimarginal principle of maximization. To maximize profits, the provider will set the price (and therefore the quantity) in each market so that (1) the *MR* earned by lowering (raising) the price in all markets is the same and (2) overall the *MR* in each market is equal to the *MC* of producing that level of output.

The derivation of the profit-maximizing prices is shown in Figure 8–3. The curve *MC* shows the provider's marginal cost for all units provided (it does not have a separate cost for each market), and the curve *SMR* shows the quantity that would be supplied overall when the firm allocated output to each market according to the specific level of *MR*. *SMR* is thus the sum of quantities in both markets at a given level of *MR*. Given the *MR* curves for the poor and the rich markets (MR_p and MR_r), at an *MR* level in both markets of 4, the corresponding quantities in the markets are 4 and 2, respectively. The *SMR* curve for those quantities will be at a quantity of 6, where $Q_m = Q_p + Q_r$.

The firm's maximum profit position will be determined by equating *MC* with the *MR* in each market. Overall, this occurs where $MC = SMR$ (at quantity 6). The corresponding outputs in each market are 4 and 2, and the prices in the two markets that equate the *MR*s are 8 and 6, respectively. Profits, which are equal to the sum of *TR* in each market less *TC*, will be greater than if the same price was set in all markets.

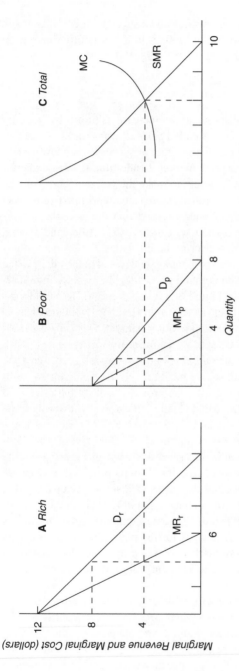

Figure 8–3 Price setting by a discriminating monopolist. If the monopolist can separate its markets into two submarkets, "rich" and "poor," the price charged in each submarket will be derived from firm-level conditions and will occur where the marginal revenue in that submarket equals the overall marginal cost to the firm. The curve *SMR* in Graph C shows the total quantity in all submarkets at each level of *MR*. Note that equilibrium occurs in each market at the same value of *MR*.

Price discrimination such as this cannot exist in a competitive market, and this is one reason why physician pricing has been characterized as monopolistic. In a competitive market, if two submarkets had different prices, "traders" would buy goods in the low price market and resell them (at a higher price but below the market price) in the second market. For many years, physicians, particularly specialists, resorted to a sliding scale of fees when setting prices, charging the richer patients more than the poorer ones (Kessell 1958). By the 1970s, physician services became more highly insured and the sliding scale all but disappeared by that time (Newhouse 1970).

8.2.4 Physician Pricing and Supply in Public Programs

A variant of the two-payer monopoly model outlined in Section 8.2.3 has been used to explain physician pricing and supply in relation to the reimbursement policies of Blue Shield (Sloan and Steinwald 1978), Medicare (Paringer 1980; Rice 1984), and Medicaid (Cromwell and Mitchell 1984; Kushman 1977; Hadley 1979) and the 1972–1975 price limitations set by the Economic Stabilization Program (Hadley and Lee 1978–1979).

The Medicare studies examined the effect of Medicare reimbursement levels (80 percent of the reasonable charges) on the assignment decision—the decision of physicians to accept the Medicare-determined fee as full payment for their services. On an individual-case basis, physicians can accept Medicare assignment of their patients. A physician who accepts the reasonable fee in full (i.e., who accepts assignment) for a specific patient receives 80 percent of the fee direct from Medicare and can bill the patient for the copayment. If the physician does not accept assignment, he or she can bill the patient whatever fee he or she chooses. In this case Medicare will reimburse the patient directly for 80 percent of its reasonable fee, and the physician must collect the entire charge from the patient. The acceptance by physicians of assignment relieves patients from the financial risks associated with higher physician fees.

The analysis is set out graphically in Figure 8–4. The physician is assumed to be a monopolist facing two submarkets: one with private patients and one with patients in a public program. (We ignore the extra billing in this analysis.) The output is defined as patients served. D_p is the demand curve for private patients, and MR_p is the related MR curve. The public agency reimburses the physicians for its patients at a fee level F_m; since the fee level is fixed, F_m is also the physician's MR for public patients. Assume that the physician's MC curve is at MC_1. Finally, assume that the physician is a profit maximizer.

According to the equimarginal principle, the physician will supply services to Q_1 private and $(Q_3 - Q_1)$ public patients, since at this output $MR_p = F_m$ and both are equal to MC_1. The private patients will be charged a price of P_m. To attract any

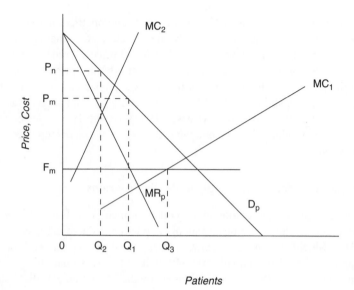

Patients

Figure 8–4 Representation of price setting by a monopolist facing a private market (with demand represented by D_p and marginal revenue by MR_p) and a publicly financed market (with a set fee and therefore a marginal revenue of F_m). With a marginal cost of MC_1, the monopolist will set the price to equate the MR in both markets. In this case, the price in the private market is set at P_m. The marginal revenue for public and private patients will be the same, MC_1. Total output supplied is Q_3, with $Q_3 - Q_1$ going to public patients. With an MC such as MC_2, the monopolist would not supply any output to the public patients; the price and output levels in the private market would be P_n and Q_2.

additional private patients, the physician would have to lower the price to private patients below P_m, which would imply an MR for private patients below that for public patients. A profit-maximizing physician will thus prefer to serve additional public patients where the MR is constant at a level F_m rather than lower his or her price and have a marginal revenue below F_m.

A lower public fee would lower the supply to the public patients (it would also cause the physician to lower his or her private fee, since the physician will now move down the MR_p curve.) A physician facing the same demand curve but with a higher MC (say, MC_2) will not supply any services to public patients and will set a private fee of P_n. This analysis demonstrates that the public and private sectors are interdependent. A public program that lowers fees will reduce the supply to the public market and will also affect the private market.

8.2.5 Hospital Cost Shifting

A model similar to the one discussed in the previous section has been used to explain hospital cost shifting, a tactic purportedly used by hospitals to raise fees on self-pay and commercially insured patients in response to low reimbursement levels by Medicare, Medicaid, and, in some instances, Blue Cross (Danzon 1982; Sloan 1984; Sloan and Ginsburg 1984).

8.2.6 Nursing Home Markets and Public Rates

The two-payer monopoly model is also suited to analyzing economic behavior in the nursing home market. Generally, in this market, there are two major groups of payers: self-pay (relatively uninsured) patients and state Medicaid agencies. Many Medicaid agencies pay nursing homes a flat rate, whereas self-pay patients are changed according to market conditions. With Medicaid agencies being economy minded and having the power to set rates, one option they have in pursuing the goal of budget containment is to set low rates.

Because the nursing homes can differentiate their products, they can develop some form of "brand loyalty" on the part of patients and prospective patients. When they have patients with some degree of preference, nursing homes will face demand curves that have some elasticity (i.e., are downward sloping). The more loyal their patients are, the more inelastic their demand curves will be.

Figure 8–4 can therefore be interpreted as pertaining to nursing home markets. In this diagram, assume that F_m is the rate that Medicaid pays to nursing homes, D_p is the demand of private pay patients, and MC_1 is a nursing home's marginal cost. At the fee level (and marginal revenue) of F_m, the nursing home will equate its marginal cost so that it is equal to the MR for each class of patients. It will therefore serve Q_3 patients, with Q_1 of these being private and $Q_3 - Q_1$ being Medicaid. If the Medicaid agency lowered its rates below F_m, fewer Medicaid patients (and more private pay patients) would be served. Shortages of Medicaid patient nursing home beds would therefore appear (Paringer 1983).

8.3   MARKET STRUCTURE AND ITS DETERMINANTS

8.3.1 Measuring Market Concentration

Market structure has a major influence on market power. Structure is usually presented in terms of an index or percentage, representing the size of the largest firm (or four firms or eight firms) relative to the overall market's output or else measuring the distribution of firm size in the market. A four-firm concentration ratio shows the percentage of the total market (in terms of sales, assets, or some other indicator of firm size) represented by the largest four firms. For example, a completely monopolized market has a concentration ratio of 100 percent; a market with 20 firms, total sales of $1 billion, and combined sales for the largest four firms of $1/2 dollars would have a four-firm concentration ratio of 50 percent. The choice of four or eight firms is arbitrary and does not indicate the concentration of the remainder of the market. A more general measure of concentration, which incorporates all firms in the market, is the Herfindahl (H) index. According to this index, concentration is measured as

$$H = \Sigma(S/M)^2 \times 10,000$$

where S is the size of each firm and M is the size of the total market. The figure 10,000 is used as a multiplier because H is usually presented as a sum of percentages expressed in absolute terms. The summation sign (Σ) indicates summation over all firms. Thus a monopolist with sales of $200 is the only firm in the market; its H index is $(200/200) \times 10,000$, or 10,000. If there were three hospitals, each with sales of $100, the H index for that market would be 3,300 $\Sigma(100/300)^2 \times 10,000$.

There is no true cutoff point for a concentrated versus a nonconcentrated market, although a figure of about 1,800 is sometimes used (Wilder and Jacobs 1986). Generally, it is thought that the greater the degree of concentration, the greater will be the ability of the leading firms to influence price, quantity, and other characteristics of output.

8.3.2 Determinants of Market Structure

Market structure can be thought of as having market and governmentally imposed (regulatory) determinants. Let us examine these in the context of the health insurance market. In the United States, the health insurance market is largely a localized market, in part because each state requires operating licenses for any insurance company operating within the state and also because of unique relations between local providers and some insurers (primarily the Blues). Aside from government insurance, health insurance has been broken down into two categories of operators, the Blues and the commercial insurance companies. The Blues comprise Blue Cross (for hospitalization insurance) and Blue Shield (for medical and other insurance). In some states the two plans are combined. The Blues are nonprofit in terms of organization. Commercial insurers include a large number of mutual (member-owned) and commercial (for-profit) firms, none of which has a substantial share of the health care market. Blue Cross and Blue Shield collect about one-quarter of the total health insurance premiums nationally, although their share of the private insurance market varies considerably by state.

8.3.2.1 Economies of Scale

Among the most important market determinants of market power are economies of scale. Let us assume that the market demand for private health insurance is D_m in Figure 8–5 and that the long-run average cost curve for a state-of-the-art insurance company is LAC. Two things should be noted in our example. First, the long-run average cost incorporates capital and other fixed setup costs as well as current operating costs; if there are high start-up costs for the industry, the LAC at

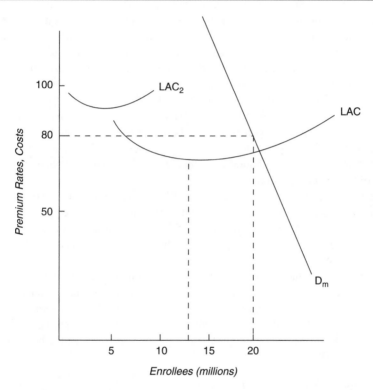

Figure 8–5 Output in an insurance market with alternative cost conditions. D_m represents market demand for insurance coverage. If the cost conditions are represented by cost curve LAC, one firm can capture a substantial portion of the market by virtue of its economies of scale and pricing policies. A producer with the cost conditions represented by LAC could set a price of, say, $80; if it did so and chose to supply 13 million policies (as shown by the dashed line), another producer with the same cost conditions could not reach a large enough scale of output to match the first producer's cost (and price). If the cost conditions were represented by LAC_2, no producer could dominate the market in this way.

low output levels will be quite high. Second, the *LAC* in our example includes insurance administration costs and the amount the insurance company reimburses the providers. The shape of the *LAC* curve in our example is such that the minimum cost is reached at a large scale of output (about 12 million subscribers).

8.3.2.2 Pricing Policies

Given certain cost conditions, one firm could capture a considerable portion of the market. To do so, however, it must resort to a second, and related, market share determinant: pricing policy. If the insurance company sets a very low price relative to costs, say, $80 per subscriber, market demand would be quite large (20 million subscribers). In this case, the insurance company would have considerable discretion in choosing its own output level; the level chosen would depend, of course, on its objectives. If it provided services for 13 million subscribers at this price, there would be an excess demand of 7 million potential subscribers. If the technology of insurance provision was known to other potential entrants, a second firm could provide insurance on a cost basis like that represented by the *LAC* curve. However, to reach a unit cost of $80, it would need to operate at a scale of 8 million subscribers. Since the potential entrant could not obtain such a volume, it might simply produce at a higher cost, charge a higher price, and obtain a smaller share of the residual market.

The final distribution of market shares will thus depend on the size of potential economies of scale relative to the potential market and also on the pricing policies of the larger firms. As seen in Figure 8–5, if the initial insurance company charged a higher price, say, $90 or $100, potential entrants would have less problem gaining an entry to the market.

If, on the other hand, the state-of-the-art cost curve was like *LAC*$_2$ (with no substantial economies of scale), no firm could obtain a substantial share of the market, and a concentration of firms would be unlikely. There is some evidence economies of scale exist in health insurance operations, but these economies are not of the magnitude that would permit a single firm to dominate the health insurance market (Blair et al. 1975).

8.3.2.3 Input Prices and Taxes

A third cause of market concentration relates not to the cost-scale relation but to the potentially different levels of cost curves for different providers. If, for example, one provider could obtain its inputs (workers, materials, etc.) at a lower cost than a second provider, its cost curve would be lower at all scales of output than the cost curve of the second provider. The first firm could capture a larger share of the market by turning its cost advantage into a price differential. One such input price differential is the discount that many Blue Cross plans receive from hospitals (Feldman and Greenberg 1981; Goldberg and Greenberg 1985), which is perhaps partly due to the special traditional relation between Blue Cross and hospitals (Blue Cross was founded by hospitals). Whereas commercial insurance companies typically have reimbursed hospitals for close to full charges, about half of the Blue Cross plans have received discounts ranging from 2 to 30 percent and averaging from 8 to 15 percent. These discounts have the effect of lowering the *LAC* curves of the Blue Cross plans relative to the commercial ones, allowing Blue Cross to gain an increased market share by charging lower premium rates. One recent estimate attributed 7 percent of Blue Cross's market share to this cost differential.

8.3.2.4 Regulation

There might also be regulatory causes of market concentration. Like the Blue Cross discount, discriminatory regulations can give one firm or type of firm a cost advantage that allows it to lower price and increase market share. One such regulation is the tax on health insurance premiums, which is imposed on commercial insurance companies in all states; in some states the Blue plans are exempt from such a tax, which is about 2 percent of premiums. In addition, the Blue plans, being nonprofit, are exempt from income taxes and, in some states, from property taxes. Such exemptions lower the Blues' total costs, giving them a cost advantage.

However, these advantages need not always result in a larger market share. As shown in Section 6.6, firms can incur costs providing on-the-job benefits for the managers. This is particularly true for nonprofit firms, whose profits cannot be directly shared by the managers. Thus any cost advantage possessed by a nonprofit firm can be appropriated by the managers rather than be passed on to consumers in the form of lower premiums. On-the-job amenities have been hypothesized to be a factor in the behavior of Blue Shield plans that were not "controlled" by physicians. Blue Shield plans deemed to be physician controlled were found to have lower operating costs. One possible explanation is that the physician-controlled plans passed on surpluses to the physicians in the form of reimbursements. Non-physician-controlled plans could appropriate potential surpluses and in the process generate higher operating costs (Eisenstadt and Kennedy 1981).

8.3.3 Market Power in the Market for Physicians' Services

Market structure and market power are not always equivalent. In the physician services market, there are a number of manifestations of market power, and yet the market structure does not have a high degree of provider concentration. For instance, for many years physicians were able to maintain a sliding scale of fees, indicating price discrimination. Also, their incomes have been well above normal, even allowing for the high cost of medical training. Yet significant economies of scale in medical practice are not present, and there is a very low degree of market concentration, conditions that normally accompany monopolistic pricing and profits levels.

The explanation of this paradox is that the medical profession developed a mechanism of control to police its members and prevent them from engaging in competitive practices such as price cutting (Kessell 1958; Rayack 1970). This control mechanism was basically in the hands of organized medical associations at the county, state, and national levels.

The key players were the teaching hospitals, the American Medical Association, the local medical associations, and practicing physicians, especially specialists (see Figure 8–6). The operation of the mechanism depended on the fact that it benefited several of the key groups: (1) interns were an important (and low-cost) input in the operation of teaching hospitals, and (2) physicians, especially specialists, needed membership on hospital medical staffs to make a good, secure living.

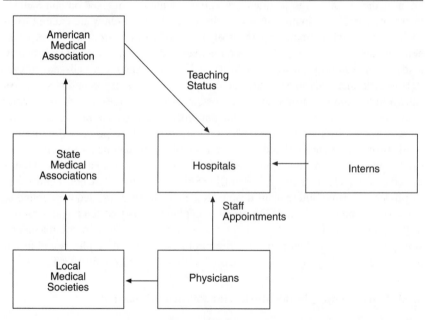

Figure 8–6 Representation of the control mechanism that existed in the medical profession. Key players included hospitals with teaching programs that required accreditation from the Council on Teaching Hospitals (AMA associated) and physicians (who benefited from staff appointments in hospitals). Membership in local medical societies was required for a staff appointment to a hospital, a regulation enforced by the AMA through its control over hospital accreditation. Local medical societies could enforce regulations (regarding pricing policies, for example) through their control over membership.

The basis of the mechanism was a convention developed by the American Medical Association (AMA) regarding the certification of teaching hospitals. According to this convention, known as the Mundt Resolution, hospitals that were certified as teaching hospitals were advised that their medical staffs should be composed only of physicians who were members of local medical societies. Since the AMA certified teaching hospitals, the resolution carried great weight.

Here is an example of how the resolution helped to limit competitive behavior on the part of physicians. County medical association members generally disapproved of price cutting and other competitive practices. One target of disapprobation was prepaid group medicine. Prepaid group practices (proto-HMOs) charged a single fee for all members, thus undermining the price discrimination system that had become prevalent. The expulsion of physicians who joined prepaid group practice staffs from county medical societies occurred in several instances (Kessell 1958), and the threat of expulsion was sufficient to make physician recruitment difficult for these practices. In addition, other competitive activities, such as advertising, were also discouraged by the organized medical profession.

The control of competitive practices by the medical profession at large has not relied solely on such formal mechanisms. With the growth of specialization, physicians have become increasingly dependent on referrals from colleagues. Physicians who engaged in competitive practices could be "controlled" to some degree if they lost referrals from colleagues (Havighurst 1978).

In recent years there has been a considerable amount of regulatory activity, especially on the part of the federal government, to contain anticompetitive practices on the part of physicians and other health care providers.

8.4 NONPRICE COMPETITION AND MARKET POWER

8.4.1 Overview

The vast majority of health care markets are neither perfectly competitive nor completely monopolistic. Consumers develop some loyalty or attachment to specific providers, but this loyalty is not complete. Furthermore, product quality or attributes other than price play a key role in the output of most health care providers; therefore, quality has a key role to play in the competitive process as well. In this section, we discuss market power and the role of nonprice competition.

In addition to price, there are many product attributes that have the potential to attract patients. Providers can increase convenience by adding office hours in order to reduce their patients' waiting time. They can build satellite facilities and clinics to cut down on their patients' travel time. Pharmacists can initiate delivery services, emergency services, family prescription monitoring records, and prescription waiting areas. Insurance companies and HMOs have a wide variety of services that might be covered and can also vary the degree to which these can be covered (e.g., through the use of copayments, deductibles, and treatment limitations). Note, however, that in all such instances additional quality is expensive to provide.

There are three relevant varieties of price-quality competition: (1) price competition alone, (2) quality competition alone, and (3) joint price and quality competition. We have already considered the first variety in Chapter 7.

8.4.2 Monopolistic Competition

Competition in both price and quality is called *monopolistic competition*. In a monopolistic competition model, we assume that there are many competitors and potential competitors (i.e., there is low-cost entry). Each firm can vary its product quality (e.g., location of facilities, operating hours, etc.) and in the process will develop some consumer loyalty (and hence market power). That is, consumers will not be as willing to change suppliers at the drop of a price as in the quality-constant perfect competition case.

Let us develop our model using the example of an HMO. We will assume that Palmedico HMO is one among a number of alternative providers (some of whom might offer more traditional insurance and fee-for-service options). Palmedico, we will suppose, is a provider of average efficiency, and we can characterize the partial loyalty of its subscribers by means of a downward-sloping demand curve (D in Figure 8–7, Graph A). Associated with this demand curve is an *MR* curve. Palmedico's cost curve will depend on the characteristics of its product: the extent of coverage, the credentials of its staff, its operating hours, the number of satellite clinics it operates, and so on. Initially, let us assume that Palmedico is a profit-maximizing institution. Given these conditions, it will set its price at the quantity where $MR = MC$. Hence, the price will be around \$750 per subscriber and the enrollment will be 5,000.

At this price Palmedico is earning excess profits, and since it is a representative firm in the industry, presumably others are earning excess profits as well. Since entry is inexpensive, other potential entrants will be attracted by the prospect of high profits. To gain enrollees, they may reduce price, and they may also offer potential enrollees a higher quality product (longer clinic hours or more clinic sites, for example). Palmedico's demand curve will shift to the left unless it responds with a higher quality and lower price, which we assume it does. As a consequence, its costs increase (because of the higher quality). The same forces will affect all firms in the market.

As long as there are any excess profits to be made, this process will continue and the quality of each firm's product will continue to rise. For each firm, demand will first shift outward in response to its higher quality and then inward in response

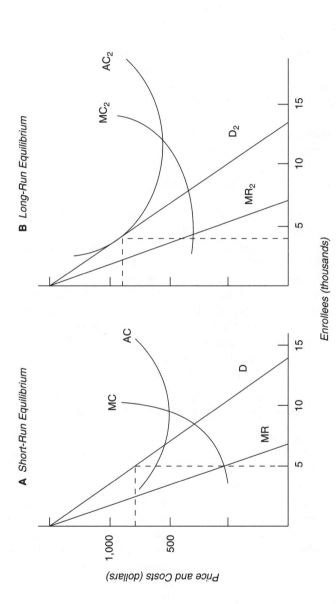

Figure 8–7 Representation of equilibrium in monopolistic competition. In the short run (Graph A), the provider's equilibrium price and quantity are set where $MR = MC$ (at 5,000 enrollees and a price around $750). In the long run (Graph B), competitive responses, including increases in quality, lead to an equilibrium where no excess profits are made (price equals average cost).

to the quality and price changes instituted by its competitors. Profit margins (the excesses of price over average cost) will continually be lowered as a result of the competition. For any firm, we cannot predict whether price will ultimately increase or decrease (i.e., we cannot predict the net result of the competitive process) because demand has shifted in both directions. For the same reason, we cannot predict the direction of enrollment. However, the final equilibrium will appear as in Figure 8–7, Graph B, where AC_2 just touches the firm's demand curve D_2. The equilibrium quantity is at the point where $MC = MR$ (i.e., it is the most profitable position Palmedico can have); in this case, Palmedico is just breaking even. All that we can say for certain about this equilibrium is that AC_2 represents a higher quality level; we cannot say for certain whether price and enrollments are higher or lower. For this reason, the monopolistic competition model has been criticized as being incomplete: It fails to make predictions on the direction of some key variables—price and quantity.

Competition between nonprofit firms would have a similar outcome. If our behavioral assumption was that the firm wants to maximize enrollees, for example, quality and price competition would still prevail and the final result would be that each provider breaks even. Models similar to the monopolistic competition model in this section have been used to explain resource allocation decisions in markets containing numerous HMOs (Christianson and McClure 1979; Goldberg and Greenberg 1980) and numerous retail drugstores (Cady 1976). The importance of nonprice factors (including quality) in these markets has been stressed. Similar models have also been used to explain the diffusion of (high-quality) technological developments in the hospital industry, such as the use of radioisotopes and intensive-care units (Lee and Waldman 1985; Rapoport 1978).

8.4.3 Monopolistic Competition and Preferred Provider Organizations

The monopolistic competition model has been used to analyze how PPOs affect hospital price and quality behavior (Dranove et al. 1986). The basic model is applied to interhospital competition, and the impact of PPOs on each individual hospital's demand curve is predicted.

A PPO is an organization that has been formed to contract with providers in order to obtain discounted prices. The PPO shops around among providers (hospitals and doctors) for lower prices and then contracts with those providers who offer better terms on behalf of insurers and/or employers. (The PPO might also institute utilization review.) The discounts are passed on in the form of lower copayments for insureds who choose the preferred providers. Consumers, in effect, are given incentives to choose providers on the basis of price. This increases the elasticity of demand facing any individual hospital, because consumers lose some of their loyalty to "their" hospital.

Using the monopolistic competition model to analyze this phenomenon, we begin with the assumption that there are many differentiated firms, each facing a downward-sloping demand curve (D_1 in Figure 8–8). We will assume that each firm has the same demand conditions and that each firm's demand curve is elastic (though the market curve can be inelastic). The implications of this will be seen below. Also, each firm has the cost conditions shown in Figure 8–8: Marginal cost is constant up to a point, then it starts to increase. The corresponding *ATC* curve is U-shaped. Initially, we will assume that short-run equilibrium is at point *A* with a price P_0 and quantity Q_0. This is based on the firm's cost conditions, demand conditions, and profit-maximizing objectives.

The change in demand conditions is the crux of this model. The introduction of a PPO will have the effect of increasing the elasticity of each individual hospital's demand (to D_2). That is, the effect of the PPO is to make each hospital more vulnerable to price changes instituted by other hospitals. With its demand elasticity increased, each hospital, assuming it acts as if all else is held constant, will lower

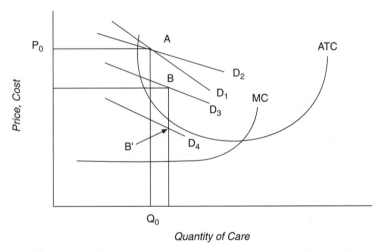

Quantity of Care

Figure 8–8 Representation of the effect of a PPO on a "typical" hospital's behavior. The initial demand curve facing the hospital (prior to the introduction of the PPO) is D_1, and the cost conditions of the hospital are represented by *AC* and *MC*. The introduction of the PPO will initially increase the elasticity of the hospital's demand curve (to D_2). In response, the hospital will lower its price. All other hospitals are facing the same situation and will do the same. As they do so, each hospital's demand curve will shift inwards. The result of these cuts is uncertain, but the demand curve could wind up at D_3 (in which case each hospital will still make a profit) or at D_4 (in which case each would operate at a loss). In the latter case, some hospitals would have to cut costs or shut down operations entirely.

its price to increase revenues and profits (this would be a profit-maximizing response of a firm facing an elastic demand curve). However, if all hospitals do the same, each hospital's demand curve will shift down (to D_3), and the new equilibrium will be at a point such as B (where each hospital shares in the larger market demand, which has expanded because of the lower price charged by all hospitals). Initially, price will fall, but hospitals in such a market may respond further. If B (on a curve such as D_3) is above the ATC curve, then the hospitals will still be making a profit after the price cut and no further change will result. On the other hand, if the collective price cuts drive the new demand curve down to D_4 (so that the equilibrium point is at B'), the hospitals will all be suffering a loss, and they will have to cut costs (by reducing services, downsizing, etc.) or some will have to leave the market. Cost cutting will shift the cost curves downward, while abandonment of the market by a few hospitals will result in a greater market share for the remaining ones. The final result will be the same: The PPO will have had an impact on hospital services ("quality") and market share.

Note that if the hospitals are operating on the constant portion of their marginal cost curves and no hospitals exit (each hospital's demand thereby remaining the same), then "downsizing" (a reduction in services and thus "quality") will be the outcome.

8.4.4 Increased Concentration

When concentration increases and providers are fewer in number, the probability of price collusion increases. Price collusion involves an explicit agreement or implicit understanding among competitors in a market to limit price competition. If there are only a few suppliers in a market and each understands that the ultimate outcome of price competition is lower prices and profits for all, the likelihood of suppliers refraining from price competition increases.

Explicit agreements to restrict price competition are illegal, but cautious pricing behavior directed at avoiding conflicts in pricing policies among competitors is not illegal. Such cautious behavior is more likely to be found when a market contains a small number of competitors, because as the number of competitors increases "cheating" is more likely. With fewer suppliers, the cost of detecting cheating is lower. Also, the impact of one supplier's price cuts is less dispersed; that is, each supplier's demand curve is shifted inward more when there are only a few suppliers.

Markets with a small number of suppliers and a significant degree of provider interdependence are called *oligopolistic*. Although vigorous price competition is not usually a characteristic of an oligopolistic market, quality competition is. In providing higher quality to attract and retain patients, the costs of oligopolistic competitors increase and profits are reduced.

Oligopolistic competition might occur when there are a few HMOs and traditional insurers in a market competing for the business of a large number of enrollees. In this case, we would expect to see rising quality but not much price competition (Hay and Leahy 1984). However, for an oligopolistic market to persist, entry by new competitors must be difficult, and the startup costs for an HMO may be low enough to make entry easy and attractive. The eventual result might be price competition. Also, buying power may discourage providers from engaging in oligopolistic behavior. In many markets, businesses play a considerable role in selecting which insurers (including HMOs) will insure their employees. If the buyer's side of the market is dominated by a few large businesses, price competition may become important despite the low number of providers.

8.4.5 Nonprice Competition

Price competition is sometimes not relevant. When patients are fully or substantially insured for a service and have a free choice among suppliers, they will choose suppliers based strictly on nonprice or quality considerations. Quality competition then becomes the only form of competition, and if the supply side of the market is competitive, costs will increase in response to quality improvements until the suppliers reach the break-even point or the limits placed by third-party reimbursers are reached. Analyses of this type of competitive process have been done for hospital markets (Farley 1985; Joskow 1980) and dialysis markets (Held and Pauly 1983). Studies across hospital markets have shown that, in market areas with greater degrees of competition (measured by the number of hospitals), hospitals are more likely to offer specialized heart surgery (Robinson et al. 1987) and specialized clinical services (Luft et al. 1986). Although these studies focused strictly on quality measures of output, there is some evidence that quality competition among hospitals is more prevalent than price competition (Noether 1988).

BIBLIOGRAPHY

Monopoly and Physicians

Havighurst, C.C. 1978. Professional restraints on innovation in health care financing. *Duke Law Journal* 1978:303–388.

Kessell, R. 1958. Price discrimination in medicine. *Journal of Law and Economics* 1:20–53.

Leffler, K.B. 1978. Physician licensure: Competition and monopoly in American medicine. *Journal of Law and Economics* 21:165–186.

Newhouse, J.P. 1970. A model of physician pricing. *Southern Economic Journal* 37:147–183.

Rayack, E. 1964. The supply of physicians' services. *Industrial and Labor Relations Review* 17:221–237.

———. 1970. *Professional power and American medicine.* Cleveland, Ohio: World Publishing Co.

Profits in Medicine

Lindsay, C.M. 1973. Real returns to medical education. *Journal of Human Resources* 8:331–348.

———. 1976. More real returns to medical education. *Journal of Human Resources* 11:127–129.

Sloan, F.A. 1976. Real returns to medical education. *Journal of Human Resources* 11:118–126.

Price Discrimination and Physician Reimbursement

Cromwell, J., and Mitchell, J. 1984. An economic model of large Medicaid practices. *Health Services Research* 19:197–218.

Gabel, J.R., and Rice, T.H. 1985. Reducing public expenditures for physician services. *Journal of Health Politics, Policy, and Law* 9:595–609.

Hadley, J. 1979. Physician participation in Medicaid: Evidence from California. *Health Services Research* 14:266–280.

Hadley, J., and Lee, R. 1978–1979. Toward a physician payment policy: Evidence from the economic stabilization program. *Policy Sciences* 10:105–120.

Kushman, J.E. 1977. Physician participation in Medicaid. *Western Journal of Agricultural Economics* 2:22–33.

Muller, C., and Ostelberg, J. 1979. Carrier discretionary practices and physician payment under Medicare Part B. *Medical Care* 17:650–666.

Paringer, L. 1980. Medicare assignment rates of physicians: Their responses to changes in reimbursement policy. *Health Care Financing Review* 1 (summer):75–89.

Rice, T. 1984. Determinants of physician assignment rates by type of service. *Health Care Financing Review* 5 (summer):33–42.

Sloan, F.A., and Steinwald, B. 1978. Physician participation in health insurance plans. *Journal of Human Resources* 13:237–263.

Hospital and Nonprofit Agency Pricing

Bauerschmidt, A.D., and Jacobs, P. 1985. Pricing objectives in non-profit hospitals. *Health Services Research* 20:153–161.

Bishop, C.E. 1988. Competition in the market for nursing home care. *Journal of Health Politics, Policy, and Law* 13:341–360.

Danzon, P.M. 1982. Hospital "profits." *Journal of Health Economics* 1:29–52.

Hay, J.W. 1983. The impact of public health care financing policies on private sector hospital costs. *Journal of Health Politics, Policy, and Law* 7:945–952.

Jacobs, P., and Wilder, R.P. 1984. Pricing behavior of non-profit agencies. *Journal of Health Economics* 3:49–61.

Johnston, W.P., et al. 1985. Interhospital variations in hospital pharmacy mark-ups. *American Journal of Hospital Pharmacy* 42:2492–2495.

Sloan, F.A., and Becker, E. 1984. Cross subsidies and payment for hospital care. *Journal of Health Politics, Policy, and Law* 8:660–685.

Sloan, F.A., and Ginsburg, P.B. 1984. Hospital cost shifting. *New England Journal of Medicine* 310:893–898.

Wilder, R.P., and Jacobs, P. 1986. Antitrust considerations for hospital mergers: Market definition and market concentration. *Advances in Health Economics* 7:245–262.

Market Power and Health Insurance

Adamache, K.W., and Sloan, F.A. 1983. Competition between non-profit and for-profit health insurers. *Journal of Health Economics* 2:225–244.

Beazoglou, T., and Heffley, D. 1994. Reevaluating the "procompetitive" effects of HMOs: A spatial equilibrium approach. *Journal of Regional Science* 34:39–55.

Blair, R.D., et al. 1975. Economies of scale in the administration of health insurance. *Review of Economic Statistics* 57:185–189.

Eisenstadt, D., and Kennedy, T.E. 1981. Control and behavior of nonprofit firms: The case of Blue Shield. *Southern Economic Journal* 48:26–36.

Feldman, R., and Greenberg, 1981a. Blue Cross market share, economies of scale and cost containment efforts. *Health Services Research* 16:175–183.

————. 1981b. The relation between Blue Cross market share and the Blue Cross "discount" on hospital charges. *Journal of Risk and Insurance* 48:235–246.

Frank, R.G., and Welch, W.P. 1985. The competitive effects of HMOs: A review of the evidence. *Inquiry* 22:148–161.

Frech, H.E. 1988. Competition among health insurers revisited. *Journal of Health Politics, Policy, and Law* 13:279–291.

Frech, H.E., and Ginsburg, P.B. 1978. Competition among health insurers. In *Competition in the health care sector*, ed. W. Greenberg. Washington, D.C.: Federal Trade Commission.

Goldberg, L.G., and Greenberg, W. 1977. The effect of physician-controlled health insurance. *Journal of Health Politics, Policy, and Law* 2:48–78.

————. 1985. The Dominant Firm in Health Insurance. *Social Science in Medicine* 20:719–724.

Lynk, W.L. 1981. Regulatory control of the membership of corporate boards of directors: The Blue Shield case. *Journal of Law and Economics* 24:159–174.

Pauly, M.V. 1987. Monopsony power in health insurance: Thinking straight while standing on your head. *Journal of Health Economics* 6:73–81.

————. 1988. Market power, monopsony, and health insurance markets. *Journal of Health Economics* 7:111–128.

Wholey, D.R., and Christianson, J.B. 1994. Price differentiation among health maintenance organizations: Causes and consequences of open-ended products. *Inquiry* 31:25–39.

Imperfect Competition

Cady, J.F. 1976. *Restricted advertising and competition*. Washington, D.C.: American Enterprise Institute.

Christianson, J.B., and McClure, W. 1979. Competition in the delivery of medical care. *New England Journal of Medicine* 301:812–818.

Farley, D.E. 1985. *Competition among hospitals: Market structure and its relation to utilization, costs and financial position*. Hospital Studies Program, Research Note 7. DHHS pub. no. PHS 85-3353. Washington, D.C.: U.S. Department of Health and Human Services, National Center for Health Services Research and Health Care Technology Assessment.

Getzen, T.E. 1983. The market and evaluation in quality assurance. *Evaluation and the Health Professions* 6:299–310.

————. 1984. A "brand name" theory of medical group practice. *Journal of Industrial Economics* 33:199–217.

Goldberg, L.G., and Greenberg, W. 1979. The competitive response of Blue Cross and Blue Shield to the health maintenance organization in Northern California and Hawaii. *Medical Care* 17:1019–1028.

————. 1980. The competitive response of Blue Cross to the health maintenance organization. *Economic Inquiry* 18:55–68.

Hay, J.W., and Leahy, M.J. 1984. Competition among health plans: Some preliminary evidence. *Southern Economic Journal* 50:831–846.

Held, P.J., and Pauly, M.V. 1983. Competition and efficiency in the end stage renal disease program. *Journal of Health Economics* 2:95–118.

Joskow, P.L. 1980. The effects of competition and regulation on hospital bed supply and the reservation quality of the hospital. *Bell Journal of Economics* 11:421–447.

Kelly, E.T., et al. 1975. An examination of the effect of market demographic and competitive characteristics on gross margins of prescription drugs. *Medical Care* 12:956–965.

Lee, R.H., and Waldman, D.M. 1985. The diffusion of innovations in hospitals. *Journal of Health Economics* 12:371–380.

Luft, H.S., et al. 1986. The role of specialized clinical services in competition among hospitals. *Inquiry* 23:83–94.

Morrisey, M.A., and Ashby, C.S. 1982. An empirical analysis of HMO market share. *Inquiry* 19:136–149.

Nyman, J. 1987. Prospective and "cost-plus" Medicaid reimbursement, excess Medicaid demand, and the quality of nursing home care. *Journal of Health Economics* 6:129–146.

Noether, M. 1988. Competition among hospitals. *Journal of Health Economics* 7:259–284.

Rapoport, J. 1978. Diffusion of technological innovations among non-profit firms. *Journal of Economics and Business* 30:108–118.

Robinson, J.C. 1988. Hospital competition and hospital nursing. *Nursing Economics* 6:116–124.

Robinson, J.C., and Luft, H.S. 1987. Competition and the cost of hospital care, 1972 to 1982. *JAMA* 257:3241–3245.

Robinson, J.C., et al. 1987. Market and regulatory influences on the availability of coronary angioplasty and bypass surgery in U.S. hospitals. *New England Journal of Medicine* 317:85–90.

Robinson, J.C., et al. 1988. Hospital competition and surgical length of stay. *JAMA* 259:696–700.

CHAPTER 9

Models Specific to Medical
Care and Health Insurance
Markets

9.1 INTRODUCTION

In previous chapters, when we developed models of medical care and health insurance markets, we supposed that both demanders and suppliers were informed participants in the market. In the competitive market model, patients were assumed to be well informed as to their conditions and the effectiveness of alternative treatments, although it was pointed out that the nature of the market may change if these assumptions do not hold. And in health insurance markets, insurers were assumed to possess adequate information to assess insured risks and hence to develop actuarially fair insurance premiums. Analysts have questioned how realistic the assumptions of adequate information are in both situations. If they are not realistic, that is, if there exists an information "asymmetry" in a market (such that either the demanders or suppliers possess better information than the other group), the market may not work properly. Indeed, in some cases it may not work at all.

In this chapter, we examine the economic effects of information asymmetry in these two markets. First we examine its effects in the market for physician services. In this market, patients enter into a special relationship with their physicians, whom they rely upon to provide them information as to their health status and prospective treatments. Physicians are thus regarded as "agents" of their patients. Ignorance on the part of the patients allows the physicians to influence their patients' tastes and hence to directly—as opposed to indirectly through market negotiation—influence demand. This phenomenon has been called *supplier-induced demand*.

Coupled with this theoretical rationale for focusing on the physician services market is an empirical (or statistical) one. There is an alleged positive relationship between the supply of physicians and the price of physician services (fees). In particular, when the supply of physicians has increased, the price has been observed to rise. This relationship is contrary to the relationship predicted by the competitive model, and the contradiction calls for additional empirical investigation as well as efforts to formulate models that make the right prediction. We examine these efforts in the next section.

A second alleged anomaly occurs in the market for health insurance. It has been posited that insurance companies may not possess sufficient information about insureds' health status to be able to assess the relative risk groupings in which these individuals will fall. Indeed, insureds can hide certain facts about their health status from the insurance companies in order to make it appear that they are healthier than they in fact are. Insurance companies are thus placed at a competitive disadvantage.

Under certain circumstances, an insurance market in which ignorance of risk is widespread will cease to operate. With the insurers unable to discriminate between risks, they become limited in their pricing options and may be forced to charge everyone the same price. Low-risk consumers may withdraw from the market (and go uninsured) whereas higher risk consumers will choose to remain in the pool. This phenomenon, where high-risk individuals are attracted to the pool, is called *adverse selection*. If it continues to an extreme, the market could be left with only very high risk consumers or, if rates grow too high, with no consumers at all. Although the relevance of the extreme version of this model has been questioned, the two versions together highlight the importance of strategic consumer behavior in the insurance market. This is viewed by many to be of paramount importance. In Section 9.3 we consider a basic model of health insurance markets with consumer self-selection.

9.2 SUPPLIER-INDUCED DEMAND

9.2.1 A Pedagogic Model

In Section 4.2.6 we focused on the asymmetry of information between consumers and providers in the medical care market. We raised the possibility that consumers may not have good information about their health status or the probable effect of medical care on their health. Although consumers are not likely to be completely ignorant, they often rely on physicians to act as agents and inform them about these variables. Physicians can, in many instances, provide information that will allow patients to form a demand curve. But this information may not be accurate. Physicians can affect the demand curve for medical care by providing information that is not wholly accurate. If physicians do induce demand unnecessarily, perhaps in response to the excess capacities of their practices, then where the ratio of physicians to population is high, demand will be shifted out more.

Ultimately, the extent of unnecessary inducement of demand is an empirical question—and a difficult one to answer.

A large number of studies have been developed that attempt to incorporate supplier-induced demand into the framework of medical markets. Many of these models focus on the provider (physician) and assume implicitly that the ability to shift demand is unlimited. Because consumers have access to information about the quality of advice they receive from their physicians, it is more realistic to recognize that limitations to demand generation may exist. We present a simple model of medical care markets that brings out some of their more important features (Pauly 1980). This model, which focuses on the individual physician, bears a resemblance to the model of monopolistic competition model presented in Chapter 8.

We assume that consumers' "taste" for medical care depends on information about initial health status (H_0); the effect of medical care on health ($\Delta H/\Delta M$ where M stands for medical care); and the impact of health on utility, incomes, and prices. It also depends on the number of physicians in the market. In particular, a lower physician to population or M.D. to population ratio (shorted to *MDPOP*) will lead to a higher demand for each physician in the market.

For each patient, we suppose there is a "true" level of H and $\Delta H/\Delta M$ that can be determined by the patient's physician. If the physician is fully truthful with the patient, a demand curve for the patient can be derived (D_{true} in Figure 9–1). This demand curve is downward sloping, which means that, for any given level of belief about H and $\Delta H/\Delta M$, the quantity demanded will be responsive to out-of-pocket price.

Of course, the physician can tell the patient that H and $\Delta H/\Delta M$ have values other than the actual ones. If the patient believes the physician, the patient's demand curve will shift outward (i.e., at any price the quantity demanded will be greater). But the physician is only one source of information, and the patient can get information elsewhere if he or she questions the physician's assessment. It is therefore likely that there is an upper limit to the physician's ability to generate demand that is not grounded in reality. We will call the demand curve at this upper limit D_{limit}.

9.2.1.1 Supply

Having specified the demand characteristics of the model, we now turn to the supply side of the market. With regard to physician behavior, the following assumptions are made:

- Each physician has an upward-sloping marginal cost (*MC*) curve (i.e., as more services are provided, marginal costs increase).
- The price of services is fixed by a fee schedule, and so fees are beyond physician control.

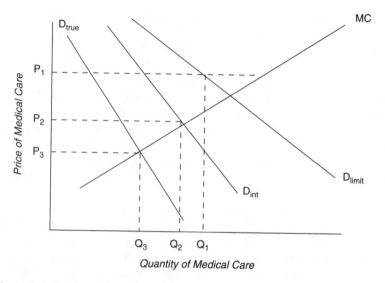

Figure 9–1 Representation of supplier-induced demand. The three demand curves, D_{true}, D_{int}, and D_{limit}, represent the demand of three successive levels of supplier inducement: no unnecessary inducement (D_{true}), an intermediate level of inducement (D_{int}), and the maximum level of inducement possible (D_{limit}). The physician's marginal cost is MC. Three alternative fee levels, P_1, P_2, and P_3, are shown. The quantity of medical care "induced" will depend on the fee level, the degree of inducement, and the physician's MC. However, at high fee levels, patient-influenced limitations may be a factor in determining utilization.

9.2.1.2 Objectives

A number of studies have identified many possible physician objectives, ranging from healing patients to maximizing profits. We will assume each physician's goal is profit maximization for the sake of convenience, not because it is the most realistic assumption. It also elucidates the "worst case" scenario and shows how the most selfish doctors will behave under specified conditions.

The model has been designed to predict the quantity of medical care provided. We will now show that this quantity will depend on the specific price received by the physician. Let us start with a high price, such as P_1 in Figure 9–1. At this price, the physician will generate demand to the limit and provide services at level Q_1. At this point, marginal revenue (MR) is greater than MC, and the physician would be able to earn additional profits if demand could be generated beyond D_{limit}. But the patient cannot be pushed further, and so this is the best the doctor can do.

If the price were lower, at P_2, the physician would generate demand up to some intermediate point D_{int} and would provide Q_2 units of service. Beyond this point,

MC would exceed *MR*, and the physician would reduce profits by inducing further demand. At an even lower price, P_3, the physician would not generate any unnecessary demand and would provide Q_3 units of service. The conclusions of even this simple model are that, with the most selfish of physicians, the quantity demanded—and the degree of demand generation—will depend on the given price.

What about an increase in the supply of physicians (i.e., an increase in the *MDPOP*)? From the viewpoint of the individual physician, such an increase would lead to a reduction in each demand curve (D_{true}, D_{int}, and D_{limit}), because these curves are the individual physician's demand curves and each physician will have a smaller market. In these circumstances each physician's quantity of services supplied will be reduced. Overall demand cannot be generated beyond the maximum, and, at a price such as P_3, there is not likely to be any change in overall services.

As pointed out above, there are a number of reasons why consumers might not be totally gullible and vulnerable to demand-generating tactics. First, consumers can obtain information from sources other than their physicians. Second, a number of studies have suggested that there is a limit to the willingness of physicians to generate demand (Rossiter and Wilensky 1984; Stano 1987), although the nature of this reticence has not been spelled out. Analysts have alternatively modelled the generation of ungrounded demand as a cost to physicians and as a cause of disutility (perhaps as a result of feelings of guilt). In either case, generating too much unnecessary demand will make the physicians (as well as the patients) worse off.

As has been hypothesized, the generation of ungrounded demand will result in higher marginal costs to the physician and, depending on revenues, may yield more profits. But what if the physician's objectives included patient well-being? The impact of this goal will be to reduce the degree to which the physician would be willing to generate demand.

The above model has dealt with demand generation and patient utilization at given prices. It presents a pedagogic treatment of the issue of demand generation and its likely degree of restriction. But it ignores the fact that, contrary to what might be expected, higher physician fees have been associated with an increase in *MDPOP*. We turn now to possible explanations of this surprising relationship between fees and supply.

9.2.2 MDPOP and Physician Fees: A Positive Relationship?

One hypothesis concerning price formation in the physician services market is that when supply shifts out, then price increases (Evans 1974). This prediction is contrary to that of the competitive model, which predicts that price will fall when supply increases. The standard competitive model (see Chapter 7) is shown geometrically in Figure 9–2. In this figure, D_1 represents an initial demand level and S_1 an initial supply level. The initial supply level corresponds to an initial supply of physicians (an initial level of *MDPOP*). Let us now increase the level of *MDPOP* to the point where the supply shifts out to S_2. Doctors, according to this theory, will offer more services, and, as supply shifts out, prices will fall and utilization will increase. This prediction does not square with the alleged empirical fact that increases in price accompany increases in physician supply (*MDPOP*). In order to fit the theory to the facts, a number of observers have contended that suppliers can shift out demand. For example, suppose the suppliers in our example could push the demand curve out to D_2. Even if the supply was to increase from S_1 to S_2, the equilibrium price would increase to P_3. Of course, supplier-induced demand can also occur when prices *fall* after an outward shift in supply. If, following an increase in supply to S_2 suppliers were only successful in shifting the demand to D_3, the price would fall even though suppliers had been successful in shifting the demand. Thus, a fall in price when supply increases is consistent with both the competitive and the supplier-induced demand theories! This makes it impossible to distinguish between them. Only when prices are observed to rise following an increase in *MDPOP* and all else stays the same can we be sure that the supplier-induced demand model is the appropriate model.

The major problem in verifying the existence of supplier-induced demand lies in the fact that other demand- and supply-influencing variables are changing along with *MDPOP*. Let us say that supply shifts from S_1 to S_2 and we observe a price increase from P_1 to P_3. In order to be sure that we are actually observing supplier-induced demand, we must be sure that we have controlled for all other variables that could affect demand and supply. If, for example, S_1 represents supply conditions in Salt Lake City and S_2 conditions in San Antonio, the demand differences between the two markets may have occurred because of supplier-induced demand or myriad other demand-influencing factors, such as health status, quality of care, insurance coverage and so on. Further, even if we have controlled for differences in *MDPOP* between the two markets, we must be sure that other intervening supply variables have not resulted in greater increases (or decreases).

A number of statistical studies have been undertaken to estimate the extent of supplier-induced demand. The majority of these have focused their attention on *utilization* of medical care, and how it has been influenced by *MDPOP*. For example, Rossiter and Wilensky (1984) studied data obtained from a national sample survey of families (known as the National Medical Care Cost and Expenditure Survey) to determine the effect of a number of variables, such as direct price, travel time, health status, and the physician to population ratio, on the number of physician-initiated visits. Physician-initiated visits, although suggested by physicians, are not the same as physician-induced visits, since the term *inducement* connotes lack of necessity. There is no way of telling from a data set such as

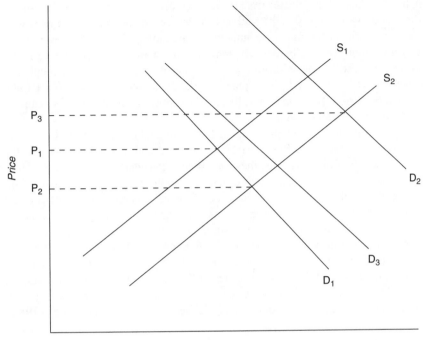

Figure 9–2 Diagram showing the difficulties in identifying the supplier-induced demand based on actual market data. An increase in the physician population will result in an increase in supply from S_1 to S_2. Absence of supplier-induced demand will cause a fall in price from P_3 to P_1, a result of a movement along demand curve D_1. However, supplier-induced demand is consistent with both an increase in price (if demand shifts to D_2) and a reduction in price (if demand shifts, but only to D_3).

that used by the authors the degree to which physician-initiated visits were unnecessary and induced by physicians for their own benefit. The results of the study indicated a very small effect of *MDPOP* on ambulatory care utilization: An increase in the ratio by one physician per 100,000 population resulted in an increase in expenditures on physician-initiated visits of only seven cents. However, the authors did not directly test the supplier-induced demand hypothesis.

   Cromwell and Mitchell (1986) and Fuchs (1978), on the other hand, did directly test for the effect of supplier-induced demand in the market for surgery by examining the effect of surgeon population ratios on surgery utilization and surgeons' fees. The data set in the Cromwell-Mitchell study consisted of metropolitan area statistics on families' characteristics and surgical utilization obtained from the Health Interview Survey of the National Center for Health Statistics coupled with Medicare surgical fee data. The authors studied how both surgical fees and surgery utilization rates differed among markets (metropolitan areas) when variables such as age distribution, education level, average coinsurance rate, the number of general practitioners per 1,000 population, and the number of surgeons per 1,000 population varied. They also controlled for the supply effect of higher fees causing more surgeons to locate in the area.

Their results indicated a price elasticity for surgical operations of –0.15 when all identified demand-shifting variables were held constant. With regard to the variable *MDPOP* for surgeons, they identified a considerable effect of this variable on surgical utilization and on surgical fees. In the case of utilization, the magnitude of the relationship was such that a 10-percent increase in surgeons in the population resulted in a 9-percent increase in surgical operations. With regard to fee increases, a 1-percent increase in surgeons in the population resulted in a .9-percent increase in surgeons' fees. The authors presented these results as indicative of a significant supplier-induced demand effect in the market for surgery. However, because of the many variables influencing supply and demand and the difficulty of controlling for these in statistical tests, there is controversy surrounding any results in this area (Dranove and Wehner 1994; Feldman and Sloan 1988).

9.3   ADVERSE SELECTION IN HEALTH INSURANCE MARKETS

In Section 4.4 the concept of self-selection in insurance coverage was introduced. Insurance plans with specific types of coverage will attract consumers who will benefit the most from the coverage. This concept and the concept of information asymmetry can be combined to define a situation that could damage an insurance market to such a degree that it ceases to exist. Although in practice economists have questioned whether this phenomenon is an empirically important one, it has drawn considerable attention in the literature (Pauly 1986).

In our insurance model, we will assume that there are three separate groups of 100 individuals. Assumptions as to their demand conditions are as follows:

- In Group 1, the healthiest, each individual has a 10-percent probability of becoming ill and requiring medical care. In Group 2, the intermediate group, the probability is 40 percent, and in Group 3 it is 80 percent.
- The cost of medical treatment for an individual in any group (i.e., the total amount of the loss in the event of illness) is $100.
- Individuals have a utility function similar to that in Table 4–1 (Chapter 4).

Based on these assumptions, the expected utility of being uninsured for any individual will be the expected utility ($E(U)$) of $1,000 (which is 100.0, according to Table 4–1) if the individual stays healthy and the $E(U)$ of $900 (which is 89.0) if he or she becomes sick. For Group 1 individuals this is (.9 × 100) + (.1 × 89.0), or 98.9. The $E(U)$s for Groups 2 and 3 are 95.6 [.6 × 100.0) + (.4 × 89.0)] and 91.2 [(.2 × 100.0) + (.8 × 89.0)], respectively. The demand for insurance for these three groups is such that each member of Group 1 would pay a premium of approximately $30 (resulting in a utility of 98.9) to be insured. For any premium above this amount, the members would accept the risk and not buy insurance. For any premium lower, they would demand insurance coverage. The indifference premium is $60 for Group 2 and $90 for Group 3.

We turn now to the supply side of the market. The relevant assumptions are as follows:

- The administrative costs, the insurance company's expenses, are $2,000.
- Total insurance company costs consist of the administrative costs plus the amount the insurer reimburses for medical care.
- The insurance company merely wants to break even, so revenues will just equal costs.

As for the pricing policy of the insurance company, which is a critical element in the model, there are a number of alternatives the company could choose. For example, it could employ an *experience rating* methodology, which involves dividing the total pool into subgroups and setting rates according to each subgroup's expected loss. In an experience rating pricing scheme, Groups 1, 2, and 3 would all pay different premiums because they have different levels of expected loss. The second type of pricing policy is *community rating*. In a community rating scheme, all individuals pay the same rate. Community rating would probably be the method chosen. For one thing, there might be an information asymmetry that would prevent the insurer from being able to distinguish between individuals in the three groups. It could not, then, charge a different premium (based on expected loss). The asymmetry occurs because, while the insureds may know which group they fall into, they will be reluctant to pass on health status information to the insurer.

Let us assume that an information asymmetry does exist. Under this condition, a single community rate will be charged to all individuals. We will now determine how the market might operate. Initially, the insurance company, wanting to break even, will charge a rate high enough to cover all the reimbursements for the three groups ($13,000) and the administrative costs ($2,000). Over the 300 individuals, this rate amounts to $50 per individual. This rate exceeds Group 1's indifference premium, and so members of Group 1 will choose not to insure. Members of Groups 2 and 3, on the other hand, will insure. With Group 1 dropping out of the market, total expenses for Groups 2 and 3 are $14,000. Again, the insurance company cannot distinguish between them, and so it must charge a single community rate, this time of $70 per individual. But this rate will be above that which members of Group 1 are willing to pay, and they will drop out of the market, leaving only Group 3. The rate will be raised to $100, but this will exceed Group 3's indifference premium. The members of Group 3 will drop out of the market as well, causing the market to collapse. This phenomenon is a joint result of adverse selection (those with the highest risks remain in the market) and community rating (chosen as a method because of the information asymmetry).

The popularity of the above model might be attributable to its doom-and-gloom prediction of market disappearance, but there is some question as to how well it fits the present market for health insurance. There is scant empirical evidence to decide its applicability, but it has drawn attention to the phenomenon of community rating and its potential role in market failure. And, in fact, in the present model the market would perform differently if experience rating was used. To see this, assume that for each group a premium is set equal to its expected medical costs plus $666 (which is one-third of the total administrative expenses). Then each group would pay a premium that was less than what it would be willing to pay. For example, Group 1 individuals would be charged $16.66 in premiums ($1,000 + $666 divided by 100 people). This is below what they would be willing to pay for insurance coverage. Thus it is the community rating pricing policy that caused the market to disappear.

There have been questions raised as to whether community rating results from informational asymmetry or other factors. Insurance companies have or can get considerable amounts of information about potential insureds by looking at age and medical history and by conducting medical exams. In fact, insurance companies use experience rating for pricing individual policies. This being the case, it may not be informational asymmetry that leads to community rating (Feldman 1987) but other causes. For example, employers may want to be equitable to all employees and so offer a single (community) rate for all—the young, the old, the sick, and so on. Employees, including low-risk employees, may accept this in part because they are happy with the idea that when they become unhealthy later in life their premiums will be community rated as well.

BIBLIOGRAPHY

Supplier-Induced Demand

Auster, R.D., and Oxaca, R.L. 1981. The identification of supplier-induced demand in the health care sector. *Journal of Human Resources* 16:327–342.

Blackstone, E.A. 1980. Market power and resource misallocation in neurosurgery. *Journal of Health Politics, Policy and Law* 3:345–360.

Cromwell, J., and Mitchell, J.B. 1986. Physician Induced Demand for Surgery. *Journal of Health Economics* 5:293–313.

Dranove, D. 1988. Demand inducement and the physician–patient relationship. *Economic Inquiry* 26:281–298.

Dranove, D., and Wehner, P. 1994. Physician-induced demand for childbirths. *Journal of Health Economics* 13:61–73.

Evans, R.G. 1974. Supplier induced demand. In *The economics of health and medical care*, ed. M. Perlman. London: Macmillan.

Feldman, R., and Sloan, F. 1988. Competition among physicians. *Journal of Health Politics, Policy, and Law* 13:239–264.

Fuchs, V. 1978. The supply of surgeons and the demand for operations. *Journal of Human Resources* 13 (suppl.):35–55.

Hay, J.L., and Leahy, M.J. 1982. Physician induced demand. *Journal of Health Economics* 1:231–244.

Hemenway, D., and Fallon, D. 1985. Testing for physician induced demand with hypothetical cases. *Medical Care* 23:344–349.

Labelle, R., et al. 1994. A re-examination of the meaning and importance of supplier induced demand. *Journal of Health Economics* 13:347–368.

Pauly, M.V. 1979. What is unnecessary surgery? *Milbank Quarterly* 57:95–117.

———. 1980. *Doctors and their workshops*. Chicago: University of Chicago Press.

Pauly, M.V., and Satterthwaite, M.A. 1980. The pricing of primary care physicians' services. *Bell Journal of Economics* 12:488–506.

Reinhardt, U. 1978. Comment. In *Competition in the health care sector*, ed. W. Greenberg. Washington, D.C.: Federal Trade Commission.

———. 1983. The theory of physician-induced demand and its implications for public policy. *Beitrage zur Gesundheitsökonomie* 4:153–172.

Rice, T.H. 1983. The impact of changing Medicare reimbursement rates on physician induced demand. *Medical Care* 21:803–815.

Rossiter, L.F., Wilensky, G.R. 1983. A reexamination of the use of physician services. *Inquiry* 20:162–172.

———. 1984. Identification of physician-induced demand. *Journal of Human Resources* 19:231–244.

———. 1987. Health economist-induced demand for theories of physician-induced demand. *Journal of Human Resources* 12:624–626.

Schaafsma, J. 1994. A new test for supplier inducement and application to the Canadian market for dental care. *Journal of Health Economics* 13:407–431.

Sloan, F., and Feldman, R. 1978. Competition among physicians. In *Competition in the health care sector*, ed. W. Greenberg. Washington, D.C.: Federal Trade Commission.

Stano, M. 1987a. A further analysis of the physician inducement controversy. *Journal of Health Economics* 6:227–238.

———. 1987b. A clarification of theories and evidence on supplier-induced demand for physicians' services. *Journal of Human Resources* 22:611–620.

Wilensky, G.R., and Rossiter, L. 1983. The relative importance of physician-induced demand in the demand for medical care. *Milbank Quarterly* 61:252–277.

Insurance Markets

Cleeton, D. 1989. The medical uninsured: A case of market failure? *Public Finance Quarterly* 17:55–83.

Feldman, R. 1987. Health insurance in the United States: Is market failure avoidable? *Journal of Risk and Insurance* 54:298–313.

Pauly, M.V. 1986. Taxation, health insurance, and market failure in the medical economy. *Journal of Economic Literature* 24:629–675.

PART III

Evaluative Economics

CHAPTER 10

Value Judgments and Economic Evaluation

10.1 INTRODUCTION

In this chapter we begin a different level of inquiry. In Part II we focused on the actual allocation of resources devoted to medical care. We were interested in explaining only the various allocations that might occur in different circumstances. We did not concern ourselves with whether any particular allocation was "good" or "acceptable" or "equitable," to mention only a few of the terms we might use to label an allocation. In this chapter we begin the task of evaluating alternative possible allocations of resources. This task will lead us to such questions as whether totally free care can be judged "better" than a provision of medical care in a simple market. Or whether and in what sense a regulated system is preferable to an unregulated one. Many of these questions, it should be pointed out, are policy issues. Indeed, evaluative analysis forms the cornerstone of policy analysis, since the ultimate goal of policy is to bring about improvements in the use of resources.

Before undertaking evaluative analysis we must lay the ground rules for conducting an evaluation. That is the mission of this chapter. In Section 10.2, the importance of having a recognizable and unvarying standard for gauging alternative allocations is discussed. The values that individual persons place on specific commodities can be used as the basis of a social evaluation. One procedure for building a social evaluation is discussed in Section 10.3. The standard that results from this procedure, which is used frequently by economists, is referred to as an *efficiency criterion*. Such a yardstick takes individuals' starting situations as given and therefore bypasses questions relating to equity and need (e.g., whether the starting positions were fair to begin with). The application of efficiency criteria to evaluate the performance of the health insurance market is discussed in Section

10.4, and policy goals emanating from this efficiency analysis are presented in Section 10.5. The relevance of the efficiency criteria as the sole benchmark of resource allocation has been questioned by many observers. An alternative approach, called *extra-welfarism*, is presented in Section 10.6. Finally, alternative measures of equity are considered in Section 10.7.

10.2   VALUES AND STANDARDS IN ECONOMIC EVALUATION

Suppose we are faced with a situation in which A has a curable cancer but is receiving no medical care and B is healthy but is spending $4,000 on surgical services for a facial lift. Would this be an acceptable allocation of our medical resources? Many would say it is unfair, but without setting forth the basic standard they used to judge the situation. Suppose, instead, that it was necessary heart surgery B was receiving. Would this change one's evaluation of the situation? Would a different standard be used to gauge its fairness?

In our example, the resources are being allocated differently in the two situations. However, unless we had a standard that did not itself vary from situation to situation, we really could not compare the two situations. That is, without an independent scale of fairness or acceptability, we would not have a measure able to gauge alternative allocations. This section presents a classification of available systems of standards, focusing on the bases on which standards may be formed.

For the purposes of economic evaluation, there are two ways of deriving a system of values and then developing a ranking of alternative uses of resources. In the first method, called *delegatory* or *top-down*, a value system is imposed on the members of society. For example, it might be imposed by a higher being, such as a deity; by an interpreter of the ultimate word, such as Moses or Mohammed; or by a dictator, who settles on some value system based on his or her values. Alternatively, someone can assume the mantle of spokesperson for society, proclaiming "society wants a decent standard of health for all" or some such alleged truth. Despite the nod toward democracy, any would-be ethical authority who chooses to speak for society without a unanimous mandate is really imposing his or her own views on society.

The second method for deriving a system of values is called *participatory* or *bottom-up*. In this method, all members of the community reach a consensus. One assumption underlying this method is that *everyone's* values must be taken into account in ranking alternative ways of using resources. Another assumption is that each individual is the best judge of his or her own welfare.

We now turn our focus to the value systems themselves. They vary tremendously, ranging from the very specific to the very vague. They can take the form of specific laws handed down by a deity or can be formulated in terms of general concepts such as *fairness*, *liberty*, and *equality*.

The field of health services analysis contains many examples of writers proposing value systems based on their own view of what seems plausible. For instance, some have posited a "right" to health or health care. One commentator used the principle of *agape* to derive this right (Outka 1974), whereas another appealed to a "strong sense in the population" that this right exists (Mechanic 1976).

Even assuming we could settle on a single value system, we would then face the problem of translating the chosen value system into a gauge or ranking scheme to assess alternative ways of using resources. This translation step can be controversial itself. Because any value system will be somewhat vague, different ranking schemes with very different implications can be derived from it. We would then run into the problem of which ranking scheme to choose. For example, the goal of "equality" can be interpreted in many ways—as equality of *health status* or as equality of *medical care utilization*. We could also decide it entails equal use of medical care for equal health status, with individuals with poor health receiving more care than individuals who are basically healthy. This may seem plausible, but how do we decide how much more care people with poor health should get? Also, if the medical care given to those in poor health is not effective; should they still receive it?

The last step, after having decided on a ranking scheme, is to apply it to actual or proposed states of resource use (e.g., distributions of health care or levels of health) to determine their desirability from a policy standpoint.

It should be stressed that value systems imposed from above are not necessarily evil. The source of such a system may be a highly respected and beloved authority, and the system may contain laudatory ideals and translate into ranking schemes that seem reasonable and compassionate. Nevertheless, an imposed scheme is not built up from the values of the members of the society and therefore retains some degree of nonrepresentativeness.

In Section 10.3 and 10.4, a participatory system of evaluation is developed. This system, well known in economic circles as the *Paretean system* (named after the famous nineteenth-century sociologist Vilfredo Pareto), allows us to arrive at a unique optimum position through examining improvements that could be made in resource allocations if we start from an initial position. This optimum holds only with reference to the initial starting point (i.e., the initial endowments each member of society possesses). We do not judge the starting point, which may or may not be fair, a consideration discussed in Section 10.5.

10.3   EFFICIENT OUTPUT LEVELS

10.3.1   Individual Valuations of Commodities or Activities

If we accept individuals' own valuations as the best indicators of their own welfare, we must then determine, at least in principle, what these valuations might be. Since our analysis is concerned with specific commodities, our task is simplified somewhat. We need only determine individuals' valuations with respect to those commodities with which we are concerned.

As seen in Chapter 3, economists have developed a hypothesis regarding an individual's valuation of units of a specific commodity. The hypothesis, which is based on our demand analysis, states that the more of any commodity the individual has, the less successive units of the commodity will be worth to him or her (as compared with other commodities). The entire analysis can be recast using money as the basic unit of value. To do this, we must assume that money is itself of constant value. That is, if an individual gives up $2, that $2 will always represent the same loss to the individual however much income he or she has. This assumption will hold, at least partially, if the outlay for the commodity in question is a reasonably small portion of the individual's total budget.

If an individual has an income of $10,000, spending $100 or $150 on a commodity is unlikely to cause the valuation of each dollar to change for the individual. However, as the amount that must be given up to obtain a commodity becomes very large relative to income, the utility of or the subjective valuation placed on the marginal dollar will change. We are making the assumption that it does not.

Given the assumption that money income has a constant value for individuals for all relevant ranges of expenditures, we can specify individual valuations of successive units of a commodity in terms of money. These valuations, it must be stressed, are the individuals' own evaluations of specific units of the commodity, and they qualify on participatory grounds for inclusion into our overall participatory social evaluation.

10.3.2 Values in a Selfish Market

To simplify our analysis, let us assume initially that there are two individuals in our market, A and B. Each has a specific schedule of valuations for his or her own consumption of medical care. Let us refer to these valuations as *marginal valuations* (*MVs*). A marginal valuation is defined as the extra amount of money an individual would be willing to pay for an additional unit of a commodity. Thus, an *MV* is a measure of what an extra unit of the commodity is worth to the individual in money terms.

In our initial analysis, both A and B derive satisfaction or value from their own consumption of medical services, and theirs is the only satisfaction that anyone in society gets from their consumption. A places a marginal value of $80 on his first unit consumed, $70 on his second, and so on, as seen in Columns 1 and 2 in Table 10–1. Note that the marginal values placed by each individual on successive units of medical care consumed diminish. Recall from Chapter 3 that all other factors, such as health status, income, and wealth, are held constant (i.e., the initial values of these variables are held constant). For purposes of social evaluation, then, we have a measure of the social worth of A's consumption of medical care (since no one else values this care other than A himself).

The assumed relation between marginal value and quantity consumed can be presented geometrically. In Figure 10–1, the curve MV_a represents A's marginal valuation of successive units of medical care. It is assumed, for ease of geometric exposition, that the units of medical care can be made very small so that the MV curve becomes smooth. A's valuation of his own consumption is referred to as the *private* (or *internal*) valuation of his consumption. On the assumption that no one else cares about A's consumption, his private valuation is the same as the social valuation (the total value placed on A's consumption by all of society).

Similarly, we present the private valuations of B in Table 10–1 and geometrically as MV_b in Figure 10–1. For whatever reason (she is poorer, more healthy, or less well educated), B places a lower value on each unit of health care than does A. Indeed, her first unit has an MV of $50, her second has an MV of $40, and so on. These valuations might seem low to us, but since B is the ultimate judge of her own welfare, we cannot question these valuations: They are simply part of the data.

According to our assumption, A and B are the only members of society who participate in the medical care market. The marginal social valuations of medical care coincide with the marginal private valuations. Column 4 of Table 10–1 lists the aggregated quantities that correspond to each level of MV. For example, at an aggregate quantity of five units of medical care (four by A and one by B), each

---

Table 10–1 Values and Costs of Medical Care

Quantity Consumed by A (Q_a)	Quantity Consumed by B (Q_b)	Quantity Consumed by A and B $(Q_a + Q_b)$	Marginal Value of Consumption (MV)	Marginal Cost of Output at Consumption Level $Q_a + Q_b$
1	0	1	$80	$35
2	0	2	70	35
3	0	3	60	35
4	1	5	50	35
5	2	7	40	35
6	3	9	30	35
7	4	11	20	35
8	5	13	10	35
9	6	15	0	35

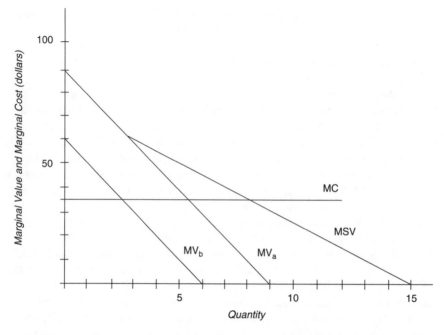

Figure 10–1 Representation of efficient output level. Individuals A and B have private marginal valuations for medical care (MV_a and MV_b, respectively). Using these, we calculate the marginal social value (MSV) curve, which relates aggregate quantity to each individual's valuation. MC is the marginal social cost of medical care. The efficient level of output is that quantity at which MSV equals the MC.

consumer's marginal value will be $50. If seven units were consumed (five by A and two by B), each individual's MV would be $40. We now have hypothesized how much each additional unit of medical care is worth to each participant. Furthermore, we have derived an aggregate-level relationship between the quantity of medical care and the marginal value to each individual if he or she was consuming at the level of consumption indicated by the MV curve. This aggregate curve, called the MSV (marginal social value) curve, shows the value to each member of the market if all individuals are consuming at the levels indicated by the curve. Because B does not have an MV above $60, for values above $60 the MSV curve coincides with A's MV curve.

An implicit assumption of our analysis is that consumer valuations are expressed in terms of a commodity, medical care. But medical care may not be valued for its own sake (except, perhaps, by a hypochondriac); it is usually *health* that is valued. In fact, each consumer's *MV* is made up of two components: an *MV* for health (termed *H*) and the marginal productivity of an additional unit of medical care (*M*) in producing health ($\Delta H/\Delta M$). Thus, the valuation of medical care is derivative, stemming from the two components. (For further consideration of this issue, see Section 10.6.)

We come next to the cost of producing medical care. Our initial assumption here is that each level of output is being produced at the minimum cost. This assumption is sometimes referred to as the *technical efficiency* assumption. It implies that, given production conditions and input prices, the lowest cost combination of inputs is used at any output level. In Column 5 of Table 10–1 and in Figure 10–1, we show the minimum marginal cost at which providers can produce medical care. We assume that this minimum marginal cost remains constant at $35 per unit as output increases. Note that the *MC* is the additional cost per unit of care; each extra unit costs $35 to produce.

One interpretation of *MC* is that it is the amount of money that must be paid to the inputs to hire them away from the next highest valued use. If medical care was not produced, something else of value to consumers would be. We can assume, then, that the *MC* is the amount we would have to pay the resources to induce them not to produce that something else. This approach allows us to put a value on unpaid resources that otherwise would appear to be "valueless" or "free." Thus the MC is marginally above (and approximates) the value that someone else would have placed on these resources in an alternative use. Viewing the *MC* in this way means that it is essentially the opportunity cost of the resources used (the value that users of other commodities would have placed on them).

10.3.3 The Socially Optimum Quantity of Medical Care

The next step in our analysis involves the definition and identification of desirable or optimum resource allocations. Since our method of evaluation is participatory, we need to identify allocations of resources that would be judged superior by all members of the community. As will be seen presently, it is possible using a participatory method to rank some allocations as superior to others, although we cannot compare every conceivable situation. Our criterion is this: The resources must be used in a way that maximizes social value. That is, if the resources are distributed in such a way that consumers are willing to pay the most for them, then output will be at the "right" or economically efficient level.

Using the valuations of A and B and the *MC* of medical care, we will be at a socially optimal (or economically efficient) level of output if the *MV*s of A and B equal the *MC* (i.e., $MV_a = MV_b = MC$). If output is at a level where the *MV*s are greater than MC, say, at an aggregate quantity of 3 in Table 10–1, then an expansion of output to 5 (an increase of 1 for A and B each) would have an MC per unit of output of $35 but would yield $50 extra in value to A and B each. Similarly, if the MC is greater than the MSV, this indicates that resources are worth more elsewhere, and so output should fall. In Figure 10–1, the optimal level of medical care is 7 units. Given our assumptions, this is how much medical care should be produced. This measure of efficiency—the distribution of output based on utility—is called *allocative efficiency*.

In reality, in a medical care market too much or too little as well as just enough medical care could be produced. Too much could be produced if the government had a policy of financing medical care and giving it away for free. At a zero price, demand will be at 15 units (where the MVs are zero); the MC of additional units will be well above this if the government is willing to ensure that all that is demanded is provided. The financing of the program could be through taxes. However, by meeting all demands, the government is clearly providing too much.

On the other hand, the market may provide too little. If medical care was in the hands of a monopolist, the monopolist would set a price well above that where $MV = MC$. If the price was $55, then three units in total would be demanded (all by A). Here the market would be producing too little care.

In addition, the optimum level of resource use could result in little or even no use of medical care by some individuals. The height of the MV curve, which is, in effect, a demand curve, will depend on health status, wealth, income, and so on. Poor people (e.g., B) may have low MVs. Indeed, if the MC was higher than in our example, a socially optimal quantity of output would be perfectly consistent with no consumption of medical care by B. (This is true, even though B may have poor health.) One might argue that this is unfair, and, indeed, depending on one's definition of fairness, it might well be. It should be recognized, however, that the root cause of the inequitable distribution of medical care is the inequitable distribution of wealth. A higher income for B would mean higher demand and MV curves for medical care. Of course, as far as the notion of economic efficiency is concerned, initial wealth and income levels for each individual are given. A redistribution of income or wealth among individuals might seem fair to many observers, but it would not be evaluated within the bounds of the present notion of economic efficiency.

10.3.4 Optimal Output with Altruism

To preserve the present notion of economic efficiency, and indeed to extend it to cover some inequitable situations, an analysis has been developed to allow for the concern of some individuals for the low medical care consumption levels of others. This analysis is related to the social demand for goods discussed in Section

4.2.2. Let us extend the previous example to allow for A's external demand for B's consumption of medical care. From A's viewpoint, it may well be that B has a level of consumption of medical care that is too low. If this is the case, we must find some representation of the value to A of B's medical care consumption. It is likely, of course, that A's concern for B's medical care consumption is not unlimited. A is concerned, but only up to a point, for A has other private and public concerns as well. In fact, as seen in Section 4.2.2, A's valuation of B's medical care consumption can be treated as any other commodity; the more B consumes, the less the marginal value to A of an additional unit. In Table 10–2, A's MV for B's consumption is \$30 for the first unit, \$20 for the second, and so on. In Figure 10–2, this external MV curve is shown as MV_a^b.

It may seem strange that A's altruistic concern for B's welfare can be translated into mercenary terms and be given a money measure. Our ability to do this rests on the assumption that commodities are scarce and A must make some choices at the margin. Even if A decided to give all his money away and use none of it for his family or own personal use, there would still be hard decisions to make. Should the money be donated to the cancer society or heart association? Should the money go toward the preservation of Newfoundland seals or bald eagles? Depending on their tastes, even the most altruistic of people must make choices regarding scarcity, and our analysis is merely a formalization of this fact. Of course, most people will engage in private consumption as well as altruistic consumption; their values can be presented by marginal valuation curves for both types of activities. The benefits to be obtained from others' consumption will be termed *external benefits,* and the values that people place on these benefits will be termed *external values.*

We can now arrive at a measure of what value society places on B's medical care. This value can be called the *social value* and is made up of all individuals' private and external values for the specific commodities. Thus the marginal social

Table 10–2 Private and Social Values of B's Consumption of Medical Care

Quantity Consumed by B	Marginal Value to B of Own Consumption (MV_b)	Marginal Value to A of B's Consumption (MV_a^b)	Marginal Social Value of B's Consumption $(MV_b + MV_a^b)$
1	50	30	80
2	40	20	60
3	30	10	40
4	20	0	20
5	10	0	10

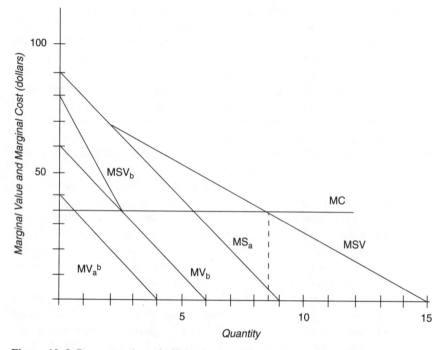

Figure 10–2 Representation of efficient output level. Individuals A and B have private marginal valuations for medical care (MV_a and MV_b, respectively); in addition, individual A places an external value on B's consumption. The marginal social value of B's consumption is the sum of the values placed on B's consumption by both A and B. The *MSV* of all medical care also reflects this externality. The *MC* is the marginal social cost of medical care. The efficient level of output is where *MSV* = *MC* (at approximately eight units).

value for B's consumption of medical care can be obtained by adding up the values both individuals place on each successive unit of medical care that B might consume. In Table 10–2, society has a marginal valuation of $80 for the first unit of B's medical care (equal to the sum of MV_b and MV_a^b), $60 for the second, and so on. These valuations are shown in Figure 10–2 as MSV_b, which is the vertical sum of MV_b and MV_a^b. By *vertical sum* we mean that each unit of B's consumption has a value to society (A and B) greater than the value placed on it by B alone. Because of this "public" dimension, we sum all values placed on each unit of B's consumption. Since each member's valuation of the commodity is measured along the vertical, or cost, axis, the summation of all members' valuations of this commodity is therefore a vertical sum.

The marginal valuation curve facing the market for medical care for A and B is *MSV*, which shows the quantity for all individuals at alternative *MSV*s for each individual. This curve is much like the *MSV* curve in Figure 10–1, except it incorporates A's valuation of B's consumption along with the private *MV*s.

The socially optimum level of output is similarly interpreted; the output is optimal at the quantity where the *MSV* for all individuals equals the *MC*. In Figure 10–2, the optimum level of output is eight units of medical care. This optimum incorporates each individual's private valuations as well as any external valuations for the poor, the needy, the sick, and so on. The optimum quantity that incorporates the external concerns of A is greater than that in which only selfish concerns appear (see Figure 10–1). However, these outcomes are results of the data, and it may well be that B's optimal consumption level is still at a low level.

The results of our extended analysis are consistent with some kind of transfer of funds from A to B for the purposes of increasing B's consumption of medical care. However, the analysis does not say what kind of transfer should take place. It may be voluntary (e.g., charitable donations given by A directly to B or to some providing agency) or tax based (e.g., taxes levied on A might be used to reimburse providers). In either case, the optimal solution allows for some transfer, although it should be stressed that any transfer can be too much or too little. The government can over- or underprovide, based on A's criteria. All that our analysis shows is that some transfer is consistent with economic efficiency.

10.3.5 Alternative Delivery Arrangements

Now that we have identified an ideal or efficient output level, we can look at alternative delivery arrangements to see how they compare to the ideal. That is, we can determine whether expected output under the alternatives is too little, just enough, or too much.

10.3.5.1 "Free" and Unlimited Care

First, assume that B is given all the medical care for free that she can consume. She would choose to consume six units of output. The social optimum is eight units for A and B, and the *MC* at this quantity is $35. Optimally, B should consume three (i.e., where $MSV_b = MC$). For every unit B consumes beyond three, the value of B's consumption is less than the cost to society (everyone). Since someone must bear the burden of this care, and since *MC* exceeds *MSV* for all units beyond three, there is a net social loss for these units. B gains handsomely (i.e., her private benefits exceed her private costs), but overall this type of arrangement may lead to a great deal of medical care being consumed with very little value attached to it.

10.3.5.2 Competitive Market, No Philanthropy

Let us look at another arrangement, that of the competitive market with no philanthropy or government programs. Recall from Section 7.3.2 that equilibrium in a competitive market will occur where marginal private cost equals price. In the example here, A will consume the right amount for himself, but B will not. B's consumption will be less than the socially efficient amount because all society would have been willing to pay more for the first four units than the marginal cost of medical care. A freely operating competitive market with no philanthropy will yield less than the optimal level of output when externalities would have justified a larger output. As for a monopolistic market, recall from Section 8.2.1 that the output of such a market will be less than the output of a competitive market, which means it will be even further below the optimal amount.

10.3.5.3 Competitive Market with Philanthropy

It has been contended that a competitive market even with philanthropy will not produce the optimal amount of output. To understand why, consider a situation in which there are many donors of medical care, each of whom places a value on the consumption of medical care by the needy. In this case some social arrangement must be found for ensuring that the values of these donors will be expressed in the market. If each of these potential donors offers to give what the output is worth to him or her, the social value will equal the sum of the private values. However, if each donor feels that the others will also give, he or she might give less, hoping to get a "free ride," that is, gain the benefit of the others' donations while giving less. It is in the interests of each private donor to initially offer less than the value he or she places on the output in the hope that someone else will pay the tab. If everyone behaves in this way, the total amount given in philanthropy will be less than the socially optimal amount. Analysts who accept the efficiency criterion frequently justify compulsory government programs as a basis for making everyone pay what the programs are worth. Of course, it is difficult to decide how much a program would be worth to each taxpayer, since the individual still has an incentive to understate the value of the program to him- or herself.

Even accepting this justification for government programs, we still must discover whether there exists an arrangement that will lead to the correct amount of medical care being utilized. As can be seen in Figure 10–2, if B was offered subsidized medical care, the efficient amount of medical care would be utilized. In this case, a charge of $30 per unit of medical care to B would lead to B's consumption of the optimal quantity—three units. The rest of society must now pick up the remainder of the tab. Since the total cost to all members of society of medical care consumed by B is $105 and since B will pay $90 of this, some arrangements must be made to collect the remaining $15 from the rest of society. This can be done in the form of taxes. Various arrangements are discussed in the next paragraphs.

We can conclude from our analysis that some form of cost-sharing arrangement can lead to the provision of an optimal or efficient amount of the product. However, other arrangements can also be efficient. One is to have needy individuals pay nothing and to impose some form of rationing. In practice, this type of arrangement requires that the rationing system used must produce the efficient outcome, and such symptoms are difficult to design and operate. Our analysis can also be extended to a case in which the needy individuals have different levels of income. If their demands differ because of these income levels, a system of variable subsidies tailored to income levels could be designed to have each member consume the right level of output (Pauly 1972).

What is critical in translating the preceding analysis into a policy prescription is a clear conception of what the external demands might be in actuality (see Section 4.2.2). Assuming that external demands for the medical care of some groups do exist and are significant, it is essential that we pin down exactly what services these external demands are for. If they are for good health, for example, then the external demanders (the As in our analysis) may demand preventive care for consumption by the potential recipients of aid (the Bs). The demands may be much more specific than that, however. The demanders might show concern only for individuals who have catastrophic illnesses requiring large financial outlays. In this case they will not want to pay for the medical care of needy individuals who have sore throats, ingrown toenails, or acne. We know very little about the nature of medical care externalities (external demands). From an efficiency point of view, however, it is necessary to know what the external demanders are concerned about before we design a delivery system that will incorporate these externalities.

Assuming that we have identified the nature of the external demands, we can then use the preceding analysis to answer our questions, as long as we have the goal of efficiency in mind. Once the demands have been pinpointed, the types of health care that might improve the situation and the potential recipients can be identified. The consumer's portion of cost sharing will be designed to ensure that there is no overuse, which is defined as any quantity beyond which marginal social benefits are less than marginal social costs. The reimbursement mechanism chosen will lead to the least cost output.

10.4   OPTIMAL HEALTH INSURANCE

The provision of health insurance requires resources and incurs costs. In the same way that there is an optimal quantity of medical care, there is an optimal degree of insurance coverage (see Section 4.3.1). We will assume that all individuals are the same in all respects except one—the amount they must pay to obtain insurance.

Let us assume that there are 900 individuals (the number is not important) who are members of a large group and 100 individuals who are members of a small group. All individuals have an initial level of wealth of $1,000. There is a likelihood of 10 percent that each individual will get sick (i.e., 10 percent of the group will get sick). For those individuals who do get sick, the medical costs are $200 per patient. The utility function for each member (all have the same tastes) is as shown in Table 4–1. This utility function can be interpreted as a measure of "consumer welfare." With regard to the supply side of the market, we assume that there is one insurer who provides insurance at cost. The loading cost to the insurer of a large group policy is $30 whereas the cost for a small group policy is $60. Our objective is to maximize the overall utility of all members without detracting from that of any single member. This is the Paretean criterion.

The framework we will use focuses on consumer welfare (utility). In general, we can assume that consumer welfare is maximized by shifting the risk onto the insurer whenever the expected utility with insurance is greater than the utility in the absence of insurance. The postinsurance utility is the net of the economic cost to the insurer of accepting the risk. Therefore, utility (welfare) is maximized whenever the risk is appropriately shifted.

In our analysis, there are two groups of individuals. Each individual faces an expected loss of $20 and each can obtain insurance at a cost that includes the expected loss ($20) plus the appropriate loading cost. For members of the large group, the full premium, including the loading charge, is $50. For members of the smaller group, the premium is $80. For members of the large group, there is a utility or welfare gain by shifting the risk: At a cost of $50, the utility will be 97.0 units, which exceeds the expected utility of not insuring, which is 95.8 units. There is a social gain from shifting the risk. The same is not true for the members of the smaller group. Since the cost of insurance for them is $80, they would be better off to remain uninsured. This would be true even if the cost of insurance for the smaller group was subsidized (i.e., if someone else paid part or all of the premiums). This is because we are using the criterion of social efficiency rather than individual efficiency. When we recognize that there is a *social* cost of insuring, then we must also recognize that there is an *optimal* degree of insurance coverage. This optimal degree may be zero if the arrangements for providing insurance are too costly.

We must also acknowledge that consumers may vary in many respects, including the following: risk of illness, income or wealth level, degree of risk aversion, and circumstances affecting the cost of illness. As each varies, the utility gain from shifting the risk of incurring medical expenses will also change. For example, individuals with a high risk of illness will gain more in utility terms from shifting their risk than individuals with a low risk of illness. Thus, a situation in which individuals who are less healthy have greater insurance coverage could be an optimal situation. That is, variations in insurance coverage between individuals can be economically efficient.

There is a confounding factor in this analysis—moral hazard. There can be a net welfare gain resulting from the shifting of risk. Once the risk is shifted, the out-of-pocket price of medical care to the consumer falls. If there is any elasticity of demand for medical care, then moral hazard will come into play and the quantity demanded of health care will increase (See Section 3.6). If the out-of-pocket price of medical care is low enough, the individual might consume care up to the point where $MC > MV$ (Section 10.3.3.) There is a net welfare loss in the medical care market that occurs when the individual is ill. There are, then, two welfare effects of insurance: the welfare gain from shifting the risk and the welfare loss from consuming beyond the optimal point when the individual is ill. True optimality requires that we consider both effects together (Gianfrancesco 1978). Usually investigators focus on the insurance market (Gianfrancesco 1983; Pauly 1990) or the medical care market (Pauly 1972) in isolation from one another.

10.5   GOALS OF HEALTH POLICY

Based on the analysis of Section 10.3, we can identify specific goals that must be met for an optimal health policy to be enacted: (1) no unreasonable demand barriers, (2) technical efficiency, and (3) adequacy of supply. Putting these together with the requirement that efficiency criteria must be met in all markets yields a fourth, higher level goal, which we will call *economic efficiency* or *allocative efficiency*. A fifth goal, although not covered in the preceding analysis, is adequacy of quality of care. A sixth goal presents itself when government provision or finance enters into the picture: restricting the size of the overall health care budget (Stoddart and Labelle 1985).

Demand Barriers. Demand barriers are impediments obstructing to the reception of care. Within the context of our present model, price is the prime impediment. One can encourage additional care demanded by lowering the direct price through the purchase of insurance, public programs, or charity. To the degree that additional medical care utilization is thought to be desirable, the effectiveness of demand barriers can be measured by the availability of insurance or the direct price faced by individuals.

However, money price is not the only factor related to demand barriers. As seen in Section 4.2.4, time costs and travel costs can also make accessing medical care more difficult. If medical care consumption is to be encouraged, these costs must be addressed, either through subsidies, relocating facilities to lower travel time and expenses, or expanding facilities and increasing operating hours to decrease waiting time.

Technical Efficiency. Technical efficiency is a measure of the cost of producing a given level and quality of output. Technical efficiency is usually expressed in terms of money costs, but care must be taken when comparing costs between facilities to be sure that all other factors (e.g., quality, input prices, case mix) have been accounted for.

Adequacy of Supply. Adequacy of supply refers to the availability of sufficient resources to provide care at the efficient level (given the level of quality). As seen in Section 6.7, adequacy of supply depends on the incentive (reimbursement) system developed, the level of reimbursement, and the adequacy of funds.

Economic Efficiency. Economic efficiency results in part from reducing demand barriers, achieving technical efficiency, and ensuring adequacy of supply. It is attained when the marginal social value in a market equals the marginal social cost, which requires the achievement of these three goals. Note, however, that overall economic efficiency requires that these goals be attained in all *relevant* markets. For example, eye surgery can be done on an inpatient and outpatient basis. If we examined economic efficiency for the inpatient market only, we would miss the opportunity of "globally" evaluating the treatment of eye care. If the same quality of care is available in both settings but is less costly in the outpatient setting, then our analysis of economic efficiency should take this into account. In this case, the marginal benefits in the two markets would be the same, but the marginal cost of outpatient care would be at a lower level than that for inpatient care.

Quality of Care. Although quality is an elusive concept, the preservation of quality of care is a matter of public concern and therefore should be a consideration in any social evaluation. In fact, quality of care is a "commodity" with economic value, and there is in theory an optimal quality of medical care just as there is an optimal quantity. It could, therefore, be considered as another aspect of economic efficiency. However, it has not yet been incorporated into the general body of health economics and so is still treated as an additional consideration.

Public Expenditure Control. Strictly speaking, the government budget does not fall within the scope of our model. Of course, a transfer of funds from A to B is consistent with a tax on A by a government body and subsequent expenditures on medical care for B. But the model says nothing about the size of the tax, the expenditure, or the difference (the contribution to the deficit). In recent years, however, the budget deficit and public spending have come under a great deal of scrutiny, and cutbacks in government programs have been widespread. Typically the rationale for cutting a program's expenditures is not lack of worthiness of the program but the program's contribution to the overall budget deficit. To the extent that cutbacks can be achieved merely through increases in technical efficiency, true savings are provided to society and there are gains in social efficiency. However, cutbacks may also result in reduced supply. This is not necessarily bad if output was greater than the socially optimum level to begin with. However, if the initial output was at the socially optimum level or below it, cutbacks will lead to reductions in social efficiency because the value of the output that is lost is greater than the savings resulting from the cutbacks.

10.6 EXTRA-WELFARISM

The framework we have used until now includes a number of value judgments and principles. A key principle is that each person is the best judge of his or her own welfare. Welfare, in this framework, depends exclusively on the utility of goods and services as valued by the individuals. If there is any "public" component of goods and services, it is introduced through external demand, which is the value some people place on other people's consumption. Beyond this, there is no justification for publicly provided health care that can be derived from the Paretean welfare framework.

The Paretean framework has come under criticism in recent years on the grounds that it does not include all that people value in life (Culyer 1990; Rice 1992). There are other sources of personal well-being besides goods and services. Many of these other sources of well-being are embodied in the characteristics of people rather than the characteristics of the goods and services that people consume. People value mobility, absence from pain, and absence from distress—and they value these for other people as well as for themselves. While it is true that there are commodities (including medical care) that are linked to these more ultimate sources of well-being, there is no automatic link between them. Consequently, a social evaluation based on commodities consumed and nothing else appears much too narrow.

"Health" is often viewed as a composite of characteristics of people, such as mobility, absence of distress, and so forth. A number of economists have asserted that health is important not only because we want it for ourselves. They regard health as one of several entities that "society" recognizes should be made available to everyone (Culyer 1993) regardless of willingness to pay. This position has often appeared in the health care literature (Fein 1972; Outka 1971). If health really is a socially recognized good, then health *services* cannot be evaluated strictly in terms of their market value. In particular, the distribution of health services must be evaluated on a social basis.

The researchers who hold this position largely avoid the question of who the judge of welfare will be, a question directly addressed in the Paretean framework. They merely assert that some decision maker, chosen (or elected) by society, should be responsible for conducting the evaluation. Thus we are no longer clear, in this extra-welfarist viewpoint, who the judge of welfare is. Indeed, extra-welfarism is consistent with the use of any social judge other than the consumers;

the approach merely posits that there are some entities whose social value is determined outside of the consumers themselves. The role of economists is to act as advisors for the distributive organization and uncover the implications of incorporating efficiency and other objectives into the economic analysis. It should be pointed out that people's direct evaluations of their health services can be included in the extra-welfarist economic calculus, as can other (nondirect) evaluations of their health care.

The extra-welfarist position is concerned with how health is distributed among all members of society. Whoever the judge of well-being becomes (the government, a community league, etc.), value judgments must still be made in order to decide how to distribute health services and health. One way to operationalize the extra-welfarist approach (i.e., turn it into an evaluative tool) is to provisionally accept the principle that health care should be distributed according to "need." If need is defined as the ability to benefit from health services (Culyer 1995), then the "decision maker" is faced with the question of how to allocate health services so as to enhance or preserve different individuals' health status. Even if this approach evades the issue (or at least leaves the issue open) of who is to decide on the distribution, this approach helps make explicit the wide array of distributions that are possible (using the principle of need and other principles as well).

Figure 10–3 is a graph that shows the health of two individuals, A and B, measured along the two axes (Wagstaff 1991). Let us make the following (non-value-laden) assumptions; individual A has a self-assessed health status of h_1 and individual B has a self-assessed health status of h_2. The health status of both can be improved, but there is a limit. Curve H shows the maximum amount of health that can be produced with the resources available for health care (assumed to be fixed for society as a whole). More health can be produced for A, but only at the expense of resources and health for B. With available resources, A's health can be increased up to h_x (with no change in B's health) and B's health can be increased up to h_y (with no change in A's health). The exact shape of the H curve will depend on how effective the additional resources are in improving each individual's health. If very little extra can be done to improve B's health, then the curve will be steeply sloped. Our curve shows that more can be done for both.

Mentioned above was the principle that health resources should be distributed according to need. There are a number of different ways to express "need."

- *Equal health status.* One value judgment is to allocate resources so that everyone ends up with an equal level of health. If this principle is used, then more resources must be provided to A to ensure that in the end both A and B are equally healthy.
- *Maximizing total health, regardless of its distribution.* A second possible principle of distribution is to allocate resources so that total health is maxi-

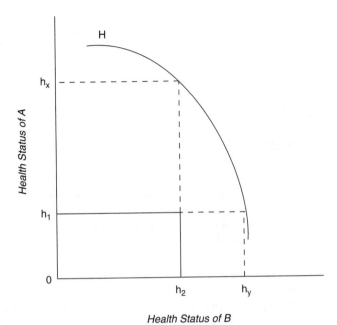

Figure 10–3 Potential health status of two individuals. The health status of A and the health status of B are currently at h_1 and h_2. Through the expending of more resources, their health status can move up to h_x and h_y respectively. However, since the available resources are finite, the limit of improvement for both individuals combined is shown by curve H.

---

mized, regardless of who gains or loses. If we chose this distributional principle, we would maximize the value of $hx + hy$, regardless of the initial values of health (h_1 and h_2). The selection of this principle is consistent with the reduction in health of any one person (say B). B's health would be reduced if, in taking away some resources from B, and adding them to B, the additional resources for A would add more in A's health status than would be detracted from B's health status.

- *Maximizing additional health per dollar of expenditure.* A third possible distributional principle would be to accept the existing distribution of health (h_1 and h_2) as a starting point 6 and to allocate additional resources to A and B so that the additional health status ($h_x - h_1$ for A and $h_y - h2$ for B) per additional dollar of expenditure would be equalized at the margin. This principle would be more in line with the Paretean efficiency principle, which states that no one will be a loser as a result of the distributional decision.

The usefulness of the extra-welfarist approach is that it allows us to go further in exploring resource allocation than the Paretean or welfarist position, and if society places special importance on characteristics such as health, then alternative distributions of health care resources need extremely careful evaluation.

10.7   MEASURES OF EQUITY

The concept of distributional equity is important in analyzing both the delivery of medical care (e.g., differences in utilization among groups), and its financing (e.g., differences in payments) and so it is essential to have measures of equity. We focus here on three types of distributional equity: intergenerational equity, vertical equity, and horizontal equity (Long and Smeeding 1984).

Intergenerational equity, in a financial context, concerns the distribution of payments among different generations. For example, if we divide up the population into retirees (who are generally over 65 and eligible for Medicare benefits), those of working age (say, those 18 to 64), and others, our classification scheme could be regarded as dividing the population along generational lines. Since the Medicare hospital insurance program is financed largely through the flow of payroll taxes into the Hospital Insurance Trust Fund, these taxes will be borne largely by individuals in the working-age group. In other words, the working-age generation is largely financing the care of the generation of retirees. The equity implications of this kind of tax are very different from the tax used to expand the Medicare program's benefits in 1988. This latter was a 15-percent tax on the taxable income of the retirees, and it proved to be so unpopular that the program expansion was repealed by Congress. This type of tax involves a minimal intergenerational transfer of funds.

It has been suggested (Feldman 1987) that current employment-based private health insurance provides another example of intergenerational transfer. All employees pay a similar health insurance premium, which is based on the average utilization pattern for all workers. If workers were rated separately by age group, according to insurance principles younger workers would have a lower premium than older workers because their utilization is less. The financing method of charging everyone in the plan the same rate (community rating) is in effect intergenerationally inequitable.

The second type of equity, vertical equity, concerns the economic burdens experienced by different income groups. For example, let us say we have three income groups: those who make under $20,000, those who make from $20,000 to $40,000, and those who make over $40,000. A tax is progressive if members of a higher income group pay a larger portion of their income in tax than those with a lower income, it is neutral if the portion is the same for all groups, and it is regressive if members of a lower income group pay a higher portion of their income in tax than those with a higher income.

An example of vertical inequity would be a flat tax charged to all individuals regardless of their income level. A fixed premium for Medicare enrollees is such a tax. Lower income groups pay the same rate as higher income groups do, and this premium amounts to a higher portion of their income.

Horizontal equity concerns the degree to which equals are taxed equally. An example of a horizontally inequitable tax is a tax on specific commodities such as alcohol, tobacco products, and hospital care. Consumption or sales taxes on the former two products fall on groups who use these products more heavily. Such taxes have been popular in the financing of health insurance programs for indigents. Even though such a tax is horizontally inequitable, it has been argued that since these individuals are likely to be less healthy and use the health care system more, they should pay higher taxes. Another type of tax that has been recommended as a way to pay for medical care for indigents is a tax on hospital admissions. Such a tax will also be inequitable, though to a large extent it will be less visible, because it will be passed on to the third parties who reimburse the providers. (Of course, the insurers, in turn, will pass the tax on by charging higher health insurance premiums.)

BIBLIOGRAPHY

Efficiency Criteria

Arrow, K.J. 1963. Uncertainty and the welfare economics of medical care. *American Economic Review* 53:941–973.

Buchanan, J.M. 1965. *The inconsistency of the National Health Service.* London: Institute of Economic Affairs.

Culyer, A.J. 1971. The nature of the commodity "health care" and its efficient allocation. *Oxford Economic Papers* 23:189–211.

———. 1977. On the relative efficiency of the National Health Service. *Kyklos* 25:266–287.

Feldman, R., and Dowd, B. 1993. What does the demand curve for medical care measure? *Journal of Health Economics* 12:193–200.

Pauly, M.V. 1968. The economics of moral hazard. *American Economic Review* 58:531–537.

———. 1972. *Medical care at public expense.* New York: Praeger.

Peele, P.B. 1993. Evaluating welfare losses in the health care market. *Journal of Health Economics* 12:205–208.

Rice, T. 1993a. Demand curves, economists and desert islands. *Journal of Health Economics* 12:201–204.

———. 1993b. A model is only as good as its assumptions. *Journal of Health Economics* 12:209–211.

Weisbrod, B.A. 1964. Collective consumption services of individual consumption goods. *Quarterly Journal of Economics* 78:471–477.

Optimal Health Insurance

Cleeton, D. 1989. The medical uninsured: A case of market failure? *Public Finance Quarterly* 17: 55–83.

Gianfrancesco, F.D. 1978. Insurance and medical care expenditure: An analysis of the optimal relationship. *Eastern Economics Journal* 4:225–234.

———. 1983. A proposal for improving the efficiency of medical insurance. *Journal of Health Economics* 2:175–184.

Pauly, M.V. 1990. The rational nonpurchase of long-term-care insurance. *Journal of Political Economy* 98:153–168.

Extra-Welfarism

Culyer, A.J. 1989. The normative economics of health care finance and provision. *Oxford Review of Economic Policy* 5:34–58.

———. 1990. Commodities, characteristics of commodities, characteristics of people, utilities, and the quality of life. In *Quality of life: Perspectives and problems,* ed. S. Baldwin et al. London: Routledge.

———. 1991. Conflicts between equity concepts and efficiency in health: A diagrammatic approach. *Osaka Economic Papers* 40:141–154.

———. 1993. Health, health expenditures, and equity. In *Equity in the finance and delivery of health care: An international perspective,* ed. E. von Doorslaer et al. Oxford: Oxford University Press.

———. 1995. *Equality of what in health policy? Conflicts between the contenders.* Discussion paper 142. York: University of York, Center for Health Economics.

Pauly, M.V. 1994. Reply to Roberta Labelle, Greg Stoddart, and Thomas Rice. *Journal of Health Economics* 13:495–496.

Rice, T. 1992. An alternative framework for evaluating welfare losses in the health care market. *Journal of Health Economics* 11:85–92.

Wagstaff, A. 1991. QALYs and the equity-efficiency trade-off. *Journal of Health Economics* 10: 21–41.

Equity and Other Social Goals

Beauchamp, D.E. 1976. Public health as social justice. *Inquiry* 13:3–14.

Daniels, N. 1982. Equity of access to health care. *Milbank Quarterly* 60:51–81.

Fein, R. 1972. On achieving access and equity in health care. In *Economic aspects of health care,* ed. J.B. McKinlay. New York: Watson Publishing International.

Friedman, L.M. 1971. The idea of right as a social and legal concept. *Journal of Social Issues* 27:189–198.

Goldfarb, R., et al. 1984. Can remittances compensate for manpower outflows. *Journal of Development Economics* 15:1–17.

Hemenway, D. 1982. The optimal location of doctors. *New England Journal of Medicine* 306:397–401.

Lewis, C.F., et al. 1976. *A right to health.* New York: Wiley-Interscience.

Long, S.H., and Smeeding, T.M. 1984. Alternative Medicare financing sources. *Milbank Quarterly* 62:325–348.

Mitchell, B.M., and Phelps, C.E. 1976. National health insurance: Some costs and effects of mandated employee coverage. *Journal of Political Economy* 84:553–571.

Outka, G. 1974. Social justice and equal access to health care. *Journal of Religious Ethics* 2:11–32.

Schwartz, W.B., and Joskow, P.L. 1978. Medical efficacy versus economic efficiency: A conflict in values. *New England Journal of Medicine* 299:1462–1464.

Stoddart, G.L., and Labelle, R.J. 1985. *Privatization in the Canadian health care system.* Ottawa, Ontario: Health and Welfare Department, Government of Canada.

Sudgen, R., and Williams, A. 1978. *The principles of practical cost-benefit analysis.* Oxford: Oxford University Press.

Thurow, L.C., 1985. Medicine versus economics. *New England Journal of Medicine* 313:611–614.

Whipple, D. 1974. Health care as a right. *Inquiry* 11:65–68.

CHAPTER 11

Financing Health Care

11.1 INTRODUCTION

There are three major methods of financing health care services—out-of-pocket payments by the consumers, insurance premiums, and taxation—and within each category there are a number of different financing techniques. For example, out-of-pocket payments include deductibles, copayments, and full consumer payments. Insurance premiums can be paid directly by the consumer or paid by the employer or the government. And taxes can be levied on income or on specific products or services. Further, the different financing methods can interact: Insurance premiums can be excluded from taxation, can be taxed, or both (as is the case in the United States).

Each method will impact differently on groups with different characteristics, such as income level or size of family. Determining how the burden of each financing method will fall is not a straightforward matter. The burden of insurance premiums that are paid out of pocket by consumers will fall on the consumers directly, but income taxes can influence this burden, and when insurance is obtained through the workplace (as is usually the case in the United States), the burden of payment is not clear-cut. Further, different kinds of taxes will have the same impact on groups with varying income levels. Economic analysis is a very useful tool for sorting out the effects of these varying finance methods. In the first part of this chapter, we examine how explanatory economics can be used to analyze the burden of the various financing methods. We also show how these varying finance methods can be assessed in terms of specific criteria or policy objectives.

Different financing methods also have significantly different costs. In the case of private insurance, there are the costs of marketing, rating alternative consuming groups, paying providers, and monitoring utilization. In the case of government finance, there are the costs of collecting taxes and administering public programs. A debate has been occurring in the United States in recent years over whether health care coverage for the population should be provided primarily through private markets (with appropriate subsidies) or public financing. In this chapter, we illustrate how economic analysis can be used to compare these options.

11.2   FINANCING MEANS AND BURDENS IN THE UNITED STATES

Currently in the United States a variety of financing mechanisms are used in health care. These mechanisms and the amounts raised through each are shown in Table 11–1. We use 1987 data in our example because a national survey was conducted in that year that provides thorough information on health insurance expenditures by households. Using data from this survey seems preferable to using data for different years that are not consistent.

As can be seen from Table 11–1, a total of $488 billion was spent on health care in 1987. Of this amount, $102.4 billion (roughly 21 percent) was financed by out-of-pocket payments by consumers. These payments constituted a larger portion of the funds spent on physician care than on hospital care.

A total of $156.2 billion (32 percent) was spent through private insurance. The majority of private insurance premiums (roughly 86 percent of all premiums) are paid through employment-provided health insurance, and the rest are paid for through individual purchases that are not employment related. Individually purchased insurance includes Medigap insurance, which individuals over 65 purchase to cover the copayments and deductibles in the Medicare program. Roughly one-half of all premiums purchased directly by individuals (i.e., not obtained through employment) are Medigap premiums.

With regard to health insurance provided through the workplace, the majority (about 83 percent) of the premiums are paid for by employers, with a smaller amount being paid for directly by employees. However, this does not mean that the employers bear the burden of the majority of the health insurance expenses. For one thing, premiums paid for by employers are workplace benefits that are not subject to income tax. There is therefore a sizable public subsidy given to employees who obtain their insurance in this way; their taxes will be lower than if they paid for their premiums directly. In addition, there is considerable evidence that, when all the wage effects are taken into account, the employees do indeed bear a major share of these premium costs, even if the picture at first glance does not show it that way.

The third form of finance that is used is public finance, or taxation. About $208 billion (45 percent) of total financing for health care involved taxation. Most of this amount went to pay for the federal Medicare program, which covers individuals over 65, and the joint federal-state Medicaid program, which is primarily for

Table 11–1 Sources of Funds for National Health Expenditures, 1987 (billions of dollars)

Private Funds			Subtotals	Total
Out-of-Pocket Expenses[a]			$102.4	
Private Insurance[a]				
Employment Related[b]				
Employer Contributed[c]	$112.5			
Employee Contributed[c]	21.8	$134.3		
Non-employment-related (self-purchase and Medigap)[b]		18.9	156.2	
Other Private Funds			21.8	
Government Funds[a]				
Federal Funds[a]				
Payroll Taxes for Part A Medicare[d]	$58.6			
Medicare Premiums for Medicare Part B and HMO Coverage[d]	7.4			
Other Federal Funds (taxation)	78.3	$144.0		
State and Local Funds[a]		64.3	208.3	
Total, All Sources[a]				$488.8

[a]Office of National Cost Estimates. 1990. National health expenditures, 1988. *Health Care Financing Review* 11(4):1–54.

[b]Vistnes, J. 1992. *Private health insurance premiums in 1987: Policy holders under the age of 65.* AHCPR publ. no. 92-0061. National Medical Expenditure Survey Summary 5. Rockville, Md.: U.S. Department of Health and Human Services, Public Health Service, Agency for Health Care Policy and Research.

[c]Cooper, P., and Johnson, A. 1993. *Employment related health insurance in 1987.* AHCPR publ. no. 93-0044. National Medical Expenditure Survey Research Findings 17. Rockville, Md.: U.S. Department of Health and Human Services, Public Health Service, Agency for Health Care Policy and Research.

[d]Petrie, J.T. 1993. Overview of the Medicare program. *Health Care Financing Review,* Medicare and Medicaid supplement, October, 1–12.

the lower income groups. These programs are largely but not entirely financed by taxation. With regard to taxation, the major federal tax that pays for the hospital portion (Part A) of Medicare is a payroll tax of 1.6 percent of wages, paid both by employers and employees. In 1987, about $58 billion was collected by this tax. In addition, there is a Medicare "premium" for medical care (physician services) and health maintenance organization (Part B) coverage, which raised $7.4 billion. Most of the remainder of the federal portion was raised through general taxation, the largest portion from direct income taxation. Of the $208 billion spent by governments on health care, $64 billion was raised from state government taxation. Most of state taxation is in the form of direct income and indirect sales taxes.

The above picture does provide an indication of where the money is coming from, but it cannot be used directly to assess the "burden" of medical care financing (defined as the reduction in real income due to payments and taxes). The complexity of the situation and the prominent role played by each of the financing methods calls for a much more detailed analysis. Each financing method imposes different burdens on different groups. We will discuss the pattern of these burdens after examining the positive economics of the burdens.

11.3 ECONOMIC ANALYSIS OF ALTERNATIVE PAYMENT SOURCES

This section presents economic analyses of alternative payment methods. The focus of the analyses is the economic impact of the payment methods on the resource owners (primarily employees and owners of companies). We will examine insurance premiums (in particular, the impact of employer-paid premiums, taxation, and mandated benefits) and taxation (the impact of payroll and sales taxes).

11.3.1 Insurance Premiums

Insurance can be obtained through the workplace or by individual purchase. Insurance obtained in the workplace can be paid for directly by the employees (through payroll deductions) or by the employers. There us no controversy over the incidence of premiums paid by employees or by individuals; the purchasers bear the cost of their insurance purchases.

The economic incidence of employer paid premiums is a little more complicated. The cost of insurance benefit packages are viewed by employers as an expense, much like wages are. An employer has a demand curve for labor and will regard the costs of various forms of compensation as monetarily equivalent. If the marginal employee is worth (has a marginal value of) $50 to the employer, then the employer will be willing to pay up to $50 in compensation, whether in the form of wages or fringe benefits (Kreuger and Reinhardt 1994). If benefits are increased, then the employer will reduce wages. Thus the economic burden of all health insurance benefits will fall on the employee either directly (out of pocket) or indirectly (through a lower wage).

11.3.2 Taxation and Insurance Premiums

Health insurance benefits paid by the employer are exempt from personal income and social security taxes. This reduces the cost to the employee of employer-paid health insurance and increases the quantity demanded for health insurance. However, we cannot assume that, once a subsidy is put into place, the quantity demanded and supplied will remain the same. To see why, consider the analysis of a tax subsidy provided below.

In Figure 11–1, the initial demand curve for health insurance (with no tax subsidies) is D_1. According to this curve, when the premium rate is $100, 75 individuals will be willing to shift their risks to insurers. Let us now introduce a 50 percent subsidy. This will in effect lower the out-of-pocket price for insurance at every premium rate. Thus, at a premium rate of $100, the out-of-pocket price to the consumer is $50, and at this price 100 individuals will be willing to shift their risks. The market demand curve will then be D_2.

According to the supply curve for insurance (S in Figure 11–1), insurers will be willing to accept 92 risks at a price of $135. Generally, a higher supplier price will be required to induce more risks to be accepted.

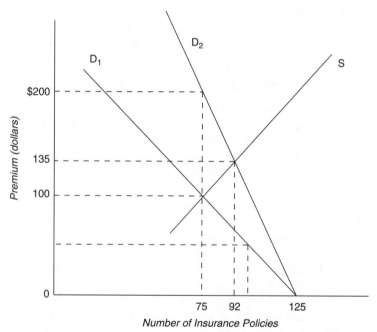

Figure 11–1 The effect of a subsidy on the quantity of health insurance. The demand curve for insurance without any tax subsidy is shown in the above diagram as D_1. This curve shows that at an unsubsidized premium rate of $100, 75 individuals will demand insurance. Let us introduce a 50-percent subsidy (e.g., at a premium rate of $100, the individual will pay $50). The market demand curve will shift to D_2. The supply curve for insurance is also shown. At a market price of $100, the insurance industry is willing to supply 75 policies (accept 75 risks). Without a subsidy, 75 individuals will shift risks to the insurers. With a 50-percent subsidy, the out-of-pocket premium price would initially drop to $50. There would be a large excess demand at this price, but the industry would not be willing to accept 100 risks at $100. The price would be increased until a new equilibrium is reached—at $135 (and 92 risks shifted).

Let us initially assume that there is no tax subsidy. Then 100 risks will be shifted at a premium rate of $100. This is the equilibrium price and quantity. Using this position as a base point, we will now introduce a subsidy on premiums of 50 percent. That is, the individuals are in a 50-percent income tax bracket and are allowed to deduct insurance premiums before calculating income taxes. A preliminary analysis of the effects of the subsidy might be as follows. The premium price would remain the same ($100) but half would be paid ($50) out of pocket by the consumer and half would fall on taxpayers (since the individual would get $50 back from the public purse). This analysis might be applied to 75 insurance policies in order to determine the "shifting" effect. However, a sounder economic analysis would result from supposing that the new quantity on which the subsidy will be based will neither be the old quantity nor the quantity demanded at a premium of $100. In order to determine the likely effects of the subsidy, we must conduct an economic analysis of the type presented Figure 11–1.

As shown in the figure, the subsidy raises quantity demanded at each price, and so more individuals will seek to shift risks at the premium rate of $100. However, suppliers (insurers) will require higher premiums in order to accept more risks. The premium rate will rise, and less risks will be shifted than were originally indicated by demand conditions alone. In our example, the final premium rate will be $135, and at this price 92 risks will be shifted.

The cost of the premium will be half-borne by the consumer and half by the taxpayer. However, the amount of subsidy will be based on the new price of $135. And the quantity of risks shifted will be the new equilibrium quantity. The final equilibrium (and the burden of the subsidy) will depend on the elasticities of demand and supply. In the extreme, if the supply curve were upward sloping, indicating no change in risks shifted, then the analysis would indicate that the premium would rise by the full amount of the subsidy. The taxpayers would pay a subsidy of $100, based on a new premium of $200, with 75 risks still being shifted. It is more likely the supply curve is horizontal, indicating an unlimited supply of risks accepted at a price of $100. Then the consumer would get a full $50 subsidy paid for by the taxpayers; in this case 100 risks would be shifted.

Our analysis does not take into account subsequent effects of the increased insurance coverage on the medical care market. Nevertheless, even this simple analysis indicates the demand and supply analysis should be considered when determining the full effects of a tax subsidy on premiums.

11.3.3 Mandated Benefits

Mandated insurance benefits are government-required coverage benefits that individuals privately purchase or employers must provide. Mandated benefits can have a considerable impact on labor markets depending on how they are viewed by consumers, and this impact will in turn affect the incidence of benefits.

We will consider an economic analysis of mandated benefits using a labor market analysis such as that presented in Figure 11–2. In the initial situation, there are no mandated benefits. The demand for labor is shown as D, and the supply of labor is shown as $S_{v=0}$. Equilibrium wages are at \$8 and equilibrium employment is at 300 workers. Such a model has been developed in Section 7.6.

We now introduce mandated insurance benefits that cost \$2 per worker. The employer's demand curve for labor in terms of total compensation will remain the same; however, when expressed in terms of the wage rate, the demand curve will shift down by \$2, since \$2 is added to the wages for each worker to calculate total compensation. The new demand curve for labor, in terms of wages, is D_2.

It would be tempting to say that the employees will bear the entire burden of the mandated benefits and take a \$2 reduction in wages, in which case employment would remain the same. Such will be the case only if the workers fully value the benefits (see curve $S_{v=b}$), the new price in this instance would be \$6.

If the workers do not value the benefits at all, there will be a reduction in wages (but by less than \$2) to \$7 (or some such amount, depending on the elasticity of labor supply), and also a reduction in employment. The burden of the mandate will then fall, to some degree, on the workers who lose their jobs. If benefits are only partially valued ($S_{v<b}$), the net result will be somewhere in between.

In an extreme case, such as a vertical supply curve, there will be no employment effect but a full wage effect. In fact, several studies have shown that these results are approximated in reality (Kreuger and Reinhardt 1994), and so the workers bear the full burden of the mandate. In sum, then, mandated benefits may have similar effects to those that might be posited without a more formal economic analysis, but this is only the case because the supply curve of labor is in reality close to vertical (zero elasticity) in the relevant ranges.

11.4 TAXATION

Much health care is publicly funded, and much of the funding comes through taxation. However configured, taxes can be regarded as reductions in income or wealth without any attached benefits. While it is true that benefits may come as a result of the use of funds, under taxation these benefits are not directly linked to the taxes. Only full-scale economic analyses using heroic assumptions can link the benefits resulting from the spending of taxes to the costs of the taxes themselves.

Taxation can be direct or indirect. Direct taxes are those that are directly levied on income. They cannot, therefore, be shifted (i.e., the burden cannot be made to fall on someone other than the taxpayer). Indirect taxes on goods and services can be shifted (in essence, avoided) to some degree. Economic analysis is useful in determining the economic impact and burden of taxation. Below we will analyze the burden of two types of taxes commonly used to finance health care: payroll taxes and sales taxes.

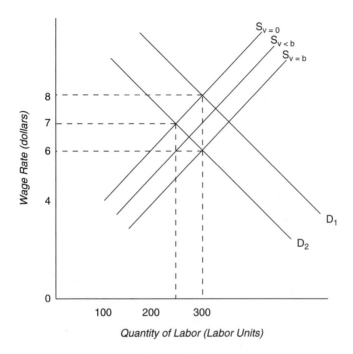

Figure 11–2 The effect of mandated insurance coverage on labor markets. The demand for labor when the employer does not provide any benefits is shown as D_1. For example, at a wage rate of $8,300 workers (the labor units) will be demanded. Let us introduce mandated benefits of $2 per worker. The employer will still value each worker's productivity the same, but at each quantity of labor the total compensation that must be paid by the employer is $2 above the wage rate. Therefore, the demand curve is shifted down by $2 at each quantity of labor (D_2). We posit three alternative supply curves for labor. The first supply curve $(S_{v=0})$ is for the situation where the mandated benefits have no value to the workers. Each employee's supply curve for labor, in terms of the wage rate, remains the same after the benefits are mandated. The second supply curve $(S_{v=b})$ is for the situation where the workers value benefits and wages equally. The supply curve relating wages to the quantity of labor supplied shifts down by the full amount of the mandated benefits ($2 in this case). The third supply curve $(S_{v<b})$ is for the intermediate situation, where the workers place some value on the benefits but less than the $2 that they cost the employer. Initially, without the mandated benefits, the market equilibrium is at a wage of $8 and a quantity of 300 workers employed. When mandated benefits are instituted, the new equilibrium position will depend on the value placed on the benefits by the workers. With full valuation, the new equilibrium will occur where wages fall by $2, but there will be no change in employment. However, if the benefits are not valued at all, then wages will fall ($7 in this case) and employment will be reduced. If some value (less than $2) is placed on the benefits by the workers, there will be an intermediate result.

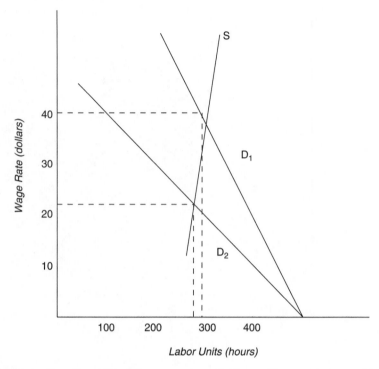

Figure 11–3   The effect of imposing an employer-paid payroll tax. Initially, the demand for labor without a payroll tax is shown in terms of wages. With the give supply curve for labor, equilibrium occurs with a wage of $40 and a quantity of employment of 300 work hours. The effect of a payroll tax of 100 percent of wages is to shift the demand curve in terms of wages down by 50 percent. For example, at a wage rate of $20, the employers pay a tax of $20, for a total payout of $40, and thus the demand with the tax is the same as it would be if the wage was 100 percent higher but there was no tax. The new equilibrium will be determined by the intersection of supply and demand for labor. In this case, the supply curve is almost vertical. There will be very little reduction in employment and an almost 50-percent reduction in wages.

11.4.1 Payroll Taxes

A payroll tax is a tax that is levied on wages. Medicare uses a payroll (social security) tax of 1.6 percent of total payroll (payable by both the employer and employee), to finance the hospital portion of Medicare. The burden of an employee paid payroll tax is quite clear: it is paid by the worker. However, because it lowers take-home wages, some workers may decide not to supply labor. Employment will therefore fall. The burden is therefore equally shared among workers.

The economic effects resulting from the imposition of a payroll tax that is paid by employers is less clear and deserves closer attention.

In Figure 11–3 we introduce the analysis of the effect of a payroll tax on labor and wages. Initially we have a competitive labor market with a given supply of labor (*S*) and a demand for labor (*D₁*). Our output measure is labor hours, and equilibrium in this market occurs with a wage rate of $40 per unit and a quantity of 300 labor hours. Note that we have drawn a very steep supply curve for labor; this indicates that workers will not change their work habits very much when wages increase or decrease. A vertical curve would indicate that they would not change their habits at all. We now introduce an employer-paid payroll tax of 100 percent of wages.

If the employers are in a competitive industry, they cannot raise the price of their output, and so their demand for labor curve cannot be increased through higher prices. The employers therefore would have to either absorb the tax themselves or lower wages. At first blush, we might be inclined to say that wages would stay at $40, taxes of $40 would be paid, and employment would remain the same. This is a very unlikely outcome given the forces behind the employment for labor. In Figure 11–3 we present the economic analysis of what will happen.

The effect of this tax is to shift down the demand curve for labor, which is based on the marginal revenue of the product that labor produces (see Section 6.8). At a wage of $20, each employer must pay a tax of $20 (which is 100 percent of the wage). Each worker costs twice as much to the firm. Therefore, whereas the employers formerly demanded 300 labor hours when the wage was $40, they will demand 300 hours of labor at a wage of $20. Note also that because the tax is expressed as a percentage of wages, the new demand for labor curve (in terms of wages) is a fixed percentage lower than the old one. The higher the wage, the greater the discrepancy between the old and new curves.

With the employers' demand curve for labor (in terms of wages) shifting downward, employees will receive lower wages. The equilibrium volume of labor and the corresponding wage rate are just under 300 hours and just over $22. This means that the quantity of labor will hardly have changed but the wage rate will have fallen by almost the full amount of the tax. The workers have not substituted away from working and have borne almost the entire burden of the tax through a reduction in their wage rate. In this case, the supply of labor curve is almost vertical, and workers would rather accept lower wages than lose employment. Other situations are possible. For example, if workers were very sensitive to their wage rates, and the supply of labor curve was close to horizontal, the labor supply would fall when wages fell. In this instance, they would avoid the tax entirely by refusing to work at lower wages. At the new wage, the tax would have been shifted to the employers, who also would hire fewer workers.

The effect of the payroll tax, then, will be to reduce employment and wages. How much of the tax will be borne by the workers (through a decrease in wages) will depend on how much they are willing to adjust their wages and their work—information summarized by the supply of labor curve.

11.4.3 Sales Taxes

A very similar analysis applies to sales taxes. A sales tax is a tax on a product or service. Most states use sales taxes as a major source of revenue. Sales taxes can be general (on all items), modified general (on most items except, for example, food and children's clothes), and specific (on gasoline, alcohol, tobacco products, health insurance premiums, etc.). In the case of tobacco and alcohol, these taxes may affect consumer behavior with regard to drinking and smoking and thus health status (and health care demand). Certainly this was the rationale for a large tobacco tax that the state of Maine imposed in order to pay for more publicly funded health care benefits in the 1980s.

In order to analyze the effects of sales taxes, we will use the example of a sales tax on prescription drugs. The initial situation, without the sales tax, is shown in Figure 11-4. There is a demand for the drugs, as is shown by the demand curve (D). This is the demand of the consumers of the drugs. And there is also a curve for the supply without the sales tax (S). In a competitive market, equilibrium will occur at a price of $4 and a quantity of 200 prescriptions filled.

Let us now impose a sales tax of $2 on each prescription, to be paid by the pharmacists. We initially might imagine that the pharmacists will simply raise the price of each prescription to $6 and collect the tax on each of the 200 prescriptions. But this would occur only if the demand curve for prescriptions was vertical and consumers would demand their prescriptions at any price. This is not a realistic scenario in the case of drugs or most other commodities. There is an elasticity of demand for drugs, as indicated by the downward-sloping demand curve.

The tax will cause the prices charged by the pharmacists to increase (if they pay the tax), and they might at first charge $6 for each prescription (though they would receive $4, as before). But there is a limit to what consumers would pay. In our case, some consumers will refuse to fill their prescriptions, thus avoiding the tax entirely. A new equilibrium will be set at $5, and only 150 prescriptions will be filled. The pharmacists will only receive $3 for each prescription and will supply less (150 at the net of tax price of $3).

The market will have shifted part of the tax onto the pharmacists, who now pay one-half of it by receiving a lower price. The consumers end up paying $1 of the prescription tax by reducing the quantity they demand. The burden of the sales tax will thus be shared. We should point out that there are other possible alternative outcomes, depending on the slopes of the supply and demand curves. However, it is not likely that all of the tax will be borne by the consumers.

As pointed out above, sales taxes are very common on a variety of products related to health. Many states impose taxes on health insurance premiums. Such a tax will have an effect on the number of risks shifted and can be analyzed using the sales tax model.

11.5 THE INCIDENCE OF ALTERNATIVE TYPES OF HEALTH CARE FINANCING

In this section we turn our attention to the incidence of alternative types of health care financing. The term *incidence* does not have a precise meaning because it has been used to indicate many things. We will use the term to denote the pattern of distribution of burdens of various financing methods (Due 1957). We will focus on one key characteristic of individuals—their level of income—and

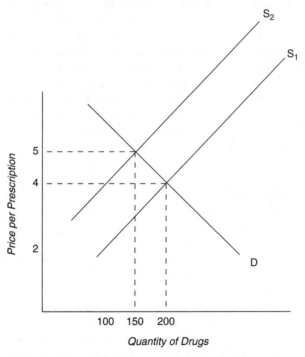

Figure 11–4 Effect of a sales tax. The supply and demand for prescriptions are shown above. Equilibrium without the sales tax is where the price is $4 and the quantity of prescriptions is 200 (where S_1 and D intersect). If a sales tax of $2 per prescription is imposed, to be paid by suppliers, the suppliers' costs will increase by exactly $2, as will the supply curve (S_2). The new equilibrium will take into account the demand elasticity. In the above case, the price will increase by $1 and the quantity sold will be reduced to 150 prescriptions. The consumers will, in effect, have shifted some of the tax onto the suppliers by reducing their demands.

four different types of financing: insurance premiums, income taxes, sales taxes, and payroll taxes. Our analysis, although highly simplified, will provide a basic understanding of the major issues.

We assume that there are four income groups each with 100 families (see Table 11–2). Each family in the lowest income group has earnings of $10,000; in the next lowest group, of $20,000; in the next group, of $30,000; and in the highest income group, of $40,000.

Each family incurs health care expenditures of $2,500. There are no differences in health care usage by income levels. However, all expenditures are financed, and the out-of-pocket cost is zero. Total medical expenses for all groups equal $1,000,000.

Each family's total consumption of commodities, including food but not medical care, is given in Column 4 of Table 11–2. The lowest income group spends all it earns on commodities, the next group spends 90 percent, the third group spends 80 percent, and the highest income group spends 70 percent. What the members of a group do not spend, they will save. If they have to pay for medical care, they will reduce other expenditures but will not reduce their savings. If they do pay for medical care itself, it will be through the purchase of insurance.

The financing problem is how to pay for the $1,000,000 in medical care expenses. There are four options: insurance premiums, a sales tax, a payroll tax, and an income tax. Our task is to determine the incidence of each type of finance on the different income groups. The conclusions we will reach are summarized in Figure 11–5.

Premiums. Each family bears the same risk of health expenses, and so it would seem reasonable to charge every family the same premium rate. There are 400 families, and $1 million in health care funds must be raised. Therefore, each family will pay a premium of $2,500.

The burden of the finance method on each family is the premium divided by family income. This would be 25 percent for the lowest income families, 12.5 percent for the families earning $20,000, 8.3 percent for the families earning $30,000, and 6.25 percent for the highest income families. The incidence of premiums are such that the burden falls steadily as income increases.

Payroll Taxes. In the case of a payroll tax, a fixed percentage of wages is charged, but there is usually a cap above which income is not taxed. We will assume that this cap is $30,000. This means that all wages up to $30,000 are taxed. The members of the highest income group, those earning $40,000, will only pay taxes on the first $30,000 of their wages. Total taxable wages are $9,000,000 for all families. In order to raise the required $1,000,000, a tax rate of 11.1 percent must be levied on all wages below $30,000.

The burden of the tax will be the same for the three groups whose members have incomes at or below $30,000. However, the highest income group only pays

Table 11–2 Income and Expenditures for Four Income Groups

Income Group	Earnings per Family	Number of Families	Total Income	Total Consumption Expenditures	Health Care Expenditures per Family	Total Health Care Expenditures
A	$10,000	100	$1,000,000	$1,000,000	$2,500	$250,000
B	20,000	100	2,000,000	1,800,000	2,500	250,000
C	30,000	100	3,000,000	2,400,000	2,500	250,000
D	40,000	100	4,000,000	2,800,000	2,500	250,000
Total		400	$10,000,000	$8,000,000		$1,000,000

$3,330 in payroll taxes per family, for an effective tax rate of 8.325 per cent. As shown in Figure 11–5, the burden of the payroll tax is the same for the three lowest groups but falls somewhat for the highest income group.

Sales Taxes. Sales taxes can be imposed on any of a variety of consumption expenditures. We will assume that sales taxes are imposed on all consumption

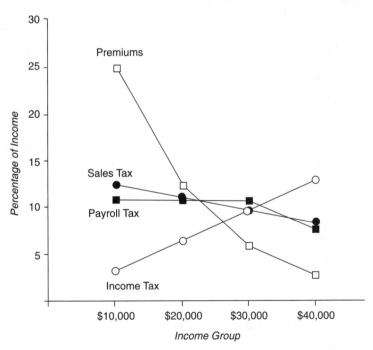

Figure 11–5 Incidence of financing methods. Premiums are the most regressive source of finance, income tax the most progressive, and sales and payroll taxes fall in between.

expenditures except on medical care. Total consumption expenditures for all families equal $8,000,000. In order to raise the required $1,000,000 in funds, the overall sales tax rate must be 12.5 percent ($1,000,000/8,000,000). The lowest income group pays $125,000 on its $1,000,000 in expenditures; the next group pays $225,000; the next group, $300,000; and the highest income group pays $350,000. The effective tax rate, or burden, for these groups is 12.5 percent, 11.25 percent, 10 percent, and 8.75 percent of income, respectively. The incidence is such that the burden continually falls as income rises. Of course, if certain "necessities" such as food were excluded from the sales tax, this pattern might change.

Income Taxation. The burden of the income tax will depend on the actual tax rates, and these are subject to policy decisions by Congress. We will assume the tax rates are such that the highest income class pays roughly four times the rate of the lowest group. This is very roughly the ratio in the United States today. Specifically, we assume that, given an average, overall rate, the lowest group will pay 40 percent of this rate (i.e., 0.4), the second group will pay 80 percent of the rate, the third highest group will pay 120 percent of the rate, and the highest group will pay 160 percent of the rate. Let x stand for the overall tax rate. The average, overall rate can be determined by solving for x in this equation:

$$.4(1,000,000)x + .8(2,000,000)x + 1.2(3,000,000)x + 1.6(4,000,000)x = 1,000,000$$

The $1,000,000 is the amount to be collected by the income tax. If we solve for x, we will find the average overall rate is 8.33 percent. Based on the ratios determined by "policy," the four groups pay 3.33 percent, 6.64 percent, 9.99 percent, and 13.33 percent of income in income taxes, respectively.

The overall incidence of the funding methods can be compared. Premiums are the most "regressive" and income taxes are the most "progressive." The other two methods fall in between (under our assumptions they are mildly regressive).

Omitted from our analysis are out-of-pocket expenditures. The use of this type of financing will result in lower overall usage (because of the downward-sloping demand curve for medical care). Thus, if families had to pay out of pocket for health care, total expenditures would likely fall below $1 million. The overall burden would depend on the response of each income group.

Our assessment of financing options will depend on our policy goals. Much of the focus in evaluating types of financing is on considerations of equity. However, efficiency issues need to be addressed as well.

11.6   THE ADMINISTRATIVE COST OF ALTERNATIVE TYPES OF HEALTH CARE FINANCING

There has been a lively debate in recent years about administrative costs associated with the health care financing system in the United States. Much of the debate has been focused on the costs associated with the marketing of health insurance and hospital services, the monitoring of utilization and the regulating of payment by insurers, the billing of third parties by providers, and the collecting of deductibles and copayments from patients by providers. Because of the complexity of the U.S. system of health care finance, more resources are devoted to these functions than in other health care systems, such as those of Canada and the United Kingdom. A study conducted using 1987 data estimated that between $96 billion and $120 billion were spent on administration in the United States, out of a total spent of $488 billion for all health care–related services (Woolhandler and Himmelstein 1991). This study primarily added up the money costs of these functions.

This debate has served to highlight the fact that a health care financing system requires resources and that different systems have different costs. The Canadian system, for example, has lower administrative costs than does the U.S. system. However, the amount of administrative costs is not the only factor that needs to be taken into account when choosing a national health care "system."

Marketing functions serve to inform potential customers about the characteristics of various health plans. Consumers can better select among health plans if they have more information. Regulation and payment functions serve to help ensure that the care that is provided is of a high quality and results in good outcomes. Although these functions are not always completely effective, nevertheless, when we evaluate a financing system, we must look at the benefits of the various financing practices in addition to their costs.

BIBLIOGRAPHY

The Burden of Insurance

Cutler, D.M. 1995. The cost and financing of health care. *American Economic Review* 85 (suppl.):32–37.

Gruber, J., and Krueger, A.B. 1991. The incidence of mandated employer-provided insurance: Lessons from workers' compensation insurance. In *Tax policy and the economy*, ed. D. Bradford. Cambridge: National Bureau of Economic Research.

Kreuger, A., and Reinhardt, U.E. 1994. Economics of employer versus individual mandates. *Health Affairs* 13:34–54.

Mitchell, B.M., and Phelps, C.E. 1976. National health insurance: Some costs and effects of mandated employee coverage. *Journal of Political Economy* 84:553–571.

Summers, L.H. 1989. Some simple economics of mandated benefits. *American Economic Review* 79:177–183.

Wilensky, G.R., and Taylor, A.K. 1982. Tax expenditures and health insurance: Limiting employer-paid premiums. *Public Health Reports* 97:438–444.

The Burden of Taxation

Aaron, H.J. 1994. Tax issues in health care reform. *National Tax Journal* 47:407–416.

Brandon, W.P. 1982. Health-related tax subsidies. *New England Journal of Medicine* 302: 947–950.

Browning, E.K., and Johnson, W.R. Taxation and the cost of national health insurance. In *National health insurance*, ed. M.V. Pauly. Washington, D.C.: American Enterprise Institute.

Burman, L.E., and Williams, R. 1994. Tax caps on employment based health insurance. *National Tax Journal* 47:529.

Due, J.F. 1957. *Sales taxation*. London: Routledge and Kegan Paul.

Feldstein, M., et al. 1972. Distributional aspects of national health insurance benefits and finance. *National Tax Journal* 25:497–510.

Gruber, J., and Hanratty, M. 1995. The labor-market effects of introducing national health insurance: Evidence from Canada. *Journal of Business and Economic Statistics* 13:163–173.

Marquis, M.S., and Buchanan, J.L. 1994. How will changes in health insurance tax policy and employer health plan contributions affect access to health care and health care costs? *JAMA* 271:939–944.

Administrative Costs

Himmelstein, D.U., and Woolhandler, S. 1986. Cost without benefit: Administrative waste in U.S. health care. *New England Journal of Medicine* 314:441–445.

Himmelstein, D.U., et al. 1996. Who administers? Who cares? Medical administrative and clinical employment in the United States and Canada. *American Journal of Public Health* 69:172-178.

Woolhandler, S., and Himmelstein, D.U. 1991. The deteriorating administrative efficiency of the U.S. healthcare system. *New England Journal of Medicine* 324:1253–1258.

CHAPTER 12

Public Health Insurance

12.1 INTRODUCTION

In this chapter, we use the evaluative framework set out in Chapter 10 to analyze selected aspects of public health insurance coverage. Health insurance lies at the heart of the health care system, and public policies related to insurance influence the functioning of the health care market. Much of the emphasis in Part II of this book is on models of consumer, provider, and market behavior that explain how these entities function under alternative insurance arrangements (e.g., copayments). In this chapter, we illustrate how explanatory economic concepts can be used to help us understand how specific policy choices (e.g., reimbursement, cost sharing by consumers, taxes, and premiums) can influence the attainment of policy goals.

Section 12.2 presents an overview of public health insurance in the United States, focusing on Medicare and Medicaid, the two major national public health insurance plans. Section 12.3 briefly discusses some of the problems that public policy faces in this area. Finally, Section 12.4 describes some of the solutions proposed in recent years and explains how each solution contributes to or obstructs the achievement of specific health policy goals.

12.2 PUBLIC HEALTH INSURANCE

Public health insurance in the United States involves a number of programs aimed at target populations. In addition, a major aspect of the issue of public health insurance is the large number of individuals who have no coverage and, as a result, frequently have low levels of access to care. In this section we discuss the two major public health insurance programs, Medicare and Medicaid, and major gaps in coverage for indigents.

12.2.1 Medicare

The Medicare program was instituted with the passage of Title XVIII of the Social Security Act, entitled "Health Insurance for the Aged." It began operation on July 1, 1966. Presently covered under Medicare are individuals 65 and over who are eligible for Social Security benefits, disabled individuals, and individuals who have end-stage renal disease. We will focus mainly on the coverage of individuals 65 and over.

Coverage for these individuals is in two parts. Under Part A, also known as hospital insurance (HI), hospitalization and limited skilled nursing facility (SNF) coverage are provided. Medicare Part A covers 90 days of hospitalization per benefit period (benefit periods are defined by the existence of a preceding specified time during which the enrollee was not a bed patient in a hospital or an SNF); in addition, each enrollee has a lifetime reserve of 60 days. Under Part B, supplementary medical insurance (SMI) is provided; coverage includes ambulatory (noninstitutional) services and supplies, such as physician services, x-ray and lab services, drugs, and medical supplies.

Because much of the aged population is covered by Medicare *and* Medicaid, a better understanding of the overall financing of public programs in the United States can be obtained by looking at a unified picture (see Figure 12–1).

With regard to Medicare hospital insurance, program enrollees pay no premiums; however, there is a deductible tied to the per diem cost of care, which has been rising steeply in recent years. In 1995, it was $716. After the deductible is met, there are no copayments for the first 60 days and a copayment of $179 per day for days 61 through 90. The public share of HI (exclusive of the deductibles and copayments) is financed primarily through a Social Security tax on *worker* payrolls (see Figure 12–1). Funds from this tax go into a fund called the Hospital Insurance Trust Fund, out of which hospitals and nursing homes are reimbursed. In 1995, this tax amounted to 1.45 percent of the payroll payable by the employer and employee each (2.90 percent in total). The base amount on which this tax is assessed has been increased considerably in recent years.

The SMI program is voluntary, with enrollees buying in with a premium. An enrollee in the SMI program receives benefits subject to a deductible (first $100 of reasonable charges in 1995) and a copayment of 20 percent of reasonable charges. The SMI premium was initially set so that the premium covered one-half of the expenditures of the SMI trust fund (which reimburses providers). Premiums ($46.10 per month in 1995) are tied to Social Security cash benefits. Recently, because of the restrictions on premium increases, premium revenues have fallen; the remainder of the SMI fund's income comes from general revenues (i.e., public expenditures). In 1966, the first year of Medicare, the SMI premium covered virtually all the revenues of the program; by 1994, the share of premiums had fallen to 23 percent, with the majority of funding coming from general taxation.

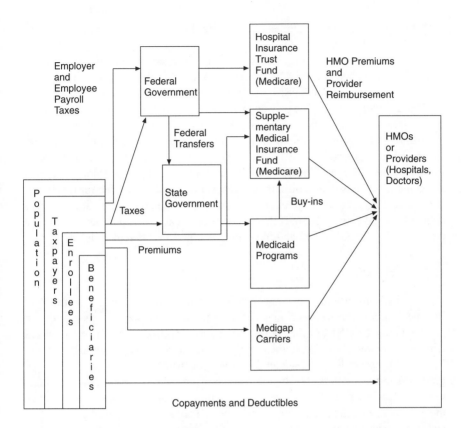

Figure 12–1 Flow of funds for Medicare and Medicaid. Because reimbursements by Medicare to providers and HMO premiums are increasing and Social Security taxes and Medicare Part B premiums are limited, additional pressure is being placed on general revenue funds. Medicaid reimbursements to providers have been increasing dramatically, which puts greater pressure on states and the federal government to raise additional revenues.

Medicare beneficiaries (those who use services) have the option of enrolling in a prepaid health maintenance organization or a competitive medical plan (an HMO-like organization that rates enrollees on the basis of past experience). The enrollee would then pay a monthly premium based on (but higher than) the Part B premium. The HMO covers the Part B deductible and copayments; total enrollee out-of-pocket costs and premiums combined would be more predictable than under the fee-for-service Part B plans. Medicare reimburses the HMO on a per capita basis; the payment to the HMO is based on the adjusted average per capita cost for fee-for-service enrollees with similar characteristics. In 1992, roughly 6 percent of

Medicare enrollees were members of a prepaid plan while the remainder were enrolled in fee-for-service plans.

There is an active private market for supplementary insurance to cover the deductibles and copayments of beneficiaries in fee-for-service plans. As shown in Figure 12–1, enrollees in the SMI program can pay premiums to private insurers for "Medigap" coverage. The private insurers then reimburse the providers for the beneficiaries' shares of their costs (i.e., the deductibles and copayments).

With regard to provider reimbursement, HI reimburses hospitals on a DRG basis and SMI reimburses physicians, the major provider group in this category of insurance, according to a resource-based relative value scale. If a doctor accepts assignment of the patient's bill, he or she accepts the Medicare fee for the procedure; Medicare then directly reimburses the doctor the appropriate amount (less deductibles and copayments). If the doctor does not accept assignment, Medicare pays the reimbursed amount and the patient is billed for the remainder.

12.2.2 Medicaid

The Medicaid program, originally designed to finance medical care for low-income families who were recipients of other financial assistance, was introduced in 1966 under Title XIX of the Social Security Act . Unlike the Medicare program, which is operated under guidelines set by the Social Security Administration, the Medicaid program is a state-federal partnership. Although the form of the program was initially determined by the federal government, state governments individually decide whether to participate in the program and determine the extent of the program. Who is covered largely depends on criteria established by individual states. In recent years federal guidelines have become more flexible, in part to allow states to impose coverage restrictions. Except for a short period in the early 1980s, states have not restricted coverage.

Individuals covered under the joint federal-state program fall into four groups: (1) cash recipients of the Aid to Families with Dependent Children (AFDC) program (dependent children and adults in AFDC families); (2) cash recipients of Supplemental Security Income (SSI) (aged, blind, and disabled individuals); (3) children and pregnant women in low income families who do receive AFDC; and (4) the "medically needy," many of whom would not qualify on an income basis but who have spent enough on medical care that their incomes net of medical care expenses fall below specific levels. In this exposition we will concentrate primarily on the covered population over 65, which falls into the latter two categories.

Federally required benefits under Medicaid include physician services, inpatient and outpatient hospital services, lab services, and nursing home services in skilled nursing homes. States can put limitations on benefits, such as on the number of inpatient days covered, authorization requirements for specific medical procedures, and so on. In addition, states can provide optional services such as intermediate care facility (ICF) stays, dental care, and physiotherapy.

The financing of Medicaid is based on a formula that incorporates state and national income levels. The minimum federal contribution is 50 percent. The state receiving the highest federal share (Mississippi) receives about 79 percent of its approved program costs from federal funds. Medicaid funds come out of general taxation revenues. Medicaid was originally designed as an open-ended program; that is, the federal share would follow the state share with no explicit limitations. In recent years a number of alterations have been proposed that would, in effect, cap the federal contribution.

Certain individuals can be eligible for both Medicare (on the basis of age) *and* Medicaid (on the basis of low income and wealth level). For these individuals, Medicaid can "buy into" SMI, paying the SMI premium as well as deductibles and copayments (see Figure 12–1). These enrollees will then be covered by Medicare for SMI and HI benefits and by Medicaid for other benefits, such as skilled nursing care and Medicare copayments and deductibles.

Medicaid state agencies reimburse physicians on varying bases, the predominant one being a fee schedule. Medicaid traditionally followed Medicare in reimbursing hospitals on the basis of retrospective costs, but recent reforms have allowed medical programs to develop prospective forms of reimbursement using diagnoses-related groups (Gurney et al. 1993). For those Medicaid enrollees who elect to enter a prepaid HMO program (about 12 percent of all Medicaid enrollees), state Medicaid agencies pay a capitation rate that is based on the cost of care for enrollees under the fee-for-service system.

12.2.3 Uncovered Care

Despite the existence of Medicare and Medicaid, many individuals either have no health insurance coverage at all or have large gaps in coverage. According to estimates by the Office of National Health Statistics, 15.9 percent of all individuals (about 40 million) had no insurance coverage in 1991 (Levit et al. 1992). A substantial number of this group were young or healthy, but the group included many who were in fair or poor health and also many children (Short et al. 1988). Further, a substantial number of these uncovered individuals were employed, which poses a problem because employment is the usual route through which health insurance is obtained (Monheit and Short 1989).

It should be pointed out that *uninsured* is not the same thing as *unserved*. Many individuals with no insurance still receive medical care: They either pay the full price for this care or receive subsidized or charity care. What is likely, however, is that they receive less care than they would if they had insurance coverage.

In addition to those with no coverage, a substantial number of individuals have gaps in coverage. The Medicare deductibles and copayments can add up to a large amount, and individuals who are covered by Medicare but do not have additional private (Medigap) or Medicaid coverage can, if they become ill, incur substantial out-of-pocket costs, including older individuals who do not have Medicaid coverage but need nursing home care. There is very little in the way of long-term care insurance coverage at present, and so individuals in nursing homes (especially intermediate care facilities) will be required to pay for such care themselves unless they "spend down" to the point where both their income less medical expenses and their assets are below the state Medicare limits.

Lack of coverage has also surfaced as a major policy issue in the area of inpatient hospital care. The burden of treating indigent patients has not fallen evenly on hospitals. Teaching hospitals, public hospitals, and hospitals that partially specialize in certain product lines (e.g., obstetrics) provide larger portions of charity care and have higher rates of bad debt (Mulstein 1984).

12.3   SOME PROBLEMS IN PUBLIC HEALTH INSURANCE

In recent years several public insurance issues have dominated the public policy scene. In this section we will briefly review these. In the following section, we discuss specific solutions and show how economic analysis can help us to develop a relation between the solutions and the goals of health policy. Keep in mind that each problem discussed is really part of a larger, overall problem, and so in discussing solutions we must be aware of spillover effects that impact other markets and groups.

Disbursements of the Hospital Insurance Trust Fund. Medicare's HI funding is tied to the growth of the portion of the Social Security tax that is earmarked for the Hospital Insurance Trust Fund. However, there is no automatic link between the growth of trust fund revenues and the growth of fund expenditures, which primarily go to reimburse hospitals (Iglehart 1992; Wolkstein 1984). The revenues are based on a percentage of payrolls and so cannot be increased by more than the increase in payrolls, unless the Social Security tax rate is increased or, as happened recently, the base on which the tax is levied is increased. In the absence of such a tax increase, large deficits have been predicted for the trust fund by the mid-1990s. Indeed, in 1994, preliminary data showed that payroll taxes directed into the Hospital Insurance Trust Fund totaled only 97 percent of disbursements, which created a greater deficit than had occurred for many years (Petrie 1993). This is because expenditures have been growing at a more rapid rate than receipts. We can illustrate the contribution of the components of this growth using the growth formula described in Chapter 2. Let us call the total reimbursements given by the fund to providers R. We can express R as the product of three variables, reimbursement per hospital discharge (p), the number of discharges per enrollee (d), and the number of enrollees (e). (In notational terms, $R = p \times d \times e$.)

In Section 2.5.1 it was shown that, when we have a variable that can be expressed as the product of other variables, the growth rate for the first variable can be approximated by summing the growth rates for the others. For example, G_R equals approximately $G_p + G_d + G_e$, where G_p refers to the growth rate for p, and so on.

Using Medicare program data (Health Care Financing Administration 1995), we can calculate that the average annual growth rate for hospital expenditures from 1972 to 1992 was 13.1 percent. The component growth was 10 percent for G_p, .2 percent for G_d, and 2.6 percent for G_e. The remainder of the difference is due to the interaction term. The major portion of the growth in total hospital expenditures thus occurred because of higher hospital costs per patient, not because of increases in the number of patients. Any solution would have to take into account this fact.

Medicare's SMI Revenues and Expenditures. SMI funds come from two main sources: premiums paid directly by the enrollees (or by Medicaid for those qualifying for Medicaid coverage) and general revenue funds. Originally, the premium rate was set so that premium revenues of the SMI trust fund were one-half of all revenues. From 1973 the growth of premiums was limited to be no greater than the growth of Social Security cash benefits. As a result, since then the premium share of total fund revenues has fallen to about 30 percent.

Reimbursements from the fund grew by about 23 percent annually from 1966 to 1994 (Health Care Financing Administration 1995). Since the number of enrollees grew by only about 2.2 percent during this period, most of this growth has been in expenditures per enrollee. As in the case of the Hospital Insurance Trust Fund, this growth in expenditures has been a major cause of concern. In this case, however, increases in tax revenues could be automatically transferred to the SMI trust to meet shortfalls of premium revenues over expenses. Nevertheless, these transfers are a drain on public funds.

Medicaid Expenditures. Medicaid expenditures have also grown substantially. From 1975 to 1992, Medicaid payments grew by an annual rate of 12.6 percent. From 1989 to 1992, the growth rate was 18.8 percent. Of this high growth rate, enrollment growth accounted for 8 percent, reflecting initiatives to enroll more pregnant women, children, and disabled persons. Much of the remainder was due to states' taking advantage of generous funding regulations for hospitals serving large shares of low-income patients. More recently, the growth in expenditures per enrollee has reverted to average historical levels. Disabled individuals have contributed the most to the growth in enrollment; these individuals have been heavy users of outpatient hospital care.

12.4 POLICY ALTERNATIVES

12.4.1 Economic Analysis and Alternative Solutions

In assessing the economic design of public health care programs we will focus on specific policies and policy instruments and determine how these might affect achievement of the policy goals that we have identified. These policies and policy instruments include the method of provider reimbursement; the level of provider reimbursement; consumer direct payments, including deductibles and copayments; and the method of financing programs (by taxes or direct payments).

The *method of provider reimbursement* affects technical efficiency, as it has an impact on the costs incurred by the provider. It may also influence the supply of a service. For example, fee-for-service reimbursement, as compared with capitation, may cause a higher volume of services supplied.

The *level of provider reimbursement* will also affect the supply of a service (in particular, a higher level of reimbursement will typically induce a greater supply). In addition, it may affect the mode of care and hence the degree of economic efficiency. A high payment level for inpatient care will encourage inpatient care and at the same time discourage outpatient care (which may be less costly). Both the method and level of reimbursement may influence the quality of care (e.g., they may motivate cost cutting and thus encourage lower quality of care). They may also have an impact on public expenditure control.

The imposition of *direct consumer payments* will influence consumer demand and public expenditure control. The effects of this policy instrument on technical efficiency and supply are not likely to be important.

By the *method of finance* for a program, we of course mean to include the degree to which consumer direct payments are incorporated into the program. Taking this into consideration, we are still left with the decision of how to collect public moneys. A number of alternative types of taxes are possible, and generally these will primarily have an impact on equity and on efficiency in other sectors. Finance methods are covered in Chapter 11.

Trade-offs between policy goals frequently occur. A policy may increase the degree to which one goal is achieved and simultaneously reduce the degree to which another one is achieved. Indeed, if such were not the case, we would hardly be faced with economic choices. Given these trade-offs, we must make an assessment as to whether the negative consequences are worth the benefits. Categorizing the consequences of policies is a very useful place to begin the evaluative process. However, economic analysis cannot make clear-cut predictions about all of the consequences of every policy. In some cases there will be gray areas, such as will occur when a cost reduction can be achieved at the expense of quality reductions and increases in economic efficiency. In these instances, we must simply recognize that the impact of the policy will depend on how much people value each policy goal. In what follows we will analyze the expected impact of a number of policies on the achievement of health care goals. Effects will be identified as "favorable," "unfavorable," or "uncertain."

We will identify the impact of each policy by making predictions using economic theory. For example, we might use the demand theory model to predict the effect of imposing a copayment. According to this model, a copayment will reduce the quantity demanded (a result generally unfavorable to the goal of increased access) but will also reduce public expenditures (thus increasing public expenditure control).

Before proceeding, a few remarks should be made about the choice of theories to use. For example, an increase in physician reimbursement rates can be analyzed using a variety of models, including the competitive demand and supply model, the monopoly model, and a supplier-induced demand model. There is no final answer as to which model to use. One rule might be, the simpler, the better. Indeed, the competitive model can go a long way toward helping us analyze the effects of many policies. But, of course, it has its limitations, and we may have to resort to other models that fit the particular circumstances better or make better predictions.

12.4.2 Policies for Medicare

12.4.2.1 Prospective Payment (DRGs)

The first Medicare policy we will examine is the implementation of prospective payment for hospitals on a DRG basis. Such a system was implemented to contain costs, replacing an inflationary cost-based system. If we base our predictions on either the profit maximization or output maximization models of Sections 6.2 and 6.4, the predicted effect of the replacement of a retrospective cost-based system with a prospective DRG system (see Section 6.7.5) will be to increase technical efficiency. These models entail the hospitals will be motivated to lower costs because the extra profits resulting from cost savings will accrue to them. Hospitals will also have an incentive to lower quality because reductions in quality will also yield cost savings. Unfortunately, we cannot say how much technical efficiency and quality will be affected.

Unless we have some idea about the actual DRG rate levels, we cannot say anything about the supply response and the overall effect on public expenditures; the higher the rates, the greater will be the supply of services by hospitals and the greater the impact on public expenditures.

The prospective payment system may also have side effects felt in the other parts of the health care system. Per case reimbursement provides hospitals with the incentives to shorten length of stay. In some cases, early discharge may result in sending patients to nursing homes (in these cases, hospital days and nursing home days are substitutes), thus increasing nursing home demand. This may in fact result in higher nursing home expenditures, possibly offsetting any reductions in public expenditures achieved by the prospective payment program.

In sum, the output and profit maximization models can be used to predict some effects, but we cannot determine the impact of the prospective payment system on the achievement of all the goals. If we add to the suppliers' goals the goal of quality (Section 6.5), we no longer have a clear-cut prediction about how quality of care will be affected by the prospective payment system. Firms will seek to preserve quality, of course, but we cannot predict how far they will go.

12.4.2.2 Medigap Premium Tax

The purpose of a tax on Medigap premiums is to make insurance that covers Medicare copayments and deductibles more expensive, thus discouraging the practice by Medicare enrollees of obtaining first-dollar coverage for medical expenses. Such a tax would raise the direct price to consumers of Medigap coverage, and, according to the theory of *insurance* demand, the demand for coverage would be reduced (see Section 4.3.1).

Although the increased price of Medigap insurance would generally be considered a barrier to demand, some might argue otherwise: First-dollar coverage may encourage the overuse of services and thus contribute to higher system costs and lower demand. With regard to public expenditures, such a tax would reduce them (1) by the amount of the tax and (2) by the additional amount of the reduction in government reimbursements due to the lower demand for medical care (Section 3.6). As for public expenditure control, this would generally benefit from the policy. It should be noted that we have an instance of desirable and undesirable effects: Public expenditure control is increased but access is reduced.

12.4.2.3 Lower Physician Fees

A lowering of Medicare's fee for physicians can be analyzed using the monopoly model. We will assume the physician-suppliers face two groups of demanders—public and private. Lower fees will result in a reduced quantity of services to patients in the Medicare portion of the market and expanded services in the private portion of the market (see Section 8.2.4). The net effect on public expenditures is favorable. However, the analysis does not predict what will happen to the patients whose access is reduced because of the reduced availability of care. They may seek assignment care (possibly of a lower quality) elsewhere or go without care.

A second type of analysis focuses on the effects of differential fee levels for medical and surgical cases. Prior to the introduction of the resource-based relative value system (RBRVS), surgeons were favorably reimbursed compared with medical specialists and primary care doctors. The RBRVS pilot studies proposed more favorable medical fees (see Section 6.7.3). However, the Health Care Financing Administration used two separate fee structures in its program, one for medical and one for surgical services (Hsiao et al. 1993). The level of surgical fees was higher than proposed.

The competitive model (Section 7.3.8) can be used to evaluate this situation. Medical and surgical services can be analyzed as constituting two separate markets. A relative increase in surgical fees will raise the quantity supplied of surgical services and reduce that of primary and medical specialty care. The overall impact on policy goals is uncertain. This is because the main effect will be a redistribution of services. Such a redistribution could best be evaluated by determining the effectiveness of different types of care in yielding better health outcomes. There is very little information at present on how better outcomes might be achieved.

12.4.2.4 Increase in the SMI Premium

An increase in the SMI premium would cause a reduction in demand for SMI coverage. This would raise barriers to demand (those who would not pay the SMI premium would now be uninsured for the medical care portion of Medicare and would have to pay full price for medical care) and reduce public expenditures. This impact would be different from that of the Medigap premium tax in terms of degree. In the case of the Medigap premium tax, a decision to switch from Medigap to no additional coverage would mean having to pay the copayments and deductibles. In this instance, the decision not to insure would mean having no coverage at all. Such reduced coverage will more likely include many more medically necessary cases than in the Medigap tax case.

12.4.2.5 Raising the SMI Copayments and Deductibles

The effect of this policy would be very similar to that of raising the SMI premium. In this case, demand could be directly choked off. Because the population affected is elderly, many negative health consequences are likely to result from the reduction in demand.

12.4.2.6 Capitation versus Fee-for-Service Reimbursement

Both Medicare and Medicaid have increased their enrollments for prepaid care. Medicare's HMO enrollments increased from 2.9 percent of all enrollees in 1984 to 6.3 percent in 1992. The increase in Medicaid HMO-type enrollments increased from 3.5 percent to 12 percent during the same period. The increase in Medicaid enrollments reflects aggressive attempts by some states to expand per capita coverage among Medicaid and welfare recipients.

Among the policy goals that capitation attempts to address are allocative efficiency and government budget reductions. Explanatory economic analysis can be used to predict whether preset capitation rates would likely achieve cost reductions (Sections 6.9.2 and 7.7.4). Using the supply model for HMOs, we predict that preset capitation rates for defined risk groups will induce HMOs to target low-cost (healthier) consumers within each risk group. Indeed, a review of Medicare HMO enrollment determined that the prior average cost of Medicare patients who enrolled in HMOs was lower than the average cost for all Medicare enrollees within the same risk category. Since Medicare-funded HMOs were being paid on the basis of an average case within the risk group, Medicare spent more under prepayment than these cases would have cost under fee for service. Medicare did not save any money by enrolling members in HMOs because the risk adjustment system was not refined enough to adjust for likely utilization patterns (Brown et al. 1993).

12.4.3 Policies for Medicaid

12.4.3.1 Limitations on Benefits

Limitations on benefits, such as maximum number of days of hospital care per beneficiary, would create a barrier to demand and reduce the public program's expenditures. However, some needs simply will not go away, and some other outlet will be necessary for these patients. For these cases, the policy simply shifts the costs from one source of funds to another.

The state of Oregon is currently instituting a benefit limitation policy. It is creating a ranking of the costs and benefits of alternative medical procedures and proposing to pay for only those procedures whose cost-benefit ratios rank high. Near the top of the list would be treatments for disorders such as bone cancer and multiple sclerosis, which, it is claimed, yield substantial benefits per dollar of cure. Lower on the list would be disorders whose treatments have a lower rate of return, including chronic ulcers and sleep disorders.

12.4.3.2 Copayments for Ambulatory Care

Copayments for ambulatory care would, according to traditional demand theory, choke off demand and thus reduce access to medical care. Choking off the demand of the poor, who are more likely to be needy cases, is more likely to have adverse health effects in subsequent periods (see Section 4.2). In this case, these individuals may obtain care as indigent patients, and so they will still cost the system something, even though the Medicaid program achieves savings. The costs would then be borne by other groups, such as payers of municipal taxes, purchasers of insurance premiums, or whomever the costs are shifted onto.

12.4.3.3 Competitive Bidding among Suppliers

Such a policy, which has been implemented by the California and Arizona Medicaid programs, has the objective of providing cost-effective care for indigents. If the buyer has a considerable degree of market power, it can extract a lower price from competitive sellers (see Section 8.2.2), and if there was any room for cost reductions, either through increasing efficiency or lowering quality, the reductions will be incorporated into the providers' responses. However, the bidding process is a complex one and may not automatically lead to savings (see Section 7.5).

12.4.3.4 *Prospective Payment for Nursing Homes*

The effect of prospective payment for nursing homes is similar to the effect of prospective payment for hospitals (Section 6.7.6), with the exception that because the lengths of stay in nursing homes are so variable, the rates must be on a per diem (daily) basis. If the nursing homes are output maximizers, we can expect lower costs because of greater efficiency and lower quality. The actual supply will depend on the level of rates that are set.

BIBLIOGRAPHY

Medicare
Berenson, R., and Holohan, J. 1992. Sources of growth in Medicare physician expenditures. *JAMA* 267:687–691.
Brown, R.S., et al. 1993. Do health maintenance organizations work for Medicare? *Health Care Financing Review* 15(1):7–23.
Congressional Budget Office. 1983. *Changing the structure of Medicare benefits.* Washington, D.C.: Congressional Budget Office.
Davis, K., and Rowland, D. 1984. Medicare financing reform: A new Medicare premium. *Milbank Quarterly* 62:300–316.
Feder, J. 1995–1996. Some thoughts on the future of Medicare. *Inquiry* 32:376–378.
Ginsburg, P.B., and Moon, M. 1984. An introduction to the Medicare financing problem. *Milbank Quarterly* 62:167–182.
Goody, B., et al. 1994. New directions for Medicare payment systems. *Health Care Financing Review* 16(2):1–11.
Health Care Financing Administration. 1995. *Medicare and Medicaid statistical supplement.* Baltimore: Health Care Financing Administration.
Hsiao, W.C., and Kelly, N.L. 1984. Medicare benefits: A reassessment. *Milbank Quarterly* 62:207–229.
Hsiao, W.C., et al. 1993. Assessing the implementation of physician payment reform. *New England Journal of Medicine* 328:928–933.
Iglehart, J.K. 1993. Health policy report: The American health care system—Medicare. *New England Journal of Medicine* 327:1467–1472.
Lee, A.J., and Mitchell, J.B. 1994. Physician reaction to price changes: An episode-of-care analysis. *Health Care Financing Review* 16(2):65–83.
Long, S.H., and Smeeding, T.M. 1984. Alternative Medicare financing sources. *Milbank Quarterly* 62:325–348.

Luft, H.S. 1984. On the use of vouchers for Medicare. *Milbank Quarterly* 62:237–250.

Petrie, J.T. 1993. Overview of the Medicare program. *Health Care Financing Review,* 1992 annual suppl., pp. 1–22.

Rice, T., and McCall, N. 1985. The extent of ownership and the characteristics of Medicare supplemental policies. *Inquiry* 22:188–200.

Smits, H.L., et al. 1982. Medicare's nursing home benefit: Variations in interpretation. *New England Journal of Medicine* 307:855–862.

U.S. Department of Health and Human Services. 1983. *The Medicare and Medicaid data book.* HCFA publ. no. 03156. Baltimore, Md.: Health Care Financing Administration.

U.S. Department of Health and Human Services. 1993. *Medicare and Medicaid statistical supplement.* Baltimore: U.S. Department of Health and Human Services.

Wolkstein, I. 1984. Medicare's financial status: How did we get here? *Milbank Quarterly* 62:183–206.

Medicaid

Battistella, R.M. 1989. National health insurance: Dilemmas and opportunities. *Hospital and Health Services Administration* 34:139–156.

Brecher, C., and Knickman, J. 1985. A reconsideration of long-term-care policy. *Journal of Health Politics, Policy, and Law* 10:245–272.

Buchanan, R.J. 1983. Medicaid cost containment: Prospective reimbursement for long-term care. *Inquiry* 20:334–342.

Congressional Budget Office. 1981. *Medicaid: Choices for 1982 and beyond.* Washington, D.C.: Congressional Budget Office.

Davis, K. 1989. National health insurance: A proposal. *American Economic Review* 79(1989):349–352.

Davis, K., and Schoen, C. 1978. *Health and the war on poverty.* Washington, D.C.: Brookings Institution.

Fox, H.G., et al. 1993. State Medicaid health maintenance organization policies and special-needs children. *Health Care Financing Review* 15(1):25–37.

Gurny, P., et al. 1993. Payment, administration, and financing of the Medicaid program. *Health Care Financing Review,* 1992 annual suppl., pp. 285–301.

Harrington, C., and Swan, J.H. 1984. Medicaid nursing home reimbursement policies, rates and expenditures. *Health Care Financing Review* 6:39–49.

Holahan, J. 1975. *Financing health care for the poor.* Lexington, Mass.: Lexington Books.

Iglehart, J.K. 1993. Health policy report: The American health care system—Medicaid. *New England Journal of Medicine* 328:896–900.

Ku, L., and Coughlin, T.A. 1995. Medicaid disproportionate share and other special financing programs. *Health Care Financing Review* 16(3):27–54.

Meiners, M.R. 1983. The case for long-term care insurance. *Health Affairs* 2 (summer):55–79.

Miller, M.E., and Gengler, D.J. 1993. Medicaid case management: Kentucky's patient access and care program. *Health Care Financing Review* 15(1):55–69.

Rowland, D. 1995. Medicaid at 30: New challenges for the nation's safety net. *JAMA* 274:271–273.

Stuart, B. 1972. Equity and Medicaid. *Journal of Human Resources* 7:152–178.

Tallon, J.R., and Rowland, D. 1995. Federal dollars and state flexibility. *Inquiry* 32:235–240.

Tudor, C.G. 1995. Medicaid expenditures and state responses. *Health Care Financing Review* 16:1–10.

Wade, M., and Berg, S. 1995. Causes of Medicaid expenditure growth. *Health Care Financing Review* 16(3):11–25.

Wycoff, P.G. 1985. Medicaid: Federalism and the Reagan budget proposals. *Economic Commentary of the Reserve Bank of Cleveland* (August).

Uninsured Care

Birnbaum, H., et al. 1979. Focusing the catastrophic illness debate. *Quarterly Review of Economics and Business* 19:17–33.

Cafferata, G.L. 1984. *Private health insurance coverage of the Medicare population.* National Health Care Expenditures Study; Data Preview 18. Rockville, Md.: National Center for Health Services Research.

Cleeton, D. 1989. The medical uninsured: A case for market failure. *Public Finance Quarterly* 17:55–83.

De Lew, N., et al. 1992. A layman's guide to the U.S. health care system. *Health Care Financing Review* 14 (Fall):151–170.

Hadley, J., and Feder, J. 1985. Hospital cost shifting and care for the uninsured. *Health Affairs* 4:67–81.

Levit, K.R., et al. 1992. America's health insurance coverage, 1980–91. *Health Care Financing Review* 14 (Fall):31–57.

Monheit, A.C., and Short, P.F. 1989. Mandating Health Coverage for Working Americans. *Health Affairs* 8 (Winter):22–38.

Mulstein, S. 1984. The uninsured and financing of uncompensated care. *Inquiry* 21:214–229.

Short, P.F., et al. 1988. Uninsured Americans: A 1987 profile. Rockville, Md.: National Center for Health Services Research and Health Care Technology Assessment.

Wilensky, G. 1987. Viable strategies for dealing with the uninsured. *Health Affairs* 6 (Spring):33–46.

———. 1988. Filling the gaps in health insurance. *Health Affairs* 7 (Summer):133–149.

CHAPTER 13

The Reform of the Health Care Market Structure

13.1 INTRODUCTION

Health reform is a term that has been applied to insurance and health care markets as well as to the total constellation of health services. In the case of insurance markets, the term refers to specific ways to make the markets perform more like a competitive market. This has meant trying to set rules to prevent insurers from engaging in "biased risk selection," a key factor in market failure, and trying to ensure that insurance is available at a "reasonable" price to those who want it.

In the case of the health care market, the main goal of reform has been to increase consumer choice (i.e., to make the health care markets more sensitive to consumer rather than provider demands). One of the key efforts has been to increase the degree of competition so that the markets work more like the textbook model described in Chapter 7.

The health care goals that market reforms seek to achieve include both equity and efficiency. The insurance market reforms have focused largely on equity (i.e., making insurance affordable to those who want it). Possible strategies include subsidies for high-risk consumers. The reforms are only secondarily concerned with increasing provider efficiency or consumer choice. Health care market reforms have focused on efficiency—on making the markets more like the competitive ideal.

This chapter examines both types of reforms. Section 13.2 reviews insurance market reforms, focusing on alternative mechanisms that have been proposed to make the insurance markets more sensitive to consumer wants. Section 13.3 explains how antitrust policy has been applied to physician, hospital, and insurance markets in order to reduce the degree of monopolization in the hope that the revised market structures will promote consumer well-being.

Note: Section 13.3 was prepared by Ronald Wilder of the University of South Carolina.

13.2 INSURANCE MARKET REFORM

13.2.1 The Need for Reform

The performance of insurance markets can be judged from the vantage point of efficiency or equity. In looking at economic efficiency performance criteria, we are essentially asking whether an optimal degree of risk is being shifted by consumers to insurers. This degree is related to the value of risk shifting to the consumers and the cost of risk shifting to insurers. If individuals are willing to pay for greater amounts of coverage (e.g., coverage for more expensive services), there are insurers who are willing to provide this coverage at the desired price, but there are some impediments to the shifting of the risks, then the degree of insurance coverage is not optimal. By the same token, if the value to consumers of shifting additional risks is low (below the cost to insurers of accepting these risks) but consumers respond to government subsidies and purchase insurance anyway because of low out-of-pocket prices, then an excess of coverage will result.

We have seen that an efficient degree of coverage may mean no coverage at all for health care expenditures. If individuals value risk shifting less than they do the cost of insurance, then they will simply not insure. However, these individuals may be very high-risk and/or low-income individuals or may work for small companies, and we may think it is inequitable for these individuals to go without insurance coverage. On grounds of equity, we might decide that something should be done to remedy the situation. In this section we examine the causes of market failure in insurance markets and the remedies that have been proposed. We present the analysis using a simple economic model to bring out the essential features of insurance market failure and market reform.

13.2.2 The Basic Model

We set out a basic model of a health insurance market in which there are seven individuals, each with a given degree of risk of being ill. The expected loss for each of these individuals is shown in Table 13–1. Individual 1, the least healthy of the lot, has an expected loss of $12; individual 2 has an expected loss of $8; and so on.

We turn to the assumptions about the demand for insurance. For each individual, there is a willingness to pay for health insurance coverage. Individual 1 is willing to pay $12, which would indicate that he or she is risk neutral (i.e., puts no additional value on the size of the loss). Individual 2 is willing to pay $10 for coverage, individual 3 is willing to pay $9, and so on. Note that individual 1 is an example of a high-risk person with limited means to pay for health insurance.

Table 13–1 The Value and Price of Insurance for Individuals

Individual	1	2	3	4	5	6	7
Willingness to pay for insurance coverage (dollars)	$12.00	$10.00	$9.00	$8.00	$7.00	$6.00	$5.00
Expected loss due to Illness	$12.00	$8.00	$7.00	$6.00	$5.00	$4.00	$3.00
Age	> 50	> 50	> 50	< 50	< 50	< 50	< 50
Employment group type (N = no group; L = large group; S = small group)	N	L	L	L	L	L	S
Cost of administering insurance in absence of pool membership	$3.00	$1.00	$1.00	$1.00	$1.00	$1.00	$3.00
Model 1 prices (experience rating by individual risk and cost of coverage)	$15.00	$9.00	$8.00	$7.00	$6.00	$5.00	$6.00
Model 2 prices (complete information asymmetry, first round)	$8.00	$8.00	$8.00	$8.00	$8.00	$8.00	$8.00
Model 3 prices (25 percent subsidy provided to all individuals, experience rating, and information symmetry)	$11.25	$6.75	$6.00	$5.25	$4.50	$3.75	$4.50

In addition to the individuals' demands, we specify personal characteristics or circumstances that will affect the insurance market in a systematic way. One such characteristic is age. In our example, we specify two separate age groups—individuals older than 50 and individuals younger than 50. We would expect, in general, that an individual whose age is above 50 will have greater expected health care costs because of poorer health status. Age is a piece of information that might be used by insurers to set premium rates.

We also specify in our example the individuals' work circumstances, as these are a prime determinant of the cost of providing health insurance and thus of the loading charge. It costs less to provide insurance coverage to individuals in a large group than to individuals who are employed by small companies or who are not employed at all. In our example, we assume that it costs $1 to supply insurance coverage to individuals in a large group and $3 to individuals in smaller employment groups or to those who must purchase insurance individually.

With regard to the supply side of the market, we will assume that there is a single supplier. This supplier knows the risks of each person (a situation referred to as *information symmetry*). The supplier sets a price for each person based strictly on his or her expected loss plus the cost of administration (i.e., the supplier engages in experience rating). Thus, for individual 1, the price will be $15 (the expected loss plus the $3 administrative cost). We also assume that the insurer has sufficient capacity to insure all consumers who are willing to shift their risks.

We now draw the conclusions of our model regarding the availability of insurance. Each individual will purchase insurance as long as the premium rate is less than or equal to what the individual is willing to pay. In our model, individuals 1 and 7 are not willing to pay up to the premium rate that would be charged by the insurer. Individuals 2 through 6 will obtain insurance at the given premium rates. It is important to note why individuals 1 and 7 did not obtain health insurance; they did not because of their particular circumstances (employment in this case). For all individuals, the outcome is the result of rational decisions. Further, this outcome is economically efficient, in that the net benefits from insurance coverage are maximized. If any additional insurance coverage was secured, the result (given our assumptions) would be a net social loss.

However, just because the outcome is economically efficient does not mean that it is "fair" or even "socially acceptable." All individuals in society (1 through 7) may agree that this outcome is unacceptable and that some solution must be found to ensure that all individuals have some degree of coverage. We will focus on a number of these solutions in subsequent sections of this chapter. However, we first focus on one of the critical assumptions of our analysis—the assumption of information symmetry. There is a considerable literature on what happens when this assumption does not hold. Our simple model will be changed to take the assumption of information asymmetry into account.

13.2.3 Information Asymmetry and Adverse Selection

In a state of information asymmetry, one group of individuals (potentially) engaged in a transaction have better information than another group (potentially) engaged in the transaction. Such a situation can lead to market failure, in that a transaction would benefit both parties but no transaction actually takes place. To see how market failure might occur, we return to our previous model except that we now assume information asymmetry exists. In this case the information is about the expected loss of the potential purchasers of health insurance. The assumption we make is that the consumers have full information about their risks but the insurer knows nothing about the health status and risks of individual consumers; it only knows about the risks of the entire population.

Given this assumption, the insurer cannot distinguish between insureds in terms of their health status, and it will therefore have to charge each insured the same premium. In total, expected costs are $45 and administrative costs are still the same, $11 for all individuals. Therefore, the insurer must collect $56, or $8 per person. Remember, we are assuming that the insurer has no way of distinguishing between individuals with regard to their risk.

At a price of $8 per person, only four individuals will insure, as the price exceeds the willingness to pay for the other potential insureds. If this situation occurs, then the expected loss per person will be determined by the loss experience of the members of the group who remain in the market. The market will not even insure individuals 1 through 4, because with the other members dropping out the price will have to increase to $9.75 to cover the cost of insuring these individuals. Indeed, the entire market can eventually disappear as people successively drop out. We should note that, except for individual 1, each individual would be willing to pay for the cost of his or her insurance. However, the insurer has no way of finding out each person's risk, and so it must charge a group rate.

13.2.4 Underwriting and Group Rating

The phenomenon of adverse selection occurs in extreme cases of information asymmetry. In fact, insurers have numerous ways of distinguishing between high- and low-risk insureds. They know or can obtain information on many characteristics associated with the risk of loss, such as age, gender, and employment (Giacomini et al. 1995; see also Section 6.7.7). Insurers can also resort to physical exams and tests to determine if individuals have certain conditions that might lead to costly health care. In addition, they have access to the past health records of their potential insureds, and these are often good predictors of future usage. Based on such risk-related information, rates can be set that reflect individual expected costs. Insurers do not have to know exactly how much each person will spend on health care; they must only be able to form separate risk pools and estimate average costs in each pool.

In cases where there are large groups, insurers need only predict the experience of the entire group. For very large groups, health care costs are quite predictable, and therefore information asymmetry does not pose a problem. Indeed, many large employers have realized this and have begun to self-insure. Of course, this does not solve the problem of those who are not members of large groups.

Nevertheless, these phenomena raise the issue of how relevant adverse selection is. Certainly, if information on projected utilization was not available to insurers, this would be a main problem in the market. But the main problem does not seem to be an absence of information. Rather it appears to be what happens when insurers *do* have accurate information about the projected utilization of potential insureds—that is, when they can set very high rates that consumers cannot afford (i.e., are not willing to pay). This leads to a situation where some individuals are selectively excluded from the insurance market. This situation, called "biased selection" or "preferred risk selection," will be discussed in subsequent sections.

13.2.5 Subsidies

The lack of insurance can come about in markets with information symmetry and information asymmetry. We will focus our attention on the former, that is, where there is complete information on the part of both groups, the insurers and the insureds. In Section 13.2.2, we concluded (under our assumed conditions) that two individuals would not insure—individuals 1 and 7. We noted that this situation, while efficient, might not be acceptable to the members of society on grounds of equity. If this is the case, we would have to devise some solution that would increase the amount of insurance purchased by the individuals who do not have insurance.

Let us, for the moment, retain our faith in the market as a mechanism for ensuring that individuals have access to health care when they get sick. Yet because the market excludes some individuals, we must devise a technique for allowing individuals to obtain insurance coverage. One such technique, widely used in the United States, is the insurance premium subsidy. According to this technique, the government provides a subsidy to individuals who purchase insurance. An example of such a subsidy is the income tax deduction for employer-paid health insurance premiums. Such a deduction reduces the value of the premium by the individual's personal income tax rate. There are also examples of states providing subsidies directly to smaller employers in order to induce them to purchase health insurance for their employees.

In our example, let us introduce a subsidy of 25 percent of the premium paid by the individual. In this case, each person pays 25 percent less than before. The postsubsidy premium rates for each individual are shown in Table 13–1. Under our initial assumption of experience rating, individual 1 now pays $11.25 (three-quarters of what was paid before), individual 2 pays $6.75, and so on. In this case, all individuals will purchase insurance. The subsidy is successful in achieving full coverage.

However, the postsubsidy situation may not be efficient from a social point of view. In those cases where the cost of insuring exceeds the individual's willingness to pay in the absence of the subsidy, the social cost of insurance will exceed the social value. Only now the cost has been shifted on to the taxpayer, and so the true cost of insurance coverage is hidden. A second problem with subsidies is they may not be successful. Studies of subsidies provided to small firms have indicated that even quite large subsidies may not be sufficient to induce the required increases in the health insurance coverage that firms provide. One study that found subsidies to be ineffective focused on small employers in New York State (Thorpe et al. 1992). However, because of the design of the subsidy, there may have been a reluctance on the part of the employers to commit to providing health insurance coverage for their employees. The subsidy was only to last for two years, after which the employers would have to pay the entire amount. Such a design might well deter employers from providing health insurance coverage because they may find after two years that they would be fully responsible for providing health insurance.

13.2.6 Cooperative Pools

The provision of insurance is less expensive when it is done in the context of a large group, usually through employers or professional associations. Individual or small group policies are much more expensive to administer. As a result, the loading charge for small group or individual policies is greater than it is for larger group policies.

There has been a recent trend toward the formation of cooperatives or insurance purchasing groups that individuals or smaller employers could join. These are called health insurance purchasing cooperatives (HIPCs). By forming a cooperative, smaller groups can be rated together as a unit and therefore receive the same rate that a larger group with the same risk profile would receive. Purchasing cooperatives have become commonplace, and a number of market reform proposals focus on this trend (Hall 1994; Reinhardt 1993).

In our analysis, let us assume that individuals 1 and 7 can join the main group. If they do so, the cost of providing them with health insurance falls to $1. If we retained the assumption of experience rating, then individual 1, at least, would not be insured. Individual 1 would still not be willing to pay $13, the premium he or she would have to pay. However, the cooperative would have increased insurance coverage (by extending coverage to individual 7) through lowering the cost of provision. This would be an efficient solution and would increase equity.

13.2.7 Community Rating and Biased Selection

One feature that has been included in some health insurance reform proposals is community rating, a scheme by which all participants pay the same premium regardless of risk. To determine the effects of community rating, let us return to our original model (see Section 13.2.2). We will initially assume that everyone pays the same premium to a single insurer. If the insurer has only to meet its full costs, including administration costs, and if all individuals are to be served, then the single community rate would be $8. At this single rate, individuals 5, 6, and 7 will not insure. This may start a spiral by which the entire market will eventually dry up.

There is another consideration in community rating. Let us assume that there are two insurers, A and B, and they are competing for business at the community rate. We will also change another assumption and suppose that the insurers want to maximize their profits. The implications of these changes are as follows. In order to maximize profits, each of the two insurers will seek out the lowest cost insureds—individuals 4, 5, and 6. They will avoid providing insurance to other individuals. There are numerous ways that the insurers could do this. They could screen insureds and, if provision is not mandatory, refuse to sell insurance to high-cost individuals. Alternatively, they could make it difficult for potentially high-cost insureds to reach them by locating in areas where younger, healthier individuals live (Light 1992).

The incentive for insurers to select low-risk individuals is indeed a powerful one, and its relevance needs to be emphasized. A key way for insurers to contain their costs is to ensure that their clients are low risk to begin with. Numerous health insurance reform proposals have been put forward, and most of them at least try to address this issue. However, under community rating, this issue is especially difficult to address because it relates directly to the profits that the insurers can earn.

Another issue relating to community rating is that, if each individual's premium is fixed, there will be no incentive for individuals to reduce their risk through health promotion and disease prevention activities. Under experience rating, individuals can be offered incentives (lower premiums) to engage in behaviors that lead to better health (e.g., no smoking). Such incentives do not exist when everyone pays the same premium.

We can evaluate community rating on two grounds: equity and efficiency. From one point of view, community rating can appear to be the most equitable rating method. After all, everyone pays the same rate. However, if everyone is not in the same risk category, then community rating involves the subsidization of the unhealthy by the healthy. If we subscribe to a notion of equity according to which equals should pay equally and unequals should pay unequally, then community rating might not seem an equitable method. On the other hand, if we view everyone as "equals" in the sense that no matter how healthy or unhealthy they are the same, then community rating will indeed appear fair.

On efficiency grounds there can be little said in favor of community rating. Community rating discourages individuals from engaging in health promotion when the social costs would warrant them to do it. Cost savings from such behavior are not passed on to the individuals who engage in it. In addition, community rating encourages insurers to seek out the lowest risk individuals, and this can cause individuals who would otherwise buy insurance not to purchase it, which eventually could lead to a drying up of the health insurance market. In response to these problems, two additional innovations have been introduced. One is a mandate requiring individuals or employers to obtain insurance. The second is risk rating—the assignment of individuals to groups according to their risks and the requirement that they pay different premiums based on these risks.

13.2.8 Mandates

A mandate is a legal requirement that some action be taken, such as the purchasing of health insurance coverage by an individual or an employer. The purpose of a mandate to purchase insurance is to block individuals from leaving the health insurance market. It is maintained that some individuals (primarily low-risk individuals) will not insure until they get older or sick and the risk of their using services increases. Only then do they insure and "take advantage" of their coverage. When low-risk individuals do not participate in the market, this causes higher group premiums and could even result in the eventual disappearance of the market. Under a mandate, everyone must purchase insurance. Many health insurance reform proposals propose introducing a mandate.

Starting with our original example, we will assume community rating and a mandate that all individuals purchase insurance. The premium rate will be $8, and all individuals are mandated to pay this rate.

Such a premium rate might impose a considerable burden on low-income individuals, and so few proposals would stop at a mandate. One way to reduce the burden would be to provide a subsidy for individuals who are designated as low income. The combined reforms would ensure that all individuals were insured and could afford insurance, since those who could not otherwise afford it would be subsidized.

The main objection to a mandate is that it imposes a welfare loss on some individuals. For example, individuals 5, 6, and 7 are not willing to pay $8 for health insurance coverage. Under a mandate, they would have to pay that amount anyway, and so they would suffer an added burden in order that higher risk and/or lower income individuals be able to obtain insurance (Hall 1994). In addition, the mandate does not eliminate the powerful incentive insurance companies have to "cherry pick" or engage in other competitive practices that enable them to select low-risk insureds. Other elements of health insurance reform must be introduced if these practices are to be curbed. The most prominent of these is risk adjustment.

13.2.9 Risk Adjustment

Risk adjustment is a technique that can be used to modify payments made to prepaid plans on the basis of characteristics of the entire group. The rationale behind this technique is that certain subgroups are more costly to treat (because they use more services) and health plans should be appropriately compensated for accepting as members these subgroups. Among the variables that have been used in risk adjustment formulas are age, gender, self-reported health status, and prior period health care use (see Section 6.7.7).

A problem with risk adjustment, in the present context, is that if a health plan discovers a variable related to health care use, it might be able to profit from the bias by selecting those low-risk individuals. For example, if body weight was associated with health care utilization, then a health plan might try to select members at least partly on the basis of their weight. Assuming it was successful in attracting lower weight members, it would benefit from having lower costs. Currently, there seem to be a number of risk factors that are not included in the risk adjustment techniques commonly used. This leaves the door open for health plans to invest in techniques that will identify potentially heavy health care users and avoid them. Such actions would reduce the effectiveness of market reforms.

13.3 HEALTH CARE ANTITRUST

13.3.1 Conceptual Framework

The economist's model of perfect competition is generally used as a benchmark in evaluating market outcomes. The perfectly competitive market, with large numbers of buyers and sellers, free entry and exit, and homogeneous products, yields a long-run competitive equilibrium in which all firms in the market are producing at the minimum long-run average cost and price is equal to marginal cost. This market equilibrium yields both technical efficiency and economic efficiency. (*Technical efficiency* refers to the tendency of firms in a market to produce goods and services at the minimum long-run average cost, a result of the price competition among firms and of the relatively small scale of each firm in comparison to market demand. *Economic efficiency* refers to the equality of price and marginal cost, which suggests that the allocation of resources could not be improved in a perfectly competitive world by moving resources from their present use to a different one.)

A second benchmark useful in examining market outcomes is found in the monopoly market model. In this market structure, because there is a single seller with blocked entry, long-run market equilibrium may yield a price greater than marginal cost. If the monopolist is a profit maximizer, technical efficiency, in the sense that the average cost is at the lowest level possible given the monopolist's choice of output, is still achieved. The monopolist, however, may not produce at the lowest average cost possible independent of the rate of output selected.

Monopoly markets also raise the possibility of shifts in the distribution of income as compared with a perfectly competitive organization of the market. Under restrictive assumptions, a competitive market in long-run equilibrium that is transformed into a monopoly market as a result of cartelization or merger would be changed in the way shown in Figure 13–1. Total market output would decline from Q_c to Q_m as a result of monopolization. The corresponding equilibrium price would increase from P_c to P_m. Monopoly profits would appear in the amount shown by the area *ABDE*. In addition to a change in the monopolist's economic well-being, there is also a change in the consumer's well-being. This change can be measured by the consumer surplus, which is the amount that the consumer would be willing to pay for the opportunity to consume a given quantity of services minus the amount actually paid. The consumer surplus is represented by the area under the demand curve above the given price. The consumer surplus would decrease from the amount represented by the area *FCD* under perfect competition to that represented by the area *FAE* under monopoly. The difference between these two levels of consumer surplus, measured by the area *ABC*, is traditionally called the deadweight loss due to monopoly.

In sum, the adverse effects of monopoly market structures are related directly to the reduction in market output from Q_c to Q_m. This reduced market output causes a redistribution between consumers and producers and also has efficiency effects in the form of a deadweight loss.

Many real-world markets, including most health care markets, are structured as oligopoly markets. Oligopoly markets are characterized by fewness of sellers and generally large numbers of buyers. Some health care markets are oligopolies on both sides of the market (i.e., both buyers and sellers are few in number). Economic models of markets structured as oligopolies tend not to yield general predictions about market outcome. Depending on whether sellers will attempt to engage in price collusion and, if not, how sellers will react to one another's price changes, the outcome in an oligopoly market may cover the entire range from monopoly on one extreme to perfect competition on the other.

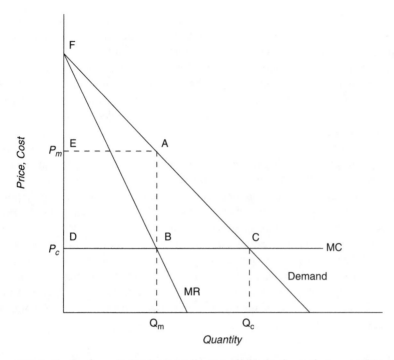

Figure 13–1 Economic analysis of monopolization effects. Under perfect competition, the price is P_c and the quantity is Q_c. Under monopoly, the price is P_m and the quantity is Q_m. Competition yields no monopoly profits and a consumer surplus of *FCD*. Monopoly yields monopoly profits of *EABD* and a consumer surplus of *FAE*.

Antitrust policy economic analysis has traditionally made an attempt to analytically define the boundaries of product markets and geographic markets and to consider whether the structure of any market so defined is close enough to a monopoly structure to suspect that performance in the market is adversely affected. This approach is reflected, for example, in the merger guidelines that have been developed over the past 25 years by the U.S. Department of Justice and the Federal Trade Commission. More recently, antitrust economists have begun to use simulation as a means of predicting the likely outcome of changes in market structure due to horizontal merger.

It should be noted that in the previous discussion of competitive and monopoly markets, perfect information on the part of consumers as well as producers is generally assumed. Perfect information entails that there is no uncertainty on the part of the consumers regarding product quality. Furthermore, since products are assumed to be homogeneous in a given market, price is the major decision variable for consumers. Health care markets do not meet this information requirement. These markets are characterized by the imperfect ability of consumers to link the acquisition of health care services with improvement in health status. Additionally, since third-party payers are dominant in most health care markets, the price of a particular health care service may be relatively unimportant to the ultimate consumer of that service. The market structure is further complicated by the fact that physicians act as agents of their patients in making decisions about whether particular services should be purchased.

As a result of these differences between health care markets and standard consumer goods markets, a discussion of antitrust policy in health care markets must take into account the particular economic characteristics of these markets. The point of view expressed here favors public policies that oppose monopoly power and promote competitive market structures. In the case of health care markets, however, there are even more caveats concerning this generalization than is true of more traditional consumer goods markets. It is often asserted that economies of scale and the possibly greater propensity of firms with monopoly power to engage in research and development may justify more concentrated consumer goods markets. In the case of health care markets, in addition to these two qualifications, high seller concentration and quantities may also be justified on the basis of better patient outcomes.

13.3.2 The Structure of Health Care Markets

13.3.2.1 Hospitals

Hospital services in the United States and Canada have historically been provided by private community hospitals. Community hospitals have traditionally been nonprofit hospitals sponsored by religious organizations, local governments, and charitable organizations. One major structural trend in the 1980s and 1990s in the United States was the rapid growth of for-profit hospital corporations.

Another strong trend in the 1980s and 1990s among U.S. hospitals was an increasing rate of mergers. Many of the mergers were related to the rise of for-profit hospital corporations. Other mergers have occurred among nonprofit hospitals in response to the rise of for-profit hospital corporations or to the increasing market power on the buyer side of the market related to the development of managed care networks (Schactman and Altman 1995).

The economic analysis of mergers suggests that mergers may be motivated by the pursuit of increased market power, the pursuit of increased efficiency, or both. The effects of changes in Medicare reimbursement policies in the mid-1980s provided a ready source of efficiency gains from mergers. The shift to prospective reimbursement for Medicare resulted in shorter inpatient stays and an increase in outpatient treatment. The general effect of these changes was overcapacity in many hospitals, which increased the likelihood that efficiency gains could be realized from mergers, especially mergers within the same geographic market. Such horizontal mergers also increase market power in given geographic markets, raising the issue of whether hospital mergers are in the public interest.

13.3.2.2 Physician Services

Physician services have traditionally been produced by physicians practicing alone or in small group practices. Before 1980, when cost containment was less prominent in the health care sector than it is now, physicians played the dominant role in the management of hospitals as well as in the management of physician group practices. The trend toward cost containment in hospitals has increased the power of hospital administrators in hospital management. The development of managed care networks is another factor that has contributed to the reduction in discretionary power of physicians in determining the price and quality of services. One response of physicians to these trends has been the formation of larger practices and other physician networks. Physicians have begun to form regional and even national practice corporations. As in the case of hospitals, the combination of physicians into large networks raises the question whether their increased market power might affect efficiency.

13.3.2.3 Health Insurers and Managed Care Plans

Health insurance in the United States has traditionally been provided as a tax-exempt fringe benefit by employers. Before about 1980, most Americans were covered by traditional health insurance, which supported fee-for-service transactions with providers. Health insurers competed with one another to obtain insurance contracts with employers. Until the 1980s, health care cost containment had a relatively low priority in the American system.

The early 1980s saw the rise of two important health care cost-containment mechanisms. First, the prospective payment system in Medicare employed purchasing power to control pricing and utilization of hospital services and physician services. Second, some states, beginning with California in 1982, began to allow payers to contract selectively with providers. This innovation enabled payers to negotiate reduced rates from providers in exchange for volume. Greater coordination of care, utilization review, and other changes caused health care management organizations (HMOs) to grow rapidly. As of the mid-1990s, HMOs enrollment totals about 50 million (Schactman and Altman 1995).

This structural change in payer markets has important implications for health care competition. In effect, increased market power on the buyer side of markets has evolved in response to market power on the provider side or to rapid price inflation due to the absence of cost-containment incentives for consumers. Mergers and consolidation among payers also raises the issue of reduced efficiency due to increased market power.

13.3.3 Antitrust Policy: History and Institutions

The most prominent piece of antitrust legislation in the United States is the Sherman Act of 1890. The Sherman Act was a legislative response to rapid changes occurring in American industry. In the last two decades of the nineteenth century, innovations in transportation and communication had transformed markets from local and regional markets to national markets. Business consolidation was a major trend, with the formation of near-monopoly conditions in some markets. The Sherman Act, building on common-law restrictions against conspiracy and monopolization, had two major sections:

> 1) . . . every contract, combination in the form of trust or otherwise, or conspiracy, in restraint of trade or commerce among the several states, or with foreign nations, is declared to be illegal . . .
>
> 2) . . . every person who shall monopolize, or attempt to monopolize, or combine or conspire with any other person or persons, to monopolize any part of the trade or commerce among the several states, or with foreign nations, shall be deemed guilty of a felony. . . .

The Clayton Act of 1914, with subsequent amendments, is the other major antitrust legislation in the United States. Two of the more important provisions of the Clayton Act are found in Sections 2 and 7, quoted in part as follows:

> 2a) . . . it shall be unlawful for any person engaged in commerce in the course of such commerce, either directly or indirectly, to discriminate in price between different purchasers of commodities of like grade and quality . . . where the effect of such discrimination may be substantially to lessen competition or tend to create a monopoly.
>
> 7) . . . no person engaged in commerce or in activity affecting commerce shall acquire, directly or indirectly, the whole or any part of the stock or other share capital and no person . . . shall acquire the whole or any part of the assets of another person engaged also in commerce . . . where in any line of commerce in any section of the country, the effect of such acquisition may be substantially to lessen competition, or to tend to create a monopoly . . .

The Federal Trade Commission Act was also passed in 1914, in part for purposes of enforcing the Clayton Act. Section 5A1 of the Federal Trade Commission Act states that ". . . unfair methods of competition in or affecting commerce, and unfair or deceptive acts or practices in or affecting commerce, are declared unlawful . . ."

There are two federal agencies that share the enforcement of antitrust law: the Antitrust Division of the U.S. Department of Justice and the Federal Trade Commission (FTC). The Department of Justice has primary responsibility for public enforcement of the Sherman Act; the FTC has primary responsibility for enforcement of the Federal Trade Commission Act and Section 2 of the Clayton Act. The two agencies combine in enforcing the merger provisions of the Clayton Act. In addition, there are areas of overlap in which the agencies share jurisdiction. Private enforcement also occurs. The importance of private enforcement is related directly to Section 4 of the Clayton Act, which provides that those injured as a result of "anything forbidden in the antitrust laws" may bring private suit and recover triple damages, including attorney's fees. The triple damages provision provides a strong incentive for injured parties to bring private suits, including class action suits.

Because of the time and expense of fully developing cases and bringing them to trial, the majority of antitrust cases are settled by consent decrees. In consent decree settlements, a court supervised agreement is worked out between the parties. In criminal suits, a settlement sometimes involves the use of a no contest plea in order that the defendant may avoid pleading guilty. In private civil cases, financial settlements, generally involving amounts less than those initially asked by the plaintiffs, are common.

13.3.4 Price Fixing and Conspiracy in Restraint of Trade

The legal tradition in the enforcement of Section 1 of the Sherman Act, which concerns conspiracy in restraint of trade, is that evidence of direct communication between competitors is sufficient to find a violation. This enforcement tradition is referred to as the *per se rule*. The Supreme Court has strongly stated that whether the prices established by conspiracy are reasonable or not is not an issue.

Despite the strong per se tradition in enforcing price fixing, legal precedent was relatively slow in extending the range of antitrust law to the professions. A landmark case in this regard is *Goldfarb vs. Virginia State Bar* (1975), in which the Court stated that the professions are not exempt from the Sherman Act's prohibition of price fixing. *Goldfarb* involved fee schedules set for legal fees by a bar association.

That the per se rule also applies to price fixing among physicians was forcefully stated in the Supreme Court's decision in *Arizona vs. Maricopa County Medical Society* (1982). In this case, two physician groups utilized relative value schedules to establish maximum prices for medical services. The Court ruled that this approach to setting maximum physician fees was subject to the per se rule against price fixing.

Maricopa clearly establishes that the health care professions fall under the per se rule concerning price fixing and conspiracy in restraint of trade. This is not to say that physicians and other health professionals may not form professional associations and discuss issues of mutual concern. Trade association activities, including some exchange of pricing information, generally do not constitute violations. The use of a common fee schedule (setting either maximum or minimum fees) would likely be a violation of the Sherman Act, however.

13.3.5 Mergers in Health Care Markets

A merger is a partial or total combination of two separate business firms. Partial mergers would include such combinations as joint ventures and intercorporate stock purchases. Complete mergers are more common. They involve the purchase of the assets or stock of one corporation by a separate corporation and usually result in the blending of the two corporations into a single succeeding firm.

Mergers are generally described as falling into one of three categories. The first type of merger is the horizontal merger, or a merger between firms that compete in the same product market and geographic market. A merger of two community hospitals in the same metropolitan area would be an example of a horizontal merger. The second type of merger is the vertical merger, which is a merger between firms that have a buyer-seller relationship. The acquisition of a physician group practice by an HMO would be an example of a vertical merger. The third type of merger is the conglomerate merger, which is a merger between firms that are neither horizontally nor vertically related. The acquisition of a community hospital by a banking corporation would be an example of a conglomerate merger.

Mergers and joint ventures have become very common in health care markets. For-profit hospital corporations such as Columbia/HCA have expanded in size and in geographic scope primarily through merger. Mergers have also been common among physician practices, as solo practitioners combine to form local and regional group practices.

The enforcement of Section 7 of the Clayton Act by the Department of Justice and FTC focuses on the seller concentration in the market before and after prospective mergers. The Hart-Scott-Rodino Act of 1976 requires that firms above a threshold size contemplating a merger ($100 million in sales or assets for one premerger firm and $10 million for the other) must notify the FTC and Department of Justice in advance of the merger. This provision of the law allows the antitrust authorities to intervene before the merger actually occurs rather than wait until asset ownership has changed hands. It also allows for modification of the assets to be acquired if seller concentration in the market justifies objections to parts of the merger.

Hospital markets tend to be local or regional in scope. In addition, because hospitals differ with respect to the array of services offered, the analysis of hospital mergers must consider both product market definition and geographic market definition. The definitions of geographic market and product market for hospitals are based on the interchangeability or cross-price elasticity of the services offered, as viewed by the consumers. Two or more hospitals are in the same geographic market if consumers (or their physician agents) consider the hospitals to be reasonably interchangeable when making decisions regarding where to seek care. Two or more hospitals are in the same product market if consumers consider their offerings of a given service to be reasonably interchangeable (Wilder and Jacobs 1987).

As noted earlier, the Clayton Act prohibits mergers where "the effect of such acquisition may be substantially to lessen competition, or to tend to create a monopoly." In the case of hospital mergers, a potential anticompetitive effect exists if there is overlap in the product and geographic markets of the hospitals prior to the merger. In general, the question of whether two hospitals are in the same geographic or product market may be more complicated for hospitals than for non-health-service firms. The geographic market definition is likely to vary depending on the medical procedure in question. Because patients are likely to be willing to travel greater distances for more complicated, more expensive procedures, the geographic market definition for hospitals is not independent of the procedure in question. In general, the geographic market is much wider for complicated procedures than for simple procedures (Wilder and Jacobs 1987).

Antitrust aspects of hospital mergers must be considered in the light of merger history. During the period 1950–1980, the enforcement agencies treated horizontal mergers very strictly, with modest market concentration levels and modest increases in concentration frequently sufficient for horizontal mergers to be successfully challenged. After 1980, horizontal merger enforcement became more lenient, as reflected in the Department of Justice and FTC merger guidelines, the most recent of which were released in 1992.

In evaluating horizontal mergers, the Justice Department and FTC use the Herfindahl-Hirschman Index (HHI) of market concentration (see Section 8.3.1). The HHI is defined as the sum of the squares of the individual market shares of all firms in the market, where market shares are expressed in percentages. For example, if there was one hospital in a geographic market, the HHI would equal $(100)^2$, or 10,000, the highest the index could be. If there were two hospitals of equal size, each would have 50 percent of the market, and the HHI would equal $50^2 + 50^2$, or 5,000. If there were two hospitals but one had 75 percent and the other had 25 percent of the market, the HHI would equal $75^2 + 25^2$, or 6,350. If there were 100 hospitals, each with 1 percent of the market, the HHI would equal 100.

According to the guidelines, the Justice Department and FTC consider both market concentration after a merger and the increase in concentration resulting from the merger. The guidelines establish three categories of horizontal mergers:

1. Post-Merger HHI below 1,000. The agency regards markets in this region to be unconcentrated. Mergers resulting in unconcentrated markets are unlikely to have adverse competitive effects and ordinarily require no further analysis.

2. Post-Merger HHI between 1,000 and 1,800. The agency regards markets in this region to be moderately concentrated. Mergers producing an increase in the HHI of less than 100 points in moderately concentrated markets post-merger are unlikely to have adverse competitive consequences and ordinarily require no further analysis. Mergers producing an increase in the HHI of more than 100 points in moderately concentrated markets post-merger potentially raise significant competitive concerns.

3. Post-Merger HHI above 1,800. The agency regards markets in this region to be highly concentrated. Mergers producing an increase in the HHI of less than 50 points, even in highly concentrated markets post-merger, are unlikely to have adverse competitive consequences and ordinarily require no further analysis. Mergers producing an increase in the HHI of more than 50 points in highly concentrated markets post-merger potentially raise significant competitive concerns, depending on the factors set forth in (other sections) of the guidelines. Where the post-merger HHI exceeds 1,800, it will be presumed that mergers producing an increase in the HHI of more than 100 points are likely to create or enhance market power or facilitate its exercise (U.S. Department of Justice and Federal Trade Commission 1992).

If hospital mergers were judged entirely on the basis of the 1992 guidelines, it is unlikely that many hospital mergers in a given geographic market would be approved. Using research reported elsewhere, Wilder and Jacobs (1987) found that the HHI for hospitals in a medium-sized metropolitan area market was on the order of 2,600 for all diagnoses together. For individual procedures, the HHI ranged from a low of 2,300 for plastic surgery to a high of 4,600 for surgeries of the nervous system.

Hospital mergers have occurred at a rapid rate since 1980. Blackstone and Fuhr state that 40 to 60 hospital mergers per year occurred in the 1980s but that the Department of Justice and FTC challenged fewer than 10 in total. In some cases, mergers were not challenged because the hospitals were not in the same geographic market. Many of the mergers and acquisitions were part of growth of firms such as Columbia/HCA. Even when hospital mergers were truly horizontal, the Justice Department and FTC applied somewhat different standards to these mergers than other horizontal mergers. This difference in standards applied to horizontal hospital mergers is apparent in the *Department of Justice–Federal Trade Commission Antitrust Guidelines for the Business of Health Care*, released initially in 1993 and updated in September 1994. The purpose of the guidelines was to provide information concerning the types of mergers, joint ventures, and other competitive activities that could be challenged by the antitrust authorities. In the area of mergers, the guidelines state that the merger of two small hospitals with low occupancy rates, even in the same geographic market, would not be challenged. They also state that two or more hospitals of any size could engage in joint ventures to buy high-technology equipment if each hospital by itself could not fully utilize the equipment.

For mergers between larger hospitals, the antitrust agencies state that they will use the "rule of reason" in analyzing mergers. In the rule of reason approach, consideration is given to whether a merger may have a substantial anticompetitive effect and, if so, whether the anticompetitive effect is offset by procompetitive efficiencies (Steiger 1995).

The primary generalization concerning the effect of antitrust policy on hospital mergers is that only a small number of mergers have been challenged by the antitrust authorities out of the hundreds of mergers that have taken place in the past 20 years. Another indication of the effect of antitrust policy on hospital mergers may be seen in the outcome of the antitrust review of the merger of Columbia Healthcare Corporation and HCA Healthcare. The merger was allowed on the condition that three hospitals in Salt Lake City and four hospitals in Louisiana, Florida, and Texas be divested. The resulting corporation, Columbia/HCA, included 191 hospitals with 39,328 acute care beds (*Value Line* 1994). Columbia/HCA subsequently merged with Healthtrust, Inc., forming a national hospital corporation with 320 hospitals and more than 100 outpatient surgery centers. This merger was approved by the FTC after Columbia/HCA agreed to sell 7 hospitals and end a joint venture with another hospital (Federal Trade Commission, 1995).

13.3.6 Monopolization

Section 2 of the Sherman Act makes it illegal to "monopolize, or attempt to monopolize." The use of the verb form (*monopolize*) rather than the noun form (*monopoly*) suggests the difficulties of enforcing an antimonopoly law. Conceptually, a monopoly is a single firm with exclusive possession of a market for a good or service. However, pure monopoly status is highly unusual. Markets with high seller concentration and partial-monopoly market structures are more commonly the object of monopolization inquiries. As a result, the enforcement of monopolization laws tend to focus on market definition, market share, and specific acts that may be taken to illustrate monopolistic intent.

A good summary of the enforcement tradition in monopolization cases may be found in the Supreme Court decision in the Grinnell case, where Justice Douglas stated that the offense of monopoly "has two elements: 1) possession of monopoly power in the relevant market and; 2) willful acquisition or maintenance of that power" (*U.S. vs. Grinnell Corporation*, 384 U.S. 563 [1966]).

Relatively little of the antitrust enforcement activity in health care has involved monopolization issues directly. Instead, most enforcement activity has taken place under the conspiracy statute, Section 1 of the Sherman Act, or the antimerger statute, Section 7 of the Clayton Act. As national hospital corporations and health care provider networks grow more important in the United States, however, the likelihood increases that monopolization issues will become more important.

The major reason that monopolization issues have been less important than other antitrust issues is that the level of seller concentration in most hospital or physician services markets, while relatively high in some instances, does not approach the level that indicates monopoly on the basis of case law. In the most direct indication of the type of market share that would be considered to be equivalent to monopoly status, Judge Hand, in the Aluminum Company of America case, stated that a market share over 90 percent "is enough to constitute a monopoly; it is doubtful whether 60 or 64 percent would be enough; and certainly 33 percent is not" (*U.S. vs. Aluminum Company of America*, 148 F.2nd 416 [1945]).

Since the Aluminum Company of America case, the only very large national corporation whose monopoly status was broken up by antitrust action was AT&T, in a case settled by a consent decree in 1982. A monopolization case against IBM by the Justice Department was dropped at roughly the same time. Because neither of these cases reached the Supreme Court, there is no clear recent judicial statement interpreting monopoly law for today's world.

There are at least three principle types of health care markets in which monopoly issues may be a future problem. First, hospital geographic markets are generally local or regional. As national hospital corporations grow and nonprofit community hospitals merge and engage in joint ventures, the market structure in some local hospital markets may evolve in such a way that a group of jointly owned hospitals reaches a market share of 60 percent. Such market evolution could lead to monopolization enforcement under Section 2 of the Sherman Act.

Physician networks represent a second area in which monopoly statutes may become relevant in the future. Physicians have been rapidly forming networks that operate as unified firms. Such networks may increase their market shares in relevant geographic markets up to the 60-percent range or greater. As their market shares rise through continued consolidation, antimonopoly law may come to be directed toward these networks.

Managed care organizations and HMOs may also become the target of monopolization statutes in the future. The development of these organizations tends to increase concentration on the buyer side in markets for hospital and physician services. As the market penetration of HMOs increases, the potential for high market shares on the buyer side of health care markets also increases. Some observers believe that the rapid increase in physician networks, hospital mergers, and joint ventures is in part a response to the increased purchasing power of HMOs and managed care organizations.

The recent Department of Justice and Federal Trade Commission (1994) statement on health care and antitrust addresses the interaction of physician networks and multiprovider networks. In general, the statement indicates that HMOs and other multiprovider networks might violate antitrust laws if the exclusion of some doctors from a dominant network in a local market makes it impossible for the excluded doctors to practice medicine. A similar argument could be directed at a dominant multiprovider network excluding hospitals in a local market.

13.3.7 Recent Developments

One of the most important trends in the health care sector during the past 20 years has been the rise of managed care plans, selective contracting, and integrated health networks. The motive behind this trend has been the desire to counteract the market power traditionally possessed by physicians and hospitals. The growth of managed care appears to have promoted competitive efficiencies in health care and has likely reduced the rate of increase in health care costs. At the same time, the rise of managed care could result in increased market power on the part of buyers or sellers of health care and ultimately raise prices to consumers (Schactman and Altman 1995).

The Clinton administration's 1993 health care initiatives, which appeared to propose greater public sector participation in health care, were not politically popular. However, the growth in managed competition recommended in the Clinton plan has proceeded despite the lack of federal legislation. In other words, the managed care revolution has been a private market dynamic rather than a legislative reaction to increasing health care costs.

Among the most recent developments in health care antitrust policy is the publication of the U.S. Department of Justice and Federal Trade Commission (1994) *Statements of Enforcement Policy and Analytical Principles Relating to Health Care and Antitrust*. These statements reflect the complexity of markets and provider and purchaser institutions in health care. They are also an indication that the antitrust authorities are seeking to adapt antitrust policy that was developed for broad applicability to the particular economic characteristics of health care markets. The provisions of the statements address the following nine areas:

1. mergers among hospitals
2. hospital joint ventures involving high-technology or other expensive health care equipment

3. hospital joint ventures involving specialized clinical or other expensive health care services
4. providers' collective provision of non-fee-related information to purchasers of health care services
5. providers' collective provision of fee-related information to purchasers of health care services
6. provider participation in exchanges of price and cost information
7. joint purchasing arrangements among health care providers
8. physician network joint ventures
9. analytical principles relating to multiprovider networks

The purpose of the statements is to reduce uncertainty concerning antitrust policy and to establish "antitrust safety zones" (conditions under which business conduct will not be challenged). For example, the merger of two small hospitals with low occupancy rates would fall in a safety zone. On the other hand, a dominant physician network might attract antitrust scrutiny by collusive agreements on price or by excluding physicians and thereby making it impossible for them to practice in the market.

Physicians have criticized the statements on the grounds that they favor insurance company and hospital networks over those formed by physicians. Comments in early 1996 by FTC Chairperson Robert Pitofsky suggested that the FTC is willing to be more lenient as regards the setting of prices by physician networks, especially in markets where insurers and HMOs have substantial market power (Pear 1996).

State governments have also become players in the antitrust policy arena. As of 1994, 18 states had enacted regulatory programs for state approval of hospital activities, including mergers, that are subject to antitrust policy. Under the state action immunity doctrine, state supervision in some circumstances replaces federal antitrust action. This development could, for example, allow some hospital mergers that would otherwise attract federal antitrust action (U.S. General Accounting Office 1994).

The health care system in the United States is being transformed structurally by the growth in managed care, selective contracting, provider networks, and large mergers. These changes have the potential to increase productive efficiency and slow the rate of health care price inflation. At the same time, they may increase market power in some product or geographic markets and lead to higher consumer prices. It is likely that as greater consolidation of providers and purchasers continues, antitrust issues will become even more important.

BIBLIOGRAPHY

Insurance Market Reform

Abraham, K.S. 1985. Efficiency and fairness in insurance risk selection. *Virginia Law Review* 71: 403–451.

Blendon, R.J., et al. 1992. Making the critical choices. *JAMA* 267:2509–2520.

Browne, M.J., and Doerpinghaus, H. 1994–1995. Asymmetric information and the demand for medigap insurance. *Inquiry* 31:445–450.

Butler, S.M. 1991. A tax reform strategy to deal with the uninsured. *JAMA* 265:2541–2544.

Davis, K. 1991. Expanding Medicare and employer plans to achieve universal health insurance. *JAMA* 265:2525–2528.

Enthoven, A.C. 1993. The history and principles of managed competition. *Health Affairs* 12 (suppl.):24–48.

Enthoven, A.C., and Kronick, R. 1989. A consumer choice health plan for the 1990s. Parts 1 and 2. *New England Journal of Medicine* 320:29–37, 94–101.

———. 1991. Universal health insurance through incentives reform. *JAMA* 265:2532–2536.

Giacomini, M., et al. 1995. Risk adjusting community rated health plan premiums. *Annual Review of Public Health* 16:401–430.

Grumbach, K., et al. 1991. Liberal benefits, conservative spending. *JAMA* 265:2549–2554.

Hall, M.A. 1994. *Reforming private health insurance.* Washington, D.C.: American Enterprise Institute.

Holahan, J., et al. 1991. An American approach to health system reform. *JAMA* 265:2537–2540.

Light, D.W. 1992. The practice and ethics of risk rated health insurance. *JAMA* 267:2503–2508.

Pauly, M.V. 1990. The rational nonpurchase of long-term-care insurance. *Journal of Political Economy* 98:153–168.

Pauly, M.V., et al. 1991. A plan for "responsible national health insurance." *Health Affairs* 10 (spring):5–25.

Reinhardt, U.E. 1993a. An "all-American" health reform proposal. *Journal of American Health Policy* 3, no. 3:11–17.

———. 1993b. Reorganizing the financial flows in American health care. *Health Affairs* 12 (suppl.):173–193.

Rice, T., et al. 1993. Holes in the Jackson Hole approach to health care reform. *JAMA* 270:1357–1362.

Summers, L.H. 1989. Some simple economics of mandated benefits. *American Economic Review* 79 (suppl.):177–183.

Thomas, K. 1994–1995. Are subsidies enough to encourage the uninsured to purchase health insurance? *Inquiry* 31:415–424.

Thorpe, K.E. 1992. Expanding employment-based health insurance: Is small group reform the answer? *Inquiry* 29:128–136.

Thorpe, K.E., et al. 1992. Reducing the number of uninsured by subsidizing employment-based health insurance. *JAMA* 267:945–948.

Antitrust Policy

Blackstone, E., and Fuhr, J.P. 1992. An antitrust analysis of nonprofit hospital mergers. *Review of Industrial Organization* 8:473–490.

Federal Trade Commission. 1995. News Release. Washington, D.C.: Federal Trade Commission, October 5.

Freudenheim, M. 1994. Health industry is changing itself ahead of reform. *New York Times*, June 27, page A1.

Pear, R. 1996. Doctors may get leeway to rival large companies. *New York Times*, April 8,

Santerre, R.E., and Neun, S. 1996. *Health economics: Theories, insights and industry studies.* Chicago: R.D. Irwin, Inc.

Schactman, D., and Altman, S.H. 1995. *Market consolidation, antitrust, and public policy in the health care industry: Agenda for future research.* Princeton, N.J.: Robert Wood Johnson Foundation.

Seplaki, L. 1994. *Cost and competition in American medicine.* Lanham, Md.: University Press of America.

Steiger, J.D. 1995. Prepared remarks of Commissioner Janet D. Steiger, Federal Trade Commission, Health Care Enforcement Issues, before the Health Trustee Institute, Cleveland, Ohio, November 9, 1995.

U.S. Department of Justice and Federal Trade Commission. 1992. *Horizontal merger guidelines.* Washington, D.C.: U.S. Department of Justice and Federal Trade Commission.

U.S. Department of Justice and Federal Trade Commission. 1994. *Statements of enforcement policy and analytical principles relating to health care and antitrust.* Washington, D.C.: U.S. Department of Justice and Federal Trade Commission.

U.S. General Accounting Office. 1994. *Health care: Federal and state antitrust actions concerning the health care industry.* Washington, D.C.: U.S. General Accounting Office.

Value Line. 1994. The Value Line Investment Survey. New York: Value Line Publishing, Inc., January 7.

Wilder, R.P., and Jacobs, P. 1987. Antitrust considerations for hospital mergers: Market definition and market concentration. In *Advances in health economics and health services research,* ed. R.M. Scheffler and L.F. Rossiter. JAI Press.

Wooley, J.M. 1993. Hospitals: Price-increasing competition. In *Industry Studies,* ed. L. Deutsch. Englewood Cliffs, N.J.: Prentice Hall.

CHAPTER 14

The Economics of Regulation

14.1 INTRODUCTION

There are several characteristics of the commodity "medical care" that might lead one to question whether the market for medical care services, in the absence of government intervention, could adequately meet the goals of health policy. First, there is the fact of consumer ignorance about health status and the effect of medical care on health. Such *ignorance* can lead to market dominance by providers over the consumers. Market behavior where information asymmetry exists has been characterized by the monopoly model and the supplier-induced demand model. Both market mechanisms can result in departures from an optimal allocation of resources, namely, low-quality care and an inappropriate supply of care (too much in the case of supplier-induced demand, too little in the case of monopoly). Second, *uncertainty* over the occurrence of illness can lead to copayments that are too low and reimbursement arrangements that are very generous. Both low copayments and high levels of reimbursement can lead to excessive supply. Additionally, overly generous reimbursement (such as retrospective cost-based reimbursement) can result in excessive quality and technical inefficiency.

In all such cases, regulation has been suggested as a solution. Supplier regulation, which is what we are concerned with in this chapter, involves the control of specific aspects of provider behavior by a public or publicly appointed agency. There are a wide variety of economic variables that can be regulated, including price, quantity of services provided, quality of care, and quantity and quality of inputs (e.g., the qualifications of providers and the standards of equipment). A widely used type of regulation in the health care field has been government-appointed self-regulation on the part of groups of providers, such as doctors. According to this model, professional groups are given the power to regulate themselves. The focus of self-regulation includes licensing, educational characteristics, and quality of care provided.

Until the early 1970s, self-regulation was a popular response to market failings. At that time, however, growing concern developed that physician self-regulation (not to mention other varieties) had a considerable degree of physician self-interest built into it and did not automatically lead to economic efficiency. In addition, there was a worry that health insurance was playing a large role in pushing up hospital costs. An obvious answer to these problems was to appeal to the political system, since it is government that sets the rules of the marketplace. One general approach to rule setting is to impose more direct public regulations on the providers. These regulations are introduced to restrict the opportunities of the producers and ensure that they act more in the public interest, and it is thus termed the *public interest approach to regulation* (see Section 14–2).

The public interest approach to regulation does require a touch of faith. It assumes that the right forces will bring pressure to bear on the political system to change the rules of the game and that the changes will cause the market to better achieve the goals of health policy. If matters do not then improve, the public interest approach calls for still more regulation.

This entire approach has been called into question, primarily because of the way the health care market has operated *under regulation*. Some argue that regulations have not unequivocally aided in the achievement of social goals and indeed that they usually will work in favor of special interest groups—in many cases the regulated suppliers themselves!

To explain this bias in regulation, another account of the role of the political process in influencing the market has been developed. This account regards the political process as a series of exchanges between consumers, producers, politicians, bureaucrats, and regulators. Out of this complex web of exchanges, policies are formulated and implemented that change the rules under which the market operates, but these rules and regulations do not necessarily favor consumers. Providers in a particular market may have enough to offer politicians that they ask for (and receive) favorable regulations in exchange. Section 14.3 examines this view of the political process.

14.2 MARKET REGULATION

14.2.1 The Market and Professional Dominance

Because of consumers' potential ignorance regarding their health status and the impact of health care on health, it has been contended that a truly free market may operate in the interests of (sometimes unethical or incompetent) providers. In addition, because of possible large losses due to illness, consumers will purchase insurance, and the lower postinsurance (out-of-pocket) price will create a disincentive for them to economize on medical care. Even if providers were fully qualified, insurance would create an incentive to use more medical care.

Let us examine these contentions in light of the flows in the hospital care market. In Figure 14–1, inside the circle are presented the flows of money and services in the hospital market. To simplify matters, the government as a financing body is left out of the picture. In the hospital market, patients receive hospital services prescribed by their doctors. These services are reimbursed for either by their insurance companies or jointly by these companies and the patients (when there are copayments). The contentions regarding the operations of a free (unregulated) market are as follows. First, the providers, both doctors and hospitals, may not be professionally qualified and may provide inferior quality services to patients. In the extreme, these services may even be harmful to the patients. Second, the flows of services from even well-qualified doctors and facilities may be excessive, in the sense that they contribute little to the maintenance of health. The public interest approach to regulation claims that, on appeal to the legislatures, regulations and laws can be brought into being that alter these flows, presumably to the benefit of the patients.

There are two ways in which these flows can be altered. One is to ensure that the proper providers are supplying the product. This amounts to preventing unqualified practitioners from supplying output and preventing excessive resources (in quantity or quality) from being used. One might say that the "right" resources will be used for the "right" job. The mechanism that regulates the qualifications of providers is the credentialing process. In the medical care market, both personnel and facilities must have appropriate credentials in order to participate in the production of medical care. In addition, mechanisms exist to determine that certain resources, notably hospital facilities, are not produced in excessive amounts. The first method of regulating the flows in the market merely determines resource availability; it does not regulate the flows of services and money once the resources are in place and supplying output.

It may be argued that the mere regulation of the quantity and quality of personnel and facilities (i.e., capital) is not enough to ensure that the market will work in the interest of the consumers. Under facility and personnel regulation, consumers may be guaranteed that, when they obtain medical care, the care will be of a minimum quality or better. However, those providers who are allowed to produce medical care may still overproduce in terms of quality, they may still provide unnecessary or excessive care, and they may still overcharge the patients or the third parties. In the response of these excesses, proponents of the public interest approach of regulation would call for further regulations—regulations intended to control the quality and quantity of medical care and the prices of these services. These regulations directly focus on the behavior of the providers and cause the market flows to be altered further. The two types of regulation are described in more detail below.

14.2.2 Regulating the Credentials and Facilities of Suppliers

In Figure 14–1, the regulating or credentialing bodies are outside the circle, and dotted arrows are drawn from these regulating bodies to the participants in the regulated market. The regulating bodies have received their authority from a legislature, either federal or state. Here we look at only a few examples of the many forms of regulation.

We begin with a description of the method of credentialing physicians. The prime method of credentialing practitioners is through state licensure, a process by which those who meet specific criteria are granted licenses to practice medicine. The criteria are determined by state licensing boards and include graduation from a medical school accepted by the physician's association and completion of one year of internship in an acceptable institution, usually a hospital. The composition of state licensing boards is of particular interest. These boards are given the power to legally determine who can and cannot practice medicine and what the practice of medicine constitutes. The members of a state are frequently recommended to the state legislature by the state medical associations. Since these state medical associations are bodies made up of practicing physicians in the state, the licensing boards in effect are organizations that represent the suppliers of medical care in the state. To put the matter another way, the credentialing of physicians amounts to self-regulation.

Other types of health personnel are also licensed by state bodies. For example, registered nurses, physician assistants, physical and occupational therapists, and optometrists all require licensure through a professional board to practice their trade. As in the practice of medicine, the licensing boards determine what credentials are required for the practice of the various professions and exactly what constitutes a professional practice (i.e., what tasks the various professionals can and cannot perform). These determinations are made in the context of state licensure laws for the practice of medicine and cannot supersede them. For example, nurses cannot normally prescribe prescription drugs, and optometrists can neither use certain drugs nor perform eye surgery. The main difference between the boards of nonphysician health professionals and physicians boards is that nonphysician boards are usually not autonomous and the laws and regulations they administer are legislated in the context of medical licensure laws. Physicians will have representation on these nonphysician state boards or will serve as advisors and thus will be in a position to influence what acts can and cannot be performed by the various kinds of health professionals.

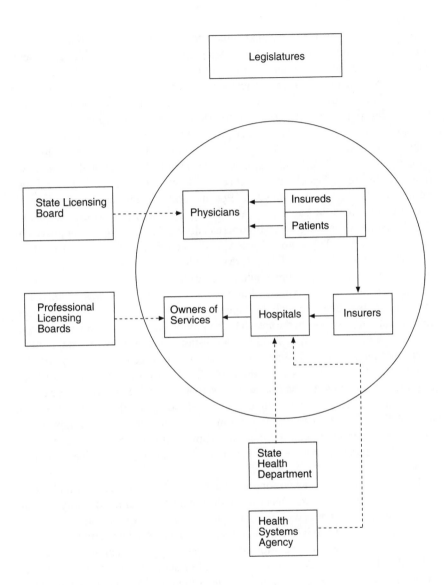

Figure 14–1 Jurisdictions of credentialing bodies. Suppliers (inside the circle) receive credentials certifying or licensing them to provide services from the credentialing bodies (shown outside the circle). The solid lines represent money flows, and the dotted lines represent regulatory control. Regulating bodies receive their authority from legislatures.

Nonpersonnel resources are also subject to credentialing processes. Hospitals must be licensed by state licensing agencies, usually the state health department. The licenses require that a minimum level of facilities and personnel be present.

A second type of regulation for hospitals is more concerned with preventing an excess of resources rather than with attaining minimum quality levels. For example, some regulating agencies attempt to limit investment (capital expansion) to types of facilities that are "necessary" in order to avoid creating duplicative or simply unneeded resources. Perhaps the best known of these are the Health Systems Agencies (HSAs), which were legitimized by the U.S. National Health Planning and Resources Development Act (Public Law 93-641) of 1974. Federal support for the HSAs was withdrawn in 1986 and only three remain in operation, all state funded. According to the HSA enabling legislation, investment in institutional facilities exceeding a certain sum (usually $100,000) had to be approved by the regional HSA. The approval was called a certificate of need (CON). If the institution did not obtain a CON before expanding, its license to operate could be withheld or, more likely, a fine could be imposed.

The membership composition of an HSA's managing board was stipulated by the enacting legislation to include a specified number of consumers and a specified number of providers in the area. These individuals acted as voting members of a voluntary board. The HSA also hired a full-time staff to study regional requirements and prepare files. The authority to grant a certificate of need lay with the board rather than with the staff of the HSA. The HSA board's vote was not final; in some cases it could be overturned by a state planning agency (often located in the state health department). Although federal funding for HSAs was terminated in 1986, 38 states still have some form of CON requirement for the approval of capital expenditures (though in most states approval is no longer routed through HSAs). In general, the role of regulation in health planning has declined in importance.

The role of the HSAs can be contrasted with the role of credentialing and licensing activities. An HSA was concerned with "too much" of either quantity or quality. Its initial concern was with restricting investment that would lead to increased institutional costs. State licensing activities are concerned with setting a floor below which quality will not be allowed to fall. Both types of activities are carried out under the auspices of legislatures, federal or state. A doctor cannot practice medicine without a license from the state licensing board and a nurse cannot practice medicine at all. In either case, if individuals violate laws, they are subject to legal sanctions. Similarly, an institution that expands without a certificate of need in a state with CON laws may be subject to legal sanctions. In addition to these legally authorized processes, certain professionally authorized processes influence the credentials of those who operate in the market.

One type of professional qualification involves the certification by a professional board of a physician in a specific specialty. For example, physicians who complete a specified time in a hospital-based residency program and subsequently pass the exams of a board that is linked to a specialty association (e.g., the examining board of the American Association of Internal Medicine) can become board-certified specialists. This form of certification does not grant them any legal privileges over and above those granted to them by the state licensing board. However, such certification is frequently a requirement, set down by members of a hospital staff, for obtaining a part- or full-time position in a hospital. The effect of extra legal certification is similar to that of licensing: It helps establish standards for those who practice in certain settings (especially hospitals).

14.2.3 Regulation of Supplier Behavior

In addition to influencing the quantity and quality of personnel and facilities, regulations exist to influence the *behavior* of providers. The reasons given for this type of regulation are that the mere regulation of credentials of suppliers and quantities of resources is not enough; suppliers may still behave in a manner detrimental to the public interest. As with the preceding types of regulations, behavior can be regulated at the legal and nonlegal levels. We will look at examples of each.

The relation of behavior-regulating bodies to participants in the marketplace is shown in Figure 14–2. Peer review organizations (PROs) were set up under the Tax Equity and Fiscal Responsibility Act (TEFRA) of 1982, an act that introduced a considerable amount of legislation related to the Medicare program. PROs are selected by the Health Care Financing Administration on a competitive basis. Preference is given to organizations that are associated with area physicians (e.g., state medical associations), as this assures some degree of local provider representation. The prime responsibility of PROs is to conduct reviews of hospital care based on random criteria. About three percent of Medicare inpatient cases are reviewed, as well as cases involving specific categories of patients (e.g., rehabilitation patients and chronic obstructive pulmonary patients). For the cases that are reviewed, there are three types of screening: a generic screening for quality of care, an admissions review, and a discharge review. The review of cases is intended to determine whether discharges were appropriate (too early or late), whether the patients got hospital-contracted infections, the causes of unexpected deaths, the circumstances in which patients returned for additional surgery during the stay, and the circumstances in which trauma occurred during a stay. Cases that do not pass the initial review are further reviewed by a physician. Admissions that do not meet review criteria following this further review are subject to claims denial. In addition, the PRO can undertake more intensive review in the future.

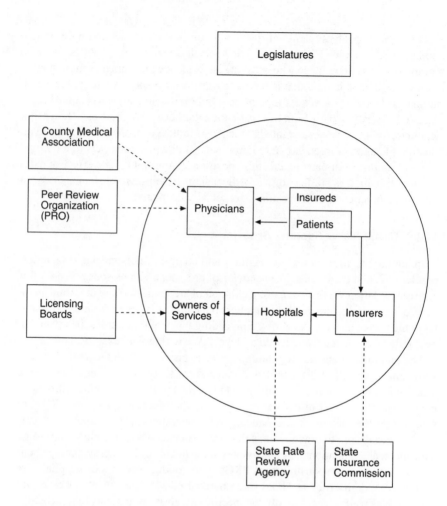

Figure 14-2 Jurisdictions of behavior-regulating bodies. Suppliers (inside the circle) have their supply behavior controlled legally and professionally by regulatory and professional bodies (outside the circle).

There is also the possibility of fines imposed by the Inspector General of the Department of Health and Human Services. PRO staff consist primarily of nurses and part-time area physicians (General Accounting Office 1988).

PROs are continuations of professional standards review organizations (PSROs), which were set up in 1973 under Public Law 92-603, the Professional

Standards Review Organization Act. Under this act, all health care institutions that received reimbursement from federal funds under Medicare or Medicaid had to submit to a review of the utilization of care conducted by the area PSRO. Any utilization deemed inappropriate would not be reimbursed for. Lack of evidence of PSRO effectiveness led to proposals by the Reagan Administration for their elimination, but concern over the quality of care under the prospective payment system resulted in a revitalization (and renaming) of these organizations.

From an economic standpoint, it is important to categorize the role of incentives in utilization review. Hospital care that is deemed to be inappropriate is penalized by a denial of claims; in the event of inappropriate care (such as an excessive length of stay), the providing hospital becomes liable for the cost of the Medicare or Medicaid patient. The review and the penalties associated with it encourage more appropriate utilization. Peer review cannot be regarded as occurring in a vacuum, however. Indeed, the very excesses that PSROs were designed to curb resulted from inducements to overutilization under the old cost-based reimbursement system (see Section 6.7.4). Not surprisingly, given the change to a prospective payment system, the more recent orientation of PROs is toward maintaining adequate quality. Of prime concern under DRGs are premature discharges (i.e., lengths of stay that are too short) and other cost-cutting measures that may adversely affect quality. As a result, some of the new initiatives of PROs include the examination of quick readmissions and the assurance of proper discharge planning.

In addition to legal types of behavior control, there are also informal types of control. Examples of informal include attempts by the medical profession to curb "unprofessional" behavior on the part of its members, such as advertising and practicing medicine in a prepayment setting. These so-called unprofessional activities have been policed at the local level by county medical societies. Until recently, membership in the local county society was frequently required for a physician to have a full- or part-time position in a hospital (Kessell 1958). Not having an association with a hospital could be financially damaging to physicians who practiced in any of a large number of specialties. Recently, the legality of such sanctions has been called into question, since they appear to be violations of antitrust law. However, whereas formal anticompetitive practices can be dealt with by law, informal ones are more difficult to curb.

Since the existing staff determine who is to have hospital privileges, physicians who behave in a manner considered unprofessional can be denied privileges without resort to legal means. In addition, they can be denied referrals by their colleagues. Since referrals constitute a large portion of business for specialists, the loss of referrals can be very damaging. As a result, physicians have generally refrained from competitive behavior and may continue to do so despite the absence of any formal mechanisms to deter them.

14.2.4 Evaluating Regulation

14.2.4.1 Background

Legally sanctioned regulations have been instituted to ensure that the market operates to the benefit of consumers and taxpayers. In the 1970s, a number of studies were conducted, both in health care and other areas, and their results have created the general impression that regulations, no matter how well meant, are not always in the public interest. In this section we will summarize the economic impact of three sets of regulations: (1) regulations prohibiting professional advertising, (2) capital expenditure regulations, review, and (3) utilization review regulations. Our summary will take into account the goals of health policy: reduction of demand barriers, technical efficiency of suppliers, adequacy of supply, economic efficiency, high-quality care, and public expenditure control.

Prior to having been curbed on antitrust grounds, laws prohibiting competitive advertising in certain professions (medicine, optometry, and pharmacy) existed in many states. The bans covered the advertising of prices for specific products or services. The rationale given for these laws was that advertising was associated with unprofessional practices, including the provision of low-quality services and products. Whether or not this was true, advertising also has another effect. It increases the flow of information to individuals about the supply opportunities available and permits them to choose a source of supply on the basis of price and other supply characteristics. Advertising also encourages suppliers to actively seek out consumers by offering low prices and product characteristics that consumers tend to want. In essence, it encourages a bidding down of prices. Bans on advertising, on the other hand, permit suppliers to behave more like monopolists, because they obstruct the flow of information to consumers about alternative sources of supply. In a monopolistic market, there is a restriction of supply and greater barriers to demand (because of the higher prices). These two conditions result in economically inefficient market arrangements.

14.2.4.2 Restricted Advertising

A study was conducted on the effects of state laws on advertising for eyeglasses. The restrictions placed on advertising according to state laws varied considerably from state to state; they ranged from a total ban on advertising to unrestricted permission to advertise. Most states fell in between the two extremes. The study analyzed the affect of state restrictiveness on the price of eyeglasses, controlling for other factors that might cause demand to increase and thus cause prices to be higher (Benham 1972). The data on price and consumer characteristics (which might influence demand) were obtained from a nationwide survey on consumer expenditures on health services. Since consumers were identified by state, the data permitted a comparison of the prices paid for eyeglasses in different states. The results of the study showed a net positive relation between restrictiveness of advertising and price. States with a complete ban against advertising had an average price paid for eyeglasses of about $33, whereas in those states with no restrictions the average price paid was about $26. The study did not adjust for all factors (both on the demand and supply side) that might influence differences in price; the necessary data were not available. Nevertheless, the study provided a good first indication of one of the effects of advertising—that it pushes down prices.

14.2.4.3 Capital Expenditure Review

Excessive capital spending can result in technical inefficiency (higher costs), excess supply, excess product quality, and high public expenditures. Capital expenditure reviews were instituted to curb spending on capital equipment so that the expensive procedures performed with the equipment would not proliferate. A study of the actual effects of certificate-of-need laws (Salkever and Bice 1976) questioned whether these effects were achieved. Between 1968 and 1972, a considerable number of states required HSA approval for capital expenditure projects and a considerable number did not. This permitted an analysis of the effects on supplier behavior of capital expenditure review. The main purpose of certificate-of-need requirements was to restrict capital expansion to those projects that were "needed"; presumably all excessive expenditures would be stopped, and the net increase in new capital stock would decline. As a result, in terms of our cost curve analysis (Section 5.4), the upward shift in cost curves (i.e., for care with excessively high technology) would be slowed, and unit costs would not increase as rapidly as when no capital review was performed.

The study examined two categories of investment: the increase in the number of beds and the dollar amount of investment per bed. The method of analysis was to separate those states that did have certificate-of-need requirements for new investment from those that did not; to control for other factors that might influence the volume of investment in these states, such as the demand for care and the availability of capital funds; and then to determine the net influence of these laws on differences in investment among states. The results of the study showed that the existence of capital review procedures had a deterrent effect on the number of new beds created (bed capacity). Given that bed overcapacity has been a problem in recent years, the associated public goal was elimination of unneeded beds. The net effect of certificate-of-need laws was in conformity with this goal.

In addition, capital expenditure review was positively associated with the amount of new investment per bed. More investment per bed means more equipment of presumably an advanced level of technology and thus higher quality care (interpreted as more technology-based care). An increase in the amount of equipment per bed is associated with greater technical efficiency or higher quality (more intensive services), but the intent of the law was to limit hospital investment and thereby contain hospital costs. In terms of this intent, the law was not successful. The net effect on public expenditure control is in doubt; fewer beds leads to a favorable outcome while more investment per bed leads to a negative one. On average, the results of this study did not create a great deal of public confidence in capital expenditure review as a means of containing cost.

14.2.4.4 Utilization Review

Analyses of PSRO activities have indicated that there have been some resulting reductions in inappropriate care (Schwartz 1981). Quality is likely to have gone up. The effect of the program on hospital expenditures is uncertain. An earlier Congressional Budget Office review (United States Congress 1979) concluded that there were no net savings from the program. However, more recent studies of utilization review in private insurance plans (Feldstein et al. 1988; Wickizer et al. 1989) indicate that insured groups in plans with utilization review have substantially lower hospital admission rates and hospital expenditures per insured than groups in plans with no utilization review. The net savings amounted to 7 percent overall and 24 percent for groups who initially had higher costs. While similar studies for PROs have yet to be released, studies such as these indicate that utilization review could have cost-saving implications in the public sector as well.

14.2.4.5 Summary

Studies of the major types of regulation discussed above have raised doubts as to whether they helped attain the social goals they were intended to achieve. It should be noted that the studies were conducted in an atmosphere (in the early 1980s) that was unsympathetic to regulation in general as a means of achieving economic policy goals. Given the negative view of regulation, explanations were sought for what was alleged to be a systematic failure of regulation.

One such explanation put forth was that regulation occurs in an environment in which it might be expected to operate systematically, at least at times, in the interests of the suppliers. The basic theory is that regulation is an integral part of the marketplace rather than the activity of independent, impassive regulators who are enforcing consumer-oriented rules of the game. According to this view, regulations can be bought and sold just like medical care and pharmaceuticals. Thus, by changing the rules of the game the governance of the market can be changed, but this is not automatically done in the interests of the consumer. The market will be altered to benefit the "buyers" of the new rules. This approach to regulation might be regarded as the political economy view of regulation.

14.3   POLITICAL ECONOMY OF THE HEALTH CARE MARKETPLACE

In this section we examine the alternative theory of regulatory activity: that this activity is the outcome of a complex series of exchanges between producers, consumers, politicians, and regulators. In a sense, this theory regards the political process as a type of market process in which participants, if the terms of exchange are right, can "purchase" from politicians laws or regulations that have a favorable impact on the purchasers' incomes. If the theory is correct, an important task is to examine the exchanges between the various participants in the political marketplace and identify the conditions under which specific exchanges favoring a particular group will occur.

14.3.1 Flows in the Political Marketplace

Figure 14–3 presents a simplified picture of the participants in a political marketplace. Incorporated in this diagram are the consumers and producers in a commodity market and their exchange of money and services. In this figure, unlike in Figures 14–1 and 14–2, there is no group outside the circle. This is because the political system, rather than viewed as a watchdog guarding the consumers' interests, is regarded as an integral part of the mechanism by which prices, quantities, and levels of quality are set. In Figure 14–3 the legislators are drawn inside the circle, and the regulators (to some extent, employees of the politicians) are also included inside the circle; the commodity marketplace has become politicized.

We can now look at the dimensions of self-interest of each of the four groups in our simplified system (i.e., what they can gain from the system and what they can offer other participants in return). The first group, the politicians, maintain their positions in office by obtaining a sufficient number of votes. Their efforts at election and reelection are aided by campaign contributions from consumer and producer groups. In return for this support, politicians can supply sympathetic legislation and regulation favoring the interests of the supporting groups. (Politicians can also supply publicly provided goods, such as fire protection services; public health services; subsidized services, such as medical care; and money payments, such as welfare payments and subsidies to producers.)

Consumers can obtain benefits through the political system from the consumption of publicly provided or subsidized commodities and services, from money transfers, and from low prices caused by strict (consumer-oriented) regulation. Their participation in the political system includes bearing some of the costs of operating the public system (this takes the form of taxes). The main types of payment that consumers can offer politicians for beneficial packages of politically provided services and regulations are votes and campaign contributions.

Providers or suppliers of commodities can gain from the system subsidies (e.g., government scholarships and subsidized loans for medical students), contracts for work provided for the public sector (e.g., Medicare and Medicaid payments), and favorable regulations and laws that enable prices and profits to be maintained at high levels and that restrict competition. Providers are also, like consumers, subject to taxes that help to finance the activities of the political system. The main

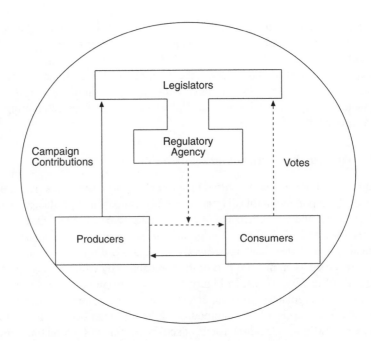

Figure 14–3 Picture of the expanded, politicized marketplace. Producers and consumers both may purchase credentialing and regulatory benefits from legislators via the political process, which is viewed as an integral part of the market mechanism. The dashed line from producers to consumers represents a service flow, and the solid line from consumers to producers represents a money flow. The dotted line from the regulatory agency represents regulatory influence, and the dotted line from consumers to legislators represents votes.

way providers can reimburse politicians for the favorable mix of political services and regulations is by making substantial campaign contributions. (Though they are voters, providers usually do not form large voting blocs.)

Regulators are appointed full-time employees of regulatory commissions. Their appointments are usually for fixed terms (e.g., three to five years). The main benefits regulators can obtain are expanded budgets and wider mandates for their agencies and good future job prospects for themselves. The former types of benefits can be obtained from the political system. Since the budgets for regulatory commissions come from legislative appropriations, regulators can offer satisfactory performance as a type of payback to their employers, the legislators. Job prospects for regulators may come from the civil service or from the industry being regulated. It is not uncommon for regulators to work for regulated industries once their terms of office have been completed.

14.3.2 Political Exchanges

Given the potential benefits and costs each group can gain and the costs it can incur from participating in the system, we now seek to explain what exchanges will likely occur in the political marketplace. We assume that all participants will follow the net benefit principle: In participating in political exchanges, they pursue their own self-interest and attempt to obtain the maximum net benefits possible from the system. Even though all participants would like to obtain favorable bundles of commodities and taxes and favorable regulations, conditions are such that some groups will be in a better position than others to obtain favorable bundles. Let us make the assumption that it is costly for an individual to participate actively in the political marketplace because of the resources (including time) needed to make his or her preferences known to the politicians, to organize blocs of voters to obtain some bargaining advantages, to make contributions, and so on. The costliness of participation varies across groups, and so some individuals or groups are more likely to bargain and strike a deal with politicians than are others.

With this perspective, we can identify two pertinent factors that influence exchanges between beneficiaries and politicians. The first is the cost of organizing a group that will bargain with the politicians of one of the political parties. The second is the incidence of the costs resulting from the exchanges made. Regarding the first factor, the costs of organizing involve identifying those individuals with similar interests, organizing these individuals into a group, bargaining for benefits with politicians, paying campaign contributions, and sharing the benefits from the system. It has frequently been asserted that the costs of organizing are substantially lower for producers than for consumers because it is very easy for producers to recognize common areas of interest and because there are fewer of them and hence it is less costly for them to reach an agreement. To the extent that this is true, producers will be more successful in obtaining favorable regulations than will consumers.

The second factor concerns the burden of providing these benefits and the manner in which the burden is borne. If one group, say a producer group, obtains favorable regulations (e.g., regulations that reduce competition and increase prices), the consumers of the industry's output will bear the cost of these regulations (e.g., by paying higher prices). If the cost is not clearly traceable to the regulations, the politicians clearly have more leeway to offer the producers regulations that lead to higher prices and profits. This is certainly true in the case of licensing, where the effect of licensing on quantities supplied (it lowers them) and on prices and producer profits (it raises them) is not clear to the consumers. The profits obtained from licensing may be considerable because of the high prices caused by restrictions on supply, but the consumers may not draw the link between high prices and licensing (and they may even applaud the protection from low-quality care that they obtain).

The role of the consumers in the political system provides a check on how far many types of political exchanges can go. They sometimes feel the effects of these exchanges, such as higher prices or taxes. When the consumers pay higher taxes, they can more directly trace the cause back to the political exchanges than when paying higher prices for regulated services. The recent interest in cost containment shown by the federal government with regard to the health care sector is associated with the major role that the federal government now plays in financing medical care. The large increases in health care costs that have occurred in recent years have a direct impact on federal taxpayers and are a source of concern to federal lawmakers. The ability of taxpayers to transfer their votes to more cost-conscious politicians has certainly placed a brake on a number of federal programs.

14.3.3 Explaining Regulatory Patterns

Some of the failures of regulation discussed in Section 14.2.4 are not mysterious when viewed in a self-interest rather than a public interest light. For example, we noted the failure of capital expenditure reviews to reduce the amount of investment per bed. At the same time, these reviews did curb new bed capacity. A political-marketplace explanation for these phenomena has been offered. Capital expenditure reviews were (and, in some states, still are) conducted by local review agencies with voluntary boards, and some of the members of these boards represented existing suppliers. If these agencies did become captives of supplier groups (i.e., hospitals), they might be expected to restrict competition by preventing new suppliers from entering the market. Their restriction of competition would show up in the stability in the number of beds. However, the agencies would not be expected to curtail the investment of existing suppliers. If these suppliers wanted to invest in higher-quality facilities rather than more bed capacity, investment per bed would not be restricted.

This analysis is merely an extension of the assumption of self-interest to all participants of the marketplace. What the political-economy approach does, in a sense, is to enlarge the marketplace. Still in the picture are providers and consumers, of course. But also in the picture are all participants whose efforts affect indirectly the demand and supply positions of the commodities in question. This includes those lawmakers and regulators who are in a position to impose (at a price) better terms for demanders or suppliers. Which group will be favored will depend on a number of factors, including the political benefits from using the political system and the costs of doing so. What is clear is that the outcome in the wider market system, in terms of quantity, cost, distribution of outputs, and so on, cannot automatically be assumed to meet the social goals of the system. However, it should also be noted that some types of regulation, most notably utilization review, have survived the antiregulation movement of the 1980s. The persistence of these types calls for further exploration into whether conditions might exist under which regulations would contribute to achieving health policy goals.

BIBLIOGRAPHY

Regulation: General

Avellone, J.C., and Moore, F.D. 1978. The Federal Trade Commission enters a new era. *New England Journal of Medicine* 299:478–483.

Dittman, D., and Peters, J.A. 1977. A foundation for health care regulation. *Inquiry* 14:32–41.

Posner, R.A. 1971. Regulatory aspects of national health insurance plans. *University of Chicago Law Review* 39:1–29.

Schwartz, W.B. 1981. The regulation strategy for controlling hospital costs. *New England Journal of Medicine* 305:1249–1255.

Regulation: Prospective Reimbursement

Anderson, G., and Ginsburg, P.B. 1983. Prospective capital payments to hospitals. *Health Affairs* 2:52–63.

Anderson, G., and Lave, J.R. 1984. State rate setting programs: Do they regard efficiency in hospitals? *Medical Care* 22:494–498.

Biles, B., et al. 1980. Hospital cost inflation under state rate-setting programs. *New England Journal of Medicine* 303:664–668.

Coelen, C., and Sullivan, D. 1981. An analysis of the effects of prospective reimbursement programs on hospital expenditures. *Health Care Financing Review* 2 (winter):1–40.

Cromwell, J., and Kanak, J. 1982. The effects of prospective reimbursement programs on hospital adoption and service sharing. *Health Care Financing Review* 4 (winter):67–88.

Detsky, A.S., et al. 1983. The effectiveness of a regulatory strategy in containing hospital costs. *New England Journal of Medicine* 309:151–159.

Farnand, L.J., et al. 1986. An evaluation of a program to regulate rural hospital costs: The Finger Lakes Hospital Experimental Payment Program. *Inquiry* 23:200–208.

Guterman, S., and Dobson, A. 1986. Impact of the Medicare prospective payment system for hospitals. *Health Care Financing Review* 7 (summer):97–114.

Hellinger, F.J. 1981. Recent evidence on case-based systems for setting hospital rates. *Inquiry* 22:78–91.

Rosko, M.D., and Broyles, R.W. 1986. The impact of the New Jersey all-payer DRG system. *Inquiry* 23:67–75.

Salkever, D.S., et al. 1986. Hospital cost and efficiency under per service and per case payment in Maryland. *Inquiry* 23:55–66.

Warner, K.E. 1978. Effects of hospital cost containment on the development and use of medical technology. *Milbank Quarterly* 56:187–211.

Worthington, N., and Piro, P. 1982. The effects of hospital rate setting programs on volumes of hospital services. *Health Care Financing Review* 4 (winter):47–66.

Regulations: Other

Benham, L. 1972. The effect of advertising on the price of eyeglasses. *Journal of Law and Economics* 4:337–352.

Christianson, J.B. 1979. Long-term standards: Enforcement and compliance. *Journal of Health Politics, Policy, and Law* 4:414–434.

Cohen, H.S. 1973. Professional licensure, organizational behavior, and the public interest. *Milbank Quarterly* 51:73–88.

Feldstein, P.J. 1977. *Health associations and the demand for legislation.* Cambridge, Mass.: Ballinger.

Feldstein, P.J., et al. 1988. The effects of utilization review programs on health care use and expenditures. *New England Journal of Medicine* 318:1310–1314.

Havighurst, C.C. 1978. Professional restraints on innovation in health care. *Duke Law Journal* 1978:304–385.

Hellinger, F.J. 1976. The effect of certificate of need legislation on hospital investment. *Inquiry* 13:187–193.

Joskow, P.L. 1981. *Controlling hospital costs.* Cambridge, Mass.: MIT Press.

Kessell, R. 1958. Price discrimination in medicine. *Journal of Law and Economics* 1:20–35.

Lave, J.R., and Leinhardt, S. 1976. An evaluation of a hospital stay regulatory mechanism. *American Journal of Public Health* 66:959–967.

Salkever, D., and Bice, T. 1976. The impact of certificate of need controls on hospital investment. *Milbank Quarterly* 54:185–214.

Shepard, L. 1978. Licensing restrictions and the cost of dental care. *Journal of Law and Economics* 21:187–201.

U.S. Congress. 1979. *The effects of PSRO's on health care costs.* Washington, D.C.: Congressional Budget Office.

U.S. Department of Health and Human Services. 1980. *Professional standards review organizations: 1979 program evaluation.* Baltimore: Health Care Financing Administration, 1980.

U.S. General Accounting Office. 1988. *Medicare: Improving quality of care assessment and assurance.* Publ. no. GAO/PE MD-88-10. Washington, D.C.: Government Accounting Office.

White, W.D. 1979. Why is regulation introduced in the health sector? A look at occupational licensure. *Journal of Health Politics, Policy, and Law* 4:536–552.

Wickizer, T.M., et al. 1989. Does utilization review reduce unnecessary hospital care and contain costs? *Medical Care* 27:632–647.

CHAPTER 15

Economic Measurement: Cost-Benefit and Cost-Effectiveness Analysis

15.1 INTRODUCTION

In earlier chapters we saw that market forces, left to themselves, do not necessarily lead to the "right amount" of medical care being utilized. Whether the amount actually produced is greater or less than the right amount depends on two things: how the market is operating and the criteria we use to measure the amount produced. As demonstrated in Chapter 10, the special characteristics of the commodity medical care, coupled with widespread third-party financing, make this market ripe for an overproduction of quality of care. On the other hand, as shown in Chapter 12, the care received by some individuals may be judged as too little.

We can hardly presume that health policy reforms will automatically correct matters. In some cases (e.g., licensure), policies intended to restrict output will be overly restrictive and unbalance the market in the opposite direction.

In this chapter we examine one tool used to measure the economic efficiency of medical care. This tool, termed *cost-benefit analysis*, provides separate measures of the economic costs and benefits of various projects and programs and permits one to determine for any level of output whether further expansion or contraction of services will yield additional net benefits or losses. It should be stressed that, in making a recommendation based on cost-benefit analysis, one is accepting the goal of efficiency as preeminent. If some other goal (e.g., fairness of distribution) overrides the goal of efficiency, cost-benefit analysis will not allow one to determine the "right" amount of medical care.

The value that people place on *medical services* varies depending on their circumstances and also on the physicians' ability to stimulate consumer wants. If individual valuations of medical care are subject to physician-induced shifts, the question "What value do consumers place on medical care?" may well be unanswerable. In fact, as the value placed on medical care shifts, the cost-benefit ratio will also shift. Because there would be no unique measure of the benefits of medical care, cost-benefit analysis would be unreliable even if we accepted the goal of efficiency.

There may be a way out of this quandary, however. Medical services are required for the restoration and maintenance of life and health. Doctors may be able to influence patients' valuation of these services by convincing them that the services are required to maintain health. It is less likely that doctors can influence consumer attitudes toward life and health. If this is the case and if these more basic sources of benefit have some degree of stability, perhaps we can find the measure of constancy we are seeking in terms of the basic entity *health*. We could then measure the outcome of medical and health care services in terms of the costs and benefits of obtaining health.

This chapter proceeds along these lines. We begin in Section 15.2 with a brief sample cost-benefit analysis. In cost-benefit evaluations there are a number of rather knotty measurement problems that, while not always accommodated in a study, should certainly be acknowledged. These problems are discussed in Section 15.3. In Section 15.4 we discuss cost-effectiveness analysis, a technique that allows one to compare the costs and outcomes of two or more alternative interventions, though it does not address the question of whether or not the intervention should be undertaken at all.

15.2   A SIMPLE COST-BENEFIT ANALYSIS

Cost-benefit analysis involves comparing the benefits of an intervention in dollar terms with the dollar value of the cost of the resources that were used in the intervention. The dollar value of cost measures what it would take to attract the resources away from a competing use. Indirectly, costs reflect the value of resources in those competing uses, and so the benefit to cost ratio is a relative measure of the value of resources in the present use compared with those in a competing use. Cost-benefit analysis, then, addresses the question of whether resources are of more value in one use than in another; that is, it addresses the question of whether the intervention is worth the effort.

For our simple example, imagine a government program designed to immunize individuals in a certain region. With a zero level of immunization, there are 500 illnesses annually. Each illness is assumed to impose a cost of $30 on the patient as viewed by the patient. These costs can be measured in terms of direct costs (medical care) and indirect cost (pay lost from missed work); pain and suffering are not assumed to be costs but outcomes. For the illness-reducing effect of levels of immunization, see Table 15–1. Immunizing the first 1,000 people reduces total illness by 100, bringing the number of illnesses to 400. Immunizing the next 1,000

Table 15–1 Data for Cost-Benefit Analysis of Community Immunizations

Number of Immunizations	Total Cost	Total Number of Illnesses	Marginal Cost of Immunizations	Net Reduction in Illnesses	Money Value of Reduction in Illnesses	Benefit-Cost Ratio
0	$1,000	500				
1,000	3,000	400	$2,000	100	$3,000	3:2
2,000	5,000	325	2,000	75	2,250	2.25:2
3,000	7,000	275	2,000	50	1,500	1.5:2
4,000	9,000	250	2,000	25	750	75:2
5,000	11,000	235	2,000	15	450	45:2

people reduces the level of illness by 75, bringing the number to 325. The next 1,000 immunizations further reduce the number of illnesses by 50, and so forth. Note that we are assuming a diminishing marginal effect from immunizations in terms of reducing illness. In Table 15-1 the total number of illnesses is shown in Column 3; the additional reduction in illness associated with each extra 1,000 immunizations is shown in Column 5; and the money value of the reduction in illness, our "benefits," is shown in Column 6. Column 6 values are obtained by multiplying Column 5 values by $30, which is the money value of losses per episode of illness.

The resources used in the provision of immunizations include a building owned by the government, a nurse whose hourly wage translates into $1 per shot, and drugs and supplies that cost an additional $1 per shot. The additional cost per shot is thus $2, and thus the variable costs for 1,000 shots equal $2,000, for 2,000 shots they equal $4,000, and so on. The total cost measures the total resource commitment made by the government in providing the services, including the use of the building. We will assume that the government could have rented out the building for $1,000, and we will use this as a measure of the economic cost of the building space. The total cost at various levels of immunization is shown in Column 2, and additional or incremental costs of each extra 1,000 shots are shown in Column 4.

Given these figures, two benefit-cost ratios can be calculated: a *total* benefit-cost ratio for each level of output and a *marginal* benefit-cost ratio calculated for any movement from one level to the next. Let us look, for example, at these ratios when 1,000 immunizations have been given. In this case, the total benefit-cost ratio is shown by total benefits created divided by total costs incurred: This is $3,000 / $3,000 (for a ratio of 1:1). The project breaks even at this level of output. Using the marginal benefit-cost ratio, the project can be shown to be cost beneficial at a level of output of 1,000 immunizations. This ratio shows the ratio of additional benefits to additional costs from producing 1,000 immunizations rather than producing none. Given that the building costs are already committed and thus fixed, the marginal costs are $2,000 and the marginal benefit-cost ratio (Column 7) is 3:2. An additional 1,000 immunizations beyond this would yield a marginal benefit-cost ratio of 2.25:2.00, which is still in excess of a ratio of 1:1 (the ratio where additional benefits equal additional costs). The third 1,000 immunizations have a marginal benefit-cost ratio of under 1:1, indicating a net social loss from expanding to a level of 3,000. Thus, the right number of immunizations is 2,000.

In identifying 2,000 immunizations as the right quantity of output, we are identifying an ideal or optimal quantity rather than an actual one. In fact, the actual quantity produced may be greater or less than the ideal or efficient quantity. For example, if the reimbursement of physicians is such that they have no incentives to offer immunizations, then, in the absence of a public health effort, very few immunizations will be provided. The actual quantity will be less than the optimal one. On the other hand, if the public health department has gotten the legislature to make immunization mandatory, 5,000 or more immunizations will be provided. From an efficiency standpoint, this is too many and would show up in the marginal benefit-cost ratio, which would be less than 1:1.

15.3 INFORMATION REQUIREMENTS AND MEASUREMENT PROBLEMS

The previous example presents an overall picture of cost-benefit analysis. The next step in our exposition is to examine in more detail the informational requirements and some of the major measurement problems in conducting such an analysis.

15.3.1 Information Requirements

Figure 15–1 summarizes the data requirements for a cost-benefit analysis in the health field. To begin with, we have the scarce resources (medical personnel and equipment) that can produce medical care, such as hospital treatment. The relation between the inputs and the throughputs (medical care) is called the *production relation*. It measures how productive the resource inputs are in producing medical care. Medical care is referred to as a throughput rather than an output because it is not regarded as the goal. The second relation is between medical care activity and the level of health. This relation, referred to as the *effectiveness relation*, measures how effective medical care is. Determining the nature of this relation is beyond the scope of economists and is usually done by medical researchers.

The two relations together form the link between resource use and health (i.e., the link measures how effective resources are in producing health). Note that resources can be ineffective because they are not used productively, the treatments produced have no influence on health, or both.

Recall that generally it is the incremental or marginal relation that is of concern to us, that is, how much more health can be produced with an extra unit of resources. We move next to the valuation process, that is, determining the worth to society of an extra unit of health. When this is done, we have a measure of the social benefits attributable to changes in the health status of the community members.

These benefits must be compared with the opportunity costs of the project to obtain a benefit-cost ratio. Strictly speaking, the opportunity costs are the benefits given up by not using the resources in the highest valued alternative use. The amount is often calculated by adding by the money cost of the paid resources and the imputed cost of the unpaid resources (see Section 15.3.4).

A complete cost-benefit analysis requires that all the preceding information be available, which is seldom the case. Because of this, a less demanding sort of analysis, cost-effectiveness analysis, has become popular. Cost-effectiveness

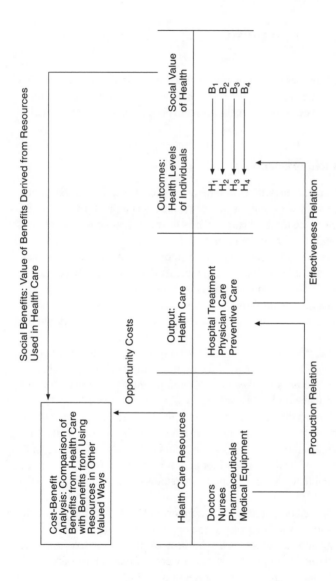

Figure 15–1 Outline of information requirements for a cost-benefit analysis of health services. A complete cost-benefit analysis involves tracing through the effectiveness of resources in producing health, evaluating the health output, and determining the opportunity costs of the resources.

studies examine the cost-output relation between alternative ways of using resources (e.g., treating kidney failure or preventing heart attacks). These studies stop short of comparing alternative objectives by placing money values on these objectives. Only a cost-benefit analysis will allow one to compare the net social value of alternative goals. By choosing broader objectives, it does become possible to compare interventions for different purposes. A number of evaluational problems must be surmounted before obtaining true cost-benefit calculations. The remainder of this section discusses some of the major problems.

15.3.2 Production Relation

The production relation represents how productive the inputs are in producing medical care. As seen in Section 1.4.1, the measurement of physician and hospital services must deal with the fact that these services vary considerably in quality, which is difficult to measure. The production relation must take this quality variance into account so as not to have technologically sophisticated medical care (resource intensive by its very nature) appear unproductive.

15.3.3 Effectiveness

To determine the relation between one variable and another, clear definitions and measures are required for both variables. As shown in Chapter 1, there is neither an unambiguous definition nor a standard measure of health. Also, numerous potential factors might influence the health of a patient in addition to medical treatment. These include the predisposition of the patient to recover on his or her own and the environment in which the care is administered. The absence of a well-defined effectiveness relation means that a key piece of information for determining the cost-benefit ratio will be missing (Cochrane 1972). Methods of determining effectiveness include the use of controlled randomized clinical trials and of large databases containing information about patients who have utilized alternative services (Drummond and Davies 1991; Simes and Glasziou 1992).

15.3.4 Opportunity Cost and Money Cost

As discussed in Section 5.3.1, the money cost is the actual payout to a resource whereas the opportunity cost is the money measure of the commitment of the resource (whether or not the resource is paid). The opportunity cost is equal to what the resource could earn in its highest valued alternative use. If, as assumed, what consumers would pay the resource in this alternative use is a reflection of what the resource is worth to them, using the opportunity cost allows us to obtain a measure of what the resource would be worth in its next highest valued use. In many circumstances, the money cost is a good approximation of the opportunity cost; that is, what resources earn in their present use and would earn in their next highest valued use are roughly the same.

To identify a resource's opportunity cost, we must first identify what the resource's highest valued alternative use is. This is by no means an easy task. Take, as an example, a radiologist in Green Bay, Wisconsin, who earns $60 an hour. If she were not practicing radiology in her particular clinic, what would the highest valued alternative be? Would she still be in medicine but in some other specialty or community? Would she work as a dentist or lawyer? There are no easy answers to these questions. Indeed, one of the most difficult tasks of evaluation economics is to identify what the resources could be doing in alternative uses. One of the main determining factors of a resource's alternative use is the time allowed for the resource to adjust to the alternative use. If our time horizon is three years, the radiologist might well retrain and become a pathologist. Her opportunity cost in such a case might be what she could earn as a pathologist. On the other hand, if we are speaking about a horizon of several months, the radiologist's highest-valued alternative may be a position as a radiologist somewhere else.

Let us assume that we are talking about the short run and that the radiologist's highest valued alternative is a position as a radiologist in a Chicago hospital where she would earn $60 an hour. This is the radiologist's opportunity cost, and in this case it equals her money cost.

There are instances when money cost will not equal opportunity cost. The money cost will be a poor guide to the opportunity cost if the resources are underpaid or are unpaid. If the radiologist donated her time for free, the money cost is zero; if we valued her resource input at zero, we would be underestimating the value of the resources used. In this case, we would use the opportunity cost as the measure of the resource commitment. Other cases where money cost falls below opportunity cost occur when buildings or equipment are donated or used but not costed.

Sometimes resources may be overvalued when measured by their money costs. Suppose Wisconsin radiologists were successful in having a law passed that placed strict limit on the number of radiologists who could practice in the state. This might drive prices up, and the radiologist in our example might be able to get $80 in Green Bay and only $60 in Chicago. In this case, the money price would be too high a measure of the resource's opportunity cost.

15.3.5 Benefits and Costs Accruing in the Future Periods

Until now, our analysis has considered only current period costs and benefits. In fact, many types of health program benefits occur in future. An individual saved by an intensive care program for heart attack victims may obtain benefits lasting a number of years.

To evaluate future benefits and costs, two things must be recognized: (1) they need to be evaluated from the perspective of the current period and (2) they need to be discounted to account for the individual's valuations of these benefits and costs. Actually, benefits are valued as of a specific point in time (say, at the end or the beginning of a time period) rather than for an entire period.

For example, when a program for 1997 is proposed, the benefits are considered as if they were all occurring at the beginning of 1997. If the beneficiaries of a heart attack program are told that benefits will occur through 2003, the benefits for 1997, 1998, and so on, are *valued* as of the beginning of 1997. (For simplicity's sake, we assume that the benefits occur on the last day of each year, 1990, 1991, etc.) That is, if $10,000 in benefits will result from the program in 1997, they will be valued at what the individual thinks they are worth to her or him on December 31, 1997. (The benefits occurring during 1997, it should be noted, are valued as if they were to occur at the end of 1997 rather than equally throughout 1997. This convention is used to simplify calculations.)

It is generally assumed that $1,000 in current benefits will be worth more to an individual than $1,000 in benefits one year from now. The value of the preference for earlier over later periods can be expressed in terms of the discount rate, called r. If an individual is asked how much money he or she would want at the end of 1997 in order to forgo $1,000 at the beginning of 1997, the person might take $1,100 at the end of the period. In other words, $1,000 on January 1, 1997, would be worth as much as $1,100 one year later. The discount rate is .1, and the equivalency of values it brings about can be expressed as $1,000 \times (1 + .1) = $1,100, or symbolically as $1,000 \times (1 + r) = $1,100. This may be rewritten as $1,000 = $1,100/(1 + r)$. This equation says that, in the individual's eyes, $1,100 one year hence will be equivalent to $1,100/(1 + r)$, or $1,000, now. The discount rate for an individual is derived largely from introspection—from a feeling of comfort with a trade-off between future amounts and lesser current amounts.

The same principle holds for comparisons between December 31, 1997, and December 31, 1998. That is, $1,000 at the end of 1997 is equivalent to $1,100 at the end of 1998 if the individual's discount rate is .10. By inference, then, 1,000 at the end of 1998 would be worth $1,000/[(1 + r) \times (1 + r)]$ on January 1, 1997 (also expressible as $1,000/(1 + r)^2$). Similarly, $1,000 on December 31, 1999, would be worth $1,000/(1 + r)^3$ at the start of 1997, and so on. Generally, improved health or added life yields a stream of benefits. That is, a saved life on January 1, 1997 will yield benefits in 1997 (valued as of December 31, 1997), 1998 (valued as of December 31, 1998), 1999 (valued as of December 31, 1999), and so on. If the benefits are $2,000 each year, the *present* value of future benefits can be expressed as

$2,000 + 2,000/(1 + r) + 2,000 / (1 + r)^2$, and so on, for as long as benefits last. The letter usually used to symbolize the annual benefits is B, with subscripts $0, 1, 2, \ldots$ for right now (0), one year hence (1), two years hence (2), and so on. In our present example, $B_0 = B_1 = B_2$, and the present value of benefits can be expressed symbolically as

$$B_0 + \frac{B_1}{(1 + r)} + \frac{B_2}{(1 + r)^2}$$

If the number of years that benefits will last is quite large and the value of the benefits for every year is the same, the present value of the benefits can be expressed as B_0/r. If benefits of $10,000 a year will last forever and if the discount rate is .10, the present value of these benefits will be 10,000/.10, or $100,000. Benefits lasting for long periods can be approximated using this formula.

The present-value formula tells us what a discounted stream of benefits is presently worth. The same formula can be applied to value costs. If C_0, C_1, and C_2 are costs of a program for the periods 0, 1, and 2, and the discount rate is i, the present value of costs is

$$C_0 + \frac{C_1}{(1 + i)} + \frac{C_2}{(1 + i)^2}$$

Note that i is used as the discount rate for costs and r for benefits. This is merely to bring out the point that the benefits may be accruing to individuals other than those who bore the costs and that these individuals may have different discount rates. In practice, we seldom make this distinction, and so we will use r as the discount rate both for beneficiaries of a program and for those who suffer the costs.

The equation used to summarize the cost-benefit ratio of a project, that is, to compare costs and benefits, is the net present value (NPV) equation, which measures the net difference between the present values of costs and of benefits. This is expressed for a three-period evaluation as

$$NPV = B_0 + \frac{B_1}{(1 + r)} + \frac{B_2}{(1 + r)^2} - C_0 - \frac{C_1}{(1 + i)} - \frac{C_2}{(1 + i)^2}$$

Given the extension of benefits and costs of a program into future periods, the analyst is faced with the problem of assigning an appropriate discount rate to the net present-value equation. Controversy exists over which rate to employ. If we believe that market interest rates clearly reflect supply and demand forces for savings and investment, it can be argued that at current levels of savings (e.g., transforming present into future wealth through bonds and mortgages), the market interest rate is an expression of the marginal consumer's discount rate. On the basis of this reasoning, the interest rate in the market for riskless bonds (e.g., most government bonds) expresses the discount rate of consumers and can be used as a discount rate for the evaluation of riskless projects, that is, those whose return is certain. For more risky projects, a higher discount rate, one incorporating a risk premium, should be used. There is a complication, however. The market interest rate reflects the discount rates of present consumers at present saving levels. The preferences of future generations are not incorporated into the picture. A generation of high-living, heavy-spending people may discount future benefits at a very high discount rate and may not care to preserve the environment for future generations or undertake projects that benefit future generations. If the benefits of future generations are to be taken into account, a lower discount rate than that which the present generation would choose in the absence of such consideration would have to be used. It has been argued that preventive programs, which are focused on longer term goals, should have lower discount rates.

An advocate of this viewpoint might place the discount rate choice in the hands of the government, which presumably would act as arbiter between the resource demands of present and future generations. However, the government can hardly be considered an impartial party. If the bureaucrats and technicians who heavily influence government decisions act to any degree in their own self-interest, they would choose a rate that is as low as possible. The reason for this is that, at low discount rates, future benefits will be valued higher relative to present consumption. By using a low rate, more long-lasting projects will be justified on a cost-benefit basis, and hence an expansion of the bureaucracy will be better justified.

In the wake of such conflicting views, analysts have established the practice of taking a neutral position on the issue of discounting by calculating the net present value using several rates and letting the policy maker choose the appropriate one. The sensitivity of the NPV to alternative discount rates can be illustrated using an example. Assume that a health program costing $43,000 (all resources used are taken from current consumption), i.e., from consumption at time period yields benefits equal to $10,000 a year for five years, beginning in the current year. Note that benefits occurring during the first year are valued as of the end of the year (B_1) and so on. To determine if the program will yield greater benefits than costs, we must find an expression for the present-value equation. With $B_1 = B_2 = B_3 = B_4 = B_5 = \$10,000$, we can apply a discounting factor to find the present value of this benefit stream. The present value (PV) equation is

$$PV = \frac{B_1}{(1+r)} + \frac{B_2}{(1+r)2} + \frac{B_3}{(1+r)3} + \frac{B_4}{(1+r)4} + \frac{B_5}{(1+r)5}$$

The values of $(1 + r)$, $(1 + r)^2$, and so on, are shown in Part A of Table 15–2 for three alternative discount rates: a low rate of 4 percent, a middle rate of 8 percent, and a high rate of 12 percent. Applying these rates to B_1, B_2, B_3, and B_4, yields the values shown in Part B of Table 15–2. The present value of the income stream is $46,298 using the low rate, $43,232 using the middle rate, and $40,839 using the high rate. Notice how the total present value of the stream falls as future benefits are given less importance (i.e., the rates of discount are higher). To determine whether the program would yield positive net benefits, we must calculate the NVP. Given that C_0 equals $43,000, the NVP is positive at a .04 discount rate, just barely positive at a .08 rate, and negative at a .12 rate. The recommendation whether or not to undertake the program will depend on the discount rate used.

15.3.6 Measuring the Benefits from Survival and Better Health

By far the most widely espoused benefits to be obtained from increased survival and better health have been the added increments of working time that better health affords. A very convenient money measure of these benefits is the earnings made by the worker during the added healthy time. If the benefits from reduced illness or reduced death last longer than one year, the future benefits can be discounted with an appropriate discount rate.

Turning this measure around, one can use it to measure the indirect cost of illness or death. In this case, the economic cost of illness or death can be estimated as the discounted money value of work time lost. Since illness also results in medical treatment, we must add the direct costs of medical care to obtain a more complete measure of the burden of illness (Rice et al. 1985). This approach to the measurement of illness costs has been called the *human capital approach.*

The human capital cost is really a lower bound to the total economic burden of illness, even if we were only counting the private costs of illness (i.e., those borne by the afflicted or forgone by the deceased). Since illness or death is accompanied by pain and suffering, the avoidance of illness and death is accompanied by the avoidance of pain and suffering. The patient presumably would place a value on avoidance over and above the value of earnings gained and medical costs avoided. Additionally, individuals "lose" nonwork time due to illness; this concept is usually omitted from human capital measures. Finally, these measures ignore the value placed by others on the avoidance of death and illness. Family members and friends do value the good health that an individual experiences. Difficult as it may be to estimate this value, it must be added to private value for calculating the social values of health and survival.

Recently, a more unified approach has been developed to obtain a measure of the private benefits of increased survival. Such an approach examines the value people place on the probability of increased survival by looking at how they value saving a "statistical life" rather than a specific identified life. One virtue of this approach is that it creates a realistic context for decision making. For instance, a

Table 15–2 Calculation of Present Value of Benefits under Alternative Discount Rates

Part A: Discounting Factors

Discount Rate	$(1 + r)$	$(1 + r)^2$	$(1 + r)^3$	$(1 + r)^4$	$(1 + r)^5$
.04	1.04	1.08	1.12	1.17	1.22
.08	1.08	1.16	1.25	1.36	1.41
.12	1.12	1.25	1.41	1.57	1.63

Part B: Discounted Present Value of Benefits ($10,000)

Discount Rate	$B_1/(1 + r)$	$B_2/(1 + r)^2$	$B_3/(1 + r)^3$	$B_4/(1 + r)^4$	$B_5/(1 + r)^5$	Present Value (row sum)
.04	9,615	9,233	8,896	8,554	8,196	44,494
.08	9,259	8,620	8,000	7,353	7,092	40,324
.12	8,928	8,000	7,029	6,275	5,602	35,834

large number of resource-allocation decisions in the health field are impersonal and involve probabilities rather than certainty. When attempting to place a value on life and health, analysts originally pursued their task by asking people how much their lives were worth to them. This puts the issue in rather a dramatic light. There have been instances when life or death decisions have been placed in the hands of society or the medical profession. For example, in the early 1950s, "life and death committees" were established to ration lifesaving dialysis treatments. Furthermore, not all, or even most, life or death decisions are made in circumstances where the outcome is certain. Individuals who would offer their souls to avoid a certain death will behave in ways that merely increase their chances of drying or becoming ill, such as smoking, eating potentially hazardous foods, and working dangerous jobs. One can only conclude that, whereas facing certain death may be intolerable, activities that increase the risk of death are often considered acceptable. They are considered acceptable because the resulting gains in income or satisfaction exceed their costs.

The willingness-to-pay approach has been used to derive estimates of the money value of increased or reduced risks of illness or death. For example, assume that a perfectly riskless occupation, folding paper airplanes and packaging them, pays a wage of $400. A second occupation that is somewhat more risky, cleaning asbestos pipes, becomes available. We assume that the riskier occupation requires exactly the same skills as the riskless one and that 3 in every 1,000 asbestos workers eventually contract lung cancer but none of the airplane folders do. If the workers in the asbestos industry were aware of these risks and were still willing to accept them, provided that they were suitably compensated for doing so, the additional compensation they would accept, called a *risk premium*, would be a measure of the value of this extra risk. If the asbestos workers were willing to accept a wage of $450 a month, then, if all other factors were held constant, the wage differential would be a measure of the value they placed on this extra risk. This value will depend on several factors, including the degree to which the workers are risk averse and the size of the risk. For example, the greater the worker's adversity to risk is, the more utility will be gained from the safe alternative. The risk premium required to compensate the individual who is more risk averse would be greater.

Investigations have been undertaken to estimate the risk premiums in risky occupations as well as the amounts consumers are willing to pay for goods that reduce the probability of death, such as seat belts and fire alarms (Blomquist 1981). The results, when extrapolated to calculate a value per statistical life, show a wide variation in such values, ranging from $300,000 to $2.5 million. Despite the wide variation, there is a considerable usefulness in such studies. The value of benefits from many health-related projects and programs can be expressed as of the reduced likelihood of illness and death. Heart attack prevention programs, early disease detection programs, water and air purification programs, and work safety measures, among others, can all have their benefits measured in terms of the reduced likelihood of illness and death (Johanneson, Johansson, Kristrom, et al. 1993; Muller and Reutzel 1984; Thompson 1986; Viscusi 1993).

15.4 COST-EFFECTIVENESS ANALYSIS

15.4.1 Introduction

Frequently, situations arise where we want to evaluate the economic consequences of alternative courses of action but we do not wish to place values on life or health. For example, if we are treating a 70-year-old woman with no financial assets for a peptic ulcer, the results of the human capital and willingness-to-pay approaches may come up short on the benefits side. It may well be that on equity grounds we have decided to go ahead and treat her. Yet if alternative courses of treatment exist, we are still faced with an economic problem, that of choosing the least-cost alternative. The object of a cost-effectiveness analysis is to rank alternative treatments on the basis of cost per unit of output or outcome.

As seen in Section 1.3, there is no unique measure of health output. The measure of "life years saved" is only useful for treatments that save lives. But one can save a life (or a statistical life) and have the patient end up in a very undesirable state of health for the patient's remaining years. In such a case, the outcome will be qualitatively different from the same number of years of good health. Many treatments do not save lives but change the quality of life (i.e., improve health status).

Cost-effectiveness analysis and cost-utility analysis are two forms of analysis that have been developed to include evaluations of quality of life. Below is presented an overview of the elements of cost-effectiveness analysis.

15.4.2 The Cost-Effectiveness Ratio

The cost-effectiveness ratio can be expressed as follows:

$$\frac{(EC_2 - EC_1)}{(EQ_2 - EQ_1)}$$

In this expression, 1 and 2 refer to alternative interventions, EC is the expected cost of the interventions occurring between two prespecified end points, and EQ is the expected health status. Both costs and outcomes are expressed in terms of probabilities, because most interventions have uncertain outcomes. The expected cost of any intervention where there are two possible outcomes (a and b) equals $P_a \times C_a + P_b \times C_b$, where P_a and P_b are the probabilities that the outcomes will occur and C_a and C_b are the costs of the outcomes. Because a and b are the only possible outcomes, $P_a + P_b = 1$.

We will now consider a hypothetical cost-effectiveness analysis of alternative interventions in the treatment of osteoporosis, a condition that is largely found in older women and is characterized by low bone mass density (BMD). BMD typically depends on age, and we will assume a woman of age 60 on average has a BMD of .8 g/cm². Osteoporosis is defined in terms of deviations from the norm; it is usually expressed as 2.5 standard deviations below the norm. For the sake of simplicity, we will express the condition as occurring when the BMD measures .65 g/cm². Osteoporosis is associated with bone fractures and very occasionally with death resulting from bone fractures. We will focus on hip fractures, although other types of fractures, notably wrist and spinal fractures, do occur.

There is a class of drugs that can be used to treat osteoporosis. These drugs have been shown to be successful in increasing bone mass, and in reducing the number of fractures. The drugs are quite expensive, however, and although we know that they are "efficacious" in treating the disease (i.e., can work under ideal conditions), we do not know how "cost-effective" they are. The following example works through the steps required to find this out.

15.4.3 Specification of the Condition and Alternative Interventions

The cost-effectiveness analysis is to be developed for a particular illness or condition in conjunction with several specific interventions. In our example, the condition is osteoporosis, as defined above. The two interventions are treatment with the (fictitious) drug alenate and no preventive treatment at all.

15.4.4 Specification of the End Points

The end points of an evaluation study define the time frame during which the costs and effects are measured. A study can focus on clinical end points (e.g., when the condition is first detected) or events and points (e.g., death) and time end points (e.g., a specific point in time when patient's condition will be measured). There can also be a combination of the two (e.g., observations can be recorded at death or else on a certain date if the patient is still alive). In our example, our beginning end point will be when a patient is diagnosed as having osteoporosis (BMD ≤ 0.65). Our final end point will be a hip fracture (event) or three years after treatment was begun (time). We will not include mortality in this example, because it is a rare event in such treatments. The patient will be assumed to take the drug for three years.

It is often useful to set out the end points of a cost-effectiveness analysis in terms of a decision tree (see Figure 15–2). A decision tree is a graphic device that illustrates the various end points and events associated with alternative interventions. In Figure 15–2, choices are represented by squares and chances by circles. There is a choice whether to treat with alenate, then there is a chance that a hip

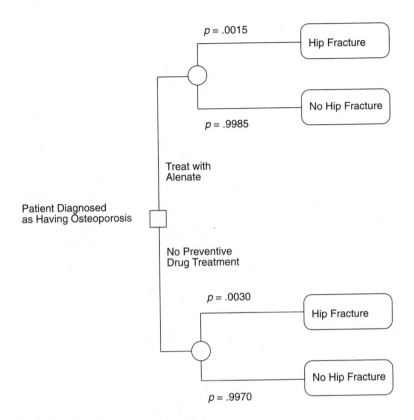

Figure 15–2 A decision tree for treatment of osteoporosis. In this figure we have the choice of two alternative interventions for osteoporosis, to treat with alenate or not to treat. In each case there are two possible outcomes—a hip fracture or no hip fracture. Probabilities associated with the alternatives are also presented.

fracture will occur. The end points are the discovery of osteoporosis and the occurrence of a fracture or the end of three years, whichever comes first.

15.4.5 Health Outcomes

Health status is measured at the end points. The difference between health status at the beginning and final end points is the outcome of each intervention. There are a variety of alternative measures that can be used to measure health status. Among these are clinical indicators, such as blood sugar level, patient weight, and cholesterol level. We could use a BMD measure as a clinical indicator but will not do so in this example.

Clinical measures are often considered inexact indicators of the effect of a treatment on a patient, and a wide variety of "outcome" measures have been proposed. For example, a clinical event, such as a heart attack, a stroke, or, as in our example, a hip fracture, could be used as an outcome measure.

Mortality rates are often used as outcome indicators in effectiveness studies, although a mortality rate usually serves as a proxy for the amount of life remaining. If the goal is to measure remaining life, then a better indicator is years of survival. Some suggest that years of survival is closer to the type of outcome patients themselves would prefer than is mortality.

There are many areas where longevity, by itself, is not a good indicator of well-being. An individual can be alive and yet suffer from poor health. A great deal of work has gone into devising indicators that are sensitive to varying health states. Currently a large number of indicators exist that focus on the quality of life of patients with specific conditions (e.g., cancer or heart disease) or generally. These indicators are based on a set of characteristics (e.g., mobility, pain, etc.) that measure varying dimensions of health (Sintonen 1981). For the individuals under study, one can scale each dimension (e.g., on a scale from 1 to 5 or 1 to 7) and then either work with the dimensions separately (Bakker et al. 1994) or weight the dimensions and combine them into a single index.

Among the indexes that measure health-related quality of life is the quality-adjusted life year (QALY). This is distinguished from other indexes by the fact that it includes death (value equals 0) and that all possible health states are valued between 0 and 1, with 1 being excellent health (Gudex and Kind n.d.). QALYs can be calculated by using the preferences of the patients, the general public, or the practitioners or by rebasing it on other available indexes (Weinstein and Stason 1977). QALYs and other indicators that directly measure patients' own preferences are called *utilities*. In our example, we do not include QALYs, although some research has been done to measure QALYs in this and other areas.

15.4.6 Efficacy and Effectiveness

Efficacy refers to the net impact of an intervention under ideal conditions. For example, if we are examining the impact of a drug, its efficacy equals its effect on health status in situations where patients are fully compliant with the directives of the physicians. Efficacy is usually what is measured in randomized clinical trials, during which patients are closely monitored by research staff.

Effectiveness is a measure of the impact of an intervention under actual or typical conditions. A drug may be efficacious, but if it has some serious side effects (e.g., headaches), patients may not want to take it, and so the effectiveness will be reduced. Effectiveness and efficacy are always expressed in terms of a comparison intervention, and so $EQ_2 - EQ_1$ would be an expression of efficacy of an intervention (if measured under experimental conditions) or its effectiveness (if measured under actual practice conditions).

In our example, we will assume a base hip fracture rate of .003 annually (i.e., a rate of hip fractures of 3/1,000 per year for patients who do not take the drug). The drug, if taken regularly, will reduce hip fractures by 50 percent, to a rate of 1.5/ 1,000 per year. The net difference $(EQ_2 - EQ_1)$ is .0015 per year; over a three-year period, this would amount to about 4.5 fewer cases per thousand.

15.4.7 Cost

The costs of each arm of the analysis include all costs related to the intervention, including all "downstream" costs that are the result of the condition. In our example, there are two sets of costs, the treatment with alenate and the treatment for hip fractures. With regard to the treatment with alenate, the annual cost of the drug is $700 and it is taken for three years. Because the treatment occurs in future years, we must discount future costs by the appropriate discount rate. We will select a 5 percent discount rate, and assume all costs occur at the end of each year. Therefore, the present value of the costs is ($700 × .95) + ($700 × .91) + ($700 × .86) = $1,904.

The expected cost of treatment for a hip fracture is based on the following assumptions: Hospitalization will cost $7,000, doctor's fees will be $1,000, and the individual will be in a nursing home for three months at a cost of $150 daily ($13,500 total). The total cost for a hip fracture will therefore be $21,500.

The expected cost of treatment will depend on the cost of treatment for a hip fracture ($21,500) times the probability of having a fracture. If the drug is taken, the probability is .0015. Therefore, the expected cost is $32.25 (.0015 × $21,500) + (.997 × $0), where .997 is the probability of not having a hip fracture and $0 is the cost of no hip fracture. The expected cost of a hip fracture if no drug is taken is $65 (using a probability of .0003).

The total cost with the drug treatment is therefore $1,904.00 + $32.25 (or $1,936 rounded off), and the cost without the treatment is $65. The net cost of the treatment $(EC_2 - EC_1)$ is therefore $1,871 (= 1,936 – 65).

15.4.8 Cost-Effectiveness

Applying our data to the cost-effectiveness equation, we obtain the following ratio: $1,871 / .0045 = $415,777. The interpretation of this figure is that, for a cost of $415,777, a hip fracture can be avoided by using the treatment. This figure (wholly fictitious) would seem quite high, but it can only be used to illuminate the alternatives. The cost-effectiveness analysis does not settle the question whether or not to use the treatment. It only tells us how much we must pay for an incremental outcome. Because of the narrowness of the concept, some investigators have attempted to broaden it by using more general measures of output, such as life years and QALYs. Such measures would allow comparison across conditions, since the outcomes are measured in the same terms. A cost-effectiveness analysis using QALYs as outcomes is sometimes referred to as a cost-utility analysis. However, many of these measures are not very sensitive to changes within a condition. For example, a case of breast cancer may not appear to be responsive on a general scale but may be very much so on a scale designed to capture different aspects of breast cancer.

The elements of a cost-effectiveness analysis are summarized in Figure 15–3. As can be seen in comparison with Figure 15–1, values are not placed on improved health outcomes. Rather the costs for each alternative are related to the physical measures of health outcomes themselves. Because dollar values are not

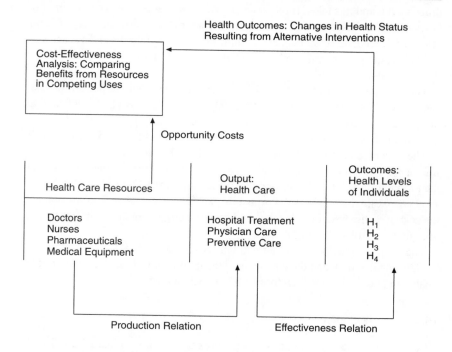

Figure 15–3 Outline of information requirements for a cost-effectiveness analysis. A cost-effectiveness analysis involves tracing through the effectiveness of resources in producing health and determining the opportunity costs of the resources. For alternative interventions to be assessed, a common outcome measure must be used.

placed on the health outcomes, cost-effectiveness analysis cannot tell us whether something is worth doing. However, when dollar measures of output are either unavailable or unacceptable, we still have a tool to gauge the economic desirability of alternative courses of action.

BIBLIOGRAPHY

Cost of Illness

Hodgson, T.A., and Meiners, M.R. 1982. Cost of illness methodology: A guide to current practices and procedures. *Milbank Quarterly* 60:429–462.

Keeler, E.B., et al. 1989. The external costs of a sedentary lifestyle. *American Journal of Public Health* 79:975–981.

Rice, D.P., et al. 1985. The economic cost of illness: A replication and update. *Health Care Financing Review* 7:61–80.

Zook, C.J., et al. 1980. Repeated hospitalization for the same disease. *Milbank Quarterly* 58:454–471.

Cost-Benefit and Cost-Effectiveness Analysis: General

Cochrane, A. 1972. *Effectiveness and efficiency.* New York: Oxford University Press.

Culyer, A.J. 1985. The scope and limits of health economics. *Okonomie des Gesundheitswesens*, new edition, 159:31–54.

Doubilet, P. 1986. Use and misuse of the term "cost effective" in medicine. *New England Journal of Medicine* 314:253–256.

Drummond, M.F. 1981. *Principles of economic appraisal in health care.* New York: Oxford University Press.

Drummond, M.F., and Davies, L. 1991. Economic analysis alongside clinical trials. *International Journal of Technology Assessment in Health Care* 7:561–573.

Drummond, M.F., et al. 1987. Methods for the economic evaluation of health care programs. Toronto: Oxford University Press.

Hatzriandrou, E.I., et al. 1988. A cost-effectiveness analysis of exercise as health promotion. *American Journal of Public Health* 78:1417–1421.

Hellinger, F.J. 1980. Cost-benefit analysis of health care: Past applications and future prospects. *Inquiry* 17:204–215.

Luce, B.R., and Elixhauser, A. 1990. *Standards for the socioeconomic evaluation of health care services.* Berlin: Springer Verlag.

Simes, R.J., and Glasziou, P.P. 1992. Meta analysis and quality of evidence in the economic evaluation of drug trials. *PharmacoEconomics* 1:282–292.

Stoddart, G.L., and Drummond, M.F. How to read clinical journals: VII: To understand an economic evaluation. Parts A and B. *Canadian Medical Association Journal* 130:1428–1433, 1542–1549.

Warner, K.E. 1982. *Cost-benefit and cost-effectiveness analysis in health care.* Ann Arbor, Mich.: Health Administration Press.

Warner, K.E., and Hutton, R.C. 1980. Cost-benefit and cost-effectiveness analysis in health care. *Medical Care* 18:1069–1084.

Weinstein, M.C., and Stason, W.B. 1977. Foundations of cost-effectiveness analysis for health and medical practices. *New England Journal of Medicine* 296:716–721.

Williams, A. 1974a. The cost benefit approach. *British Medical Bulletin* 20:252–256.

———. 1974b. Measuring the effectiveness of health care systems. *British Journal of Preventive and Social Medicine* 28:196–202.

Health-Related Quality of Life and QALYs

Bakker, C., et al. 1994. Cost effectiveness of group physical therapy compared to individualized therapy for ankylosing spondylitis. *Journal of Rheumatology* 21:264–268.

Erickson, P. 1966. Modeling health-related quality of life: The bridge between psychometric and utility based measures. *Journal of the National Cancer Institute*, monograph 20, 17–20.

Gudex, C., and Kind, P. n.d. *The QALY Toolkit.* York, England: Center for Health Economics.

Sintonen, H. 1981. An approach to measuring and valuing health states. *Social Science and Medicine* 15C:55–65.

Torrance, G.W., and Feeny, D. 1989. Utilities and quality adjusted life years. *International Journal of Technology Assessment in Health Care* 5:559–575.

Weinstein, M., and Stason, W.B. Foundations of cost effectiveness analysis for health and medical practices. *New England Journal of Medicine* 296:716–721.

Williams, A. 1985. Economics of coronary bypass grafting. *British Medical Journal* 291:326–329.

Value of Health and Life

Blomquist, G. 1981. The value of human life: An empirical perspective. *Economic Inquiry* 19:157–164.

Fisher, A., et al. 1989. The value of reducing risks of death. *Journal of Policy Analysis and Management* 8:88–100.

Johanneson, M., Jonsson, B., Borquist, L. 1991. Willingness to pay for antihyperintensive therapy—results of a Swedish pilot study. *Journal of Health Economics* 10:461–474.

Johanneson, M., Johansson, P.-O., Kristom, B., et al. 1993. Willingness to pay for antihypertensive therapy—further results. *Journal of Health Economics* 12:95–108.

Landefeld, J.S., and Seskin, E.P. 1982. The economic value of life: Linking theory to practice. *American Journal of Public Health* 72:555–566.

Mooney, G. 1977. *The valuation of human life.* New York: Macmillan.

Muller, A., and Reutzel, T.J. 1984. Willingness to pay for a reduction in fatality risk. *American Journal of Public Health* 74:808–812.

O'Brien, B., Viramontes, J.L. 1994. Willingness to pay: A valid and reliable measure of health state preference? *Medical Decision Making* 14:289–297.

Rice, D.P., and Hodgson, T.A. 1982. The value of human life revisited. *American Journal of Public Health* 72:536–538.

Schelling, T.C. 1968. The life you save may be your own. In *Problems in public expenditure analysis*, ed. S.B. Chase. Washington, D.C.: Brookings Institution.

Shogren, J.F., Shin, S.Y., Hayes, D.J., et al. 1994. Resolving differences in willingness to pay and willingness to accept. *American Economic Review* 84:255–270.

Thaler, R., and Rosen, S. 1975. The value of saving a life. In *Household production and consumption*, ed. M.E. Terleckyj. New York: National Bureau of Economic Research.

Thompson, M.S. 1986. Willingness to pay and accept risks to cure chronic disease. *American Journal of Public Health* 76:392–397.

Viscusi, W.K. 1993. The value of risks of life and health. *Journal of Economic Literature* 31:1912–1946.

Viscusi, W.K. 1978. Labor market valuations of life and limb. *Public Policy* 26:359–385.

Zeckhauser, R. 1975. Procedures for valuing lives. *Public Policy* 23:419–464.

Specific Cost-Benefit and Cost-Effectiveness Analyses

Berwick, D.M., and Komaroff, A.L. 1982. Cost effectiveness of lead screening. *New England Journal of Medicine* 306:1392–1398.

Bloom, B.S., and Jacobs, J. 1985. Cost effects of restricting cost-effective therapy. *Medical Care* 23:872–880.

Doherty, N., and Hicks, B.C. 1975. The use of cost-effectiveness analysis in geriatric day care. *Gerontologist* 15:412–417.

Elixhauser, A. 1989. The cost effectiveness of preventive care for diabetes mellitus. *Diabetes Spectrum* 2:349–353.

Evans, R.G., and Robinson, G.C. 1980. Surgical day care: Measurements of the economic payoff. *Canadian Medical Association Journal* 123:873–880.

―――. 1983. An economic study of cost savings on a care by parent ward. *Medical Care* 21:768–782.

Hammond, J. 1979. Home health care cost effectiveness: An overview of the literature. *Public Health Reports* 94:305–311.

Lave, L.B. 1980. Economic evaluation of public health programs. *Annual Review of Public Health* 1:255–276.

Russell, L.B. 1986. Is prevention better than cure? Washington, D.C.: Brookings Institution.

Scheffler, R.M., and Paringer, L. 1980. A review of the economic evaluation of prevention. *Medical Care* 18:473–484.

Weinstein, M.C. 1983. Cost-effectiveness priorities for cancer prevention. *Science* 221:17–23.

Weisbrod, B.A. 1971. Costs and benefits of medical research. *Journal of Political Economy* 79:527–544.

Weisbrod, B.A., et al. 1980. Alternative to mental hospital treatment. *Archives of General Surgery* 37:400–405.

Economic Evaluation and Technology Assessment

Detsky, A.S. 1985. Using economic analysis to determine the resource consequences of choices made in planning clinical trials. *Journal of Chronic Diseases* 38:753–765.

Drummond, M.F., and Stoddart, G.L. 1984. Economic analysis and clinical trials. *Controlled Clinical Trials* 5:115–128.

Weinstein, M.C. 1981. Economic assessments of medical practices and technologies. *Medical Decision Making* 1:309–330.

Glossary of Health Economics Terms

access. Potential and actual entry of a population into the health care delivery system (U.S. Congress 1988).

acute care. Inpatient diagnostic and short-term treatment of patients.

adjusted average per capita cost (AAPCC). An estimate of the average cost incurred by Medicare per beneficiary in the fee-for-service system, adjusted by county for geographic cost differences related to age, sex, disability status, Medicaid eligibility, and institutional status.

adverse selection. The systematic selection by high-risk consumers of insurance plans with greater degrees of coverage. The insurers who offer these plans end up with insureds who incur greater than normal costs.

agency (agent). A group (individual) that has been delegated authority to make decisions and perform activities on behalf of those doing the delegating. Physicians are often said to act as agents for their patients, indicating that the physicians make decisions about treatments based on their knowledge.

all-payer system. A system of reimbursing providers in which all separate insurers coordinate to set uniform payment policies. Individual providers will then receive the same reimbursement from different insurers for cases with similar characteristics.

alternate level of care (ALC). A non-acute treatment patient occupying an acute care bed would be viewed receiving an alternate level of care—a level other than the appropriate one.

ambulatory care. Care rendered to individuals under their own cognizance any time when they are not resident in an institution.

Acknowledgments: The author would like to thank Carl Asche, Chris Houston, Dev Menon, and Tom Noseworthy for their help in compiling this glossary.

ambulatory care groups (ACGs). A case-mix classification system incorporating related ambulatory care visits, based on ICD-9-CM diagnostic codes and patient age and sex (Weiner et al. 1991).

ambulatory visit groups (AVGs). A classification system by which ambulatory care visits with associated procedures are classified into similar resource-using groups based on diagnosis, procedure, age, and sex.

appropriateness of care. The extent to which the expected health benefits of a procedure exceed its expected negative consequences by a sufficiently wide margin that the procedure is worth doing. Considerations of cost are excluded (Chassin et al. 1987, 2534).

atypical patients. Patients who exhibit patterns of care different from typical cases, either because they do not complete a full and successful course of treatment in a single institution or because their length of stay exceeds the statistical trim point.

availability. The supply of services, generally in relation to the demand for the services.

average cost (AC). The unit cost for a selected volume of output; total cost divided by total quantity of output. The average cost is equal to the average variable cost plus the average fixed cost.

average fixed cost (AFC). The unit fixed cost for a specific volume of output. The average fixed cost is equal to the total fixed cost divided by the volume of output.

average length of stay. *See* **length of stay**.

average variable cost (AVC). The unit variable cost for a specific volume of output; total variable cost divided by quantity of output.

bed days. The number of days in a period that beds are available. In a year, bed days are 365 × the number of available beds.

biased selection. The deliberate choice, by a provider or insurer, of a group of patients (insureds) with preselected characteristics associated with low utilization of health care.

burden. With reference to a tax, the reduction in real income resulting from the tax (Due 1957, 6).

capacity. Capacity is a measure of the output that can be reached when existing resources are fully and efficiently used.

capital. Human, physical, and financial means of production.

capitation. A payment system in which the entity financially responsible for the patients' health care services receives a fixed periodic sum for each patient that covers the costs of utilization by the patient. The sum can be adjusted for specific patient characteristics, such as age and sex.

case management. A collection of organized activities to identify high-cost patients as early as possible, locate and assess alternative treatment methods, and manage health care benefits for these patients in a cost-effective manner (Scheffler et al. 1991).

case mix. An index or measure of the average level of resource requirements for a group of cases sorted and weighted according to type of case. The weights represent the estimated resource use for each type of case.

case-mix groups (CMGs). A Canadian system for classifying hospital inpatients into groups using similar quantities of resources according to selected patient characteristics such as diagnosis, procedure, age, and comorbidity. CMGs are maintained by the Canadian Institute for Health Information.

charges. A price set for a product by the supplier. Charges may not equal cash received because some payers may receive a discount or fail to pay.

coinsurance. A system of provider payment in which the patient is responsible for a portion of the payment and the insurer or third party is responsible for the rest.

community care. Care provided in a noninstitutional setting, including in the home or in the patient's "neighborhood."

community rating. A method of setting insurance premiums for health care coverage. In this method, all insurers in the group pay the same premium regardless of their risk-related characteristics, such as age or health problems.

comorbidity. A disease or condition that is present at the same time as the principal disease or condition of the patient.

competition. A state of competition exists in a market if no single firm or consumer is large enough to influence the market price. This state usually occurs if there are many buyers and sellers in the market.

competitive price. The price at which demand and supply are in equilibrium in a competitive market.

complements. Two goods or services that are consumed together, such as surgeons' services and operating room services. The economic relevance of complementarity is that a change in the direct price of a complement will cause a shift in the demand curve of the other service.

complications. Adverse patient conditions that arise during the process of medical care.

concurrent review. A process of ongoing review while the patient is undergoing treatment in the hospital, and of certifying the length of stay that is appropriate for the approved admission (Scheffler 1991).

consumer's surplus. The difference between what an individual is willing to pay for a given quantity of a good or service and what is actually paid. This is equal to the area under the demand curve between no consumption and that specified quantity minus the amount paid for all the units (price times quantity).

consumption. The use of services to satisfy current wants.

continuing care. A system of service delivery that includes all of the services provided by long-term care, home support, and home care. This term reflects within it two complementary concepts, i.e., that care may "continue" over a long period of time and that an integrated program of care "continues" across service components, that is, that there is a continuum of care. Continuing care is still in the process of emerging from its acute care, social services, and public health roots into a separate system of delivery, i.e., a distinct, separate, and major "product line" in the overall health care system (Hollander 1994).

copayments. Out-of-pocket payments for health services made by users as their share of the providers' total reimbursement.

core services. In Canada health services which must be available to every resident of a province (Saskatchewan Health 1993). *See also* **insured services.**

cost. The value placed on the goods and services. *See* **opportunity cost** and **money cost.**

cost benefit. The relationship between the dollar impact of an intervention and its opportunity cost. It can be expressed as a ratio or as a net value (benefits minus costs).

cost curve. The relation between cost and volume of output. It can be specified in terms of total costs, average or unit costs, and marginal costs. *See* **long-run cost curve** and **short-run cost curve.**

cost effectiveness. The relationship between the additional cost and the additional health outcome (expressed in physical terms) of one intervention as compared with another.

cost function. A behavioral relationship between cost (viewed from either a marginal, average, or total perspective) and the variables that influence cost, including volume of output, quality of output, input prices, and variables affecting organizational efficiency. *See* **cost curve, long-run cost curve,** and **short-run cost curve.**

cost sharing. The joint payment or sharing of a price by the consumer and the payer (insurer).

cost shifting. The charging of different prices for differentially insured patients, usually including the subsidization of care for nonpaying patients.

cost utility. The relationship between the additional cost and the additional health outcome (expressed in terms of a utility index) of one intervention as compared with another.

critical care. See **intensive care.**

day procedure groups (DPGs). A classification system for ambulatory patients in which patients are assigned to classes according to principle procedures that use similar resources. The DPG system was developed from New York's PAS system and is used by the Canadian Institute for Health Information.

deductible. A fixed amount that a consumer must spend out of pocket before insurance coverage begins. If the deductible is $200, the individual must pay for the first $200 of medical expenditures out of pocket.

demand. Consumer willingness to purchase alternative quantities of services at various specified prices, represented by the position of the demand curve.

demand curve (schedule). A schedule indicating the quantities of a service that an individual or group is willing to purchase at different prices of that service, all other factors (income, tastes, other prices) held constant.

diagnosis. A determination of the specific physical ailment of an individual.

diagnosis-related groups (DRGs). A system of classifying hospital inpatients into groups using similar quantities of resources according to selected characteristics such as diagnoses, procedure, age, and any complications or comorbidities. DRGs are used for hospital reimbursement in the U.S. Medicare system (Fetter 1991).

direct cost. (1) In social cost accounting, the cost of all resources incurred by providers of health care; usually refers to paid resources. (2) In hospital cost accounting, the cost of resources (doctors, nurses, lab techs) that are directly involved in the provision of care; overhead costs are excluded.

direct price. See out-of-pocket price.

direct teaching costs. As regards hospital care, the costs in a teaching hospital that can be directly traced to educational rather than patient care functions. These include resident and intern salaries.

discharge planning. The process of assessing a patient's needs for treatment after hospitalization and effecting an appropriate and timely hospital discharge impact of Blue Cross and Blue Shield plan utilization management (Scheffler 1991).

discount (time discount). A constant applied to future costs and benefits in order to value them equivalently to costs and benefits occurring in the present period.

disease prevention. *See* **prevention.**

disequilibrium. A state in which a market is not in equilibrium. As a result of a shift in demand or supply, a market will be in disequilibrium until the price and quantity adjust to the new equilibrium levels. A state of disequilibrium can be permanent if there is some barrier (e.g., government price control) that permanently maintains the price at a level above or below that of equilibrium.

DRG. *See* **diagnosis-related groups.**

economic cost. *See* **opportunity cost.**

economies of scale. Reductions in operating costs associated with larger scale operations.

economies of scope. Reductions in the operating costs of two or more related services (e.g., home care and hospital care) associated with joint production (e.g., production of both services by the same organization).

effectiveness. The relationship between an intervention and its health outcome, usually measured in physical units (e.g., life years saved). Some definitions specify that effectiveness is a measure of the ability of an intervention to bring about an outcome under actual practice conditions.

efficacy. The relationship between an intervention and its health outcome under ideal (usually experimental) clinical conditions.

efficiency. (1) Technical efficiency is a measure of how close a given combination of resources is to producing a maximum amount of output. (2) Allocative or economic efficiency is a measure of how close a given combination of resources is to yielding maximum consumer satisfaction.

elasticity of demand. The quantity of a service demanded in response to the out-of-pocket price of a service or product. Elasticity is calculated by dividing the percent change in the product divided by the percent change in the direct price. The price and quantity in terms of which the change is measured can be the original price and quantity (point elasticity) or an average of the original and the new prices and quantities (arc elasticity).

emergency care. Emergency care involves immediate decision making and action to prevent death or any further disability for patients in a health crisis.

encounter. A single visit to a provider (sometimes used as an output measure).

episode of care. A series of temporally contiguous health care services related to treatment of a given spell of illness or provided in response to a specific request by the patient or other relevant entity (Hornbrook et al. 1985, 171).

episode of illness. A single unbroken interval of time during which the patient suffers from a continuous spell of signs and/or symptoms that are perceived as sickness or ill-health (Hornbrook et al. 1985, 170).

equilibrium. A situation in which all forces are in balance so there is no tendency to change. (1) **consumer equilibrium** occurs where the individual consuming unit has acquired a composition of goods that gives the unit its maximum attainable satisfaction (utility) given the constraints (prices, incomes) it faces. (2) **producer or provider equilibrium** occurs when the firm is producing the level of output that achieves its objectives (e.g., maximum profits, maximum output). (3) **market or competitive equilibrium** occurs when all buyers and sellers simultaneously achieve their maximized positions; demand and supply are therefore in balance at these determined levels of price and quantity.

equity. Fairness (e.g., in the provision of health care). *See* **horizontal equity** and **vertical equity**.

experience rating. A method of setting health premiums for health care coverage. In this method, each insured in the group pays a premium that is based on his or her risk-related characteristics.

extra billing. Billing for an insured health service rendered to an insured person by a medical practitioner in an amount in addition to any amount paid for that service by the provincial or territorial health insurance plan (Canada Health Act 1984).

fee-for-service reimbursement. The type of reimbursement in which payment is made for each item or service.

factors of production. *See* **resources**.

firm. A self-contained organization that engages in the production or provision of a service or product. The production can occur in more than one facility. *See* **plant**.

fixed costs. Costs that remain the same despite changes in the volume of output.

fixed inputs. Inputs that, within a selected range, do not vary with output. Examples include office space and equipment.

flat-of-the-curve medicine. Medical care that has no impact on health status. The allusion is to the curve relating medical care inputs to health status output. Eventually, if medical care is provided in large enough quantities, its additional effectiveness is hypothesized to be zero (i.e., the output will be constant and the curve will be flat).

full cost. The cost that a provider incurs in producing services. The total cost covers *all* inputs, direct and indirect, used in the production of the services.

funding. A payment made to a provider to cover expenses for services rendered. The funding is not necessarily related to the costs incurred for specific patients or services.

global budget. A fixed annual operating grant paid to a provider that is to cover all services provided to all patients who are treated.

gross domestic product (GDP). The money amount of all final goods and services (consumer, investment, and government) produced within defined geographical boundaries. A standard measure of relative health expenditures for a given state, province, or country is total health spending divided by GDP.

group model HMO. A health maintenance organization in which the HMO contracts with an independent group practice to provide care for its members. The contractual arrangements are usually on a per capita basis.

group practice. A medical practice in which several practitioners share some inputs, such as office staff and space.

health. (1) A complete state of physical, mental, and social well being, and not merely the absence of disease or illness (World Health Organization). (2) A state characterized by anatomic integrity; ability to perform personally valued family, work, and community roles; ability to deal with physical, biologic, and social stress; a feeling of well-being; and freedom from the risk of untimely disease (Last 1988, 6).

health care. A range of services and products whose end purpose is the preservation or enhancement of health.

health insurance. The payment for the expected costs of a group resulting from medical utilization based on the expected expenses incurred by the group. The payment can be based on community or experience rating.

health insurance purchasing cooperative (HIPC). An insurance organization that acts as a broker between payers of health insurance (households, businesses, governments) and health care providers. The HIPC sets standards for health care services and seeks competitive bids for these services; the consumers can then select from among the competing providers.

health maintenance organization (HMO). An organization in which a provider or management group takes on the responsibility for providing health services to a specific group of enrollees in exchange for a set annual fee for each enrollee. The HMO can be the provider or it can contract for services with outside providers.

health plan. An organization that acts as an insurer for an enrolled group of members (Prospective Payment Assessment Commission 1993).

health promotion. Education and/or other supportive services that will assist individuals or groups to adopt healthy behaviors and/or reduce health risks, increase self-care skills, improve management of common minor ailments, use health care services effectively, and/or improve understanding of medical procedures and therapeutic regimens (American Hospital Association 1991).

health-related quality of life (HRQOL). A measure of health status that can incorporate physical, emotional, social, and role functioning; pain; and many other factors. It is usually based on the responses of patients to questions in professionally devised instruments.

health status. *See* **health-related quality of life**.

health technology. All procedures, devices, equipment, and drugs used in the maintenance, restoration, and promotion of health.

health technology assessment. A comprehensive form of policy research that looks at the technical, clinical, economic, and social consequences of the introduction and use of health technology.

home care. Care provided in the home, for a wide variety of purposes, including health maintenance, preventive care, and substitution for acute care (Hollander 1994). *See also* **home support.**

home support. Home and community based long-term care services, provided by persons other than professionals, such as nurses or rehabilitation therapists (Hollander 1994).

horizontal equity. Fairness in the treatment of individuals who are at the same level with regard to some scale (e.g., people who are equally wealthy or have the same degree of health).

hospice. A combination of services for terminally ill patients and their caregivers that is based on a humanistic philosophy of care.

inappropriate care. *See* **appropriateness of care.**

incidence. The pattern of the distribution of the burden of a tax, among various individuals or groups (Due 1957, 9).

incremental cost. The additional cost resulting from a change in output by one or more than one unit.

indemnity. A type of insurance contract in which the insurer pays for care received up to a fixed amount per episode of illness.

independent practice association (IPA). In this type of HMO, the organization contracts with independent physician practices to provide health care for the enrollees. Payment to providers is usually on a fee-for-service basis.

indigent. An individual who cannot pay for his or her own care.

indirect cost. (1) In social cost accounting, the cost of time lost due to illness (i.e., resources that are not directly paid for). (2) In hospital cost accounting, the cost of resources not directly related to patient care.

indirect teaching costs. The additional costs that a teaching hospital incurs in the process of training interns and residents. These costs cannot be measured directly because they are inseparably joined with treatment costs.

inputs. *See* **resources.**

intensity of care. The amount of resources and services embodied in a unit of care (e.g., a day of hospitalization, a hospital stay, or a physician visit).

intensive care. The clinical speciality that treats patients with threatened or established organ failure through the employment of highly technical equipment by specially trained staff.

intermediate care facility (ICF). A facility providing a lower level of nursing care than a skilled nursing facility. Medicare no longer pays for ICF-level care.

international classification of diseases, ninth revision (ICD-9). A comprehensive disease coding system developed by the World Health Organization.

international classification of diseases, ninth revision, clinical modification (ICD-9-CM). A two-part medical information coding system used in abstracting systems and for classifying patients for DRGs. The first part consists of a comprehensive list of diseases with corresponding codes compatible with the World Health Organization list of disease codes. The second part contains procedure codes that are independent of the disease codes. ICD-9-CM was developed in the United States based on the World Health Organization system, and is the U.S. coding standard. Some Canadian provinces also use ICD-9-CM diagnosis and procedure codes.

intervention. A task or set of tasks performed by a health professional with the object of influencing health status.

investment. The employment of physical or human capital to create the conditions for further production.

loading charge. The portion of an insurance premium that is over and above the amount expected to cover payment for insured services.

long run. A period over which all inputs can be increased, including capital stock and specialized labor.

long-run cost curve. The relation between the cost of production and volume of output or scale of plant for a period during which all inputs, including capital equipment, have sufficient time to vary.

long-term care. Services that address the health, social, and personal care needs of individuals who, for one reason or another, have never developed or have lost the capacity for self-care. These services may be continuous or intermittent, but it is generally presumed that they will be delivered indefinitely.

managed care. Any system of health service payment or delivery arrangements where the health plan attempts to control or coordinate the use of health services by its enrolled members in order to contain health expenditures, improve quality, or both. Arrangements often involve a defined delivery system of providers who have some form of contractual arrangements with the plan (Physician Payment Review Commission 1994).

managed competition. A manner of funneling payments for health services from a collective insurance fund to competing providers (Enthoven 1993; Reinhardt 1993).

marginal cost (MC). The change in cost resulting from a change in output by one unit. Since fixed costs do not change with output, marginal cost is related only to variable cost.

marginal productivity. The additional output due to the application of one or more units of an input or resource, holding all other inputs constant. Marginal productivity can be increasing, constant, or diminishing.

marginal revenue (MR). The additional revenue that a firm obtains from selling one more unit of a service.

market. A network of buyers and sellers whose interaction determines the price and quantity traded of goods and services.

market structure. Those organizational characteristics of a market that determine the relations of sellers to sellers, buyers to buyers, and sellers to buyers.

Medicaid. A federally aided, state-administered program that provides medical assistance to certain low-income people.

medical care. A component of health care. A process or activity, guided by medical practitioners, in which certain inputs or factors of production (e.g., physician services, medical instruments, and pharmaceuticals) are combined in varying quantities to yield an output (medical care services) or outcome (health status).

Medicare. (1) In the United States, a nationwide, federally administered program that covers hospital and physician care and some related services for eligible persons over age 65, persons receiving Social Security disability insurance payments, and persons with end-stage renal disease. (2) In Canada, the health insurance system that is jointly financed by the federal and provincial governments and administered by the provincial governments.

money cost. Expenditures incurred (paid out) at a given volume of output.

monopolistic competition. A state of monopolistic competition exists in a market if there are many sellers but each is able to achieve a certain degree of customer loyalty and thus has some influence over price.

monopoly. A state of monopoly exists in a market if there is a single supplier. The supplier will then have control over prices in the market.

moral hazard. The risk to an insurer that its insureds will increase their consumption of insured services because of the reduction in the out-of-pocket price resulting from the insurance coverage.

morbidity. Illness. The morbidity rate is the rate of illness in a population.

mortality. Death. The mortality rate is the rate of death in a population.

most responsible diagnosis. The ICD-9 code identifying the disease or condition considered by the physician to be most responsible for the patient's stay in the institution. In the case where multiple diseases or conditions may be classified as most responsible, it is the one responsible for the greatest length of stay (Canadian Institute for Health Information). This is the Canadian coding convention. For the U.S. convention, see **principal diagnosis**.

multiproduct firm. A firm that produces a variety of products with different specifications (e.g., types of medical services).

need. A quantity of services that an expert (doctor, planner, etc.) judges that a patient or group of patients ought to have in order to achieve a desired level of health status (Boulding 1966).

network. A health maintenance organization comprising several different medical groups that are under contract to provide care to enrollees. Usually, the contract is on a fee-for-service basis.

nonprofit (not-for-profit). A nonprofit organization has as its prime purpose the providing of services to a specified population rather than the earning of profits for shareholders.

nursing home. A nursing home is an institution providing supervised, personal care for people who are not ill enough to require hospitalization in an acute care or auxiliary hospital but who require assistance with the activities of daily living.

opportunity cost. The value of the alternative use of resources that was highest valued but not selected. With some exceptions (e.g., when resources are overpaid), this equals the market value of all resources used to produce a given volume of output.

outlier. A patient who has a long length of stay (or a long length of treatment) as compared with other patients with the same diagnosis.

out-of-pocket price. The price that is directly paid for health care services by the consumer and is not subsequently recovered from an insurer or government. The out-of-pocket price is the burden that directly falls on the consumer as a result of his or her use of medical care.

outpatient care. Hospital-provided care that does not involve an overnight stay.

output. An activity or process during which a patient is treated or "cared for" by health care resources with the object improving the patient's health.

patient days. The number of days that patients are under inpatient hospital or nursing home care during a year.

per capita payment. A fixed annual payment per person made to a provider or health maintenance organization. The totality of payments is intended to cover the cost of care for all enrollees during the year.

per diem payment. A flat-rate payment to a hospital or other institution for each day the patient is an inpatient in the institution.

plant. A single facility engaged in production. *See* **firm**.

point-of-service plan (POS). A health maintenance organization plan that allows members to use providers not on the organization's rolls. To gain access to such providers, the members must pay an added premium or out-of-pocket payment.

preadmission certification. The prospective review and evaluation of proposed elective hospital admissions using acceptable medical criteria as the standard for determining the appropriateness of the site or level of care and certifying the length of stay required (Scheffler 1991).

preferred provider organization (PPO). An arrangement in which a group of health providers agrees to provide services to a defined group of patients at an agreed-upon rate for each service (de Lissovoy et al. 1986, 7).

premium. The payment made to an insurance company in return for insurance coverage.

prepaid group practice (PGP). A group practice that charges patients on an annual per capita basis and bears the risk for providing the insured services.

prevention. Any intervention that reduces the likelihood that a disease or disorder will affect an individual or that interrupts or slows the progress of the disorder. Primary prevention reduces the likelihood that a particular disease or disorder will develop in a person. Secondary prevention interrupts or minimizes the progress of a disease or irreversible damage from a disease by early detection and treatment. Tertiary prevention slows the progress of the disease and reduces the resultant disability through treatment of established diseases (Spitzer 1990).

preventive medicine. That aspect of the physician's practice in which he applies to individual patients the knowledge and techniques from medical, social, and behavioral science to promote and maintain health and well-being and prevent disease or its progression (Hilleboe and Lairmore 1965; Last 1988).

price. An amount of money paid or received per unit of a service or commodity.

price discrimination. The charging of different prices for the same product to different customers, made possible by the inability of consumers to resell the product to each other. The charging of different prices is usually due to the existence of different demand conditions for different groups of customers.

price taker. A supplier that has no influence over the price of the services or commodities it sells. However many units it sells, the price is taken as given.

primary care. A type of medical care that emphasizes first contact care and assumes ongoing responsibility for the patient in health maintenance and therapy for illness. Primary care is comprehensive in scope and includes overall coordination of treatment of the patient's health problems.

principal diagnosis. The diagnosis that, after investigation, is found to have been responsible for the patient's admission to the hospital. This is the U.S. coding convention. If a patient is admitted to the hospital for a minor TURP (trans uretheral resection of the prostate) procedure, and it is discovered he or she has carcinoma of the lung, the prostate diagnosis would be the one coded under this convention. For the Canadian convention, *see* **most responsible diagnosis**.

procedure. An operative or nonoperative intervention.

production. The act of combining resources to yield output.

production function. A quantitative relationship expressing how outputs vary when the quantity of inputs changes. Also called **production relation**.

production relation. *See* **production function**.

productivity. The ratio of physical inputs to physical outputs. The inputs can be one single input (e.g., labor), with others held constant, or all inputs combined.

products of ambulatory care (PACs). An ambulatory care classification system developed in New York State primarily for the funding of nonsurgical, nonemergency ambulatory care visits, based on body parts and purpose of visit (Tenan 1988).

products of ambulatory surgery (PASs). An ambulatory surgery classification system developed in New York State for funding ambulatory surgery procedures, based on similar resource-using procedures (Kelley et al. 1990).

profit. Total revenue minus total cost. Accounting profit is defined as total revenue for a period's sales minus costs matched to those sales. Economic profit is total revenue minus economic costs.

prospective payment. Payment to (usually institutional) providers based on predetermined rates unrelated to current or past costs.

provider. A supplier of health care services.

public health. The combination of science, practical skills, and beliefs that is directed to the maintenance and improvement of the health of all the population. It is one of the efforts organized by society to protect, promote, and restore the people's health through collective or social actions (Last 1988).

quality-adjusted life year (QALY). A numerical assessment of the proportion of an individual's state of full health experienced over a year. QALY values generally range from 0 (assigned to death) to 1 (full health), though certain states of health can be valued at less than 0. QALY values can be directly derived from individuals' utility measurements or can be based on existing values of health states.

quality of care. The degree to which the process of medical care increases the probability of outcomes desired by patients, and reduces the probability of undesired outcomes, given the state of medical knowledge (U.S. Congress 1988).

quality of life (QOL). The degree to which an individual enjoys everything. It has been defined, by a philosopher, as the possession and enjoyment of all the real goods in the right order and proportion. Nonphilosophers, *see* **health-related quality of life (HRQOL)** or **health status** for terms only slightly less stratospheric.

quantity demanded. The quantity of a service that an individual or group is willing to buy at one specific rate.

quantity supplied. The amount of a service a supplier or market is willing to supply at any one price.

rate. The price per unit charged by an institution for its services.

rate setting. The setting of institutional prices by a paying or regulatory agency.

refined diagnosis-related groups (RDRGs). Also called **refined group numbers (RGNs).** A classification system in which resource use patterns and secondary diagnoses are used to refine the assignment of patients to severity classes (RDRGs).

regulation. (1) A regulation is a law or rule imposing government or government-mandated standards and significant economic responsibilities on individuals or organizations outside the government establishment. (2) The process of regulation is carried out by government or mandated agencies through such means as setting or approving prices, rates, fares, profits, interest rates, and wages; awarding licenses, certificates, and permits; devising safety rules; setting quality levels; enacting public disclosure of financial information regulations; and enacting prohibitions against price, racial, religious, or sexual discrimination (U.S. Domestic Council 1977).

reimbursement. The payment made by an insurer to a provider for specific services provided to an insured patient. Reimbursement is usually associated with payments based on a service-by-service, or patient-by-patient basis.

relative value. A value placed on a specific unit of service (e.g., a follow-up office visit, a blood test, or an inpatient cholecystectomy) expressed in relation to some standard (e.g., a minute of lab test time or physician care).

resource-based relative value system (RBRVS). A resource weights service classification system that aims at setting resource weights according to the total relative cost of each service, including "psychological" costs of the provider, time costs, and training costs.

resource intensive weights (RIW). Canadian relative weightings for inpatient groups. RIWs combine Canadian length of stay and U.S. cost per day data to form hybrid cost per case weights. Separate weights are calculated for "typical" and "atypical" cases.

resource utilization groups (RUGs). Clusters of nursing home residents, defined by residents' characteristics, that explain resource use (Fries et al. 1994, 668).

resources. Resources are defined as the means used in producing services. Resources can include physical capital (beds and equipment) and human capital (physicians, nurses, etc.). Also called *inputs* and *factors of production*.

retrospective payment. Payment to a provider for services provided based on actual costs incurred by the provider. Since the payment is based on costs incurred, the amount to be paid must be determined after the service has been provided (i.e., retrospectively).

retrospective review. A review of claims after the episode of care is concluded and the claim is submitted to the insurer (Scheffler et al. 1991).

returns to scale. The relationship between total output and scale of operations, which are measured as proportional increases in all resources. Because all resources are allowed to increase in proportion, this is a long-run relationship.

revenue. Income earned from the provision of services. Gross revenues equal income earned overall, while net revenues equal income earned minus costs or expenses.

risk. Uncertainty as to loss; in the case of health care, the loss can be due to the cost of medical treatment or other losses arising from illness. Risk can be objective (relative variations between the difference between actual and probable losses) and subjective (psychological uncertainty relating to the occurrence of an event) (Greene 1977). *See also* **risk averse**, **risk neutral**, and **risk taker**.

risk averse. A person is said to be risk averse if losses of a given amount create more disutility than the utility that comes from gains of the same amount (and so losses will tend to be avoided).

risk factor. Behavior or condition that, based on evidence or theory, is thought to directly influence the level of a specific health problem.

risk neutral. A person is said to be risk neutral if he or she values losses and gains of the same amount equally.

risk pooling. The sharing of the costs incurred by members of a population. The payment method can vary but will not be based on the risk of individuals.

risk taker. A person is said to be a risk taker if, for that person, the utility of gains is greater than the disutility of losses of equal value. A risk taker is therefore predisposed to gamble.

second surgical opinion. Patients are sometimes required to get a second or even a third consulting opinion for specified nonemergency surgical procedures (Scheffler et al. 1991).

secondary care. Specialist-referred care for conditions of a relatively low level of complication and risk. Secondary care can be provided in an office or hospital and can be diagnostic or therapeutic.

selective contracting. A procedure whereby an insurer can legally exclude providers from its list of participating providers (Melnick and Zwanzinger 1988, 2669).

short run. A period in which all of the inputs cannot be adjusted (increased or reduced). Those inputs that cannot be adjusted are called "fixed" and include capital stock. *Short run* also refers to lengths of time insufficient for new firms to enter a market or industry.

short-run cost curve. The relation between cost and volume of production of a plant during a short adjustment period in which only some inputs are variable (and the rest are fixed).

shortage. An excess of supply over demand at a given price.

signout case. A patient who leaves the hospital against medical advice.

single-payer system. A reimbursement system in which there is a single payer or one dominant payer.

single-product firm. A production unit that produces a single, homogeneous product. Exists only in economic theory.

skilled nursing facility (SNF). A facility that provides short-term, subacute posthospitalization care and rehabilitative care.

social cost. The cost to all members of society of any activity or service. Can be the sum of private and external costs or of direct and indirect costs.

solo practice. A one-doctor medical practice.

staff model HMO. A health maintenance organization whose practitioner staff are employees of the health plan. Usually the practitioners are paid on a salary rather than fee-for-service basis.

standardized mortality rate (SMR). A single mortality rate for a large group of individuals who are in different age and sex categories. The total rate for the entire group is made up of the rates in different age and sex subgroups, which are weighted or averaged according to a given structure of a standard population (e.g., the population of an entire country or the population in a base year).

substitutes. Goods or services that compete with each other, such as Aspirin and Tylenol. The direct price of one of the substitutes will cause a shift in the demand curve for the other.

supplier-induced demand. The amount of shift in the demand for services resulting from the suppliers' influence on consumers' tastes (intensity of desire for the services).

supply. A supply curve. The quantity supplied at each price.

supply curve. (1) For a single firm, the quantity the firm is willing to supply of a service at alternative prices of the commodity. (2) For the market, the relationship between the quantity that all firms are willing to supply and alternative prices of the service.

supply function. (1) For a single provider, a quantitative relationship between the quantity the supplier is willing to supply and a series of variables that influence the supplier's behavior, such as price, technology, case mix, quality, and input prices. (2) For a market, the quantitative relationship between the quantity that all suppliers in the market are willing to supply and a series of variables that influence all of the suppliers' behavior, including price, technology, case mix, quality, input prices, and the number of suppliers in the market.

surplus. (1) For a nonprofit firm, total revenue minus total expense (the counterpart of profit for a for-profit firm). (2) For a market, the excess of quantity supplied over quantity demanded at a given price.

tastes. Consumer preferences for goods and services expressed in terms of an index of satisfaction or utility. Taste is a catchall concept for everything other than prices and incomes that affect demand, including health status, age, sex, level of education, and so on.

technology. *See* **health technology**.

technology assessment. *See* **health technology assessment**.

tertiary care. Highly specialized care administered to patients who have complicated conditions or require high-risk pharmaceutical treatments or surgery. Tertiary care is provided in a setting that houses high-technology services, specialists and subspecialists, and intensive care and other highly specialized services.

third-party payment. Payment by a private insurer or government to a medical provider for care given to a patient.

time cost. The value of time required to conduct an activity. This variable has two components: value per unit of time and time actually spent in the activity. Value per unit of time is taken as equivalent to lost earnings or the value placed on forgone leisure activities.

total costs (TC). The sum of fixed and variable costs. All of the costs required to produce a specified level of output.

total fixed costs (TFC). All of the fixed costs required to produce a specified level of output.

total product. The total amount of output produced.

total variable costs (TVC). All of the variable costs required to produce a specified level of output.

transfer case. A hospital inpatient who is admitted from or discharged to another institution.

transfer payment. A payment made to an individual that is unrelated to resource use.

trim point. A point, calculated using a statistical formula, applied to all lengths of stays (or cost per case) within a single DRG (or CMG) in order to separate outlier cases from the rest.

typical patient. A patient who receives a full, successful course of treatment in a single institution and is discharged when he or she no longer requires acute-care services.

utility. (1) An index comparing various levels of an individual's satisfaction with alternative quantities of specified goods, services, or situations under certainty. The index that allows the quantification of differences between the levels is called *cardinal utility* (Pigou 1960). (2) A ranking of alternative bundles of goods and services under certainty, on the basis of better, equal, or worse, with no indication as to *degrees* of satisfaction (ordinal utility). (3) A ranking of alternative risky situations on the basis of an individual's own preferences regarding probabilities (von Neumann-Morgenstern utility) (Torrance et al. 1995).

utilization. The actual use of services by consumers (the services must be demanded and supplied).

utilization management. A set of techniques used by or on behalf of purchasers of health care benefits to manage health care costs by influencing patient care decision-making through case-by-case assessments of the appropriateness of care prior to provision (Institute of Medicine 1991).

value judgment. A pronouncement that states or implies that something is desirable (or undesirable) and is not derived from any technical or objective data but instead from considerations of ultimate value, i.e., ethical considerations (Nath 1973).

variable costs. Costs that change in response to changes in output. Variable costs can be expressed as total, average, or marginal.

variable inputs. Inputs that can vary in quantity during a specified time period.

vertical equity. Fairness in the treatment of individuals who are at different levels with regard to some scale (e.g., people who fall into different income classes).

volume. The number of cases (or other service units) provided.

wants. Consumer tastes or desires.

BIBLIOGRAPHY

American Hospital Association. 1991. *Health statistics.* Chicago: American Hospital Association.

Boulding, K. 1966. The concept of need for health services. *Milbank Quarterly* 44:202–223.

Chassin, M.R., et al. 1987. Does inappropriate use explain geographic variations in the use of health care services? *JAMA* 258:2533–2537.

de Lissovoy, G., et al. 1986. Preferred provider organizations. *Inquiry* 23:7–15.

Due, J.F. 1957. *Sales taxation.* London: Routledge and Kegan Paul.

Enthoven, E. 1993. The history and principles of managed competition. *Health Affairs* 12 (suppl): 24–48.

Fetter, R.B., ed. 1991. *DRGs: Their design and development.* Ann Arbor, Mich.: Health Administration Press.

Fries, B., et al. 1994. Refining a case mix measure for nursing homes. *Medical Care* 7:668–685.

Greene, M.R. 1977. *Risk and insurance.* 4th ed. Cincinnati: South-Western Publishing Co.

Hilleboe, H.E., and Lairmore, G.W. 1965. *Preventive medicine.* 2nd ed. Philadelphia: W.B. Saunders.

Hollander, M.J. 1994. The cost effectiveness of continuing care services in Canada. Ottawa: Queen's University of Ottawa Economic Projects.

Hornbrook, M.C., et al. 1985. Health care episodes. *Medical Care Review* 42:163–218.

Institute of Medicine. 1991. Quoted in Scheffler, R.M., et al. The impact of Blue Cross and Blue Shield plan utilization management programs, 1980–88. *Inquiry* 28:263–275.

Kelley, W.P., et al. 1990. The classification of resource use in ambulatory surgery. *Journal of Ambulatory Care Management* 13(1):55–63.

Last, J.M. 1988. *Public health and human ecology.* New York: Appleton and Lange.

Melnick, G.A., and Zwanzinger, J. 1988. Hospital behavior under competition and cost containment policies. *JAMA* 260:2669–2675.

Physician Payment Review Commission. 1994. *Annual report to Congress, 1994.* Washington, D.C.: Physician Payment Review Commission.

Pigou, A.C. 1960. *The economics of welfare.* London: Macmillan.

Reinhardt, U.E. 1993. Reorganizing the financial flows in American health care. *Health Affairs* 12 (suppl):172–193.

Saskatchewan Health. 1993. *A guide to core services.* Regina, Saskatchewan: Saskatchewan Health.

Scheffler, R.M., et al. 1991. The impact of Blue Cross and Blue Shield plan utilization management programs, 1980–88. *Inquiry* 28:263–275.

Spitzer, W.O. 1990. The scientific admissibility of evidence on the effectiveness of preventive interventions. In *Preventive disease,* ed. R.B. Goldbloom and R.S. Lawrence. New York: Springer-Verlag.

Tenan, P.M., et al. 1988. PACs: Classifying ambulatory patients and services for clinical and financial management. *Journal of Ambulatory Care Management* 11(3):36–53.

Torrance, G., et al. 1995. Multi-attribute preference functions. *Pharmaco-Economics* 7:503–520.

U.S. Congress, Office of Technology Assessment. 1988. *The quality of medical care.* Pub. no. OTA-H-386. Washington, D.C.: U.S. Government Printing Office.

U.S. Domestic Council. 1977. *The challenge of regulatory reform.* Washington, D.C.: U.S. Government Printing Office.

Weiner, J., et al. 1991. Development and application of a population-oriented measure of ambulatory care case mix. *Medical Care* 28:452–472.

Index

Note: Page numbers in *Italics* indicate material in figures and tables.